THE STORY OF THE TWELFTH

OUR THREE COMMANDING OFFICERS

**LT.-COL. (Hon. Col.) L. F. CLARKE,
D.S.O., V.D.**

**MAJOR-GEN. SIR J. GELLIBRAND,
K.C.B., D.S.O.**

**LT.-COL. C. H. ELLIOTT,
C.M.G., D.S.O., V.D.**

THE STORY OF THE TWELFTH

A Record of the 12th Battalion, A.I.F.
during the Great War of
1914-1918

BY

L. M. NEWTON
(Late Lieutenant and Adjutant 12th Battn., A.I.F.)

The Naval & Military Press Ltd

Published by
The Naval & Military Press Ltd
5 Riverside, Brambleside, Bellbrook
Industrial Estate, Uckfield, East Sussex,
TN22 1QQ England
Tel: +44 (0) 1825 749494
Fax: +44 (0) 1825 765701
www.naval-military-press.com
www.military-genealogy.com
www.militarymaproom.com

In reprinting in facsimile from the original, any imperfections are inevitably reproduced and the quality may fall short of modern type and cartographic standards.

FOREWORD

THE narrative of the doings of the 12th Battalion in the Great War is designed to help the veterans of the Battalion to live over again the long years spent in the Valley of the Shadow, or, at the best, only a short march away. With the memory of those days there will also arise a mental picture, more complete than any book could create, of the spirit of the Battalion, second to none in the glorious traditions of the A.I.F.

Of the gallantry and endurance displayed by the 12th Battalion in the many actions fought on the soil of Gallipoli, France and Belgium, there is fortunately no lack of adequate description and recognition in official and unofficial documents. It is very open to doubt, however, whether a due tribute has ever been paid to the discipline of the 12th. No one could claim that either the original members or the reinforcements joined up imbued with all the virtues of the perfect soldier and the desire to salute. Yet from the first days of its existence the Battalion settled down to work in the same dependable fashion that was maintained to the end, taking duty seriously and nevertheless getting what fun there was out of daily life. Probably the most trying period during the war for the A.I.F. was the time spent on the Canal defences after the evacuation of Anzac. Coupled with the discomforts of life spent on the hot sand, shortage of water, and torments of every wind that blew, were the aggravations of heavy labour constructing defences that disappeared with every sand-storm, and the disappointment of an enemy who never appeared at all. Under such conditions of life it would not have been difficult to find excuses for military offences, yet at this period, as the regimental records show, offences in the 12th were conspicuous only by their extreme rarity.

Each unit in the A.I.F. had, undoubtedly, its own characteristics and temperament—at times so marked that it was said one might distinguish the men of each battalion on a bathing parade. Looking back to the days spent with the 12th, the outstanding feature seemed to be that the men came nearer than most to the soldier's ideal regiment—"a happy band of brothers," the sort of brother that knows and does his job and has every intention of making others do the same.

General Sinclair-MacLagan was a man of very few compliments, but for all that he paid a singularly high tribute to the 12th at Tel-el-Kebir whilst watching them at training. "Look at them! Good old 12th! How on earth they do it I don't know. They don't seem to move, and yet they always get there on time." As a matter of fact, the 12th, without knowing it, followed the pleasant example of Nelson's captains, and by anticipating orders, avoided even the appearance of hurry or fuss.

Envy is a failing that few soldiers will confess to, yet there are many who cherished that feeling towards Colonel Elliott. He commanded the 12th for over three years.

(Sgd.) JOHN GELLIBRAND,
Major-General.

AUTHOR'S PREFACE

Comrades,

In submitting "The Story of the Twelfth" to you, I feel that some explanation is necessary, both with regard to its tardy appearance and the form it has taken.

The question of writing a record of the unit has been under consideration, at intervals, ever since our return from the war, but the task was so enormous and called for such literary talent, that none of us considered ourselves competent to undertake it.

However, at a reunion of the 12th Battalion Association held at the Town Hall, Hobart, on November 16th, 1923, the question of compiling the history again arose, and Colonel Elliott and I once more explained the reason why we had not attempted it. But the members present were distinctly of the opinion that a history should be written, and it was suggested that it might take the form of a chronological diary.

Regarding the wish of the meeting as an instruction, I, as President of the Association, took the initiative and commenced some experimental efforts for consideration of the Committee.

About four years ago, while events were still fresh in my memory, I started to write my own reminiscences, merely for my own personal use, pleasure and reference, and starting from the time we left Egypt in 1916, I got as far as Pozieres. I now attempted a chronological diary covering the same period, and submitted both efforts to the Association Committee for consideration. They were unanimously of the opinion that if I could continue on the same lines as the reminiscences a readable record should be the result.

Narrative.—In the compilation of this work, I have to thank Lt.-Col. D. A. Lane for writing Chapters VI. and VII., covering the occupation of Anzac, as during the larger portion of this period I was away from the unit wounded, and did not feel myself competent to record this important part of its existence.

For a similar reason, Colonel Elliott assisted me by writing Chapter XII. (Pozieres and Mouquet Farm), which could not, under any circumstances, be attempted by anyone who did not actually participate in the engagement.

Useful information, such as reports on companies, platoons and individuals in various operations, details concerning supply and transport, medical work in the field, etc., has been furnished by Lt.-Cols. J. L. Whitham, C.M.G., D.S.O., and R. A. Rafferty, D.S.O.; Major W. W. S. Johnston, D.S.O., M.C.; Capts. J. E. Newland, V.C.; C. N. Richardson, M.C.; D. McLeod, M.C.; H. E. Spotswood, M.C.; Lieuts. G. Vaughan, M.C.; R. D. Radford and G. W. Turner, D.C.M., M.M.

The following N.C.O.'s also rendered material assistance by furnishing me with incident and detailed information concerning their platoons and companies:—C. J. Allen, M.M.; J. Allen; E. T. Domeney, M.M.; P. O. Hay, M.M.; J. Kitson; W. E. Phillips, M.M.; S. J. Rowles; F. H. Ripper, and E. G. Garlick.

The Defence Department made the War Diary of the 12th Battalion available for my use, while Capt. C. E. W. Bean, the official historian, forwarded me a copy of his own notes concerning the operations in which the Battalion participated.

Illustrations.—The photographs selected all have a direct bearing on the Battalion's existence and the text itself.

In addition to the Official War Photographs, exclusive photographs have been loaned by Colonel C. H. Elliott, C.M.G., D.S.O., V.D.; Capts. C. H. Stubbings and R. M. W. Thirkell, M.B.E.; Lieut. A. J. Lovett (late 3rd A.L.H.), and J. W. Beattie, Esq. The London "Graphic" also allowed me to reproduce one of the late Lieut. Booth's sketches which appeared in their paper.

The pictorial insets at the beginning of each chapter and the coloured wrapper are contributed by Cpl. H. G. Kelly, and have helped in no small way to make the book more attractive.

Editorial.—The task of reading the manuscript and rendering literary assistance to a very inexperienced narrator has been generously performed by Chas. Barrett, Esq., of the Defence Department, Melbourne (Chapters I.-IV., VIII.-XI., and XIII), and Chas. S. King, Esq., of Hobart (Chapters V.-VII., XII., and XIV.-XXI.).

"The Story of the Twelfth" does not aspire in any way to be a complete history of the 12th Battalion. Very many acts of bravery, fortitude and determination which were performed in almost every engagement, though well worthy of record, were known to but the few who participated therein, while many others are irrevocably lost through lapses of memory in the effluxion of time.

Of over 8,000 members of the Battalion only a very few, of course, can receive mention by name in such a book as this, and I trust I may be forgiven if members of the unit with long and honourable service who might expect to figure prominently in the work, find their names unintentionally omitted.

Every member of the Battalion, at some time or other, must have received a parcel whilst on active service, and eagerly cut the string and unfolded the wrappings to disclose some cherished article within. Let this book be accepted in that light—the language in which the story is couched represents the paper and string, while the facts recorded are, in short, the things which really matter.

L. M. NEWTON.

Lindisfarne,
    Hobart, Tasmania,
        1/1/1925.

CONTENTS

Chapter		Page
I.	The Birth of the Battalion	1
II.	Troopship Life	13
III.	Mena Camp	24
IV.	Lemnos	43
V.	The Landing	62
VI.	The Occupation of Anzac	98
VII.	Lone Pine and Return to Lemnos	117
VIII.	Camps at Sarpi, Tel-el-Kebir and Serapeum	137
IX.	Arrival in France	165
X.	Fleurbaix Sector	183
XI.	The Road to the Somme	204
XII.	Pozieres and Mouqet Farm	218
XIII.	The Winter of 1916	246
XIV.	The German Withdrawal—Spring, 1917	282
XV.	The Summer of 1917	327
XVI.	The Battle of the Ridges—Autumn, 1917	356
XVII.	The Winter of 1917	391
XVIII.	The German Offensive—Spring, 1918	421
XIX.	The Defence of Strazeele—Summer, 1918	446
XX.	The Final Advance—Autumn, 1918	465
XXI.	Conclusion	491

LIST OF ILLUSTRATIONS

Our Three Commanding Officers	Frontispiece	
The Official March through Hobart	Face Page	10
Troopship "Geelong" Leaving Hobart	,,	16
The Sphinx and Pyramids	,,	32
Sketch by the late Lieut. J. L. C. Booth	,,	48
Anzac Beach	,,	64
The "Sphinx" Rock, Anzac	,,	112
12th Battalion Bivouac, Anzac	,,	128
Pontoon Bridge over the Suez Canal	,,	160
The Trenches in the Fleurbaix Sector	,,	176
Aerial Photograph of the Fleurbaix Sector	,,	192
Albert Cathedral	,,	208
Gibraltar Strong Post, Pozieres	,,	224
Switch Trench, near Gueudecourt	,,	256
The Village of Boursies	,,	304
Our V.C.'s	,,	336
Typical Country in Sector in Front of Ypres	,,	368
Cloth Hall, Ypres	,,	400
Pradelles Church	,,	432
Ruins of Strazeele	,,	448
Village of Chuignolles	,,	480

Chapter I.

THE BIRTH OF THE BATTALION

IT seems hard to believe that such a quiet and unassuming township as Pontville should have been the birthplace of the A.I.F. as far as Tasmania was concerned, but such was the case, as the concentration camp was opened at this spot on August 15th, 1914, and volunteers were at once enrolled and allotted to the arms of the service to which Tasmania was at this time contributing her quota. They consisted in the first instance of one squadron of Light Horse, one battery of Artillery, Headquarters and four single companies of Infantry, one field company of Engineers, one section of Field Ambulance, and one company of A.S.C.

A staff from District Headquarters were not long in establishing the camp, after which drafts of men, varying in number, commenced and continued to arrive at Brighton Junction, which was the nearest station to the camp.

The journey to Pontville, as experienced by the majority of recruits, did not vary very much, except in detail. It generally consisted of a long train journey, in company with a carriage full of genial companions, who revivified old patriotic and South

African War songs and sang them with great gusto. For those who travelled at night, sleep was out of the question, as everyone was unconsciously suffering from suppressed excitement and preferred to discuss the subject which was uppermost in their minds.

Under circumstances such as these, I arrived at Brighton Junction, with about forty companions, on the morning of August 25th. A cross-country walk of about two miles brought us to the camp, when we reported to the Brigade tent. After a short wait, an officer came out (who afterwards proved to be Major R. P. Smith, the Camp Commandant) and briefly interrogated us individually. Those with previous experience were at once allotted to that branch of the service in which they had been trained, whilst those with experience in the handling of horses were drafted to either Light Horse or Artillery Units. The remainder, in which I was included, were led off in a straggling formation to that portion of the camp allotted to the "gravel crunchers." Sergeant Frank Wilson was Orderly Sergeant on that particular day and met our party as we neared the Battalion lines and escorted us to the Orderly Room, where Claude Lyne (a few days later being appointed Battalion Orderly Room Sergeant) took from us such regimental particulars as were necessary at this stage.

Those of us from the north of the Island were posted to "B" Company and afterwards paraded to the Q.M. Store, where R.Q.M.S. Jim Newland issued us each with a palliasse and showed us a heap of straw with which to fill it. We were next issued with three blankets, shown to our tents and told to deposit the few worldly possessions we had brought with us. We were not left alone long, for the Orderly Sergeant soon grabbed three or four for fatigue work, namely, to clean up the camp lines —our first job as soldiers in the Great War. The majority of us were totally ignorant of military etiquette and affairs generally at this time, and did not know an officer from an N.C.O., but called them all "Sir." Frank Wilson, however, told us to "Cut out the rough, as 'Sergeant' was good enough for him."

Everything was very strange to me at first, such as tent orderly duties, cook-house, tatoo bugle calls, lights out, etc., but I slept the sleep of the just on that first night, and required very little rocking. It took me some few moments, however, in the morning to remember where I was when the sounding of "Reveille" awoke me in darkness, and immediately afterwards the band struck up and marched up and down the lines. One of the tent party said, with a yawn, "Who the —— is going for the coffee?" and although someone left the tent, I thought it an attempt at cheap sarcasm. But not so, for almost immediately a dixie of hot, black coffee was brought in and we all participated. I began to think that army life was not so bad. Then for the morning wash—and what a crowd there was down at the tap—it was "hop in for your cut" with a vengeance. At 7 a.m. we "fell in" and were marched off by warrant officer instructors for an hour's physical training, better known as "physical jerks." I suppose we were keen in those days and enjoyed it, but that soon wore off, and it was not long before the early morning parade was a thing to be dreaded and avoided.

It did not take long to accustom myself to the new surroundings, military terms, routine regulations, and within a fortnight I could take my part in close and extended order drill with credit to the company of which I was already beginning to feel proud.

By this time I knew myself to be No. 262 Pvt. L. M. Newton, "B" Company, 12th Battalion, 3rd Inf. Brigade, 1st Aust. Division. The "Australian Imperial Force" was not known much in those days by that name, and we were generally referred to as the "First Contingent" or the "Australian Expeditionary Force."

The senior personnel of the Battalion consisted of the following:—

Headquarters:
    Commanding Officer—Lieut.-Col. (Hon. Col.) L. F. Clarke, D.S.O., V.D.
    Second in Command—Major (Hon. Lieut.-Col.) S. Hawley.
    Adjutant—Lieut. J. Northcott.
    Quartermaster—Lieut. N. D. Fethers.
    Transport Officer—Lieut. L. M. Mullen.
    Signalling Officer—2nd Lieut. S. R. Houghton.
    Medical Officer (attached)—Capt. V. R. Ratten.
    Chaplain (attached)—Capt. the Ven. Archdeacon R. H. Richard.

"A" Company (recruited from Hobart and South of the Island):
    Company Commander—Capt. C. H. Elliott.
    Subalterns—2nd Lieut. I. S. Margetts, 2nd Lieut. T. E. Weavers.

"B" Company (recruited from Launceston and N.E. Coast):
    Company Commander—Capt. E. H. Smith.
    Subalterns—Lieut. H. A. MacPherson, 2nd Lieut. J. A. Foster.

"C" Company (recruited from N.W. Coast):
  Company Commander—Capt. D. A. Lane.
  Subalterns—Lieut. J. P. Patterson, 2nd Lieut.
    R. A. Rafferty.
"D" Company (recruited from West Coast):
  Company Commander—Capt. J. L. Whitham.
  Subalterns—2nd Lieut. H. Massey, 2nd Lieut.
    A. Green.

Machine Gun Section: 2nd Lieut. W. H. Room.

Headquarters:
  R.S.M.—R.S.M. W. Kennedy.
  R.Q.M.S.—R.Q.M.S. J. E. Newland.
  M.G. Sergeant—S.S.M. J. T. Bryant.
  Signalling Sergeant—S.S.M. R. Jerrett.
  Orderly Room Sergeant—Sgt. C. H. Lyne.
  Transport Sergeant—Sgt. W. F. Wilmot.
  Sergeant Cook—Sgt. T. S. Yanner.
  Band Sergeant—Sgt. W. J. Smith.
  Pioneer Sergeant—Sgt. C. Dand.
  Armourer Sergeant—Sgt. E. Hynds.

"A" Company:
  Colour Sergeant T. Selwyn.
  Sergeants J. Cooper, F. C. Wilson, L. T. G.
    Chambers and V. A. Jacques.

"B" Company:
  Colour Sergeant F. Herbert.
  Sergeants W. A. Connell, C. N. Richardson,
    G. W. Thorpe and W. L. Garrard.

"C" Company:
  Colour Sergeant J. V. Pickett.
  Sergeants T. S. Stott, L. J. Birkett, W. C. Jackson and A. A. Skinner.

"D" Company:
  Colour Sergeant C. H. Stubbings.
  Sergeants W. N. Fisher, A. J. Hearps, A. H.
    Sanson and H. V. R. Fraser.

The first essential thing to be done was to equip the Battalion ready for war, and it was not long before some new article of clothing or equipment was being issued every day. Needless to say, almost the first issue was that of web equipment and a rifle, and although I intently watched Staff Sergeant-Major Harris put a set of equipment together I inwardly vowed that it would be many a day before I would take mine to pieces, fearing that its reconstruction would be almost beyond my powers. But even this soon proved a simple task compared with the problems that were to face us in the future. I shall never forget the motley crowd our Company looked still wearing their civilian clothes with web equipment and rifle. Before dismissing we were instructed how to slope and order arms, and when the Company was taken over by Capt. Smith prior to dismissing us, he called out, "Private Newton." I sloped arms, paraded myself and saluted by bringing my hand to the peak of my cap. "No, no, my lad, that's not the way to salute when you have a rifle at the slope," said Capt. Smith, and he forthwith instructed me in the proper method. In answer to his query, I told him that my civil occupation was that of a clerk, and after some little interrogation I was detailed to carry out the duties of Company Orderly Clerk. I saluted (correctly) and returned to my position in the ranks, and after dismissal was collared by the Colour Sergeant, who told me to bring my gear up to his tent, at the head of the lines.

It was not long before I familiarised myself with my duties, which consisted of preparing daily states for headquarters, parade states, ration states, compilation of nominal rolls, filling in attestation papers as the new recruits were drafted to "B" Company, recording all equipment, clothing and stores received from the Q.M. Store and supervising its issue to the men, obtaining signature for everything (how precise and conscientious we were in those days) and preparing pay rolls. Within a few days my promotion to Corporal appeared in Battalion Orders, dating from 1/9/1914.

In the meantime, training was proceeding and progress was rapid. I was allotted a section in Lieutenant MacPherson's right-half company and attended parades on every possible occasion. We quickly proved ourselves efficient in squad and section drill, and soon carried out Company movements. Similarly (thanks largely to a big percentage of militia men) we mastered extended order drill and were soon tramping all over the surrounding country as advance guards, fighting a rearguard action over Brighton racecourse, taking up outpost positions and attacking imaginary enemies at every point of the compass.

Then we carried out our musketry practices, which necessitated a day's journey to Sandy Bay Rifle Range. Each Company was allotted a day in rotation, and a fatigue party would be detailed for range duties, and set out before daylight. The Company would follow somewhat less than an hour later and march to Brighton Junction where we entrained, and on arriving at Hobart, marched to the range and carried out a good day's firing. On return to the camp, musketry returns were compiled and forwarded to Headquarters, and all those who did not qualify were passed out as not being up to the required standard of the first contingent.

"B" Company's firing was exceptionally good, and, indeed, Lieut. MacPherson told us that our half-company had obtained the best results in the

Battalion. But probably every officer in the Battalion was telling his men the same story—it does no harm, and tends to engender a spirit of *esprit de corps*.

The next phase was Battalion training, when the Commanding Officer, Col. Clarke, would take charge of us. This generally necessitated us carrying a mid-day ration, and we would either go for a long route march, or carry out an attack practice across the Apsley railway line and up the slopes beyond. At the conclusion we would probably do some Battalion drill movements. Who among us can forget the day that the Adjutant, Lieut. Northcott, took charge of the Battalion and gave us some drill movements? None, I think. After giving several orders, which apparently were not carried out to his satisfaction, he closed the Battalion into "close column of companies," and after a short rest gave the command, "Slope arms." (Pause). Then, in a stentorious voice, "Keep—those—rifles—*still*. They—are—waving—about—like—a—crop—of—*corn*." Later on, we were marching in column of companies when he gave the command, "Advance in column of squads." This command in Battalion drill proved too much for the troops and the result was chaotic. Again, that penetrating voice, "Battalion—*halt*. The organisation—of the Battalion is—*rotten*. In some cases—the companies—were not even told off into—*squads*."

Those criticisms sank deep into the mind of every man on that parade, and during later years of the campaign were frequently recalled when a few of the "originals" gathered together and talked over old times.

On September 26th, the two single companies that

were recruited in South Australia, namely, "E" and "F" Companies, arrived at the camp. They were organised and commenced their training at Morphetville Camp, just outside Adelaide, and were largely comprised of Port Pirie miners. The Battalion lined up and gave them a cheer as they came into camp, but although they were mostly all of large physique, they did not look too sprightly on their arrival, as during their trip from Adelaide in the "Geelong" they experienced some very severe weather when coming down the West Coast, and many of them were still suffering from the effects.

Their officers and senior N.C.O.'s were as follows:—

"E" Company:
  Company Commander—Capt. L. E. Burt.
  Subalterns—Lieut. W. R. Jorgensen and 2nd Lieut. A. H. Fraser.

"F" Company:
  Company Commander—Lieut. J. A. W. Kayser.
  Subalterns—2nd Lieuts. T. Holland and G. A. Munro.

"E" Company:
  Colour Sergeant P. J. Mildren.
  Sergeants P. B. Ballard, P. H. Weston, L. H. Lewin, and Percy.

"F" Company:
  Colour Sergeant W. C. Burford.
  Sergeants J. C. Moller, G. D. Stuart, A. J. Seaman and K. G. Jacob.

There are many things upon which I could enlarge, but which must give way to matters of more importance, but a mere mention will bring back memories—the church parades, camp fire concerts at night, leave parties into Hobart, evenings spent in Pontville itself (cut abruptly short by the entrance of the piquet), forty-eight hours final leave that was given long before embarkation, shifting camp on to the high ground, the excellent quality of the dust which permeated everything—including the stew—the particular Sunday when R.S.M. Kennedy had to use his authority to induce some lady visitors to leave the camp, the roast sucking pig that one of "B" Company tents enjoyed (duly paid for), the fire in the township of Pontville when Pvt. Townsend distinguished himself, and so I could continue.

It was soon evident that our day of departure was drawing near, for kit inspections were held almost every other day. The method employed was for half the company to gather round in a semi-circle with sufficient space between the men to render it impossible for one article to be owned by two men during the inspection—then all our goods and chattels were tipped out on to a waterproof sheet. The officer would go down the list, calling out "Forage cap," and we would all hold it up and the names of those who were short were taken. And so on, with singlet, shirt, socks, underpants, trousers, tunic, jersey, boots, laces, puttees, braces, hat, chin-strap, towel, soap (we were frightened to use our issue cake), housewife, brush, comb, tooth-brush, holdall, cap comforter, shaving brush, razor, knife, fork, spoon, dungarees, white hat, sea kit-bag, etc. I don't think a force was ever equipped so thoroughly and efficiently as the first Australian Expeditionary Force.

The official march through Hobart took place on 4th October, when the Battalion entrained at Brighton Junction at 8 a.m. and proceeded to Moonah,

OFFICIAL MARCH THROUGH HOBART, OCT. 4th, 1914

(*Photo. by J. W. Beattie, Esq.*)

where we detrained. We then marched along the Main Road as far as Augusta Road, where we halted and fixed bayonets. It was a particularly hot day and the march through the city with rifles at the slope was long and tiring. However, the constantly changing crowd which lined the streets and packed the verandahs all along the route was sufficiently interesting to make us forget the fatigue, although the lack of enthusiasm which was displayed tended to prove that the seriousness of the war was not appreciated in those early days. After the march we dismissed on the Domain and were given a bun and a cup of tea, but most of the fellows who had friends enjoyed a more substantial repast. About 6 p.m. the Battalion, or at least the greater portion of it, re-assembled at the station and returned to camp, tired out.

We were somewhat disappointed a week or two later, at Albany, when we heard of the enthusiastic welcome that was given to the New Zealanders at Hobart, when they carried out a similar march a few days after our troopship had left.

Another indication that our departure was fast approaching was the fact that parties were detailed almost daily to proceed to the troopships "Geelong" and "Katuna" for loading purposes. It was then that the boys first got to know Capt. Clogston, of the Engineers, who, with his monocle in his eye, told the "bally blighters" to get a hustle on with their work. The loading was eventually completed and our sailing day was fixed for 20th October. On that morning we had a particularly early "reveille," about 4.30 a.m., and breakfast shortly after. Blankets were rolled and stacked, tents struck and the camp left generally clean and tidy before we marched out for the last time. The troop train took us right on to the Ocean Pier, where the "Geelong" was berthed, and we commenced embarking soon after 10 a.m. We had had implicit and detailed instructions regarding the embarkation and were all marched down to our respective troop decks and allotted our mess tables. Only those who have been down a troop deck know how crowded they are, especially when every man is wearing full marching order; there was barely room to move, and being a particularly hot day, the atmosphere soon got stifling. By ones and twos we got on to the top deck and commenced looking for relations and friends amongst the crowd on the pier. Almost the whole of Hobart was there, but no one from the country or outlying districts, for our departure was kept very secret and no mention of it was made in the press. The troopship commenced to hoot about 2 p.m., but it took some time to collect the stragglers who had eluded the sentries and got away for a last bit of liberty and to enjoy a last drink at their favourite hotel. The calling of rolls was impossible, and when the piquets at last came back and reported that everyone that could be found had been brought or ordered aboard, it was assumed that the troops were all mustered, and at 4 p.m. the ropes were cast off and we drifted away amid cheers and wishes of "God speed." I watched the crowded pier recede and listened to the band playing "Rule Britannia" and "The Girl I Left Behind Me," until the sounds were lost in the intervening distance.

Chapter II.

TROOPSHIP LIFE

THE army, however, knows no sentiment, and before we had passed the Iron Pot we were fallen in and received our issue of mess utensils, hammock and blankets. I well remember that, as dusk was falling, in company with Sergeants Frank Wilson and Jethro Bass, I leaned over the ship's side and watched the receding shores of Tasmania, and wondered when we would see them again. Little did any of us know!

The trip across the great Bight was not bad, considering the weather one does encounter at times in this sea, but the old "Geelong" rolled pretty well and was quite sufficient to make the majority of the men sick until they got their sea legs. It used to cause great joy on the troop deck at meal times, during this period, as the companion-way which led from the top deck to the troop deck was very steep. One day we had curry for dinner, and the mess orderly had to carry a brimming dish of liquid curry, together with a dish of vegetables. It was alright until he commenced to descend the steep ladder, and then the boat gave a roll, upon which he overbalanced and fell to the bottom—curry and all. The greasy curry on the deck now made matters worse. Three mess orderlies suffered the same catastrophe on that particular day. The next person to descend was the Battalion Orderly Officer, Lieut. Rafferty, and his descent was watched by the whole troop deck with bated breath, and, sure enough, as soon as he touched the slippery deck his feet went from under him and he measured his length, amidst an uproar of laughter from the troops.

When we were a few days out, we were all innoculated against typhoid fever (I think), Sisters King and Radcliffe, who were now aboard with us, taking prominent parts. We were afterwards innoculated so many times for so many diseases that we ceased to be interested. One or two of the fellows aboard refused to be innoculated, and were sent home from Albany.

We reached Albany about 28th October, and found some of the troopships already assembled there. Others continued to arrive daily until the convoy was complete, consisting of twenty-eight Australian troopships and ten New Zealanders.

Our troopship was situated well into the centre of the harbour and in consequence we could see very little of either the township or surrounding country, which appeared to be flat, uninteresting and more or less devoid of vegetation. Nevertheless, we envied those units whose troopships occupied positions at or near to the wharf and who were enabled to carry out short route marches on shore. We contented ourselves by watching the arrival of troopships and the constant movement of motor boats as they darted from ship to ship on official business.

On Sunday, 1st November, we set sail in three long lines, the "Orvieto" with Divisional Headquarters aboard being the flagship, the "Geelong's"

NOVEMBER, 1914

position fifth boat in the port file or column, and the whole convoy disposed as follows:—

"Wiltshire"	"Ovieto"	"Euripides"
"Medic"	"Southern"	"Argyllshire"
"Ascanius"	"Pera"	"Shropshire"
"Star of England"	"Armadale"	"Afric"
"Geelong"	"Saldanah"	"Benalla"
"Port Lincoln"	"Katuna"	"Rangatira"
"Karroo"	"Hymettus"	"Star of Victoria"
"Marere"	"Suffolk"	"Hororata"
"Clan MacCorquodale"	"Anglo-Egyptian"	"Omrah"
		"Miltiades"

"Arawa"	"Maunganui"
"Athenic"	"Hawkes Bay"
"Orari"	"Star of India"
"Ruapehu"	"Limerick"
"Waimana"	"Tahiti"

We were escorted by battleships, amongst which were the "Melbourne," "Sydney," "Minotaur," "Hampshire," "Aboukir," and after we were out a day or so we were joined by one or two

Japanese warships. The speed of the convoy, of course, was the speed of the slowest troopship, namely, the "Southern," which suffered much abuse in consequence.

We soon settled down to regular routine work—meals, parades, drawing rations, boat drill, sweepers' parades, and drawing of hammocks were all carried out automatically.

Of course, there was not sufficient deck space for all the units to parade at the same time, and therefore a roster was drawn up and the different decks were allotted to different units at varying times during parade hours. Parade work generally consisted of physical exercises, rifle exercises, musketry, lectures, and kit inspections. The signalling section used to carry out continual duty, in reliefs, on the bridge, and received all messages from the flagship and other vessels. We often received messages from Major Hawley, who was in command of the troops on the horse-boat, the "Katuna," and who had with him—as far as the 12th Battalion was concerned—Lieutenant Mullen and the transport section.

At night there was not a light to be seen in the whole convoy as you looked astern, the only light the troopships carried being one at the rear of the stern masthead. Even the striking of matches to light pipes and cigarettes had to be done behind cover. At one period of the voyage matches became extremely scarce and warning was always given when one was being lit, and immediately pipes were loaded and cigarettes taken out and as many as possible utilised the services of the one match before it eventually went out.

The one outstanding feature of the voyage, of course, was the sinking of the "Emden." It had

DEPARTURE OF THE 12th BATTALION
Troopship "Geelong" leaving Ocean Pier, Hobart, Oct. 20th, 1914
(Photo. by J. W. Beattie, Esq.)

always been known that she was in the Southern Seas somewhere, but no one realised that she was actually in our vicinity. At 7.30 a.m. on 9th November, the "Sydney" was seen to belch forth volumes of black smoke and dash off across our front and disappear over the horizon, whilst the other battleships, although they did not leave the convoy, appeared "excited." There was much conjecture among the troops, and it was not until some hours later that we knew officially that the "Sydney" had actually engaged the "Emden" and defeated her. As stated previously, the speed of the convoy was that of the "Southern," the slowest boat, and although she suffered much adverse criticism at times (because we thought we would never get to the front before the war was over), nevertheless the safety of the convoy was probably due to her tardiness in this instance. The "Emden" apparently knew we were in the vicinity and was on the look-out for us and had crossed our course ahead only a few hours earlier. Had she crossed astern, what might have happened?

A few days later we reached Colombo, where the "Sydney" had already arrived, but we were instructed not to cheer as we passed her, as some small token of respect to the prisoners who were there, and who had put up such a clean and sportsmanlike fight throughout. We did not go ashore at Colombo; in fact, we anchored outside the breakwater, and under these circumstances were rather pleased that we did not stay long there as the weather was extremely warm.

The usual routine was continued, the monotony being broken by concerts, sports, boxing, etc., and a tour of duty on guard about every five or six days. Interest was also roused on one occasion by the band going "on strike" and refusing to play at the officers' mess.

One morning we woke to find the "Ascanius," which was two boats ahead of us, laying off on our port bow and apparently in difficulties. It transpired that just before dawn the "Shropshire" had run into her (the disposition of the troopships having altered since leaving Colombo), and although the troops had to don their lifebelts and man the boats no material damage was done, and she very soon regained her position in the convoy. When we were going through the Red Sea the "Geelong" and the "Orvieto" detached themselves from the column and slowed up. We lowered one of the ship's boats and rowed over to the "Orvieto" and received a stock of cigarettes, tobacco and matches, our own stock being entirely exhausted.

It was not until we were within a day's sail of Suez that orders came through that we were to disembark in Egypt to complete our training. We were quite certain now, in our own minds that the war would be over before we could get to the front, and considered ourselves very hardly done by. Just as we were entering Suez Roads, we saw an Indian convoy coming up astern of us, containing 40 boats and consequently 78 transports were anchored at Suez at the same time—a truly wonderful sight. Our turn eventually came to enter the Canal and although monotonous the trip through was very interesting to everyone aboard.

The Canal was fortified at intervals by strong posts and block houses, garrisoned by English and Indian troops. Questions were freely asked as we slowly passed, which gave plenty of scope for witty and humorous replies. Of course, the stock question was, "Who are you?," and on one occasion a wag from the top boat deck replied, in a shrill, falsetto voice, "We are the Light Horse," which brought forth a roar of laughter. The climax, however, was reached one evening when out of the darkness someone asked, "Where are you from?," to which we naturally replied, "Tasmania," and felt very humiliated when the unknown voice again asked "Where's that?"

It was a very hot passage through the Canal, a hot wind blowing across the desert carrying with it a fine, sandy dust, which made the atmosphere very parched. Port Said was at last reached, which proved a source of immense excitement and interest to the troops. The boat was soon surrounded by Gyppos in dinghies, selling goods of all descriptions — fruit, jewellery, post cards, scarves, Turkish delight, and one hundred and one other things. The natives were either particularly shrewd by nature, or else had quickly learned their lesson from the troopships which had already passed through. The biggest trade was done in fruit, which was particularly acceptable to us after our five weeks of troopship fare, and bartering was soon in full swing for oranges, dates, figs, tomatoes, etc. And what a din of noise! It would sometimes take as long as five minutes to come to terms over a handful of oranges, the purchaser roaring out his offer from the troop deck and the vendor offering an alternative price from the dinghy. One lesson the natives had learnt well—never to allow goods of any kind aboard on appro., for they seldom, if ever, made a reappearance. On the conclusion of a bargain a basket was pulled up on a string and you were instructed to "put de money in de basket," which was then lowered and the purchased goods substituted and pulled up.

There were some three or four battle cruisers and torpedo boats at Port Said whilst we were there, and I think most of us saw a hydroplane for the first time, which flew over the port and finally took to the water just as it was passing the "Geelong." We stayed at Port Said for a few hours only, and then went out past the breakwater and anchored in the Mediterranean Sea about a mile off the shore, in order to make way for the other boats, which were coming through the Canal in a continuous stream. We now knew that our port of disembarkation was Alexandria, but it necessitated a wait of a couple of days at our anchorage before we could proceed, as the accommodation at the wharves was taxed to the uttermost and we had to wait our turn.

However, we finally came alongside the wharf on the morning of 9th December, and it was not long before unloading was in full progress. The 12th Battalion was the last unit to disembark, and it necessitated spending the night aboard, which was extremely objectionable owing to the excessive heat and noise. A line of sentries was placed along the wharf, but even with this precaution some of the men managed to get away into the town and obtain some vile concoction which was called "whiskey"—it was even put up in bottles bearing the names of well-known distillers—but its effect on the men was so disastrous that the medical officers caused some to be analysed and found it to contain some abominable ingredients.

The next day, 10th December, we disembarked and entrained, and wended our way up the Nile Valley. This journey was a source of wonder to all of us, and every few minutes some new sight, now on one side of the carriage and then on the other, would require the attention of everyone. That which surprised most of us was the nature of the country. The very word "Egypt" seems to suggest unending sand and desert, and yet the country through which we were passing was green with pasture and other vegetation. On every side, and as far as one could see, were fields of maize, rye, lucerne, cabbages, and many crops of which we did not yet know the name. Irrigation channels intersected the fields freely in all directions, and the bullock carrying out his never-ending route march round the water-wheel was a source of continued interest to the men. The native villages which were scattered everywhere brought forth more comment than anything else. One never saw an isolated house anywhere; they were all grouped into villages and miniature native towns, and, almost without exception, were made of mud or clay, or some composition used only by the natives, and huddled together in filth, dust and mud. Now and again one would see a better class house, probably occupied by a merchant or more wealthy native, which would be of better structure and surrounded by a garden or trees, many of which were in bloom, and formed a striking contrast to the hovels which surrounded it. The Diggers often would generally give a wave or a shout to the man tilling the soil with a primitive wooden plough drawn by oxen; the hail generally was returned, whilst the numerous boys which lined the route at intervals more often responded with some lewd gesture. The women, wearing a long, loose-flowing black garment, with a veil, and either carrying a baby at her side, leading a child by the hand, or carrying a water-jar or some huge bundle on her head, was much commented upon and received her share of wit and welcome as the train passed, but generally acknowledged it with silent contempt and disdain.

As the train stopped at the various stations it was soon crowded with natives selling fruit of all kinds, which was freely purchased by the troops and whom, I am sorry to say, were taken in on all sides by their ignorance of the Egyptian currency, a half piastre (a nickel coin worth about 1¼d.) being palmed on them in many instances for a shilling. But this state of affairs did not last long, for the Australian, with his usual sagacity and inventive power, soon gave the coins a name of his own until better informed and ascertained their approximate exchange value. It was also found that the natives were secreting bottles of that vile "whiskey" beneath their flowing garments and disposing of it at a fabulous price. After the experience of the previous night at Alexandria it is a marvel that the men bought it, but they did, and the officers and N.C.O.'s at once took action to prevent its sale. Every time a bottle made its appearance it was commandeered and broken on the wheels of the train, and when the natives realised that we were determined in our efforts they went for their lives as soon as an officer or N.C.O. appeared.

We arrived at Cairo about 4 p.m. and commenced detraining and unloading at once. We were each given a pannikin of tea, a roll and saveloy, from a stall which had been erected in the station yard and which proved very acceptable. Having left a guard to look after the baggage and stores, the remainder of the Battalion were put on to trams which were awaiting us outside the yard, and proceeded through the outskirts of the town on to the Mena Road, where we obtained our first glimpse of the Pyramids in the glow of the sunset. The Mena

Road is a wonderful piece of engineering work, being a raised road lined on either side with beautiful trees and running from Cairo fully six miles into the desert, to the very foot of the Pyramids. The road is wide and well built, with a double tram line on the left of the road (going out) and on the outer side of the trees. By the time we arrived at Mena it was quite dark, and the walk of about a quarter of a mile over the loose sand proved very tiring after the long day. However, we marched on to our camp site and bivouaced in the sand for the night. And, by Jove, wasn't it cold! Egypt may be hot in the daytime, but the change of temperature is very great, and it's equally cold at night.

There was not much difficulty in rousing the men in the morning, for very few of them had slept much and were only too glad to be on the move and to get warm. The first thing one saw was the immense Pyramid, which appeared to be almost on the top of us, and, indeed, so it was, for it was only about half a mile from the camp site. For the first few minutes after observing it, I am sure everyone was silent, either from awe, contemplation or respect, but it was not long before we were promising ourselves an early visit and tour of inspection.

Chapter III.

MENA CAMP

THE first day, of course, was spent in laying out the camp and pitching the tents, after which a living chain was made, stretching from the camp to the Pyramids, and stones were passed along and used to form the camp boundaries. The lay-out of the camp was approximately as follows:—

Pyramids

To Cairo	C A N B E R R A R D.		
		Mena Hospital	
A.S.C.		Engineers	2nd Inf. Brigade	1st Inf. Brigade
		Infantry Road	
		3rd Inf. Brigade	
Artillery			

After we had been in camp a couple of days we were joined by our two West Australian companies,

"G" and "H" Companies, which had received their early training with the 11th Battalion in Blackboy Hill Camp, near Perth.

The personnel of these Companies were as follows:—

"G" Company:
    Company Commander—Capt. J. P. Lalor.
    Subalterns—Lieut. J. L. C. Booth and 2nd Lieut. J. Evans.
    Colour Sergeant J. P. Castles.
    Sergeants J. Allen, J. A. Williams, W. P. Nevitt and A. E. Churchus.

"H" Company:
    Company Commander—Capt. E. T. Leane.
    Subalterns—Lieut. E. Y. Butler and 2nd Lieut. A. S. Vowles.
    Sergeants T. C. Ross, H. Thomas, W. H. Karn and A. Love.

As soon as we settled ourselves in camp, we were allotted company training areas about a mile away and carried on our training. The route to the training grounds was very heavy going, over loose sand in which you would sink ankle deep, and which made progress very slow, but the training area itself was on a high ridge and covered a good area of hard gravel. During our voyage from Australia we had become more or less soft in condition and cramped from lack of exercise, and in consequence, for the first week our training was steady until we got back into our old form, and consisted of rifle exercises, section, company and extended order drill.

Our first morning parade was at 8.30 a.m., and we would take a mid-day meal with us, carry out a day's training and return to camp at 3 p.m.

During our first leisure hours the Battalion went almost *en masse* to carry out a tour of inspection of the Pyramids and Sphinx. The "good guides" offered their services all the way along the route until they became a nuisance, and in many cases were dealt with forcibly. I went with a party, including Roy Scoble, Windred, Jack Adams, Lucas, Keith Terry and Norm. Ransom, and together we climbed to the top of the Pyramid and explored the interior, for which purpose we had to take our boots off and go in stockinged feet. This was because some of the passages are on a steep incline and the constant passage of feet over thousands of years has made the surface so smooth and slippery that it would be impossible to climb them with boots on. Our guide took us into both the King's and the Queen's Chambers, charging five piastres every time he lit a small piece of magnesium wire, and in the course of his rapid and almost incoherent description of the various places, repeated parrot-fashion, I am afraid he made many statements which were of doubtful origin.

Although individual members had been into Cairo, either on special leave or duty, the first general leave given to the Battalion was on Sunday, 13th December, and, needless to say, almost everyone availed themselves of the privilege. The trams were packed, many of the men riding on top, and the conductor found it very difficult to collect all the fares.

On arrival in Cairo each one went his own way to see the sights, make various purchases and enjoy himself generally. Esbekieh Gardens, Kasr-el-nil Bridge, Zoological Gardens and the Museum were all visited in turn. The first thing to be done by many of the men was to get their boots cleaned, after which they went in search of a good meal to relieve and supplement the camp fare. Most of them would patronise one of the restaurants kept by Italians and Greeks, whilst the officers dined more sumptuously at the Grand Continental or Shepherd's Hotel.

The day being hot, most of us would wander about in small parties, having a drink at one of the *alfresco* restaurants which abounded everywhere and which appealed to the Australian, whilst others would venture into one of the native wine shops, from whence a continual stream of barrel-organ music issued and in which dancing girls were seen flitting to and fro. Others delved still farther into the heart of this lively city and explored the mysteries of the Wozza itself.

As the evening drew to a close, tracks would be made back to camp—some by tram, some by *gharri* (or cab), and others by taxi. What races we used to have along the Mena Road! The occupants of two rival *gharris* would encourage their drivers to urge their horses by offering them huge prize money if they could race their opponents back to camp—in many cases the troops would relieve the driver of his office and take the reins themselves. The same thing applied to the taxis where the splendid condition of the road—and often the lateness of the hour—was the cause of many a speed limit being exceeded. This practice, however, became so dangerous and was the cause of so many accidents that orders were issued forbidding the racing of taxis and *gharris*, and limiting the speed of the former.

Before we had been in camp very long special attention was given to the messing, as during the first ten days or fortnight the men had to partake of their meals in their tents, which was neither comfortable nor sanitary. The sand was so fine, that on a windy day it would penetrate into all the food and at all times got mixed up with the dixies, plates, mess-tins and cups, and as it was not of the cleanest variety after being trampled upon by the occupants of a tent, the staff (probably urged by the medical officers) soon brought about a better state of affairs. This was done by the erection of four mess sheds per battalion, at the head of the company lines. These were quickly built by a big squad of natives, and allotted as follows:—

> No. 1 Shed—H.Q. Details "A" and "C" Companies.
> No. 2 Shed—Sergeants' Mess, "B" Company and half "D" Company.
> No. 3 Shed—Half "D" Company, "E" and "F" Companies.
> No. 4 Shed—Space for Q.M., "G" and "H" Companies.

The cook-houses were situated between the mess sheds and the Battalion parade ground, and I'm afraid the cooks carried out their duties under trying conditions. They had to do their cooking in the open, in the heat of the mid-day sun and in the face of the sand-laden winds, from which we suffered much during our sojourn in the camp. The only cover they had was one shanty between two companies, in which to keep and cut up the meat. It was somewhere in the vicinity of the "B" Company cook-house that the regimental pet was lodged. This was a Tasmanian devil—a devil by nature as well as by name, for it was so vicious that it would allow no one to go near it, and it was not long before everyone ceased trying. Its caretaker was "Bluey" Thompson, "D" Company cook, and both on the "Geelong" and at the camp he was about the only one that could get anywhere near it. It was a centre of interest to the civilian visitors who came out from Cairo to see the camp—in fact, a representative from the Cairo Zoological Gardens suggested purchase, but "Bluey," knowing how "attached" the Battalion was to the beast, refused the offer.

The officers' mess was situated on the far side of the parade ground and consisted of a large marquee tent. They contracted with a local caterer to run the mess, and suffered rather badly in consequence.

The officers certainly got the better end of the stick on the "Geelong" with regard to rations, but making due allowance for the messing fee which the officers had to pay, the men themselves scored at Mena Camp.

The rations at this time were not bad, although perhaps we might have complained a bit (the Diggers always considered it a sound principle to find some fault at which to work up a grouse) if we had been unable to get into Cairo once or twice a week to dine sumptuously off roast chicken and salad (our favourite meal). The bread ration was good and plentiful, and also the jam. Our meat issue was always converted into stews and curries, which are nice in their way but tend to become monotonous after a few weeks without change.

Vegetables were almost an unknown quantity—in fact, an allowance of 6d. per man per day was made to each company in lieu thereof. The Company Quartermaster Sergeant (as he afterwards became), in collaboration with the Company Commander, had the spending of this money, and generally made his purchases at the British Expeditionary Force Canteen. Needless to say, he tried to vary them as much as possible, and obtained rations which were suitable to take out for a midday meal whilst training, such as biscuits, saveloys, eggs, sardines, etc., also rice, raisins, figs, prunes, etc., for puddings.

The sergeants had their mess in No. 2 Shed, and it was really a continuation of the mess which had been established at Pontville and again constituted on the "Geelong," both of which I was a member, having obtained a Lance-Sergeant stripe before embarkation. Sergeant Sanson was mess caterer, and put on a good table. The messing fee was 6d. per member per day, and, supplemented by the profits arising from the wet canteen attached to the mess, the financial position should have been good, but I regret to say that it was entirely the reverse, and when the mess broke up at the end of the camp there was a deficit which Colonel Hawley caused to be made good from our pay.

On January 1st, 1915, the A.I.F. adopted the double company organisation and thus we became a Battalion of four companies instead of eight: "A" and "C" Companies combined to form the new "A" Company commanded by Major C. H. Elliott (now promoted), with Selwyn as Company Sergeant Major and Pickett as Company Quartermaster Sergeant. "B" and "D" Companies combined to form the new "B" Company commanded by Major E. H. Smith (also promoted), with Herbert as C.S.M. and Mildren as C.Q.M.S.

"E" and "F" Companies combined to form the new "C" Company under Capt. J. L. Whitham, with Stubbings and Burford as his senior N.C.O.'s and

"G" and "H" Companies formed the new "D" Company under Capt. J. P. Lalor, with Castles and Allen on his Coy. H.Q. Staff.

Having mastered platoon drill and the new movements in Company and Battalion drill, we again continued our Battalion training and very soon exceeded the efficiency attained at Pontville. This phase of our training was carried out at a locality known as Tiger's Tooth, and which I am afraid was the cause of many an inflated sick parade, attended by a large percentage of faint-hearted johnnies and pointers, in the hopes that the R.M.O. would put them on "light duty."

Tiger's Tooth consisted of a line of high, jagged rocks which rose abruptly out of the ocean of sand, miles away towards the west, and were silhouetted against the horizon. We had seen them many times from our companies' training grounds—in fact, they were a landmark to be seen from all the high ground—and had commented freely upon them, little thinking that in the near future we would be dragging our weary way through the loose sand, carrying full marching order, and eating a mid-day meal in the close vicinity, or even worse, shivering in the cold dawn on their rocky slopes, waiting for the sun to rise.

We paraded at 8 a.m. from now onwards. The band would play us out with our regimental march, "When the Empire Calls," after which we would carry out march discipline until we reached the scene of our day's operations, for Tiger's Tooth was fully five to six miles from camp. Our training, needless to say, was varied and thorough, comprising advance guards, battalion in attack, outpost positions, rearguard and retiring actions, flank guards, and so on.

The country over which we worked was very difficult and deceptive, and was the means of excellent training for the Scouts. For about 400 to 500 yards in front of a company or platoon the ground would appear to be as flat as a billiard table, and yet after making a reconnaissance it would be found to be full of dead ground capable of giving good cover to a couple of hundred men. During these manoeuvres, conducted by the Commanding Officer (Colonel Clarke), Colonel Hawley was always to be seen riding all over the country rounding up sections and platoons which had gone astray, surprising the company signallers and runners who had taken up a position in some dead ground and were having a spell and keeping a watchful eye on operations generally.

We would knock off about noon for the mid-day meal, and as soon as we had piled arms and broken off into small parties a host of natives, mostly women, would appear from nowhere—for there was not a sign of them until now—selling fruit, chocolate, etc., and their cries soon became familiar and were imitated by the troops when they wanted to make a purchase, such as "Orangis—big one, gibbit two for half," "Nes-les chocolates, verra gude," "Flag cigarette, gibbit *baksheesh*," "Eggser-Cooked," "Cake Cairo."

Having finished our meal and cleared up the mess we would carry out about half-an-hour's company or battalion drill and then wind our weary way back to camp about 3 p.m., or a bit earlier if it was the Battalion's turn for general leave into Cairo.

During the whole of this period the specialists were receiving training with their respective sections. Lieut. Houghton would take his signallers "flag-wagging" along the Valley of the White House,

THE SPHINX AND PYRAMIDS, MENA

(Photo. by Lieut. L. M. Newton, M.C.)

or instruct them in the use of the heliograph, which could always be seen flashing from the high ridges. Lieut. Room and his Vickers Machine Gun Section also attained a high degree of efficiency during their training at Mena. This was carried out either by means of lectures in the mess sheds or by drill and tactics in the vicinity of the camp. A lot of time was needed for cleaning the guns, due to the sand penetrating the mechanism during the training, or even on their being exposed to the wind to any great extent.

Lieut. Patterson was responsible for the training of the Company Scouts in their various duties, although this branch of specialist training was not taught in such detail as was the custom in later years in France. Another specialist was the rangefinder, who received instruction in the use of the mekometer under company arrangements.

The stretcher-bearers were left in camp frequently for duty with the Regimental Medical Officer, who put them through their stretcher drill and gave them invaluable instruction in first aid. Even the buglers were not exempt from training, for on arrival at our training area it was usual to send them to some far off gully to practice their calls, and they found it difficult to shirk their training, for as soon as the bugle calls ceased for any length of time, a messenger was sent by the C.O. to know the reason why. At the same time, I've a shrewd idea that they used to carry on by reliefs and thus get their spell that way, for though only five months "old" we were fast becoming old soldiers.

The next phase of our training was brigade training, and I think the time now opportune to make some mention of our Brigade Staff.

The Brigadier was Col. E. G. Sinclair-MacLagan, D.S.O.; the Brigade Major, Major C. H. Brand; and the Staff Captain, Capt. A. M. Ross, all of whom had seen previous service in the field. It would have been a difficult task to have found a more competent and efficient combination that that just mentioned. The Brigadier was a stern disciplinarian, but he was respected by all ranks, and everyone realised that although it was almost impossible to hide an error, defect or omission from him, yet he never complained or roared without good cause and was always amenable to reason. He knew the Section Commander's duty as well as he knew that of the Battalion Commander. Whilst we were practising a Battalion in attack, he would ride over the horizon with his orderly, approach a section, and enquire from the Section Commander what the Battalion was doing, point angrily to a man with his safety catch back, question a man as to the range of a certain object, complain at the fitting of equipment, ascertain if every man had a haversack ration and a full waterbottle, and then ride off to confer with the C.O. before we had properly realised who he was.

The Brigade Major was similar to the Brigadier in many ways; he, also, was very keen on the discipline of the Brigade, and a good look-out was always kept for his approach during periods of training. It was generally believed by the men that the Brigade Major never slept, and was always on duty. He was always to be seen after "lights out" where least expected, either turning out a guard, pulling up late arrivals into camp and commandeering their passes, or investigating some noise in one of the Battalion lines. And yet he was always out before "reveille!" I well remember one evening that I went to the cinema at the back of the Transport lines. There had been an afternoon show and we were waiting to go into the next one about 6.30 p.m. or 7 p.m. As soon as the first house commenced to come out the mob wanted to get in and there was a deadlock; then, by a concerted effort the crowd began to sway and eventually we all swarmed into the shed—needless to say, without paying. Whilst we were congratulating ourselves on a cheap evening's entertainment and calling on the management to begin, the Brigade Major jumped on to the stage and there was at once silence. "Stand up the men who paid to come in," he said, but no one moved. "Are you aware that a portion of the profits from this cinema go to your own regimental funds and that you are robbing yourselves? I refuse to allow the performance to commence until everyone has paid." And as the management came round we meekly handed out our piastres.

The Staff Captain was not known to the rank and file quite so much in those days, although afterwards we got to know him better and admired his pluck and courage. Much of his time at Mena, no doubt, was taken up in the Brigade Office, but even so he often accompanied the Brigadier on his tour of inspection of training. He was also to be seen in camp after the Battalion had left, and was the bane of the Battalion Orderly Officer and Sergeant, making minute inspection of the cook-house, mess sheds, Q.M. Store, and the Battalion lines generally.

Brigade training was very little different to Battalion training as far as the rank and file were concerned, and generally we knew far less of what we were doing or what particular function the Battalion was holding, but we all appreciated the fact that the training was primarily for the officers.

After the conclusion of the operation the "Officers" call would be blown, and either all officers or perhaps just company commanders would parade before the Brigadier and the day's training would be criticised, errors pointed out and, I am sure, helpful advice given.

On the morning of January 26th, 1915, long before it was light, an alarm was given and we all had to dress and turn out in full marching order. Officers, Sergeants Major, and platoon sergeants were soon on the scene urging the men to hurry, and many an uncomplimentary remark was passed about the war in general and individuals in particular. Within less than half-an-hour the Battalion was on the parade ground, and, to our disgust, we marched off, taking a course straight into the desert towards Tiger's Tooth. Our hearts sank within us! Before long we discovered that we were not the only unit out in the cold morning air and very soon the whole Brigade was complete and as dawn broke we halted about half-way to Tiger's Tooth and received the command to break off independently and march back to camp. It was merely an example showing how quickly a whole Brigade of some 4,000 men—wholly unprepared—could be turned out, if necessary, at a minute's notice.

Another day the Battalion was taken out under Brigade arrangements (to Tiger's Tooth, of course) to carry out a billeting scheme stage-managed by the Staff Captain. A village was laid out by means of tape and signalling wire, and guides were sent to meet the Battalion as they approached and led their respective companies to billets in barns, halls, houses, granaries, schools, etc., each indicated by a small notice board. We were instructed in the posting of billet guards, the position and use of alarm posts, and many other details. Altogether, we enjoyed it and found it a relief to the ordinary routine of training.

Another big event in our training was a divisional route march with all 1st line Transport, which was carried out on February 1st, 1915. We were waiting on the parade ground a long time and it seemed as if the column would never pass, as the 12th Battalion was at the tail of the Infantry. The route was down the Mena Road about three miles, and then we went north across a country track and made a circular detour back. It was very interesting all the way through the cultivated fields and passing the native villages, but the day was very hot and the road exceedingly dusty, and as we were at the tail of the column, our pace was very erratic and we were continually halting, which as every soldiers knows is tiring in the extreme. We finally passed through a grove of date palms, and as the White House came into view we knew that we were not far from camp. Altogether, it was supposed to be a very satisfactory march, although our Battalion suffered more fatigue owing to its position in the column, and yet we had only one man drop out, half a mile from camp, and that was Sgt. Dand, whose duties had precluded him from carrying out the intense training which the rest of us had been experiencing for some weeks.

The greatest excitement which prevailed in the camp was during the first week in February, when news came through that the Turks had attacked the Suez Canal on February 3rd, 1915, and had attempted to make a crossing at Tusoom and El Kantara. The Arab boy was eagerly awaited with his paper, as he cried, "Egyptian news to-morrow, very gude," and so on. It was the first time that we had been in an actual theatre of war, almost within sound of the guns, and we wondered whether we would be called upon to assist. The 3rd Field Company Engineers had already been on the Canal for some period preparing defensive works, and excitement was at fever heat when two battalions of the 2nd Brigade marched out. The attack failed miserably, and ere long the two 2nd Brigade battalions came back, having got only as far as Ismailia. The Engineers, however, were more or less in the thick of it, and we were afterwards interested to know that our sisters of the "Geelong," Sisters King and Radcliffe, were moved into the fighting zone and did duty in the only stationary hospital on the Canal, through which the wounded were evacuated. The pontoons in which the Turks attempted to cross the Canal, riddled with bullets, were afterwards exhibited in the Cairo Zoological Gardens.

The health of the Battalion was distinctly good during our sojourn in Egypt, largely due, no doubt, to the intense training which we carried out. However, the Mena Hotel, at the tram terminus, had been converted into Mena Hospital, staffed by Australian doctors and nurses, and was usually fairly full. This was due principally to the abnormal number of cases of pneumonia, believed by the medical officers to be caused by our training in full marching order in the sun and getting very hot and wet with perspiration, and when a spell was given, the men used to take off their equipment and in consequence many caught a severe chill. However, as soon as the cause was detected, caution was taken to avoid a recurrence, with good results. It was at Mena that the Battalion suffered its first losses, for two of our comrades succumbed to their illnesses and were buried in Mena British Cemetery, Old Cairo, with full military honours. On February 4th, 1915, our ranks were further depleted, when a number of men, who had been classed as "medically unfit," left the camp and proceeded to Ismailia, where they embarked on the H.S. "Kyarra" for return to Australia. To compensate these losses, however, our first batch of about 100 reinforcements arrived in camp on February 9th, under the command of Lieut. H. C. Orbell, who was himself posted to "B" Company, whilst his reinforcements were distributed amongst the companies.

Attached to the Mena Hospital were some very fine swimming baths, which were allotted to battalions and other units in rotation. Many of the men used to make a point of having a bath every time they went into Cairo, but, of course, we were not all built that way, and in consequence these swimming and bathing parades were of great importance in such a hot climate as the presence of vermin had already been detected amongst some of the men, and it was of the utmost necessity to teach them to keep down this pest whilst we were living under comparatively good conditions.

What more can be said of Mena? One could tell of our visits to the Citadel and Mahomed Ali's Mosque, Matirieh, the Mokattam Hills and Sakharra Pyramids, of the town piquet, the Redcaps, of our night operations, our field firing (again at Tiger's Tooth), of the bursting of the reservoir and the swamping of the camp which necessitated the calling out of the inlying piquet, of the church parades at the mound in rear of the camp, of the bugle bands and bagpipes which used to play other units in and out of camp, of divisional duties which used to swallow up the whole Battalion strength, of the avenue of native shops—known as the "Strand"—at the back of the camp with the wet and dry canteens and the cinema near by, but these brief references will be sufficient to refresh the memories of those who sojourned with the 12th Battalion in the shadow of the Pyramids.

Our training was brought to its zenith near the end of February, when we participated in divisional operations under the command of Major-General Bridges, C.M.G. For this purpose the Battalion, with its headquarters, specialists and gear, marched up the dusty road past the Pyramids and Sphinx and out on to the plains beyond. The 3rd Brigade carried out the role of Reserve Brigade, and whether the Brigade itself was called upon for any assistance I do not know, but certainly the 12th Battalion did not become enveloped in the attack and we had an easy day in consequence, returning to camp about 3 p.m.

The last days of February brought hurry and bustle, loading and packing, wonder and excitement, and, above all, curiosity. The 12th Battalion had received its orders to move! The news quickly spread through the whole of the camp, and very soon enquiries were rife as to the authenticity of the rumour. We soon learned that the 3rd Brigade was the only brigade to receive the orders, and our excitement and curiosity were even increased. Why were we so selected? Where were we going? Was it for more training, or really to test the training we had already received by carrying it into practice?

We moved on a Sunday. (It was already becoming a by-word that all our arrivals and departures occurred on Sundays, and as the narrative continues it will be seen how consistently this happened). On February 28th we made an early start to pack our gear, hand in our blankets, and strike tents generally. This was all completed by noon, although we did not move off until about 4 p.m. Then the fatigue parties commenced to clean up the camp, and if we cleaned it up once we must have cleaned it up a dozen times. The Orderly Officer would commandeer a party of some twenty men and advance them in extended order right across the camp site, picking up paper, tins and rubbish as they went, but a strong westerly wind—almost a gale—was blowing, and as soon as the fatigue party finished all the paper and rubbish from the 9th, 10th and 11th Battalion lines would be blown along and our work would be in vain. However, we fell in on the Battalion parade ground for the last time at 4 p.m., so that we could carry out our march into Cairo in the cool of the early evening, and as we marched off, Canberra Road was lined with men from all branches of the service, who wished us good luck and who probably envied us our departure; the Sisters also came out from the Hospital and bade us a cheery farewell. Many a sigh of relief was given as we passed the main guard outside the hospital for the last time, for there was hardly a member of the Battalion who had not some lively recollection of that same guard, either a wearisome twenty-four hours of duty with much presenting of arms, or a "Stand and deliver" after "lights out" when he was out of camp without a leave pass.

We swung round into the Mena Road and on the left-hand side saw some of our own fellows that we were leaving behind, as they were in a kind of convalescent camp situated in a hollow on the corner, and who were not sufficiently recovered from their illnesses to come with us. On looking down the column one could not help thinking what a wonderful body of men the Battalion appeared as they marched down the Mena Road with full marching order and little galvanised billies swinging from the supporting straps. The marching was excellent, our spirits high, and many were the *"saiedas"* given to almost everyone we passed, for after six months we believed that we were really on our way to one of the fighting zones.

Cairo was again our entraining point, needless to say, and we pulled out just after dark, and in consequence there is nothing of importance to record of our train journey up to Alexandria, where we arrived next morning. The train took us right on to the wharf and we then knew that we were again to sample the joys of troopship life, our future home on this occasion being Troopship A3, known in civil life as the P. & O. S.S. "Devanha."

On the morning of March 2nd we set sail under sealed orders, and it was said, on good authority, that the captain himself did not know our destination until he broke the seal of his orders after he had been two hours at sea.

We set a northerly course and proceeded without escort, and maps soon made their appearance and we wondered where our destination could be. During the latter part of the next day we were passing numerous little islands, some of them near and some away on the horizon, and consequently we knew ourselves to be in the Grecian Archipelago —in fact, information had by this time penetrated to the troop deck that our destination was the Greek island of Lemnos.

Chapter IV.

LEMNOS

ON the morning of March 4th we were up betimes, and it was evident that we were making for an island which lay immediately ahead, and at 7 a.m. we entered the narrow entrance and found ourselves in the huge land-locked harbour of Mudros. When one remembers what a hive of shipping this harbour afterwards contained and what a tremendous base it formed for the Gallipoli campaign, we may recollect with justified pride that the "Devanha" was the first troopship to arrive there.

The harbour itself was very large and we proceeded to the farther end, passing the village of Mudros on the way. It was surrounded by hills in all directions, many of which had three, four, and sometimes five windmills on their crests. They were quaint structures, these windmills, with about eight arms, but nothing to indicate how the wind could operate them, until later in the morning, when peasants apparently took advantage of the breeze which had sprung up, and commenced to set them in motion. This was done by unrolling some canvas on to a framework and thus forming eight small sails, which set the mill in fast motion, and when the day's work was completed the sail was again rolled up and made fast round the respective arms.

During the day the other troopships arrived, bearing the other units of the Brigade, namely, "Suffolk," "Ionian," "Malda," and the "Nizam," the latter being the horse boat. We were now called the Detached Force, and Col. MacLagan was in complete command.

We remained on board for some few days, carrying out such training as is practicable on troopships, and wondering all the time what our destination and objective were to be. Knowing that the Navy had been busy for some weeks back in bombarding the forts of Gallipoli with a view to forcing the Narrows, we naturally supposed that we would be utilised for one of two purposes, either (1) to effect a landing and assist in forcing the passage of the Dardanelles, or (2) occupy the forts after they had been silenced or even to continue the advance.

In the meantime other troopships were continuing to arrive with the Royal Marine Light Infantry (R.M.L.I.—better known to us by the substituted words, "Run, My Lad, Imshee") and other units of the Naval Division.

When we had been here about a week, or may be less, the 9th Battalion, which was very cramped for room on the "Malda," was taken ashore and put in a tented camp just outside Mudros. The transports of all units were also taken ashore and given exercise. This was an indication that it was possible that we might be remaining at Lemnos for some short period, and it was not long before our Battalion used to go ashore in boats every morning at 8.30 a.m., carry out a full day's training ashore and return to the boat about 4 p.m. Our first day ashore will certainly be remembered by everyone. We carried out a route march some three miles round the harbour, with Col. Clarke and the Battalion band at our head, and before we had gone far numerous kiddies from the neighbouring villages joined us, and one youngster, bearing a large Greek flag on a pole, proudly headed the column and accompanied us for some two miles. A pen and ink sketch of this circumstance appeared in the London "Graphic," having originated from the pen of Lieut. Booth.

Our life on the "Devanha" during this period formed a distinct phase of the Battalion's career and is deserving of comment. Troopship routine and discipline was very much the same as on the "Geelong," but the monotony of training was relieved by our daily landing and carrying out operations on shore. Rations, however, were deplorable, and the memory of them mars what was otherwise a more or less pleasant period of our military existence. Complaints were made at every meal and all our Company Officers did their uttermost to bring about an improvement, but their efforts were useless, for the Quartermaster could only tell us that we were now on Admiralty rations and were receiving our full issue.

Bread was the first trouble. To begin with, we were allowed only 1 lb. a day per man, and owing to the fact that they had some trouble with the bakers aboard it was turned out in a shocking condition. In fact, it was not bread at all, but solid lumps of dough, and uneatable. To compensate, we were given a ration of ship's biscuits, but to us they were as uneatable as the bread, for our teeth could make no impression on them whatever, and they would not even break after being treated with the helve of an entrenching tool. We were at our wits' end to know what to do, but at last we managed to chip off a few bits with our bayonets and soaked them in water and ate them that way. That was the manner in which we afterwards used to treat them—having learned by experience. We broke them in small pieces with the bayonet and then put them through the mincing machine in the cook-house and afterwards made them into a pap, either with water or with milk, if procurable. These biscuits were put to various uses; they were bowled along the deck, hurled across mess-tables as missiles, and one humorist who was handy with the paint-brush painted a cross over a soldier's grave on one, with the inscription, "Oh God, our help in ages past," and hung it on the handle of one of the officers' cabins.

However, this state of affairs did not last too long, for the trouble in the bake-house was apparently satisfactorily arranged, and decent bread again made appearance.

Of our rations the tea, sugar, milk, oatmeal (for breakfast) and meat (sufficient for one meal only) were handed straight to the cook and were never seen by us. All the platoon sergeant had to issue was one 1 lb loaf per man and 2 ozs. of jam. This constituted our day's ration, and considering the training we were doing at this time it is marvellous that we kept so fit.

It was really a farce the Company and Battalion Orderly Officers making their inspections at meal times, and one could honestly say that although we all growled and complained every time they came round the majority of us felt sorry for them, knowing that their own rations were particularly good at this period and yet they were helpless to bring about a better state of affairs for the men, although they one and all conscientiously made an effort to do so.

The troop decks on the "Devanha" were more crowded than those on the "Geelong," and many of us used to sleep on the promenade deck. Almost all the sergeants used to adopt this practice, and I remember Richardson and myself always shared a "possie" with Garrard next to us on one side and Pearson, from "C" Company, on the other. And will we ever forget the cold winds? We thought it cold during the nights that we spent in Egypt, but is was certainly nothing to the icy, penetrating winds that blew across Mudros harbour. We would lie and listen to the Artillery blowing their mounted "reveille" and dread throwing back the clothes and exposing ourselves to the cold air—in fact, we used to put our trousers on under the blankets. However, we quickly had to make a move when the ship's crew came round the corner and started to wash down the decks, and we rapidly collected our blankets and hammocks and rolled them up and tied them in platoon bundles and stacked them in the hammock bins, ready for the evening time again.

Every day at 8.30 a.m. we would commence to go ashore, getting into the boats either by the ship's companion-way or down rope ladders. Volunteers having been called for rowers, we would put our backs into the rowing and quickly cover the 400 to 500 yards to the shore, and the Battalion would assemble at a place called Taligna Point. Each boat-load, as it arrived, formed up on the beach and then marched off to an assembly point and waited until the Battalion was complete. Whilst this was in progress we were soon surrounded by a crowd of pedlars—men, women, boys and girls, of all ages and sizes—each eager to dispose of their wares, which consisted almost entirely of eatables such as oranges, dates, strings of figs, nuts, chocolate, Turkish delight, cigarettes, bread, and cheese made from goats' milk. It is superfluous to say that they did a roaring trade and very soon sold out, only to return with a fresh supply ready for us when we embarked again in the afternoon.

The Battalion having assembled, we would then march off and carry out a day's training, which consisted either of a route march under company or battalion arrangements, or a company or battalion in attack.

It was during these days that we became acquainted with the country and people. The latter were of the peasant type and lived more or less under miserable conditions, although they appeared happy enough. The men wore a very baggy pair of pantaloons, generally blue in colour, with a sheepskin jacket, leggings made from sacking and tied round with string, and boots made from goats' skin or bullock hide. Their chief occupation appeared to be tending goats, whilst others cultivated isolated plots of ground with oxen and a primitive wooden plough.

The women were either very timid or very modest, for one saw very little of them. Their was nothing particularly characteristic about their dress, except perhaps a handkerchief of varying hues which was worn over the head and the ends generally held together in their mouth. They worked hard both in the fields and in their homes.

(Photo. by "The Graphic," London)

Facsimile of a sketch drawn by the late Lieut. J. L. C. Booth, 12th Battalion, which appeared in the London "Graphic" (by whose courtesy it is reproduced) in May, 1915. It illustrates the route march carried out by the 12th Battalion at Lemnos, referred to on page 45, when two lads, with a Greek flag, headed the column.

The younger women and girls would rush inside as soon as they saw any troops approaching, but the older women would remain at their doors, spinning flax on to a top, or knitting huge stockings, or other articles of apparel.

The country, as mentioned previously, was nothing but hills, large and small, ranging one behind the other, and it was not long before we realised it when once we recommenced our training in earnest. The ground was very rocky and stony and was cultivated only in small patches in the low-lying districts. In the hills the goat herds could be seen or else heard by the tinkling of their bells. There appeared to be only about one well-made road, which followed the harbour round from Mudros well round to the other side, and all other communications were by indistinct and primitive roads or else mountain tracks. There was hardly a single isolated house to be seen at Lemnos; they were all grouped into compact villages and generally situated in a valley with hills all round them, probably for safety and protection from the weather.

And still our training continued—adopting artillery formations, forming a firing line, calling up reinforcements, assaulting a crest of a hill, consolidating the line, reorganising after the attack, pursuing a fictitious enemy down the slopes of a hill, changing direction half-left to avoid a village, re-assembling for the mid-day meal, and in this manner day after day we gradually became as hard as nails and almost as fit, physically, as any body of troops within the knowledge of mankind.

The only troops that were left aboard during this period were the company cooks, headquarters orderly room staff, Q.M. staffs, troop deck sergeants and a fatigue party reduced to a minimum for cleaning up the troop decks and for work in the cook-house. One day "Bluey" Thompson, one of "B" Company's cooks, lost his pipe—a pipe noted for its age and strength—and it resisted all "Bluey's" efforts to find it. Such a commotion was caused that all the cooks and the cooks' fatigue party joined in the search, but still the pipe refused to be discovered. At last the Battalion came home, tired and hungry, and you may well believe that "Bluey" got very little sympathy for the smokeless day he had put in. Stew was for tea that day (as usual), and mess orderlies paraded to the cookhouse for the dixies and the platoon sergeant or mess corporal proceeded to issue it to the men. The Battalion Orderly Officer then appeared with his stereotyped "Any complaints?," but knowing how powerless the officers were to assist us, we had realised the futility of complaining, but on this instance there was a "Yes, sir" from a distant troop deck and the Orderly Officer went along. It was a "D" Company mess, and on being asked what was wrong the corporal said, "We don't mind making an effort to eat the stew, sir, but I'm dashed if we're going to tackle *this*." And he held up "Bluey's" pipe!

The only ration which was at all plentiful on the "Devanha" was tinned milk. Of this we had plenty —in fact, "B" Company found it too much. We used it for porridge in the morning and for putting in the tea, and yet there was always some left over, and so C.Q.M.S. Mildren used to accumulate it until we had a case full. This was then smuggled into the boat and taken ashore and Garney Rundle and I were allowed to remain off parade, hire a donkey, and take the milk into Mudros. We there discovered a storekeeper who could speak

French. I at once got to work and struck a bargain with him and exchanged the milk for either one, one-and-a-half or two sheep's carcases, according to the amount of milk we took in, which we transported back to the boat and eventually to "B" Company's cook-house. Of course, the whole thing was irregular and had to be kept very quiet, but at the same time it meant the supplementing of a very inadequate ration, and so it was considered by all concerned that the end justified the means.

It was on these occasions that I got to know Mudros, the principal village on the island. It was situated on the eastern shores of the harbour and consisted of fairly well-built houses of the peasantry type. The outstanding feature of the village was a recently built Greek Orthodox Church right in the centre, on the village green—if Grecian villages can boast of such a feature. The inside of the Church was disappointing in its bareness, the only ornaments being of a cheap, tawdry and tinsel description. The main street led down to a small wharf, but the largest boats belonging to the native population that I saw there were not much bigger than an ordinary rowing boat capable of carrying a sail. The wharf was guarded by Greek soldiers, who lolled about in a very haphazard way and did not seem to bother as long as nothing happened to disturb them. The jetty formed the landing place for all the French troopships which were now in port, and one could see a variety of uniforms—blue-grey of the infantry, red trousers and blue jackets of the artillery, pom-pom hats of the sailors, and last, but not least, the smiling black faces of the Senegalese troops.

On the northern side of the village, just near the 9th Battalion camp, a hospital was established, and it was here that "B" Company suffered its first casualty. Douglas Carlson had been evacuated with measles, but other complications set in and he died on 24th March and we buried him in the Greek cemetery about a quarter of a mile out of the village, with full military honours, both Greek and Australian padres officiating at the graveside.

On 17th March the Colonel made a grave mistake. A deputation from the troop deck was paraded to him and the members requested that a holiday should be given to all the Irishmen of the Battalion in honour of St. Patrick's Day, and in a weak moment the Colonel granted their request. Fully half the Battalion suddenly remembered that their father or their father's father—or someone—hailed from the Emerald Isle, and in consequence rapidly developed an Irish brogue. The other half of the Battalion reluctantly paraded on the top deck and got into the boats to go ashore, inwardly cursing their tardiness in not discovering a strain of Irish blood running through their own veins.

And what a spectacle greeted our eyes when we returned to the boat in the afternoon! And what a victory St. Patrick had! Green ribbons, rosettes, Irish flags, harps of Erin and green handkerchiefs had appeared from nowhere, whilst Tiny Anderson was leading a jazz band, composed of mess utensils and buckets, by standing on one of No. 8 Platoon's mess-tables with a green tam o' shanter on his head.

Needless to say, many of them—Irish or otherwise—were very glad next morning that St. Patrick's Day came only once a year.

It was now known by our commanders that our destination was to be Gallipoli; the nature of the country over which we would have to fight was also known, and orders were accordingly issued that the troops were to be exercised as much as possible in hill-climbing. Up hill and down hill, up the next one and down the other side the Colonel took us, and although some of the grousers began to wish they had never enlisted, yet the Battalion's respect for their commanding officer grew day by day, for in spite of his years he led the column through all this strenuous climbing, and yet at the end of the day appeared to be almost as fresh as when he started. I well remember one day; it was a bright, crisp, sunny morning, we had been climbing hills since we landed and on reaching the summit of a particularly high one a glorious view presented itself. We could see the coast line of half the island, and the snow-clad summit of the island of Samothrace, forty or fifty miles away to the north, glittering in the sun. One of the men in the leading platoon, pointing with his finger, said, "Doesn't Samothrace look beautiful this morning?" This brought an angry retort from somewhere in the rear of the company, "Put your blanky finger down; the Colonel will see which hill you're pointing at!"

On 29th March the Battalion (less "D" Company) landed and proceed to a three-day bivouac about a mile and a half out of the village, which proved an acceptable diversion from troopship routine. Being detached from the Brigade, we were issued with 120 rounds of ammunition per man (for the first time) in case of emergency. Whilst at the bivouac we carried on with our training—route marching, hill climbing and battalion in attack. Every man will remember the day that the Colonel took us for a route march, and as we were marching along a valley with a very high hill with a sheer slope on our left, he gave the command, "Platoons, left wheel." We could hardly believe our ears; surely he was not going to ask us to climb to the top of *this* hill! But as soon as each platoon had completed the wheel and was clear of the track, he halted us and told us to sit down and have a spell as he wanted us to attempt the climb in one go—and we did it! It required a tremendous effort, though, with a full pack up, and everyone was just about done when we reached the top and most of us stretched out on the broad of our backs and took a long breather. We had dinner at the top, during which time we admired the magnificent view which was visible, and afterwards we formed up in mass formation and the Colonel addressed us somewhat on the following lines:

"Officers, N.C.O.'s and men, we have now been training together for seven months and have reached a very creditable state of efficiency. However, at this present moment we are standing on foreign soil, you are carrying 120 rounds of ball ammunition per man, and if you look out to sea you will observe in the far distance Gallipoli and the Narrows, with the battleships patrolling the entrance. We are only forty miles off and you can hear the sound of the naval guns. This is the nearest most of us have ever been to the war, and when the time comes for us to take a closer and more active part I wish you all the best of good luck and would only remind you that the honour and fair name of the Battalion are in your hands."

For a while there was not a sound, as every man strained his eyes to see as much of our future objective as possible, and reflected on the Colonel's remarks, but the reaction soon set in and there was a buzz of voices as the situation, as it now presented itself, was discussed by all ranks. Afterwards, Lieut.-Colonel Hawley put us through some rifle exercises and then we descended the slope and returned to the bivouac, well satisfied with the result of our very strenuous climb.

It was about at this time that Lieut. Green was detached for duty. No one exactly knew what his duty was, but he could always be seen careering round the harbour in a motor or steam launch, or towing lighters or barges from jetty to troopship, and the ease with which he substituted nautical orders for military words of command gained him the nickname which has stuck to the present day, namely, "The Admiral."

During our stay at Lemnos the following order was issued, which is of interest and worthy of note:—

> "Company Commanders will ensure all ranks being warned against any interference or communication with Turkish women during the forthcoming operations. These women are to be known by the fact that they wear the Turkish veil. Good treatment of women will be of great value to the force in its military operations and will facilitate information, supply and transport, besides the enhancement of British prestige, and curtailment of the period that operations may last in Turkey. The O.C. Detached Force wishes all ranks to realise that on each man rests the great responsibility of keeping the honour and good name of the British race unsullied in its operations in enemy country, *and that it is his bounden duty to report any delinquents at once.*"

About the end of the first week in April other

Units of the Division commenced to arrive, as well as the British 29th Division, so that the harbour presented a wonderful sight with such a mass of merchant ships, and in addition the super-dreadnought "Queen Elizabeth," as well as cruisers and destroyers, almost too numerous to mention.

As the different Australian troopships passed the "Devanha," unit would recognise unit and greetings were exchanged, but every boat overwhelmed us with the one question—"Have you heard of the battle of the Wozza?," a subject on which we were very soon enlightened.

Regimental colour patches were issued to us on 13th April, but very few of us realised at the time their full significance, nor their relation one to the other. Neither did we know the depth of sentiment which would ultimately surround them, for many have been the toasts proposed to "the old blue and white," toasts received with the greatest of pride and reverence.

We were next issued with two little white linen bags, each to carry a day's ration when we landed, consisting of a tin of bully beef, a tea and sugar ration, a cube of oxo, and a quantity of small biscuits. The first thing we did was to stain the bags a khaki colour with permanganate of potash, coffee or hot tea, otherwise they would have been an excellent target for the sniper, as our only means of carrying them was to hang them on to our equipment. We were also issued with Field Service caps similar to those worn by the British soldiers, from which we were instructed to take the steel wire which kept it in shape. This was to destroy the sharp contour of the hat and thus offer a less disdistinguishable target to the enemy.

On 19th April we made our first move to take up

our dispositions prior to the actual landing. "B" Company was transferred to the "Ionian" and attached to the 10th Battalion, "C" Company was transferred to the "Malda" and attached to the 9th Battalion, and "D" Company to the "Suffolk" with the 11th Battalion. Battalion Headquarters and "A" Company remained on the "Devanha."

The next few days were spent more or less in a leisurely manner and the men were given as much rest as possible, knowing what was before them. Platoon inspections were held every day to ensure that every man's equipment and gear were complete particular attention being paid to field dressings, and final issues were made, amongst which were canvas water bottles capable of holding ½ gallon of water, which were given to the buglers to carry, and 2 bandoliers of ammunition, each containing 120 rounds.

The day before we landed a full set of equipment was weighed, including pack, rifle, 2 extra bandoliers of ammunition and three days' rations, and it turned the scale at 82 lbs.

On 22nd April a full-dress rehearsal of the landing was carried out—torpedo boat destroyers came alongside and all ranks, with full marching order, went aboard, either down the gangway or by rope ladders thrown over the ship's side. The destroyers then steamed to a point near the entrance of the harbour and slowed up about 100 yards from the shore, when we got into rowing boats and quickly rowed ourselves ashore, where we formed up rapidly under our respective commanders. This was considered sufficient, as the only object of the practice was to ensure complete unison between the army and the navy during the forthcoming operations, and so we re-embarked and returned to our respective troopships.

The following order from General Birdwood, embodying excellent advice and giving the men an insight into future conditions, was issued about this time and read to all ranks:—

"Officers and Men,—

"In conjunction with the navy, we are about to undertake one of the most difficult tasks any soldier can be called upon to perform, and a problem which has puzzled many soldiers for years past. That we will succeed I have no doubt, simply because I know your full determination to do so. Lord Kitchener has told us that he lays special stress on the role the army has to play in this particular operation, the success of which will be a very severe blow to the enemy, indeed, as severe as any he could receive in France. It will go down to history to the glory of the soldiers of Australia and New Zealand.

"Before we start there are one or two points which I must impress on all, and I most earnestly beg every single man to listen attentively and take these to heart.

"We are going to have a real hard and rough time of it until, at all events, we have turned the enemy out of our first objective. Hard enough times none of us mind, but to get through them successfully we must always keep before us the following facts. Every possible endeavour will be made to bring up transport as often as possible, but the country whither we are bound is very difficult and we may not be able to get our waggons anywhere near us for days, so men must not think their wants have been neglected if they do not get all they want. On landing it will be necessary for every individual to carry with him all his requirements in food and clothing for three days, as we may not see our transport till then. Remember, then, that it is essential for everyone to take the very greatest care, not only of his food but of his ammunition, the replenishment of which will be very difficult. Men are liable to throw away their food the first day out and to finish their water bottles as soon as they start marching. If you do this now we can hardly hope for success, as unfed men cannot fight, and you must make an effort to try and refrain from starting on your water bottles until quite late in the day. Once you begin drinking you cannot stop, and a water bottle is very soon emptied.

"Also, as regards ammunition, you must not waste it by firing away indiscriminately at no target. The time will come when we shall find the enemy in well entrenched positions, from which we shall have to turn them out, when all our ammunition will be required; and remember:

"Concealment whenever possible.

"Covering fire always.

"Control of fire and control of your men.

"Communications never to be neglected.

(Sgd.) W. R. BIRDWOOD."

At last the day arrived for which we had been training so long, for at 2 p.m. on 24th April, 1915, the transports of the 3rd Australian Infantry Brigade weighed anchor and threaded their way through the maze of shipping in the harbour, and we were cheered by the various troopships (Australian, British and French) as we passed.

We finally cleared the entrance of the harbour and each troopship took up its appointed position which, with the battleships, cruisers and destroyers leading (H.M.S. "Queen Elizabeth" in front), were in the formation known as "line ahead."

The convoy proceeded to the island of Imbros, and anchored after dark behind the shelter of some dark hills which loomed in the distance. At about 9 p.m. we were given our last meal before we landed, and it seemed to have an additional relish. On the "Ionian" it was a bully-beef curry with plenty of fine large onions cooked whole, and, my word, didn't we enjoy it! And there was plenty for a second helping, which most of us accepted without a murmur.

The torpedo-boat destroyers came alongside, one on the port and one on the starboard side, at 11 p.m., and the Battalion embarked as under:—

From T.S. "Devanha":
    H.Q. and "A" Company ....   H.M.S. "Ribble"

From T.S. "Ionian":
    1 Company 10th Battalion, "B" Company 12th Battalion (5 and 8 Platoons) ....   H.M.S. "Scourge"

    1 Company 10th Battalion, "B" Company 12th Battalion (6 and 7 Platoons) ....H.M.S."Foxhound"

From T.S. "Malda":
    1 Company 9th Battalion, "C" Company 12th Battalion (9 and 10 Platoons)   H.M.S. "Colne"

1 Company 9th Battalion, "C" Company 12th Battalion (11 and 12 Platoons)	H.M.S. "Beagle"

From T.S. "Suffolk":

1 Company 11th Battalion, "D" Company 12th Battalion (13 and 14 Platoons)	H.M.S. "Chelmer"
1 Company 11th Battalion, "D" Company 12th Battalion (15 and 16 Platoons)	H.M.S. "Usk"

At last we were all packed aboard and made an effort to make ourselves as comfortable as possible under the circumstances, for we knew that we would be aboard for a few hours. All round the ship's side were sacks of coal-dust, which we rightly assumed were to give us cover as soon as we got under the enemy's fire. As the ship's quartermaster on the troopship struck "eight bells" indicating midnight, so the two destroyers silently and slowly left the ship's side. A few of the troops remaining behind in hospital, R.Q.M. Staff and the ship's crew (including two Belgian stewardesses on the "Ionian") leaned over the side to see us leave, but not a sound was heard as we glided away, and not a farewell exchanged; even those most devoid of sentiment must have felt the suppressed excitement with which the atmosphere seemed to be charged. And so we disappeared into the night.

Chapter V.

THE LANDING

WE were particularly favoured as regards weather, for it was a beautiful moonlight night, with sufficient cloud to prevent the visibility being of a dangerous nature. The air was somewhat keen when the destroyers were steaming at all fast, but otherwise there was a pleasant freshness in the air. For a few hours the flotilla of destroyers steamed slowly towards the Peninsula—without lights, needless to say—and then went dead slow for some long period waiting for the moon to go down.

The morale and general bearing of the men was wonderful, and resembled that of old campaigners rather than untried troops. They loosened the belt of their equipment and sat down with their backs against the sacks of coal and other deck fixtures and conversed freely in an undertone on a variety of subjects, whilst expressions of opinions were gratuitously given as to the probable fate of various members of the Battalion within the course of the next hour or so. About 2 a.m. the crew of the destroyers came round with buckets full of hot steaming cocoa, which was liberally distributed and consumed with a relish. Even the men who had attempted to snatch a few minutes' sleep allowed themselves to be disturbed without the usual complimentary remarks, when they discovered what was awaiting them.

About 3 a.m. the moon went down and it began to get intensely dark, and we again proceeded towards our objective. As we began to get near the shore our progress was made by short spurts or rushes. We went "full speed ahead" and then slowed up whilst a sailor, detailed for that purpose, took a sounding and reported to the bridge; by continuing in this manner we were enabled to "feel" our way along in the darkness.

The various courses of the battleships and destroyers were now converging to the prearranged landing place, and in consequence we could see, at intervals, other destroyers and the hull of a huge cruiser (from which other units of the Brigade were landing) looming up black in the darkness. By this time the boats from which we had to land and which had been towed from the stern, were brought alongside and the rowers were ordered to get into them. On the "Foxhound," as the destroyers made one of those sudden spurts previously referred to, a boat on the port side was taken by surprise and crashed into the side of it and capsized. Willing hands were at once given for rescue work, and we pulled the saturated rowers, as well as a sailor, back on to the deck, when they were quickly replaced in the boat.

At last, at about 4.30 a.m., the destroyers made a final spurt and took us within 100 yards of the shore. At this moment the first shot was heard from shore, followed immediately by a veritable fusilade of bullets, which fell in the water all round us.

Whilst this was happening the first boat-loads of troops were proceeding ashore as fast as possible. Those from the "Ribble" were towed six at a time by a steam pinnace, within 50 yards of the shore, and then the crews rowed for their lives. Those from the other six destroyers had to row the whole way.

It was not long before a rousing cheer was heard coming from the left flank, and we knew that Australians had set foot on Turkish soil. On most of the destroyers the 12th Battalion Company had to allow the Battalion to which it was attached to land first, and in consequence we had to wait fully ten minutes on the destroyers before any boats were available to land us. During this time we were subjected to heavy rifle and machine-gun fire from the hills in front, and also shrapnel from the guns at Gaba Tepe. It was still dark and we could not see the shore in front of us, but the hundreds of flashes from the rifles, high up in the air, were an indication to us of the nature of the country. As the bullets passed over our heads with that distinctive "crack" which became so familiar to us in later days, a heated argument was started by the men on several of the destroyers as to whether or not the enemy was using explosive bullets, but a well-placed burst of shrapnel soon scattered them and made them seek shelter behind the sacks of coal, which now proved their usefulness. As the boats came alongside—some bringing casualties—they were quickly filled with 12th Battalion men, an officer or N.C.O. accompanying each load, with a middy steering in the stern and a sailor lending a hand with an oar ready to take the boat back again. Each boat load also carried a box of ammunition, which would be so much in demand before the day was over.

ANZAC COVE

(Photo. loaned by Lieut. A. J. Lovett, late 3rd A.L.H.)

As soon as we were within a yard or so of the shore we all jumped out without ceremony—up to our waists in water—in fact, some of the men who had to jump out from the stern actually went right under and had to flounder ashore the best way they could.

During our baptism of fire the Battalion had received its fair share of casualties, either whilst awaiting to disembark from the destroyers or whilst being rowed ashore, or on the beach itself. Lieut.-Colonel Hawley was badly wounded as he stood with an oar preventing his boat from drifting away from the beach as the troops jumped ashore. Sergt.-Major Bryant also received a nasty wound in the face as he was being rowed ashore, and Lieut. Northcott (Adjutant) was wounded almost as soon as he got on to the beach.

The Battalion landed approximately on a frontage of 500 to 600 yards, in order from the left, "A," "D," "B" and "C" Companies—"A" and "D" Companies on North Beach, and "B" and "C" Companies round the point in Anzac Cove.

This was not the prearranged landing place, for the spot selected by General Sir Ian Hamilton and his staff, and embodied in the operation orders received by General Birdwood, was the beach immediately north of Gapa Tepe, where the slopes were far less precipitous. However, by an act of Providence, the navy made an error of nearly a mile, due, no doubt, to the strong currents and the intensity of the darkness immediately prior to the final advance into the shore, and in consequence we were landed too far to the north and had to scale the cliffs of Sari Bair. It afterwards transpired that the Turks had prepared a network of submerged barbed wire entanglements running far out to sea, at and around the very spot where the landing was to have been made, while on shore our advance would have been checked by a garrison of troops established in well-sited trenches made of concrete. It has since been authoritatively stated that a landing at this spot under these formidable conditions would have been verging on the impossible. Hence, as I remarked before, the navy's error was nothing less than an act of Providence, for which we were profoundly grateful.

It has been said of the landing "that the doings of the 12th Battalion for the first day on Gallipoli resolves itself into personal reminiscences of small bodies of troops. The nature of the country prevented any combined movement, and the Battalion, after landing, advanced inland in small parties led by officers for some considerable distance." This statement is so true that the only method of recording the part played by the whole Battalion is to endeavour to follow each Company from the beach to its ultimate position in the firing line. Even so, it must be remembered that a Company did not land on the beach intact, but dribbled ashore in small boat-loads, so that an officer or senior N.C.O. did not necessarily advance with his whole command, but just gathered all troops in his vicinity and rushed headlong for the cliffs on which the enemy was situated, and from which he must be dislodged.

The boats from the "Ribble" landed Battalion Headquarters and "A" Company almost on the extreme north of the Divisional front, at the foot of the well-known landmark on Russell's Top, known as "The Sphinx." This portion of the beach was under direct machine-gun fire, apparently coming from the lower slopes of Walker's Ridge, or perhaps further north from the vicinity of Fisherman's Hut. Some of the men from the previous tow of boats had not yet been able to advance over the fifty to sixty yards of scrubby country between the beach and the slopes of the cliff, but Col. Clarke quickly urged them forward in spite of the fire, himself leading the way. He had with him at this time Lieuts. Margetts, Patterson and Rafferty and from fifty to sixty men, mostly "A" Company 12th Battalion. As they neared the foot of the cliff the machine-gun still worried them considerably, and the Colonel ordered Rafferty to take his platoon and endeavour to silence it. Rafferty, however, had had a specific duty allotted to him immediately on landing, namely, to utilise his platoon as an escort to the Indian Mountain Battery until in position. He therefore reminded the Colonel of this fact, but the latter, no doubt thinking that if the machine-gun was not disposed of very quickly, the Mountain Battery might not have an opportunity to land at all, instructed Rafferty first to locate and then to dislodge the machine-gun before reporting to the Battery Commander.

In the meantime, the grey dawn had developed into broad daylight, and the strength of the party grew and diminished as they became separated and then met other parties advancing through the thick scrub, which was anything from waist to shoulder high. At last the slopes of Walker's Ridge were reached, which proved to be of a gravelly formation, capable of giving a decent foothold, with good substantial bushes which were utilised in pulling oneself up from foothold to foothold. Half-way up the slope, Cpl. Laing, of "D" Company, came across the Colonel, almost out of breath, struggling up with a heavy pack, and advised him to throw it away; but this the Colonel was loath to do, so Laing took it for him. The top was eventually reached, and it was here that the party saw its first Turk. Margetts rushed ahead with his revolver, followed by several excited and out-of-breath Diggers yelling "*Imshi, yallah,* you ——," but the Commanding Officer quickly called them back and told them to get into a regular formation and advance in skirmishing order, clearing the bush as they went along.

Whilst this had been happening, Major Elliott had landed close by, and, following approximately the same course, with a party of men reached the ridge much about the same time as Colonel Clarke. The whole party then moved forward and passed over a trench, from which the enemy had apparently just retired. It was well made, with the parapet carefully flattened and screened by half-dead bushes, and a quantity of ammunition and equipment had been left behind in the rapid evacuation. Without waiting to examine the trench they passed on, as the enemy could be seen retiring up the slopes of a prominent hill some 600 or 700 yards to their right front. This proved to be Hill "Baby 700," which was won and lost after much severe fighting on this first day. It was about at this moment that the Colonel took out his message book and commenced writing a report to Brigade Headquarters when he was shot through the heart. His batman rushed over to his assistance, but had barely reached him when he became the second victim of the Turkish sniper. Pvt. Moggridge, an old South African campaigner, noticed that the spot where they had fallen was on a well-worn track, and warned everyone clear of it. Major Elliott, however, who had heard of the calamity but not Moggridge's warning, came up to take over command and became the third casualty, being wounded through the shoulder and receiving a fracture of the left arm. He quickly appreciated the situation and told no one to come near him, and himself waited an opportunity before crawling away from this danger spot.

The loss of a commanding officer in the field is the heaviest blow that can befall any unit, and the 12th Battalion formed no exception in this instance. We realised that it was only during the last few weeks of training at Lemnos that we had begun to know and understand Col. Clarke, and, incidentally, to value him. Although he was stern and somewhat reserved, we knew him to be full of grit and a soldier to his finger-tips, and on this memorable morning he had proved himself to be a brave and gallant gentleman, who did not know the meaning of fear. The wonderful achievements of the Battalion at Anzac and in the later years of the campaign constituted the finest monument which any unit could erect to a commanding officer, who had laid such a splendid foundation.

These casualties left Patterson and Margetts with about fifty men, and the former officer took charge of the party. After a short conference they decided to send some scouts forward to discover if the enemy occupied any of the ground between them and the slopes of "Baby 700," and Margetts promptly selected his two best, namely, George Vaughan and Tilley. These two went forward, and after passing the "Nek" signalled back "All clear." Just as Patterson was about to advance, Capt. Burt came up with more men and advocated a proper reorganisation, which was promptly done, officers taking charge of their platoons and N.C.O.'s being allotted to sections. They then commenced to advance in extended order until nearing the "Nek," when they were joined by Capt. J. P. Lalor, of "D" Company, with nearly half of his Company, and Capt. Tulloch, of the 11th Battalion, with some of his Battalion. The former officer at once assumed command, and realising that the role of the 12th Battalion was that of Reserve Battalion, he wisely decided that it was of paramount importance to establish a strong position astride the "Nek" rather than to allow his men to become absorbed in the irregular advance. In accordance with this decision, it was agreed that Capt. Tulloch, of the 11th Battalion, should take his men forward, while the 12th Battalion, under Lalor, dug a semicircular trench astride the "Nek" and commanding the gully on either side, capable, if necessary, of covering a retirement of our own troops, and of repelling an enemy rush down the slopes of "Baby 700." It was now between 7 and 8 a.m.

After Tulloch and his men had gone forward, the position, as far as Lalor and his party were concerned, became quiet; there was no enemy this side of "Baby 700" and all rifle fire appeared to be going well over their heads. Major Robertson, of the 9th Battalion, had by this time joined them on the "Nek," and it was then agreed that another advance should be made over the top of "Baby 700." Margetts took his men up the slope, passing many dead Turks at the position they occupied after retiring from Walker's Ridge when Colonel Clarke and his party first made their appearance earlier in the morning, and with Major Robertson, took up a position in the scrub on the northern slope of the hill, where they were subjected to heavy rifle fire. In endeavouring to locate the spot from which this fire originated, Margetts freely used his field glasses and discovered a communication trench on the slopes of Battleship Hill, some 700 to 800 yards away, down which the Turks appeared to be advancing in considerable force. He at once brought concentrated fire to bear upon this trench, but it was so sited that with little difficulty the Turks were able to reach dead ground in an adjacent gully, where undoubtedly they assembled for a severe counter-attack. During this time, casualties were becoming very heavy from frontal fire, and also from a machine-gun which enfiladed them from the flank, when, to crown everything, word was passed along the line that our troops were falling back on the left. It was only too true, and the Turks could be seen advancing in force from the gullies on the flank of Battleship Hill. Margetts had no option but to withdraw his men round the slope of "Baby 700" back towards the "Nek."

Whilst this had been happening, our Brigadier had established his headquarters on McLaurin's Hill, where he had an uninterrupted view of "Baby 700," and saw the advance over the summit and the subsequent retirement. He realised the importance of holding this hill, which was of the greatest strategic importance. He urgently appealed to the Divisional Commander for reinforcements to be sent to this spot, but the 1st and 2nd Brigades had already landed and had been absorbed into the battle. One company of the 1st Battalion, however, was diverted and sent over Russell's Top to the "Nek" to reinforce Lalor, Margetts and Patterson.

These troops quickly deployed and, picking up the fragments of the 9th and 12th Battalions in their advance, gallantly rushed the hill, and for the second time established a line on the forward slope of "Baby 700," many of the men with Margetts occupying the same position as before.

The fighting on the forward slopes of this hill continued fiercely right through the morning and well into the afternoon. Again we were driven off it, and, reinforced by New Zealanders, again we re-established our position. The ammunition was beginning to become a serious question, and Margetts left the line to endeavour to find Lalor and make some arrangements as regards replenishing it. Just near the "Nek" he met Patterson, who told him that Burt had gone back some time ago to get ammunition and reinforcements and should return at any time. Margetts was absolutely exhausted, and Patterson therefore insisted on him remaining at the "Nek," whilst he himself went forward with some dozen or twenty men. This he did, and arrived in the line just as the Turks launched a heavy counter-attack, and was never seen again.

Lieut. Patterson was one of the greatest assets the Battalion possessed, for he was a born leader of men, who instinctively trusted him to the uttermost. His youth, vitality, strength and daring had endeared him to all men who had trained under him in Tasmania, Egypt and Lemnos, and who had accepted his leadership on this April morning. He was the only officer of the 12th Battalion, up to this time, who had originated from the Military College at Duntroon, and his every action reflected credit on the years of training he had received there. He had now given his life for the country that had bred and trained him—surely an ample repayment!

Margetts found Lalor in a forward position and was instructed by him to take a man and go back to get ammunition, supports and stretcher-bearers.

Taking Bugler Quantrill with him, Margetts left Lalor about 3.30 p.m.

Lalor then moved forward on to the seaward slope of "Baby 700," where the fighting was thickest. Although the mental strain and anxiety which he had experienced since landing early in the morning had been enormous, he nevertheless rallied his men and, waving his arms, shouted, "Come on, the 12th." The words had hardly passed his lips when he fell dead, and "the 12th" (the last words he uttered) lost one of its most gallant and capable officers.

It will readily be seen that "A" Company as a Unit had now ceased to exist, its members being either casualties or hopelessly separated along the front and absorbed into the command of officers and N.C.O.'s of various battalions. The only platoon whose exploits have yet to be recorded is that of Lieutenant R. A. Rafferty, who, soon after landing had been ordered by the Commanding Officer to locate and silence a machine gun on the extreme left flank which was inflicting numerous casualties as the troops left the boats and had crossed the beach into the scrub.

Rafferty had with him about twenty men of his own platoon and about twenty men of other units and commands whom he had collected on his way from the beach. It was now necessary for him to advance 700 to 800 yards across comparatively flat country, covered with only a low scrubby growth. They advanced in extended order until they came to a dry creek bed, about six feet deep, in which it was hoped to rest for a moment and reorganise, but as soon as they reached it a machine gun opened up from the right flank—in the vicinity of No. 1 Post—and hopelessly enfiladed them. There was nothing for it but to push on. In front lay an open field, quite devoid of any cover, which had to be crossed before a position could be taken on a sandy knoll which would give them a commanding position overlooking the country around Fisherman's Hut. Had Rafferty any doubts in his mind as to the course of action he should take, they were quickly dispelled by the fact that at this moment four boats could be seen making for the shore at this spot laden with troops. It was, therefore, of paramount importance that he should advance on to the knoll and cover their landing. He gave the signal to advance, and as they doubled across the open field a storm of bullets met them, causing heavy casualties right along the line, to such an extent that only Rafferty, Sergeant Skinner and six others reached the cover of some rising ground on the far side of the field. Lieutenant Rafferty crawled up to the crest of the hill and discovered that the boats had landed and that the men had taken up a position on the beach, but there appeared to be a strange absence of any movement, so he called for a volunteer to go over to them. Private A. H. Stubbings offered to go, and, crossing the beach, took cover behind one of the boats. His worst fears were confirmed, for almost every man lying on the beach was dead and it was some time before he could find even a wounded man from whom he could gather some news. They belonged to the 7th Battalion, and their officer, Lieut. Layh, with a few survivors, lay in the grassy tussocks on the foreshore. Stubbings took this information back, and as the fire from Fisherman's Hut had ceased for some time, Rafferty decided to go back with his survivors and arrange for stretcher-bearers for Layh's party and then to carry on with his particular job of escorting the Mountain Battery. This he eventually did, picking up the Battery on the beach and escorting them to White's

Valley, just to the right rear of Johnston's Jolly, where they opened fire about noon.

"B" Company were landed from the destroyers "Foxhound" and "Scourge," and reached the beach at the northern end of Anzac Cove, just near the spit, Ari Burnu, which separated the Cove from North Beach. As soon as we floundered ashore, we rushed to the cover of an overhanging cliff and dropped our packs, which were hanging loosely from our shoulders by the supporting straps. The boxes of ammunition were carried well away from the water's edge and dumped together. We then looked round for an officer to give us our direction, and the first one I saw was Capt. Whitham. "Straight up the hill," he said. "You can't go wrong if you go inland." Loading our magazines as we went, we made for the hill, which we afterwards knew as MacLagan's Ridge. A very thick growth of shrub, heavy with the morning dew, covered the hill, and enabled us to pull ourselves up the slope. Many a time a man would slip back, smothering those below him with a shower of *debris*. The top was reached and most of us were well out of breath, so we halted for a few moments before crossing the crest, and waited for the remainder to come up, utilising the time by taking out the bolts of our rifles and cleaning out the dirt and sea water with which they were soiled. Lieut. MacPherson now joined us, and with high spirits we crossed the ridge and advanced down into Shrapnell Gully, after passing an evacuated trench and some dead Turks. At the bottom of the gully was a small running stream, with a notice board near it, upon which were Turkish characters and an arrow pointing towards some tents. Some of the men wanted to explore the latter, but received strict orders to the contrary, and so the advance was continued up to the second ridge in perfect order. The line was moving in such splendid formation, and our training and discipline of Mena and Lemnos were being carried out in such detail, that when Corporal Harry Webber inadvertently fell and his rifle went off, Lieut. MacPherson immediately roared out, "Who's that —— fool with his safety catch forward? Don't you know the first thing to do after loading your rifle?" The top was reached and we found ourselves on a large plateau (Johnston's Jolly) fully 300 to 400 yards across and at once came under fire. There were some troops already about fifty yards in front of us, and by means of short rushes we quickly joined them and stiffened up the firing line.

Movement could be seen in some scrub about 200 yards to our right front, but we were afraid to fire as we did not know whether they were our own troops or not. As far as one could judge, it was now about 6 a.m., or perhaps a little later, and we remained here for about an hour, advancing the line a few yards by making individual rushes. Then the Turkish batteries opened fire from the high ground on the extreme left flank, and simply peppered the plateau with shrapnel. At first, their range was not exact, but this they soon corrected and we had to lie in the open with no possible chance of cover, with the pellets and shell cases falling all round us. One particular shell burst right over us and a shot penetrated my waterbottle on my back, so quickly turning to Jack Adams on my left, I told him to undo it. This he did, and about four or five of us had a drink before the water all ran out; it was too precious to be wasted. The manner in which the men lay unflinchingly under this hail of shrapnel was a splendid example of fire discipline, but Sgt. Richardson came over to me and suggested that if we thinned the line out a bit by taking some of the men fifty yards to right and left, many of the casualties which we were receiving would be averted. This advice seemed so sound that I agreed to do so. I took some half-dozen men with me and darted off to the left, when someone called me. It was Lance-Corporal Rod. McElwee, with a wound in the face, from which the blood was flowing freely. I ripped out his field dressing, quickly bound him up in an amateur way, and then darted off to the left, where the rest of my section had gone. A voice, which I at once recognised as Major Smith's, said, "Is that you, Newton? Get hold of a half-dozen men or so and go and reinforce on the left." I got hold of "Darky" Dennis, Schwartzkopff, Tim Willis and some others, and darted off again still farther to the left and found myself next to Sgts. Hearps and Will and Cpl. Freddie Carroll. We certainly missed the shrapnel fire, but the machine-gun bullets were whizzing close over our heads, cutting off the leaves and twigs of the bushes like a sharp knife. The Turks were entrenched in a splendidly concealed position about 300 yards away and only very occasionally did a target offer itself, but the opportunity was never missed. About noon, the Indian Mountain Battery opened fire from our right rear, and a very encouraging sound it was, too. After they had been firing for some little time, a message was passed along the line, "From the Brigadier to the Commander of the Mountain Battery. That last shot was very good; keep to that range." It was the first time that we knew our Brigadier was so close to us, and the fact in itself was reassuring. Shortly after, the Brigade-Major

—Major Brand himself—walked right along the line, making no effort to take cover of any kind. He was flicking his leggings with a little short cane, and kept saying, "Give it to them, boys! Give it to the ——! Every shot a bull's eye!"

The day seemed interminable and the afternoon particularly long, and we were all beginning to feel the effect of the nerve strain. About 5 p.m. the enemy attempted a counter-attack on our right front, but it soon crumpled away as our thin, ragged line crackled with rifle fire. The casualties were gradually mounting up, and the cry of "Stretcher-bearers wanted on the right (or left)" became more persistent. Our position, however, was so exposed out on the plateau that it was impossible for the stretcher-bearers to get out to us, and so we could only encourage the wounded to wait until dark, and make them as comfortable as possible.

Whilst this had been happening, Sgt. W. A. Connell, of No. 6. Platoon, with a few of his men, had become detached and found themselves in the middle of one of the 10th Battalion's companies situated on Johnston's Jolly. At about 10 a.m. an order was passed along the line by Major Hurcombe (10th Battalion) for that portion of the line to advance in small parties. Connell collected a few of his remaining men—certainly less than a section —together with some of the 10th Battalion in his immediate vicinity, and commenced an advance across the northern portion of Johnston's Jolly in short rushes. As they advanced, Turks were seen to jump up in front of them and retire rapidly to the far side of the plateau. Connell led his party in south-easterly direction towards Owen's Gully, on the slope of which he noticed a short trench held by a party of Turks with a machine-gun. At the moment, their attention was engaged by troops advancing across the plateau, when Connell outran the remainder of his party in their efforts to dislodge the garrison and capture the gun. They were seen at the last moment and an attempt was made to fire on the rapidly advancing troops, but only resulted in a few ill-aimed shots, after which the Turks picked up the gun and fled. Connell and his party attempted to occupy the trench but were apparently seen by a Turkish battery, which commenced firing shrapnel at them and forced them to take cover in the thick scrub in Owen's Gully, from whence they afterwards moved into an old trench near Lone Pine. From here they had an excellent view of Gun Ridge, and on one occasion, during a counter-attack which was taking place farther north, they saw some gun teams trying to get into action, and attempted some long range rifle fire which had the effect of making the gun team limber up again and change its position. Connell was one of the few men who advanced to the far side of Johnston's Jolly, and for his bravery, leadership and initiative on this occasion was awarded the Distinguished Conduct Medal — the only decoration received by the 12th Battalion for the operations on 25th April.

At last the sun began to sink behind the island of Imbros, and we looked forward to a few hours of respite, in which we could dig some trenches and obtain some relief from the constant artillery and rifle fire. Our hopes were soon dashed to the ground, however, for as the darkness deepened so the machine-gun fire increased, until it was almost an act of suicide even to get on to one's knees. As a unit, "B" Company was fairly well concentrated, but was wedged into the middle of the 10th

Battalion, and all night long messages were being passed backwards and forwards from Capt. Jacob to Capt. Lorenzo, of that Battalion. Attention was paid to the ammunition, and men were detailed to scour the country, both in front and in rear, and to take all ammunition and water bottles from the men who had been killed during the day, of which there were only too many. The stretcher-bearers worked gallantly during the night, taking great risks in exposing themselves to the rifle fire, which never ceased the whole night through. We were also instructed to dig ourselves what cover we could with our entrenching tools, and very little encouragement was needed to make us do this. It was far from comfortable lying on a particularly prickly holly undergrowth, with which the plateau was covered.

At one time during the night, the message was persistently passed along the line, "Don't fire, the Indians are advancing on the right." It afterwards transpired that this same message was used on almost every section of the front during the first day and night, and since the gunners were the only Indians we had with us on that first day, there is very little doubt that the enemy had some good linguists, probably wearing similar uniform, mingling in our ranks, who passed this order along in order to withhold our fire.

There was a machine-gun in front of us during the greater part of the night, which was extremely irritating. It appeared to be one of our own guns firing about ten or fifteen yards in front of the line, and the detonation from it was deafening and nerve-racking. Every time it stopped and one's voice could be heard, the gunner was urged to come in, but the only answer was another deafening burst of fire. At last an order was passed along from an officer nearby, ordering him to come in. The only reply was another burst of fire, even more penetrating than before. At last, one of our fellows volunteered to go out and find the gun and bring it in, but although he went well out in front no trace of it could be found. A message was then passed along the line, "Take no notice of the machine-gun in front; it is an electrical contrivance of the enemy." When we later on became more experienced in warfare, we knew that deafening sound to be bullets passing very close over our heads—a very familiar sound in France when the Germans used to traverse the parapet with machine-gun fire. It was probably just as well we did not know it on that first night.

Never at any time during the night did the continuous line of flashes from the enemy's rifles diminish—a good indication in itself of the strength with which he held his line. Towards dawn, the message was passed along the line, "The enemy is preparing to attack and is crawling towards us; fix bayonets!" Just as the first flush of dawn could be observed in the east, the Turk did make an attack on our front, although the full force of it was launched against a position more on the right of the plateau. He advanced, yelling "Allah! Allah!" but was greeted with rapid fire right along the line with such deadly result that, as the light strengthened, he could be seen retiring into his trench in extreme disorder, leaving many casualties behind. And so the remnants of "B" Company commenced their second day on Gallipoli.

"C" Company disembarked from the destroyers "Colne" and "Beagle" and landed on the southern portion of Anzac Cove, towards Hell Spit. Their experiences on the destroyers, whilst waiting for boats to land them, were very similar to those recorded in other companies, although information afterwards collected seemed to indicate that rather more casualties were sustained whilst rowing ashore. On reaching the beach the men jumped into the water, many of them waist deep, and rushed for the shelter of the overhanging cliffs. Instructions were rapidly issued for packs to be taken off and dumped clear of the water's edge, which was quickly carried out by all ranks. A few of the men, who were of a methodical turn of mind, carefully placed their packs—containing, no doubt, many cherished belongings—in concealed positions, in the vain hope that they would afterwards recover them.

In the meantime, the Company Commander, Capt. J. L. Whitham, had reported to the Brigadier, who was already ashore, in a small *nullah* near the beach. He instructed Whitham first to deposit at that spot the Brigade reserve of entrenching tools, which "C" Company had been detailed to carry, and then to take his company, less one platoon, over MacLagan's Ridge (as it was afterwards called) and occupy the ridges running eastwards from Hell Spit. Lieut. A. H. Fraser, in command of No. 11 Platoon, was detailed to occupy a point some fifty yards inland, which overlooked the Brigade's temporary headquarters, and from which some sniping had apparently been directed on to the beach.

"C" Company were fortunate in the fact that the whole unit landed on an approximate frontage of sixty yards, although the operation was somewhat protracted owing to delay in return of the boats which had first landed portion of the 9th Battalion and Brigade Headquarters from the same destroyers. Lieut. G. A. Munro and No. 10 Platoon had already proceeded in a southerly direction with some of the 10th Battalion and occupied a position on McCay's Ridge. A message, however, was incorrectly delivered to him, which resulted in his temporarily withdrawing his men, but they were joined in Shrapnel Gully by Whitham, who was advancing with No. 9 Platoon (Lieut. T. Holland) and No. 12 (Sgt. P. H. Weston). The three platoons, therefore, moved forward in a more or less organised formation and took up a position on McCay's Ridge with a frontage of 200 yards, almost in the same spot previously occupied by Munro. During this advance a couple of shells fell, but did not burst, near the company on the southern slope of MacLagan's Ridge, and rifle fire was encountered when crossing the crest of the ridge and other exposed positions, and appeared to come almost directly from the rear. No doubt it originated from Plugge's Plateau before the enemy was dislodged by troops on the left flank. Corporal Ring proved himself of great assistance by displaying wonderful coolness and keeping his section well under control. Several of the men who had become separated from their own command voluntarily attached themselves to his section, as by his crisp words of command and sensible advice, he quickly inspired confidence in his men.

Whilst the company were occupying the position on McCay's Ridge, shells were heard to pass overhead from the Gaba Tepe batteries, but did not worry them at all; occasional rifle fire came from the left flank and left rear, but was not of a serious nature. The company were now facing Gaba Tepe and Bolton's Ridge, and trenches could be plainly seen on the forward slopes of the latter, but appeared to be unoccupied.

Munro and No. 10 Platoon were now sent forward to reconnoitre the gully in front and to ascertain if the slopes of the ridge in front were occupied by the enemy. He was marvellously cool as he conducted the advance through the thick scrub, and resembled more an officer carrying out a peace time reconnaissance or exercise than one who was actually leading troops in action for the first time. His whistle blasts could be distinctly heard as the platoon advanced across the bottom of the gully, whilst section commanders' reports—"No. 5 all correct," "No. 7 good-oh"—indicated his constant enquiry after their welfare.

In the meantime, Whitham was endeavouring to ascertain with accuracy his position on the map, assisted by C.S.M. Claud Stubbings and a rangefinder, who together took several ranges on to prominent landmarks.

Just as Munro reached the crest of the next ridge and signalled all clear, heaving firing could be heard on the left and the line could be seen advancing in the vicinity of Johnston's Jolly. Almost at the same moment, the position along McCay's Ridge was reinforced by several units of the 2nd Brigade, so Whitham decided to take advantage of the fact and co-operate with his flank in advancing the line in a south-easterly direction. Finally, he occupied the northern portion of Bolton's Ridge with Munro and No. 10 Platoon on the left (with whom was Capt. Kayser), Holland and No. 9 in the centre, and Weston with No. 12 on the right. During this advance, the strength of the company, as a composite unit, was somewhat weakened and many of the men became detached in their progress through the thick scrub, and were afterwards located in isolated parties as far distant as the Daisy Patch to the north. One of these parties, consisting of Pvts. Jim Parker, Tom Dunham, Clarry Webb and some three or four others, remained out in an exposed position until well into the afternoon. An attempt was made on one occasion to return to the main line of defence, but in doing so they were fired upon by our own men and so were forced to remain in front, and to obtain additional cover they moved into one of the gullies at the head of Sniper's Ridge, where they were joined by Capt. Kayser during the latter portion of the afternoon. He told them to dig in, but the ground was so hard that very little impression could be made with entrenching tools. They remained here until after dark, when they filtered back individually and joined the main line on Johnston's Jolly.

Whitham and his company, however, occupied Bolton's Ridge some time between 9 a.m. and 10 a.m., and became subjected to rifle fire at long range, the origin of which could not be located. Fire was brought to bear on some apparent trenches on the forward slope of Pine Ridge, but no enemy fire was drawn from this direction.

Additional reinforcements from the 2nd Brigade gave another opportunity for an advance, which was commenced with the object of occupying Pine Ridge, although, ultimately, an intermediate position was taken up on a subsidiary ridge about halfway, afterwards known as Knife Edge. During the descent from Bolton's Ridge, across the southern extremity of Allah Gully, heavy machine-gun fire was encountered, and by the time the Knife Edge was reached the organisation of the company was rather broken up. Just before leaving Bolton's Ridge, Lieut. Holland was wounded in the head by a rifle or machine-gun bullet, which completely parted his hair down the centre and put him out of action for the day: Munro still had No. 10 Platoon under fairly good control as he crossed Knife Edge, but the sections of Nos. 9 and 12 Platoons were weakened, separated, and hopelessly intermingled with other units.

During this period, the Turkish batteries were pouring shrapnel on to 400 Plateau, and as the troops were seen to occupy Knife Edge and adjacent ridges, the range was lengthened in order to rake the valleys on the southern slopes of the high ground; and a shrapnel bullet from one of these bursts wounded Whitham in the left arm, between the elbow and shoulder, about 11 a.m.

Munro, Corporal Austin, and several men from their own platoon as well as other units, still continued to advance, and there is every reason to believe that they reached a point on Weir Ridge, if not the western slopes of Pine Ridge itself, although the information afterwards obtained was not sufficient to locate definitely the extent of the advance. The outstanding feature of this forward movement was Munro's attitude throughout, for his dash and born leadership inspired confidence in the plucky band of men who followed him. Their advance was finally checked by encountering a well-concealed position in the scrub, which was held by a strong party of Turks. The party put up a valiant effort to dislodge the enemy, and many of the men were killed in the attempt, including Lieut. Munro, who was shot whilst firing his revolver at some Turks within twenty to thirty yards of him. At a later date, when casualties were reported and commented upon, everyone realised that the Battalion had lost a first-class officer in Munro. He was a school teacher by profession, and most thorough and unobtrusive in everything he did. He rarely expressed an opinion unless it was asked for, and, when given, it invariably proved to be well thought out, terse, and to the point. He was a strict disciplinarian and administered his platoon impartially, the two qualities combined causing him to be respected and beloved by his men.

The loss of their leader disorganised the small attacking party, who withdrew in twos and threes to various parts of the line.

Capt. Kayser also went forward from Knife Edge, and, in his endeavours to gain touch with the enemy, carried out some valuable reconnoitring work. As previously stated, he came across an isolated party of "C" Company who had been separated from their company since early morning. Between 4 p.m. and 5 p.m., the fire on this portion of the front increased considerably and men of the 2nd and 3rd Brigades holding advanced positions were forced back. Kayser came back with some of these men and reported that the enemy held a strong position on the western slopes of the next ridge and that it would be utterly useless for any portion of the line, with the number of men then available, to attempt to dislodge them. As soon as darkness fell, the line was straightened out and organised, and a defensive position was dug along Knife Edge and Silt Spur, thus joining up the troops on 400 Plateau. In these trenches the shattered remains of "C" Company, in most cases, occupied individual positions.

It is only necessary now to record the doings of "D" Company, which landed from the T.B.D.'s "Usk" and "Chelmer."

The manner in which the boats proceeded from

the destroyers to the shore differed only in detail from those already described in other companies. Commander England was an outstanding example of fearlessness on the "Chelmer" as he remained on the bridge and gave his orders with cool precision under a hail of bullets.

Casualties were sustained before any of the troops commenced disembarking, among the first being "Banjo" Reeves, and shortly afterwards L.-Cpl. Martin, whose wounds proved fatal.

As soon as the 11th Battalion were clear, the boats returned for "D" Company, and Capt. J. P. Lalor (or "Little Jimmy," as he was affectionately called by his men, on account of his diminutive figure) was among the first to get in. He almost seemed to be enjoying himself, in spite of the hostile rifle and machine-gun fire, which was increasing every minute, and cheered the men as they rowed by singing "It's a Long Way to Tipperary." He was carrying with him a fine old sword (a family relic) bound round with hessian to prevent it glistening in the sun. It was lost during the stress of fighting and afterwards picked up by L.-Cpl. Freame, 1st Battalion, who, in his turn, lost it during the counter-attacks in the evening.

On the "Usk" a wonderful impression was made upon the men by one of the sailors whose duty it was to stand in the bows of the boats as they were being brought alongside to prevent them bumping against the ship's side. Quite oblivious of the danger he was incurring by remaining in the open the whole time, he helped the men into the boats and reassured them by constantly saying, "You'll be orlright now, me 'earties, you'll be orlright now." C.Q.M.S. Jack Allen landed with this half of the company and was seriously wounded as he was in the act of jumping from the boat on to the beach, sustaining a fractured thigh. He had been an N.C.O. in the Imperial Army, with a considerable amount of service to his credit, and the fact that he became an early casualty on this first day was a great loss to his company, which appreciated him at his full value.

Lalor and Booth rallied their men as soon as they had landed and had quickly deposited their packs on the beach, to allow easier movement, and made for the scrub in the direction of Walker's Ridge. After proceeding some 150 yards, Lalor sighted a Turkish sniper concealed in a bush and quickly pulled him out by the leg. The sniper made frantic signs to indicate that he had not fired at our men, and pointed to his rifle which was clean, but one of the men near by discovered his ramrod with a piece of rag in it covered with powder. Lalor detailed one of the men to take him back to the beach, but it is very doubtful whether he reached there as the escort arrived back in a very short time.

On reaching the crest of Walker's Ridge, they were met by Lieut. E. Y. Butler and half of his platoon, and almost immediately came under heavy fire from snipers. Lalor then detailed some half-a-dozen men (Pvt. J. Kitson being the only one of the party who can now be definitely traced) to locate and dislodge the Turks, who were beginning to inflict too many casualties. They crawled through the thick undergrowth, and after half-an-hour's exciting skirmishing managed to clear the slope in front, although in their effort to do so two of the party were killed.

By this time, the portion of the company acting under Lalor's orders had reached the "Nek" and joined Burt, Margetts and Patterson with a percentage of "A" Company. Lalor immediately assumed command and gave instructions for a defensive position to be dug astride the "Nek," which was of considerable tactical importance in the event of a withdrawal. He told Butler to take his men forward to the next slope with Capt. Tulloch, of the 11th Battalion, in order to cover their consolidation. This party moved forward with great caution, picking up isolated sections in their advance, and eventually reached a spot on the eastern slope of Battleship Hill, from which the Narrows were visible, and which was the farthest point reached on the northern portion of the Anzac Corps' front. They had not advanced this long distance without striking opposition, but determination and a skilful method of advancing forced the Turks back. On their reaching the slopes of Battleship Hill, however, machine-gun fire became severe, and an enfilade gun was causing many casualties. It is believed that Sgt. Kidson was killed at or near this spot. A very heavy fire was now heard to come well from the rear, and Tulloch (who was in charge of the party) was afraid of being cut off, and therefore decided to withdraw. They were told off into four sections and withdrew two at a time, the stationary sections giving covering fire to those who were moving backwards, in accordance with our training at Mena. They arrived back to find a fierce battle in progress on "Baby 700" and were soon absorbed into the fighting, in the course of which Butler was wounded in the right hand, which resulted in the amputation of his thumb.

Lalor, meanwhile, had dug his defensive position, organised the men under his command, and had voluntarily accepted the responsibility of a large sector of the line. He was essentially a man of movement, and merely occupying a position with no fighting attached to it, whilst men were being killed out in front, was not to be considered. About 8.30 a.m., therefore, he ordered an advance on to the forward slopes of "Baby 700," and the men required little or no encouragement to conform to the order, but were only too willing to follow their company commander. He was known to everyone in the Battalion as the grandson of Peter Lalor, of the Eureka Stockade fame; it was known that he at one time joined the British Navy and deserted; that he subsequently joined the French Foreign Legion, and afterwards took an active part in a South American revolution; and with such a leader they would have gone to the ends of the earth.

The progress of the Battle of "Baby 700" has already been recorded, and the fierceness of the fighting which continued throughout the morning. Lalor was the person to whom everyone looked throughout the engagement, and proved himself to be indefatigable in his efforts to save useless casualties and yet force the attack to a successful issue. The hill had been won and lost twice during the morning and early afternoon, and about 3.30 p.m. he decided to make another effort to recover it by moving across Malone's Gully and attacking round the northern shoulder. The enveloping movement was half completed when the Turkish batteries sighted them and opened up a deadly shrapnel fire. This caused so many casualties that Lalor decided to advance once again, and passed the cautionary word of command along the line. Just before 4 p.m. he commenced to lead the advance by leaping to his feet and shouting, "Come on, the 12th," but he had hardly gone a couple of yards before he was killed by a Turkish bullet. His death was a severe blow to the men with him at the time, as it was to his whole company when they afterwards reformed. Although small of stature, "Little Jimmy's" heart was large, whilst his vitality was almost inexhaustible. Coming from a fighting family as he did, and adopting a military profession, it would be difficult to discover a more appropriate resting place than that which was allotted him—a soldier's honoured grave.

From this time onwards it has not been possible to trace the doings of "D" Company as a unit on this particular part of the front, and it is more than probable that they suffered a fate similar to the other battalions and became irreparably separated.

Nos. 13 and 14 Platoons, under the command of Lieuts. J. L. C. Booth and J. A. Evans respectively, landed immediately to the north of Ari Burnu, and after leaving their packs in a protected spot, they made for the steep slopes in front of them. The climb was particularly stiff, but pluck and perseverance got them to the top. Evans took the lead and advanced over the rear of Plugge's Plateau. It was somewhere about here that the party saw its first Turk, carefully concealed in a thick bush and busily employed in sniping. Digger Watson was the first to sight him, when only about two paces away, and instinctively brought his rifle and bayonet to the "on guard" position, following by a "long point," which satisfactorily accounted for the Turk.

Going forward, down into a steep gully and up the other side, they eventually reached a position near to Lone Pine. Here some Turks attempted to block their progress with a machine-gun, but they were apparently only fighting a rearguard action, for on being pressed they quickly vacated their position, taking the gun with them. Evans halted his men at this spot in order to ascertain his own position and that of any flanking troops. Whilst doing this, some of the men noticed a small Turkish trench about 150 yards to the left, and almost immediately someone shouted, "Look at Bill Michie!" Together with Pvt. Griffin and one other man, he could be seen rushing the trench, and these three privates together tackled a Turkish trench, from which only two of the enemy escaped.

Hostile shrapnel fire now worried the party considerably and casualties were becoming frequent, so Evans decided to make another advance, and as far as can be ascertained took up a position on the next ridge, which would probably be Sniper's Ridge. During the whole of the morning, Evans had received wonderful assistance from his N.C.O.'s, the most noticeable being Sgt. J. Williams and Cpl. Donald McLeod. The latter could always be seen doing the work of two men, keeping his men well under control, giving orders with his broad Scotch accent, and on all occasions personally leading his men with the full conviction that they were following him to a man. At this juncture, Lieut. Evans was severely wounded in the small of the back by the nose-cap of a shell, and McLeod was quickly on the spot and carried him over the crest of the ridge to a place of safety.

Anxiety was now felt regarding some dead ground on the right front. Scouts were sent forward to reconnoitre, and they returned and reported that fully two companies of Turks were formed up ready to attack. It was quickly realised that the strength of the defending party on the ridge was totally inadequate to withstand such a strong attacking force, and immediate steps were taken to get as many of the wounded back as possible.

The attack eventuated and "D" Company's party was gradually forced back by force of numbers, until they met the advanced units of the 2nd Brigade, who strengthened the line and maintained a position which afterwards formed part of the main line of defence. In this withdrawal, McLeod's party became separated and attached themselves individually to officers and N.C.O.'s of various units in their immediate vicinity.

Booth's platoon kept a little to the left of Evans' party as they advanced and became more separated, Booth himself, with about half of his men, being located somewhere near Courtney's Post, whilst others were known to have joined up with Lalor's party during the morning. It was discovered that he and his party were successful in assisting to beat off a heavy counter-attack during the morning, but details were never obtained from him as he received a severe wound in the head, and afterwards died on 28th April on the Hospital Ship "Itonus." He was a man who had seen considerable war service as an artist-correspondent in the South African War, and afterwards in Bulgaria and Turkey in 1904 and 1909, being on the staff of the London "Graphic." He has been aptly described by one of his fellow officers as a "happy, genial comrade, full of quiet courage, whose presence brought comfort. His kindly insight into human nature made him the big brother of officers and men."

Pvt. Stanistreet did good work on that first day, for although wounded in the head during the early part of the morning and sent down to the beach for evacuation, he refused to go aboard the lighter. He was afterwards seen again in the firing line, brandishing a revolver he had discovered. During the afternoon many of the men were craving for water, but no one volunteered to descend the gully, which was subjected to heavy fire from secreted snipers. "Give me your bottles," said Stanistreet, and with a string of bottles over his shoulder he started for the beach, only to become a victim of the deadly snipers.

Cpl. E. W. D. Laing occupied a position almost on the extreme left of the line, near the head of Malone's Gully, with a few isolated men of "D" Company, and for a long time was the senior N.C.O. of a party of sixty men of mixed units. Very fierce fighting took place on this flank (doubtless a continuation of the struggle for "Baby 700"), and during the morning and early afternoon he and his party charged no less than five times over the scrubby slope in front of them, only to be forced back on each occasion. The men were now suffering very much from nerve strain, and after the last charge the Turks were seen to withdraw into cover. Laing immediately ran over to an officer near by and asked to be allowed to take his men forward in a bayonet charge and definitely settle the matter. Permission, however, was not granted, and when darting across a few minutes later to repeat the request he was wounded in the thigh. The line afterwards retired and he was forced to crawl back through the scrub in order to gain safety.

Other men of "D" Company who made themselves conspicuous by acts of gallantry and powers of leadership were:—Cpls. Whaley, Hale, McKiver,

McLennan; Pvts. MacKenzie, Cook, Munday, Roberston, Dickson, Elliott, Rowles, Howard, Redrop, Roberts and White.

The Signalling Section spent a very tiring and hopeless day endeavouring to establish visual signalling stations, but were unsuccessful in obtaining communication in this manner, and Lieut. S. R. Houghton ultimately employed his section as runners.

Lieut. W. H. Room handled his Vickers Machine-Gun Section with cool precision, and on reaching a position in the firing line he squatted behind a bush with his watch in his hand and quietly told the gun team that he had rarely seen them mount the gun more quickly during their period of training. Casualties in the section were inevitably heavy, as the gun was in action in the front line the whole time with cover from view, but not cover from fire. During the evening of the first day the last of the gun team became a casualty and volunteers were called for to keep the gun in action. Pvt. Geo. Tostevin, of "B" Company, came along with blood streaming down his face, and during the whole of that night and the next day he kept the gun firing in an extremely exposed position and assisted in repelling a heavy counter-attack.

The A.M.C. details worked hard all day on the beach, under the command of Major J. M. Y. Stewart (Capt. Ratten having returned to Australia from Mena), who tended to the wounded as they were brought to him, although suffering from a dislocated knee. Regimental Medical Officers and Field Ambulances worked in conjunction on this first day, with their various staffs. The beach soon became congested with stretcher cases, and as the Turks began to rake the foreshore with shrapnel

APRIL, 1915

it became necessary to carry as many of the men as possible into sheltered spots, or to build protective walls with the numerous packs which littered the beach.

The casualties suffered by the 3rd Brigade at the landing (April 25th-30th) were as follows:—

	Killed		Wounded		Missing		Total	
	Off.	O.R.	Off.	O.R.	Off.	O.R.	Off.	O.R.
Bgde. H.Q. ..	—	—	—	1	—	—	—	1
9th Battn.	7	25	11	229	1	242	19	496
10th ,, ...	5	45	8	224	—	184	13	453
11th ,, ...	2	32	7	183	—	154	9	369
12th ,, ...	4	69	15	224	2	191	21	484
Total	18	171	41	861	3	771	62	1803

A considerable number of the "missing" were subsequently found to be wounded and evacuated on to hospital boats without notification reaching the unit. The remainder were all killed in action, for of the 4,931 casualties suffered by the First Australian Division at the landing, only one man was taken prisoner.*

---

*Vide Bean's "Official History of Australia in the War of 1914–1918," Volume I., Page 586.

Chapter VI.

THE OCCUPATION OF ANZAC
NARRATIVE CONTINUED BY LIEUT.-COL. D. A. LANE

AFTER the turmoil, anguish and exhaustion of the few days after the Landing, a line of defence having been established and re-organisation effected, the Battalion settled gradually down to "trench warfare," a form of warfare not taught in the training manual and quite foreign to the half-company skirmishes practiced at Pontville or the Brigade exercises against Tiger's Tooth and the shivering night outposts in White House Valley.

The first entrenchments were only knee-deep and narrow, without much in the way of communication trenches. Less than two days saw a marked difference, trenches being deepened to give cover when standing, and communications improved. Support trenches were very soon established, and by the beginning of May the Battalion's position was well consolidated. A well constructed firing line skirted the crest of the ridge, while on the reverse slope the support trenches were deep, wide, and well provided with shelters, "possies," Company Headquarters, cookhouses etc. Battalion Headquarters were snugly placed in the hillside at the head of the valley. Although the term "dug-out" was the common appellation to the shelters in general use, yet the same must not be confused with those elaborate, deep-sunk residences which were later so well known in France. The Gallipoli "dug-out" was not as a rule a bomb-proof one, but consisted principally of a recess cut in the hillside, or trench walls, completed with a couple of layers of sandbags, and, if the owner was a C.Q.M.S., officer, or lucky, roofed with iron. The poorer class of citizen had to be content with a water-proof sheet covering. "Possie" was the more general term applied to the habitation of the rank and file.

What a transformation had been effected in the appearance of that Battalion which had a little over two months previously marched out of Mena Camp, every man equipped to the last numeral and "INF." The weather was hot, intensely so, and clothing was discarded or retained in conformity with the temperature. Some men wore putties and some did not; tunics, when worn, were unbuttoned. It was no longer a "crime" to appear on parade unshaven, and the regulations forbidding the hair at the back of one's neck exceeding half an inch in length were sadly disregarded. Dirty faces were common. Chin straps had gone out of fashion and even puggarees were fast disappearing. But every man retained complete his rifle, bayonet, equipment and smile. Though the smile might be in the midst of a dirty face, yet the rifle always showed clean and bright as in old Pontville days. The Landing and subsequent days has proved to the soldier his dependence on his weapons, and the rifle and bayonet were regarded as his inseparable companions.

The days now rapidly developed into a fixed

routine. Each company had its frontage in the line held by one or two platoons, with platoons in support. Digging had been the order of the day from the jump, and dig they did. The rabbits at York Plains or Ross in far-away Tassy would have marvelled at the work performed by the men who erstwhile earned a living at dragging *them* from their burrows. There was no slacking, every man doing his bit willingly and well. It is a pity that one cannot remember the crude remarks and jokes that were bandied about. Abdul was the principal subject of chaff.

Early in May the Battalion was well settled in position. The 3rd Brigade occupied the right of the line at Anzac, overlooking Gaba Tepe, facing south, and facing east confronted by Gun Ridge held by the Turks. The 9th Battalion was on the right, next the 12th Battalion, and on our left was the 10th Battalion. There was little to complain about as regards the weather at this period. The days were indeed hot, but not uncomfortably so. The sea was like a sheet of crystal below us, where transports lay well out from shore and trawlers and pinnaces kept up a busy traffic.

W. O Kennedy had received his commission and was now for a while acting as Adjutant. Tostevin, of the Machine Gun Section, had also received his commission and had filled the vacancy of O.C., M.G. Section.

It was not really a "merry month of May." A most novel mode of living was being entered upon, and the cheery, uncomplaining spirits that made up the brotherhood—for into such had the fierce scourge of battle and death welded the survivors of the first week—vied with each other in constructing comfortable "possies" and making light of danger and discomforts. There are those who deride the discipline of the A.I.F.; there are those who scoff at the military methods of discipline. Let it now be said, once and for all, that never was there more urgent need for rigid discipline than at this time, when with their backs to the sea, a few hundred yards in their rear, with no comforts and little water, and always tired, these men of the 1st Division faced the trained army of Turkey. And let the traducers of those men know that unselfishly and loyally those men rose to, and maintained the high order of discipline which was demanded. If proof is required, then suffice it to say that a weak-disciplined unit could not have maintained its position against the Turk. Officers, N.C.O.'s and men lived as companions and yet maintained that degree of respect that varying ranks demand. Was there never any growling? Of course, there was, and emphasised by Gallipoli-born adjectives, but this in no wise impaired the efficiency of the job which the growler slaved at whilst emitting his growl. And then the sense of humour invariably prevailed in the end, and the growler was forced to grin. "Furfies" and "Latrinograms" were always in the air. Grim and hard was the work before all, and yet humour prevailed. Nevertheless, over all there hung that deep feeling of loss sustained during the first few days, for it must be remembered that every man had lost some bosom pal or friend.

So the first few weeks saw the Battalion settle down, in every sense of the word, into what was now a well established line of defence. The firing line, it goes without saying, was fully manned day and night. Snipers' posts were established, ammunition recesses prepared, fresh communication trenches commenced and existing ones improved. "Dig" was the order of the day, broken by the four principal events of the twenty-four hours—"Stand-to" an hour before dawn, and then—ah!—"Stand-down"; then "Stand-to" at dusk, with its follower of "Stand-down."

During the day, Padre Richard in his brush-covered "possie" solemnly censored the many letters awaiting the post, and how many times did he read, "I hope this finds you as it leaves me at present"? For the personal comfort of the recipient let us trust that it never did! Meanwhile, Lieut. Sid Houghton, Battalion Signalling Officer, would be squatting behind the Padre's "possie," talking flags to his devoted section. And all will agree that the Battalion signallers were a splendid and efficient section, never failing to carry out the important duties assigned to them.

Practically every night brought its action away on our left, at Quinn's or Courtney's, or some such post, when often one was held spell-bound by the terrific and fascinating crash of musketry and machine-gun fire. But the front held by the 12th was strong and the Turk had so far made no desperate effort to break it.

About this period—the middle of May—Oratunga Sap, leading from near the left of the Battalion's frontage, was commenced. It was the first move in a scheme to establish a concealed line of trenches about 100 yards in advance of the front line and lower down the hill. Probably every 12th Battalion man who served on Gallipoli knows something of Oratunga Sap, and yet there was nothing particularly striking or remarkable about this trench. Perhaps it was simply because of it being the first effort made to sap forward, and because of the added danger (however small) which such a proceeding involves.

Oratunga Sap had proceeded for some fifty yards or more when a diversion occurred in the form of a Turkish attack, delivered with the intent to drive the Australians into the sea. This was on the night of 18th-19th May, 1915. Furious and sustained musketry and machine-gun fire broke forth about 9 p.m. away to our left, and it was known that Abdul was going all out to it. Throughout the night the Turkish attack was maintained, gradually working towards the right of the Anzac line. Then, as the first streak of dawn was appearing over Gun Ridge, heavy fire broke out from the trenches of the 10th Battalion on our left. All was keen expectancy along the 12th frontage. Every firing recess and loophole was manned, and through practically every loophole a pair of eager eyes gazed out toward the dawn. "Here they come." In an instant every rifle was ready, but early training still held good, and, apart from a few shots fired by too eager spirits, fire was withheld till the order was received. The dawn had sufficiently advanced to show up the attacking troops, and after a scrutiny over the parapet by the Company Commanders, the order was given, "Commence firing," and Bedlam broke loose. There were more troops manning the trenches than there were loopholes, and so eager were our men to get their shot in, that step holes were dug in either side of the trench, and, standing with legs astride the trench, ardent fellows delivered their fire from this precarious position. One or two others leapt on to the parapet and were instantly ordered down, while others sat pick-a-back on a comrade's shoulders, and so got in a few rounds. Very few Turks reached the trench, and from the spirit displayed by the troops manning it, it was fortunate for the Turk that he was driven back before arriving at his objective. Nevertheless, let no disparaging remark be passed as to the gallantry of the Turkish attack. The disadvantage was all theirs, and they pushed forward against a well sustained and well directed fire. It must not be forgotten that great attention had been paid to musketry instruction, and as a body, the men of the 12th were good shots.

During this attack use was made of the Gallipoli jam-tin bomb. Corporal Craig essayed to throw one of these at some Turks who were lying in the corn close to the firing line. After lighting the five-second fuse he became a little apprehensive about pitching the missile, but was urged in very forceful and profane language from his immediate neighbours to "chuck it." In a flurry he did so, and then realised that the direction he had thrown was that of Oratunga Sap. There followed first an explosion of gun-cotton, and next a more alarming explosion of oaths from the occupants of the Sap. Corporal Craig, realising that he had possibly caused physical hurt to one of his own Company, and knowing that he had caused mental injury, peered over the parapet, regardless of the hostile fire, and called, "Did I hit anyone?" Even the occupants of the Sap laughed. Sergeant-Major Tom Selwyn was at the head of that Sap, and in his thirst for gore thought to get a few infidels as they rushed from the corn field on his left. He first took the precaution of detailing a soldier to watch for any Turk who might happen to be lying in the low scrub to the right of the Sap. Tom stuck his head up and got busy, and so did someone else, and before he knew it a bullet had ploughed its way along the side of his skull and "A" Company's Sergeant-Major became a casualty. It was dangerous to stick one's head above the scrub in those parts.

After this attack the Turkish dead lay thick on the slopes in front, and some of the wounded were rescued from the corn field two days after the action. On the 21st, an effort was made by parties under the Red Cross and Crescent flags to bury dead and search for any wounded still lying on the field, but hostile fire caused the attempt to be abandoned.

The weather was distinctly warm, and the air was pungent with the odours of the dead. At evening the stench was at times most oppressive, and there was no escape from it. Add to this the ceaseless domestic war waged with the "grey-backs," and life held few of those amenities worth living for. But again the sense of humour prevailed over all discomforts. Small diversions of a domestic nature with a humorous side were of continual occurrence, such as when "Scotty" Williamson and "Jock" Gracie, both good soldiers, would start frying their bacon in the entrance to Company Headquarters and awake Capt. Kayser from his morning snooze. Then something would be doing. Many a one was grateful to those two soldiers for creating amusement when everything seemed hopeless.

An Armistice was arranged for the 24th, from 7.30 a.m. to 4 p.m., for burial of the dead. Parties of our people and the enemy, bearing white flags, proceeded along the front, midway between the hostile lines. About every 100 yards a flag-man was halted and thus formed a line of demarcation. Parties of the enemy then proceeded to clear the ground of all dead on their side of the line and parties of Australian troops cleared our front. The stench during this operation was awful, and the cessation of all fire had a rather weird effect. About 4.30 p.m., when all parties were withdrawn, the war recommenced.

The following day at 12.20 p.m., H.M.S. "Triumph," lying off Gaba Tepe, was seen to be torpedoed. The sea was calm and glassy at the time. As the vessel quickly settled to port, a destroyer dashed alongside and took off the crew. In ten minutes she was floating bottom up, and eventually disappeared at about 12.55. Destroyers from all directions dashed to her assistance and a posse of pinnaces raced out from Anzac Cove to the doomed vessel and assisted in the rescue of the personnel. The "Triumph" and "Bacchante" had become as old friends to us, and it was with feelings of deep sorrow and regret that we saw the good old "Triumph" sink to rise no more.

However, it is an ill wind that blows no one any good. Some days later three or four hogsheads were discovered on the beach, and they were full of cider. Many impromptu and unofficial fatigue parties, consisting of anything from one man to half-a-dozen, proceeded with water-cans, petrol tins, water bottles, or any description of vessel that would hold liquid, to the common *"rendezvous."* Cider flowed free, and as the assemblage on the beach was like to draw shrapnel, our zealous Staff Captain Holmes dashed into the throng with an axe and grievously wounded the casks. However, many jubilant soldiers bore back to the lines quantities of the precious fluid. Alas! the sounds of violent vomiting which proceeded that evening from many a homely "possie" gave forth proof that the salt water had had first "go" at the cider. That was indeed an ill wind.

Patrols were constantly in demand both by day and night, and a few of the regular members of these were Sgt. Joe Cooper and Pvt. Vaughan, of "A" Company, Sgt. Don McLeod, Corporals Fred

Brine, Duncan Forbes and Dickenson, of "D" Company. Sgt. Will, of "B" Company, figured largely as that Company's patrol-leader, and, apart from personal distinction, helped in no small degree in building up the Battalion's record for patrol work. Of "C" Company, Capt. Rafferty's "Greyhound Patrol" was the most famous, and, led by that daring officer, one doubts whether they would have stopped short of seeking the person of Liman von Sanders himself, had they been so required.

Sergeants McLeod and Cooper were particularly conspicuous for effective patrol work. On one occasion, Sgt. McLeod led a patrol consisting of himself, Corporals D. Forbes and Potts. A machine-gun from the unit on our left fired upon them, Cpl. Forbes being hit and Potts stunned; nevertheless, Sgt. McLeod, in the face of great danger, stood up, and eventually by signals indicated to the machine-gunners that they were an Australian patrol. This done, he gave first aid to Cpl. Potts and succeeded in bringing him back to consciousness. Then, placing Cpl. Forbes, who was breathing his last, on to his (McLeod's) back, he carried him into our lines under a heavy hostile fire. Could more be desired to demonstrate the soldierly qualities of such a man as Sgt. McLeod?

Cpl. Potts and Pvt. Robertson later figured in a neat little affair when, whilst on patrol, they captured and brought in three Turks.

The first days of June saw uncomfortably hot weather settling in with the attendant swarms of flies. And they were "some" flies—not like the ordinary house fly, but a cross between a bee and a blue-bottle; only these fellows were a bright shiny green. Such pernicious brutes it would be difficult to match. They fought the soldier and each other for every scrap of food, after having gorged themselves flabby on the Turkish dead. They settled in swarms on one's back and took cheap rides. It was impossible to sleep during the afternoon, owing to their tormenting habits. They were productive of more bad language than the "grey-backs," water fatigue, mule transport, and every other language producer put together.

The shortage of water now became very serious and caused a great deal of distress. The ration per man was well under two quarts per day for all purposes, and washing was out of the question unless permission was obtained to visit the beach. In the evening, Brighton Beach presented the appearance of a popular seaside resort, minus, however, bathing sheds and costumes. How those evening swims were enjoyed, until the Olive Grove batteries one evening opened on the bathers, causing many casualties, and it was thus that Pvt. Buckpitt lost his life. He was an excellent soldier, who knew no fear.

The nightly drawing of rations was a strain on the temper of the fatigue parties detailed for this duty. The Battalion's quota of biscuits, cheese, Fray Bentos and S.R.D. was piled in a neat little stack and duly signed for. Then the N.C.O. of the party had his work cut out to prevent pilfering by Q.M.S.'s or private pirates, whilst waiting for the string of mules to arrive. Then followed the packing and loading of these restless, kicking brutes. It was not uncommon for a load which had taken twenty minutes to hook, to be bucked off in two. On these trips, one made the acquaintance of Capt. Littler, Beach Commandant, who often strolled round during the evening to "see how things were going."

About this time, Cpl. Hancox, of "A" Company, was killed in the trenches, and his loss was keenly felt by many old comrades, as Hancox was a splendid N.C.O. and had he survived would undoubtedly have gained rapid promotion. Another incident, luckily not attended with very serious results, occurred when a shell dropped on the parapet directly in front of Sgt. Naylor and his brother Ivor. The Sergeant was a bit shaken and Pvt. Naylor was evacuated with some nasty wounds in the head.

After the attack of 19th May, matters had settled down again to the continual "stand to arms"; dig, dig, dig; fatigue parties to carry water, which was now drawn from wells in Shrapnel Gully; and interludes when "Gallipoli" stew was cooked by enterprising individuals in their mess-tins. Fatigues were arranged with monotonous regularity. If one wasn't digging, one was carrying water from Shrapnel Gully, or sandbags from the beach. It was arranged that each man should have a few hours in the day to himself, in which he could clean his rifle and attend to his own personal comfort and cleanliness.

The cap which had been issued in addition to the *saieda*—as the Australian hat was called—provided insufficient cover to the neck from the scorching sun, and an issue of cap flaps was made. These flaps fitted to the back of the cap and much resembled the shade used by the troops during the Indian Mutiny. Shorts had become the fashionable mode of dress, and it was not at all uncommon to see a newly issued pair of fine mounted pattern breeches operated upon with the butcher's axe and amputated above the knee. In fact, the practice became so prevalent that orders were eventually issued prohibiting such destruction of good clothing. Some months later, when the cold weather set in, many regretted the loss of the lower half of their breeches.

On 16th June, the 5th reinforcements, including Lieut. C. H. Perkins and 114 other ranks, arrived and were taken on strength. Three days later work was commenced at night on the new position on Holly Ridge, afterwards known as Tasmania Post, and on the 21st the post was garrisoned.

Previous to this, a new concealed line had been constructed from Oratunga Sap on the left and extending towards the right of the Battalion sector. This line consisted of a tunnel from which fire recesses were opened out at intervals, the parapets being carefully screened with shrubs.

About this time, water being a scarce and much desired commodity, Pvt. Cassanova began sinking a well a little below Battalion Headquarters. He received ample encouragement in his labour, and, incidentally, a great deal of chaff. Each day found him, hot and perspiring, sinking deeper and deeper into the earth, but his efforts were not crowned with success. However, he excavated a monument to himself, known as "Cassanova's Well." He felt certain that he would strike water in the Valley of Despair. Others thought that he would at least strike trouble, as the valley in question was in "No Man's Land," and right under the Turkish lines.

The amount of spade work performed on that small area of ground occupied by the 12th Battalion was astounding. The trenches were well constructed and the company officers instilled a spirit of competition amongst the four companies respecting the cleanliness and order of their lines. A match on the trench floor was regarded as a terrible eyesore. Novelty and invention were not wanting. The little niches made in the trench wall for carrying ammunition, jam-tin bombs, etc., all showed the varying characteristics and ingenuity of the men who made them. About this period the first respirators, for use in case of gas attacks, were issued, and numbers of spare ones were placed at intervals in carefully constructed holes in the trench walls. Balls of hemp, soaked in tar, were also distributed along the trenches. These were also for use in case of gas attack, the instruction being to light them and place them along the parapet, the hot air arising therefrom dispelling the gas cloud as it passed over. Fortunately, it was never necessary to use these on the Peninsula.

Major E. H. Smith, temporarily commanding the Battalion during this period, was an officer keen on engineering, and the excellent trench work performed was largely due to his active supervision. He took a pride in the construction of these lines, which made itself manifest throughout the unit.

The Battalion suffered a decided loss when a shell dropped one morning into "B" Company's trenches, killing Pvt. Smith and seriously wounding Lieut. H. C. Orbell, one of whose legs was badly shattered. Although so grievously hurt, he retained his *sang froid* and smoked a proffered cigarette.

Work in Tasmania Post had been unceasing. The ground on which this post was constructed had been first reconnoitred by Major Clogstoun, O.C. Engineers, and Capt. Rafferty, and the line roughly marked by broken twigs where the front trench was ultimately to be placed. The post was situated on a flat-topped rise about midway between our original front line and the hostile lines. Two saps were pushed forward, and what were ultimately the

support lines of the post were first constructed on
the edge of the flat top nearest the 12th's trenches.
Saps were then again pushed forward and laterals
driven to form a front line trench on the far
edge of the flat top. Unfortunately, these laterals
were driven prematurely before the saps had
been sufficiently advanced. The effect was to
shorten considerably the field of fire, giving no
command over the Valley of Despair. It was an
error that caused considerable trouble later.

Ten days after the first trenches in Tasmania Post
had been garrisoned, and within a couple of days of
occupying the front line trench, the Turks were
heard at night working on their edge of the flat top.
A ruse was practised by which the enemy disclosed
the existence of a covering party, clearly indicating
that something was going on. Next day the 11th
Battalion, on our left, reported that Abdul was
constructing a line of trench in opposition to Tasmania Post. On the 10th July, a local enterprise
was carried out with the object of harassing the
Turks in the construction of these works, but by
then they were well established, and little, if anything, was achieved.

Two days later, a demonstration was carried out by
the 3rd Brigade and Light Horse on our right, to
keep the Turk in his lines and prevent reinforcements being sent to the southern zone, where the
8th Army Corps was attacking. The 12th
Battalion's part consisted in sending forward a
covering party of one officer and twenty men in
advance of Tasmania Post, and then rushing parties
of men over the parapet of the support trenches
(main line of defence) across the valley into Tasmania Post to simulate an attack on the Turkish
trenches on Holly Ridge. These men were then to

THE "SPHINX ROCK" AT ANZAC, SHOWING THE NATURE OF SOME OF THE COUNTRY
(Copyright by Australian War Museum)

return by the communication trenches. At 8.15 a.m. the first party hopped over, and were followed at intervals of three to five minutes by four more parties. At first the enemy's fire was weak, but increased as each party appeared. Lieut. T. Weavers led the covering party of twenty men from Tasmania Post, and they were exposed to a heavy machine-gun and rifle fire. They remained out for twenty-five minutes and then withdrew. Lieut. Weavers was badly wounded in the arm and ten others were wounded. The operation was very well carried out, and achieved the desired result.

By the middle of July, the weather was extremely hot and unpleasant, and life in the trenches became sweltering. Dysentery was very prevalent and the health of the troops generally was bad. Our men were worn out by continual fatigues, poor food and dysentery, and it was impossible to get the same amount of digging done as in the earlier days. The warfare was becoming extremely monotonous and the humour now coming forth was more of a cynical nature. But discipline did not relax, and the high standard of cleanliness of the trenches and lines was maintained. And then, to everyone's annoyance, inoculation for cholera was commenced. It was undoubtedly a safe precaution, but its unpopularity was proclaimed in unmeasured terms.

However, through it all, the war proceeded. Night after night Sgt. Joe Cooper, of "A" Company, would sneak out with a patrol and scavenge round for arms and accoutrements left on the battlefield in our front. He brought kudos to the Battalion for the salvage work he carried out.

Patrols were frequently pushed out at night, and in this respect Pvt. Vaughan, one of the scouts trained by Lieut. Patterson, effected some excellent work, as also did Sgt. D. McLeod. The Battalion was more than once complimented on the results of its patrol work, thanks to those eager spirits who performed this dangerous, though exciting, duty.

Preparations were always maintained for dealing with possible gas attacks, and gas helmets were now issued in addition to the old respirator. These were not the elaborate cylinder-and-tube contraptions which made their appearance later in France, but just the old cloth "P.H." helmet with mica windows and rubber mouthpiece.

On the night of the 18th July, two parties leapt out from Tasmania Post with intent to surprise and capture working parties of Turks engaged on their trench in front. The Turks retired and six of the 12th Battalion were wounded. Lieut. C. Blakney, who lived to see long service later with the 52nd Battalion, commanded one of these sallies, with much credit to himself and the Battalion. It was such little enterprises as these that broke the monotony of trench warfare, and provided a safety valve for any pent-up savagery. However, although spirits were as high as ever, the general physical condition of officers and men alike did not permit of violent exertion of any long duration.

Towards the end of July it was generally anticipated that the enemy was about to deliver a vigorous attack, and preparations were accordingly made for meeting it. All posts were keyed up to the highest pitch of alertness, and in addition to standing to arms at sunset and dawn, "Stand-to" was ordered for moonrise or moonset. This big attack, however, did not materialise.

When it became apparent that the enemy had firmly established himself on his edge of Holly Ridge, preparations were put in hand for ejecting him, and to this end the Engineers commenced three tunnels forward from Tasmania Post against the hostile trench. By the 27th these tunnels had been pushed forward adjacent to Abdul's line, and mines laid and connected. On this date, the 11th Battalion, detailed to deliver the attack against the Turkish trench, relieved the 12th Battalion, who withdrew into bivouac in rear of the 9th Battalion.

As the doings of the 12th Battalion are so intimately interwoven with Tasmania Post, it is necessary to diverge from the Battalion's narrative and follow for a moment the events which led up to the extension of that post.

On the 31st July, the 11th Battalion exploded the mines against Turkey Despair (as the hostile trench on Holly Ridge was called) and carried the position by storm. As Capt. Leane, of 11th Battalion, led this attack, the captured trench was thereafter known as "Leane's Trench."

The following night, a company of the 12th Battalion garrisoned Leane's Trench, and after daybreak were relieved by a company of 11th Battalion. Again, on the night of 2nd August, a company of 12th Battalion garrisoned Leane's Trench. The tunnels, run forward for the mines, provided three excellent communications with the old front line of Tasmania Post, which now formed part of the support system of trenches. To the left of Leane's Trench was a Turkish communication trench, which apparently was only garrisoned by the Turks at night. Immediately darkness fell, Major Lane, commanding the company of the 12th Battalion, pushed a patrol forward into this trench and forestalled the Turkish garrison, which was then moving forward. A barricade was erected; a further party with picks and shovels stole quietly forward to reinforce the patrol, and digging operations were commenced with the object of connecting the recently acquired trench with Leane's Trench before dawn. By working furiously throughout the night, the party completed connection just as day broke, the last obstacle being the removal of a small tree. This tree was one of those which had been marked by the Engineers when the reconnaissance was made of Holly Ridge and the position of the front line trench roughly indicated. The trench now acquired, together with later extensions, was ultimately known as "Leane's Trench."

On 5th August, the Turks attacked and captured Leane's Trench, but by a vigorous counter-attack of the 11th Battalion were driven out.

Chapter VII.

LONE PINE AND RETURN TO LEMNOS

THE part played by the 12th Battalion in the Lone Pine attack is not commonly recognised. The Battalion was detailed as part of Divisional Reserve, and the sole reference in the Commander-in-Chief's despatches to the work done by it during the action is contained in the bare statement, "Part of the 12th Battalion, the Reserve of the 3rd Brigade, had therefore to be thrown into the *melee*."

For some days before 6th August, many troops had been landing over-night, including some units of Kitchener's New Army. The valleys in rear of our positions were filled with these troops, and it became evident that "there was something doing."

On 5th August, Company Commanders were assembled, and details of an attack on Lone Pine, which was to be made next day by the 1st Brigade, were gone into. Company Commanders during the afternoon reconnoitred the trenches and positions which they would be required to occupy in event of the Divisional Reserve being required. These trenches were at that time occupied by battalions of the 2nd Brigade. Arrangements were completed for leaving the area occupied by us, as it was thought possible that the results of the action would bring about a general advance. All gear and material that it would not be possible to take forward was stacked in company or battalion dumps. A spirit of eager anticipation pervaded all ranks, and the general idea that an advance would mean more or less open warfare was very acceptable, as everyone was weary of simply manning trenches.

Early on 6th August reinforcements for the Battalion arrived, and their welcome was a warm one, both by friend and foe. Lieut. T. Haslam was in command of these reinforcements, and was appointed to "D" Company. The Battalion at the time was very weak as regards strength of officers.

During the morning of the 6th, orders were issued for all ranks to sew on to their tunics armbands of white calico six inches wide, one on each sleeve, and a patch six inches square behind the right shoulder. These were to serve as distinguishing marks, and any person not wearing these marks was to be treated as an enemy. Company Commanders were, therefore, very careful to ensure that all men under their command complied with this order.

Before mid-day, final arrangements had been completed and everyone took to his "possie" and awaited developments.

At 4.30 p.m. our artillery commenced a heavy bombardment of the Turkish trenches, paying particular attention to Lone Pine and other points to be attacked. In the valley below the 12th Battalion position was a howitzer battery of the Lowland Division, and for over an hour the infantrymen from their more or less secure retreats watched the gunners going down under the Turkish counter-battery fire. Major G. B. Carter, Medical Officer to the 12th Battalion, calmly walked down to the battery position and applied first aid to the wounded, regardless of the terrible shrapnel fire that was drenching the battery.

At 5.30 p.m. three battalions of the 1st Brigade assaulted Lone Pine with the bayonet. The position was a remarkably strong one. The trenches were provided with overhead cover and were protected by wire. The ground to be traversed by the assaulting troops was a slight decline, varying from sixty to one-hundred-and-twenty yards wide. This was swept by a hail of rifle, machine-gun and shrapnel fire. The wire had been greatly destroyed by the artillery bombardment, but the overhead cover had been smashed in only a few places. After a short but bloody struggle the position was captured.

The actual attack and capture of a position is not always the most difficult and costly part of an operation. Counter-attacks by the enemy are sure to be made, and holding a position against these counter-attacks is often the hardest and most trying work of all. It was so in the case of Lone Pine.

At 6 p.m. the 12th Battalion received orders to move to their allotted positions in close support in Gun Lane. Platoons fell in and rolls were called in record time, companies moving independently to their positions. While passing along Artillery Road they came under a hail of shrapnel, meant principally for our batteries at the Pimple. The area covered by this fire was passed at the double, and the Battalion assembled in Gun Lane. Here they lay, whilst the Turkish shells constantly fell on the parapet, but fortunately not one struck actually in the road. This fire was drawn by the batteries at the Pimple, which was only a short distance from where the Battalion was lying. Considering the intensity of the hostile fire, the casualties suffered by the Battalion while waiting for three hours in Gun Lane were remarkably light. Lieut. Ogilvy, of "A" Company, was, unfortunately, amongst those killed.

About 9 p.m., "A" Company was ordered to reinforce the troops in Lone Pine, and was followed immediately by "D" Company. These companies filed through tunnels to an underground firing line, which formed their jumping-off point.

The area over which they had to advance was the same as that over which the troops had charged to the attack about three-and-a-half hours previously, and the dead and dying encumbered the ground in all directions. In some places they lay in groups where machine-guns had caught them. Hostile machine-guns still played across this ground, and shrapnel enfiladed it. However, Lone Pine was reached with little loss. Unfortunately, amongst those killed was Sgt.-Major Williams, of "D" Company, who led the last line of that company and was shot through the heart before reaching the objective. He was a fine and gallant soldier, and had been recommended for a commission. A few days after the action of Lone Pine, his name appeared in orders to the effect that he had been gazetted as 2nd-Lieutenant.

The trenches in the captured position presented an awful appearance. Dead literally carpeted the ground, and in some cases blocked the trenches. Tunnels and communication trenches were crowded with wounded and dead to such an extent that communication became extremely difficult. It was almost impossible for a Platoon Commander to maintain control of his platoon, and in the inevitable confusion command was exercised by officers over men of such units as chanced to be in their vicinity. The Turkish batteries during this period maintained a steady fire on the position.

It is difficult to follow the operations of the two companies of the Battalion without taking the part played by each separately. The first task for the Company Commanders was to collect their men, who arrived at various places in the support trenches (originally the Turkish firing line). This was accomplished, and "A" Company, commanded by Capt. L. M. Mullen, was collected in the left of Lone Pine, and early next day occupied a portion of the firing line and successfully resisted the repeated counter-attacks made by the Turks during the 7th and the night of 7th-8th. "D" Company, commanded by Major D. A. Lane, was collected in the support trenches in the right of Lone Pine, and spent the night of 6th-7th and the morning of 7th in clearing the dead from the trenches and communications to the firing line.

Another good N.C.O. was lost to "D" Company in Sgt. (afterwards Capt.) Don McLeod. This most excellent soldier, who had figured so prominently in patrol work, unfortunately, had a hand blown off with a bomb. Holding his injured forearm in his sound hand, with the thumb pressed firmly on the artery, he quietly requested another soldier to apply first aid. This was done effectively, and for some hours Sgt. McLeod stood there in the trench, waiting for an opportunity to pass to the rear. He must have been in great pain, but he never murmured or appeared downcast. His bearing was a most inspiring example, at a critical hour, to those about him.

At dawn on the 7th, Cpl. Rule, of "A" Company,

was lost. His section had, during the hours of darkness, climbed on to the parados of a support trench in order to direct their fire more effectively against any counter-attack. As day broke, Cpl. Rule passed the order to descend into the trench, and although some of his men believed that he also descended, he was never again seen, and was reported "missing."

During the morning of the 7th, the enemy succeeded in regaining a portion of the Lone Pine trenches on the right, held by the 2nd Battalion, and about 2 p.m. "D" Company was ordered to reinforce that battalion. Communication between O.C. "A" and "D" Companies with Battalion Headquarters was difficult, and orders were issued to them by G.O.C. 1st Brigade direct.

As already mentioned, the Turkish firing line had become our support line, and as the enemy had prepared elaborate overhead cover, the passage to the firing line resembled passing through a tortuous tunnel. The Company passed along the firing line till contact was gained with the enemy where they had effected a lodgment during the morning. The trenches here were extremely narrow and not well traversed. Our own and Turkish dead lay anywhere and everywhere, and in some instances our own wounded were still lying at the bottom of the trench. All that afternoon a terrific bomb battle was maintained, the bombs being the old jam-tin type, lit by a fusee or match.

Soon after nightfall the Turks made a vigorous attempt to recapture their lost trenches, and a hard and bloody fight set in. In this the two companies of the 12th Battalion were hotly engaged the night through. The men were in poor physical condition, due chiefly to the ravages of dysentery, but they stuck to their positions, and by dawn the Turkish counter-attack was beaten back. It was during this fighting that Sgt. McLennan was badly wounded through the premature explosion of a bomb. He had done excellent work throughout the afternoon, and N.C.O.'s such as he could ill be spared at this time.

During the 8th, "A" and "D" Companies of the 12th were withdrawn, and later "B" Company, under command of Lieut. H. Massey, was sent into the Pine. This company met with some stiff fighting and, unfortunately, lost Lieut. Woodhouse, who was reported missing after the action.

"C" Company of the 12th were utilised during the action of Lone Pine in stretcher-bearing; thus the whole Battalion took part in the action. Two officers were killed, and both Major Lane and Capt. Rafferty were wounded, but remained on duty.

On being withdrawn from Lone Pine, the Battalion returned to its bivouac in Clarke Valley.

On 12th August, nine newly commissioned 2nd-Lieutenants from the ranks of the Battalion were posted to the various companies and acting N.C.O.'s appointed. Next day, the 12th relieved the 11th Battalion in our old position on the right flank of Northern No. 1 Section of Defence. The Battalion was now greatly reduced in strength by casualties suffered during the recent operations and through sickness. The total strength was 26 officers and 712 other ranks (including A.M.C. details and 130 reinforcements). Back in the old familiar lines, the usual trench routine was adopted, but in a different spirit to their earlier occupation. The energy, good humour and chaff that marked that period were now lacking. The men were worn out and weary. Their health was so undermined that any prolonged exertion was impossible, and digging was not effected with the old rapidity or vim. However, watchfulness was in no wise relaxed, but it became necessary to shorten the period of duty for sentries.

The Battalion observation post during this period, and to the end, was in charge of L.-Cpl. N. B. Lane, "A" Company. The reports forwarded from this post repeatedly drew complimentary remarks both from Brigade and Divisional Headquarters. The artillery O.P. was close behind, and there existed splendid co-operation between the artillery and infantry, due in no small way to the constant communication between O.P.'s.

Despite the heat and the poor physical condition of all ranks, work on saps and communication trenches was continued. From Leane's Trench, tunnels were being pushed forward with the object of constructing a new line on the slopes of the Valley of Despair, and the work of connecting Oratunga Sap with the left of Leane's Trench was commenced. On the 18th, a change was made in the frontage occupied by the battalions of the Brigade, the 12th Battalion now occupying from the 10th Light Horse trenches on Holly Ridge to the north end of Leane's Trench and Tasmania Post. The Post, which had at first formed only an advanced position of the Battalion's frontage, had now so grown in size and importance as to be garrisoned by the whole Battalion. Improvement of front line and communication trenches was carried on incessantly and the forward saps gradually extended.

Some mention may now be made of the many ruses carried out to draw the enemy's fire and induce him to expend ammunition, of which his supplies were believed to be short. Sometimes these ruses were organised on a large scale by Brigade Headquarters, when all battalions in the line participated. Flares would be lighted at different parts of the main line of defence and answered by flares from forward posts; the blowing of whistles and issuing of loud words of command; rattling of bayonets and accoutrements in the most forward trenches, and then the sudden opening of rapid fire. Tricks of this nature seldom failed to produce heavy and sustained firing from the Turkish lines. Then again, the ruse would be purely a battalion or company affair, such as sounding whistles simultaneously along the line and every man jerking his bayonet up, whilst burnt jam tins with stones in them were thrown from the forward bomb-holes. These operations were, as a rule, carried out at night.

On the 29th August, the Battalion strength was 23 officers and 605 other ranks, of whom 34 were sick and off duty. On this day the Turks heavily shelled behind Tasmania Post, and in the evening an aeroplane came over and dropped a couple of bombs. However, there were no casualties in the Battalion.

By the end of the month, the forward tunnels from Leane's Trench being sufficiently advanced, preparations were made for the construction of fire pits. At this time the Battalion was just able to maintain the requisite number of rifles to man the firing line and to provide the reliefs, after making provision for continuous working parties. The men were twenty-four hours on duty and twenty-four hours off. The heat and the flies prevented those off duty from obtaining any adequate rest during the day, so that the men, who were so worn out as to require more than ever a sound night's rest seven times in a week, were reduced to a sleep every second night. Yet, such was their spirit, that they answered to every call made upon them.

Good salvaging work was still being effected and the slopes of the Valley of Despair were cleaned up by our patrols.

Second-Lieut. J. W. Christophers joined up, and was posted to "C" Company, in the beginning of September, and about this time information was received that the Turks would probably attack on or before the 5th of the month. All defensive arrangements were reviewed, but matters were always in such a state of preparedness that little improvement could be made. The attack did not eventuate.

On the 10th September, the 4th and 7th L.H. Regiments took over our position and the 12th Battalion withdrew from Tasmania Post for ever, "A" and "B" Companies moving into support trenches of original main line of defence and "C" and "D" Companies going into bivouac at head of Clarke Valley. The whole history of the 12th Battalion on Gallipoli revolves round Tasmania Post. Commenced at first as an advanced post, garrisoned by two platoons and then a company, it soon became a centre of dire strife and bloodshed. Although at various periods it was occupied by other units, yet the 12th seemed to keep touch by sending in a company as garrison on occasions. By captures from the enemy the Post was extended, and by incessant toil day and night its defences were improved. Then the 12th, weak in numbers and with officers and men so worn out, that it is doubtful whether they could have doubled fifty yards in marching order, moved into their old post as a unit, and were barely able to man the firing line adequately. No regrets were expressed on withdrawing, although certainly at the time no one was aware that the Battalion would never garrison the Post again. Even if it had been known that their withdrawal was final, the men of the 12th Battalion would have had no regret. On the contrary, they would have felt greatly relieved; so unpleasant had conditions made their experiences in the Post.

The withdrawal into bivouac was the commencement of better times. The weather was cooler, ration supply was better, and the strain of observation duty ceased. At this time (11th September) the strength of the Battalion was 21 officers and 573 other ranks, including Medical Officer and five A.M.C. details. Rumours were abroad regarding a projected relief of the 3rd Brigade for a rest at Mudros. It sounded too good to be true, but a couple of days later crystallised into fact, when orders were received that the 12th were to provide 150 rifles every forty-eight hours to battalions in the firing line, who would be withdrawing certain of their personnel.

On the 15th, the Battalion commenced supplying the 150 rifles to battalions in the line, and on this day Lieut. Connell, with twenty-six other ranks, went to Imbros as a guard at G.H.Q. This was regarded as a holiday by the men concerned. Four days later, Major C. H. Elliott returned from hospital and assumed temporary command of the Battalion. Although for some months he was not appointed to permanent command, this marked his first actual command of the Battalion, which he was destined later to lead through all the vicissitudes of Egypt and France, till its final demobilisation at the conclusion of the war.

A few days later, our Orderly Room Sergeant, Roy Latta, was evacuated sick, and Sgt. L. M. Newton was appointed in his stead, thus commencing a career on Battalion Headquarters Staff that was later to see him Adjutant, and as closely associated with the history of the Battalion as its revered Commanding Officer.

At the end of September, Lieut. A. H. Appleby and twenty-four reinforcements joined the Battalion, together with twenty-one other ranks returned from hospital. Every addition to the strength was now gladly welcomed, for although life in bivouac was far pleasanter than the trenches, a great deal of fatigue work was required of the Battalion.

On 30th September, the strength of the Battalion on the Peninsula (excluding guard at Imbros) was twenty officers and 571 other ranks. The weather was now much cooler and the general health of all ranks was improving. The expected relief was always a popular topic of conversation. We were still providing relief for the battalions in the line, and it amounted to having forty-eight hours in the line and forty-eight hours rest in bivouac. Better food and conditions had soon brought back the vivacious good humour, which had marked the earlier period of the occupation before trying experiences had made the men cynical. In the evening, Pvt. Percy's call of "'D' Company, here for your flap-jacks and down below for your rice" (referring to the cook's "possie") always called forth a volley of humorous replies. The arrival of extras from the Comforts Funds was as welcome as a mail from home, and never failed to produce a buzz of interest and anticipation.

On the 1st October, Major J. L. Whitham was evacuated sick and a spell was afforded to Capt. I.

12th BATTALION BIVOUAC: ANZAC

(*Photo. loaned by Capt. C. H. Stubbings*)

Margetts and twenty-six other ranks, who left for Imbros to relieve Lieut. Connell's guard at G.H.Q. Capt. Margetts had been on the Peninsula without a break since the Landing, and had earned a respite, if only for two or three weeks. There were at this time five officers and 112 other ranks of the Battalion who had been at Anzac continuously since the Landing.

Although in support, the 12th usually had one or two companies in the line relieving companies of other battalions, and it now fell to their lot to garrison the Ledge and Black Hand trenches. In anticipation of a wet winter, efforts had been made to provide drainage for the trenches, and to effect this in many places the trench floors were about fifteen feet deep. The system of tunnels with fire recesses broken out was fairly common and provided dry and covered communication along the line. A great number of the communication trenches were tunnels, pure and simple. In order to provide accommodation for supports close to the front line, a system of "bakers' ovens" was commenced. These "ovens" were recesses cut back for about eight or ten feet from the side of tunnels, with a ledge on either side and across the end. These ledges were beds for the lucky occupants. Although the residents of "the catacombs" regarded themselves as fortunate in their shelter, they suffered severely from the cold and from the bitter wind which swept through the tunnels. The method of lighting at night was also a page from the dark ages. A piece of tow stuck into a jam-tin of oil sufficed. This, of course, was only possible in the covered trenches where lights would not be visible from the hostile lines.

Demonstrations to draw the enemy's fire were

still kept up at irregular intervals, and the Turk did not hesitate to try a few tricks on us. At one time a report was circulated that he was using gas, but it afterwards transpired that incendiary bombs, thrown by the enemy into Lone Pine, and failing to ignite, had given off a dense smoke, and this had caused the "furphy" of "Gas."

Brigade Orders of 10th October contained the notification of Major Elliott's promotion to Lieut.-Col. (temporary), thus marking another stage in the service of the officer whose name was later to be so closely associated with that of the 12th Battalion.

The weather was now becoming decidedly chilly, and those who had earlier converted their breeches or trousers into shorts, now wished that they had retained the severed portions. A heavy thunderstorm made everyone appreciate what open bivouac would mean during the winter, and although "evacuation" was not common knowledge, the projected spell on Lemnos was, and it became more and more the topic of conversation.

"Beachy Bill," the Turkish gun at Olive Grove, never failed to put his mid-day *strafe* on to the beach. Although responsible for not a few casualties amongst carrying parties, this gun came to be regarded as an integral part of life at Anzac, and was the theme of much banter among the troops.

Only one year and three days had passed since the Battalion sailed from Hobart, when it relieved the 11th Battalion in the line, for what was generally believed to be the last stretch of duty prior to leaving for the much-discussed and longed-for spell. That year had seemed more like five years, and it could hardly be credited that such a vast change could, in so short a space of time, have come over the eager, fresh troops that had sailed in the "Geelong." Lean, gaunt and weather-beaten, and inured as they were to grim duties, hard work and trying conditions, it was difficult to realise that these were some of the same men. And now orders were received that it was impossible to relieve the 3rd Brigade just yet! Then the yarn began to spread that a tourist visiting Anzac in 1940 came across two hoary-headed old fellows sitting in a fire recess. "Hallo," he said, "who the blazes are you and what are you doing here?" "We belong to the 12th Battalion and are waiting to be relieved," was the reply. "But, my good fellows, that war finished years ago." "Cripes, Bill, the 3rd Brigade has been forgotten again." This and similar yarns became common and helped as a safety valve to the bitter disappointment of postponed relief. Another slight diversion was the introduction of the "wallaby" rifle standard, by which a rifle could be registered on to points of the hostile lines, and during the hours of darkness accurately aimed on to those points. Lieut. Connell was given charge of these "standards" and enjoyed himself in causing casualties among the infidel host.

On the 25th, an extra issue of rum was served to celebrate six months on the Peninsula. Round the convivial dixie lid, yarns of the good old times at the Landing were swapped, and truth was strangely intermingled with fiction.

As October wore out and November crept along, the question, "When are we going to be relieved?" became more and more persistent. As a variation in the daily routine, practice in the use of gas helmets became more general, although on Gallipoli the full meaning of a "gas attack" was not realised. Cold weather made the "possies" less homely than in summer months, when shade and attempted refuge from flies and shrapnel were their principal functions. Now protection from wind and rain was required and the beloved "possie" failed to meet requirements. However, all hearts were cheered and hope rose anew when, on 14th November, orders were received that the 1st and 2nd Brigades would relieve the 3rd Brigade in the line. As an offset to excessive optimism, the embarkation of the 9th and 11th Battalions were at the same time postponed on account of rough weather. It appeared as though someone in the Battalion must have killed a Chinaman, as the weather continued rough and stormy, with strong wind. Two days later, however, the long-talked-of and eagerly-awaited relief appeared to be materialising, as an advance party of ten men left with the 9th and 11th Battalions for Mudros, and orders were received for the 12th Battalion to hand over to the 2nd Brigade on the morrow. The air was now electrical with the hope of a speedy exit from Anzac; and without a doubt a rest was urgently required, for the physical condition of the men could not withstand the bitter weather now setting in. After being relieved by the 2nd Brigade, the 12th moved into their old bivouac area, where a heavy thunderstorm that night added to their misery. Many "possies" were flooded, and every little valley carried a turbulent stream of water. Clothing and equipment was washed away, and even a jar of rum — genuine S.R.D. — was swept out of a C.Q.M.S.'s store. Next morning, although the day broke fine and sunny, everything was wet and sodden, and individuals were wandering about looking for lost property. But we were to be off that night, so what matter! Such material and belongings as it was impossible to take away with the Battalion were buried, to be recovered on the expected return in six weeks or two months, and the immediate expectancy of "pastures new" could be read in the gaunt and bronzed faces. Then word was received that the Battalion would not go that night, and that there would be no movement of troops for two or three days. Down went the mercury in Hope's thermometer. Grim and ghastly yarns were originated, and satire replaced humour. It was told how the Battalion was doomed to be marooned till every third man had died of melancholia for the sin of the Light Horse in shaking the Gippo saddler's bits at Mena. Although everyone knew that it was only a temporary disappointment, impatience was very evident, but as the day wore on and clothing and ground dried, the spirit of good humour returned. Strange to say, despite the heavy rains, only half rations of water were available, it being out of the question to use surface water owing to contamination.

On 25th November, the day which marked seven months' continuous work on the Peninsula, orders were again received that the 12th was to embark that night for Mudros. The news, although so long and eagerly expected, when it did come, seemed too good to be true. Excitement ran high. The optimists recounted the number of beers they would consume on arrival at Mudros, whilst the pessimist predicted that something fresh would crop up to postpone the move. At any rate, optimist and pessimist bustled round completing final arrangements, cleaning up cook galleys and lines, and for once every ear listened while Battalion Orders were read proclaiming how and when this wonderful move would be carried out. The evening meal was served earlier than usual, and after a final inspection of the bivouac areas, companies were given the order to "fall in." This is an order usually received reluctantly, but on this occasion men were waiting half-an-hour before, with equipment on and arms close by. There was no need for the N.C.O.'s to urge the backward to "get a hustle on." This "fall in" was carried out almost as rapidly as that preceding the attack on Lone Pine. Rolls were called and platoons reported "All present and correct." At 5.45 p.m. the order was given, "Move to the left in file," and with light hearts, though heavy tread, the Battalion began the night march to the beach.

The embarkation was to take place at William's Pier, on the north of Anzac, near the spot where the 12th Battalion effected their landing, and the march was via Shrapnel and Rest Gullies. So weak were the troops and for seven months so unused to marching in full "marching order" that frequent rests were necessary. In February, the Battalion could have effected this march without a halt or without one man falling out, but before half the distance was covered many men showed signs of distress. The thought of what was in store, however, kept everyone moving.

On arrival at the beach it was necessary to wait till orders were received to commence embarkation. The Battalion was halted in a sunken road, through which the chilly winds whistled, and it was cold to the marrow. After two or three hours of stone-cold waiting, the order was received at 12.30 a.m. to embark. Silently, and in good order, the companies filed along the pier and on to the "beetles," as the huge, decked-in, flat-bottomed punts were called. "Beachy Bill," as a last farewell, sent along a few rounds which, luckily, burst short of the pier. The "beetles" pushed off, and in a short time, after a scramble up the Jacob's ladders, all were embarked on the S.S. "El Kaliera." The vessel was uncomfortably crowded, and sleeping space could barely be secured on the open decks. But what matter! Barring submarines or accident, a short shift now would see Mudros again.

For collective and individual acts of good service, the following awards were given in the Battalion during its service on Gallipoli:—Major E. H. Smith, C.B.; Major J. L. Whitham, C.M.G.; Sgt. Connell and Pvts. Vaughan and Yaxley, D.C.M.; Sgts. Cooper and Will, M.M.

The following appointments to commissions were made from the ranks during the period the Battalion was on the Peninsula:—R.S.M. Kennedy, C.S.M.'s Williams, Newland, Stubbings and Richardson, Sgts. Connell, Blakney, Love, Holyman, Weston, Hart, McLeod, Webster, Bass and Jacob, Pvts. McElwee, Tostevin, Nicholas, Ogilvie and Von Bibra. Reinforcement officers joining up during the progress of the campaign were Lieuts. C. H. Perkins, Appleby, Teakle, Christophers, Aspinall, Haslam and Woodhouse.

Before this part of the Battalion's history is concluded, a word of appreciation must be said of the services of the A.M.C. The value of their work is apparent when one remembers that the physical condition of the troops was low for the greater part of the period of occupation, and that all the elements of a disastrous epidemic were present— uncovered dead, flies by the million, bad water, and poor and uncovered food. That such devastation did not occur was undoubtedly due to the efficient supervision and organisation of the Medical Service generally and its officers in particular.

Many a soldier of the 12th during this campaign

benefitted in a quiet way by the kindly thought of two "unofficial" members of the Battalion, who were adopted during the voyage on the "Geelong." These were Army Nursing Sisters J. Radcliff and A. G. King, who, during the many trips they made to Alexandria on hospital ships, seized the opportunity of procuring mosquito netting and such-like boons, which were distributed in the Battalion and greatly assisted in alleviating the discomforts of bivouacing with the flies and other pests.

Besides the personal exploits narrated, many a good and gallant deed was performed of which the particulars are now so uncertain that, even if space permitted, it would be impossible correctly to record them in this narrative. The Battalion existed, in these early days, more as four separate units, as represented by the companies, and it requires a recorder to come forward from each company before merit can be correctly allocated. Individual acts of heroism have now escaped the memory of the writer, and others that should be mentioned are crowded out through lack of space, so let the reader remember that this and the previous chapter are purely attempts to outline the general life and doings of the 12th Battalion on Gallipoli, and do not for a moment purport to record all the details and actions, which went to make up the life and history of this last, but not least, of the battalions of the 3rd Australian Infantry Brigade.

Among the officers and men of the 12th Battalion, although now long disbanded, the spirit of comradeship and *esprit de corps*, founded at Pontville, Morphetville and Blackboy Hill, cemented on Gallipoli and consecrated in the blood of so many good and true comrades who have "gone west," exists to this day.

Chapter VIII.

CAMPS AT SARPI, TEL-EL-KEBIR AND SERAPEUM

NARRATIVE CONTINUED BY LIEUT. L. M. NEWTON, M.C.

THE Battalion was embarked on the Z37, S.S. "El Kaleira," by midnight on 25th-26th November (the Battalion having completed its seven months' occupation to the day). We left the pier, went north, and lay off Suvla Bay until daybreak. It was bitterly cold, and most of us unrolled our blankets, lay down, and attempted to sleep for a few hours. We sailed at dawn next day, and for the last time saw the sun rise over Gallipoli—it was thought at the time that we were going to Lemnos for a spell, and the news of the evacuation during our sojourn there came as a distinct surprise. With mixed feelings we watched the shores of Anzac recede into the distance, that of relief being predominant, especially with those members of the Battalion who had spent the whole seven months of hardship there. As we got out to sea, the breeze freshened, and we had a choppy passage over to the island, many men being seasick. The harbour was reached soon after midday. It presented a wonderful appearance—it seemed as though the merchant service of the whole world had assembled there, for on rounding the point a forest of masts and funnels came into view. The most prominent vessel was the gigantic liner "Olympic," which had been converted into a hospital ship. There were also battleships, cruisers, destroyers, troopships, other hospital ships, store and depot ships, and a heterogeneous collection of minor craft. We proceeded to the far end of the harbour once again and landed in lighters on the side of the harbour opposite to the principal village of Mudros. And what a different spectacle the foreshore presented! Instead of bare fields, there now appeared camps of all kinds, tented hospitals, flying the Red Cross flag, workshops, ordnance stores, generating plants, distilleries, and many other camps and buildings which we could not designate by a casual glance.

When the Battalion had landed, at about 3.30 p.m., we marched in column of route to our camp at Sarpi, about a mile distant. We presented a very weird spectacle to the troops who watched us march past. Some of us had Australian tunics much the worse for wear, some "Tommy" tunics, others wore "shorts," and some converted "Tommy" slacks. Australian hats in various states of age and condition were worn by the majority, but a number had the British service cap with the wire frame removed. A varied collection of scarves, mittens, cap comforters, cardigan jackets, rabbit-skin jerkins and other weird articles of winter clothing "not on issue" completed the motley parade. Our marching and march discipline was anything but good. We had not been on a parade ground for more than seven months, we were cold, tired and hungry, and the majority almost as weak as kittens from the effects of dysentry and the conditions of life generally during the past few months. It was amusing to see the packs that some of the men carried, laden with cherished souvenirs which they were loathe to leave behind—Turkish packs and rifles, caps, shell cases, bombs, etc. Private Tilley was generally considered to have the best collection, under which he laboured heroically; he had not only his own, but also many of Captain Rafferty's, who was well known as a connoisseur of souvenirs.

The march of only a mile seemed long to these tired war-worn troops, and men soon commenced to fall out and straggle until it appeared as though the Battalion was marching in single file. A pitiful sight was presented when we marched through one of the hospitals which lined the road. Some of the patients had just been to draw their rations and were standing on the roadside watching us pass, with bread and other dry rations in their arms, when three or four fellows broke off and rushed over to them, offering to exchange some of their souvenirs for a loaf of bread.

We eventually reached the camp, where our advance parties were waiting for us, and as the stragglers arrived they were directed to their platoon tents. A hot meal was soon issued and before long the Battalion was once again in high spirits—refreshed and ready for a night's sleep to be enjoyed with a sense of security that we had not experienced for a long time.

Next morning we woke "independently," if I may put it that way, for no Reveille was sounded, and the men were allowed to sleep just as long as they liked. We now looked around, and discovered that our camp was composed of hospital marquee tents which were pitched on the side of a hill, sloping down to a backwater which separated us from the 3rd Australian General Hospital. At low tide it was possible to wade across, the water not coming above one's knees, otherwise it meant a good half mile march round the head of the bay.

The day was spent in calling platoon rolls and cleaning clothing, rifles and equipment generally, while lists of shortages and requirements were prepared and forwarded to the Quartermaster (Lieutenant W. Kennedy) in the hope that the articles would soon be forthcoming. A large batch of reinforcements under Lieutenants Hubbe and Peters, which were already in the camp awaiting our arrival, were also absorbed into the Battalion and allotted to companies on 28th November.

During the next few days the weather was trying —a piercing wind from the North penetrated every nook and corner of the camp. It was the first time we had encountered such cold, even worse than that experienced during our last week on the Peninsula, and the men could not find enough clothes to put on. A fall of snow might have had its usual effect of warming the atmosphere, had not the wind increased in strength and keenness. The majority of the men of the Battalion were still suffering from acute dysentry, and one of our greatest hardships at this time was due to the fact that the Battalion latrines were situated quite 200 yards from the camp and on the crest of the hill, thus receiving the full blast of these icy winds. This may have been highly desirable from a point of view of sanitation in normal times, but in existing conditions the discomfort and inconvenience suffered by the men could easily have been ameliorated.

On 4th December another batch of ninety-four reinforcements arrived under Lieutenant R. M. W. Thirkell, while Lieutenants A. S. Vowles and J. A. Foster reported back from hospital.

For the next week or two the Battalion had a very easy time, resting and recuperating, calling of rolls, reorganising companies and appointing new N.C.O's., absorbing reinforcements, and as much recreational training (especially football) as possible. All guards and fatigues were supplied by the newly arrived reinforcements. It was also generally said that the first question the R.M.O. (Major G. B. Carter) asked the men on sick parade was—"What's your regimental number?" If it was a "peninsula" number, he was marked "No duty" without more ado, but if not, the medical inspection was continued in the orthodox manner, and the individual in question took his chance of getting "Duty," "Light Duty" or of joining his "Anzac" cobber.

December 8th was a red-letter day for the Battalion, for it was then that Lieutenant-Colonel J. Gellibrand p.s.c., arrived and assumed command. We knew that we were fortunate in obtaining such a commander, for his ability as a Staff Officer on 1st Australian Divisional Headquarters was already well known, and the fact that he was a Tasmanian made him all the more welcome.

The personnel of Battalion Headquarters and Company Commanders at this period was as follows:—

>Commanding Officer—Lieut.-Col. J. Gellibrand.
>Second-in-Command—Major C. H. Elliott.
>Adjutant—Capt. I. S. Margetts.
>Quartermaster—Lieut. W. Kennedy.
>Signalling Officer—Lieut. R. M. W. Thirkell.
>Machine Gun Officer—Lieut. G. Tostevin.
>Transport Officer—Lieut. J. E. Newland (at Mex).
>O.C. "A" Company—Capt. L. M. Mullen.

O.C. "B" Company—Capt. H. A. MacPherson.
O.C. "C" Company—Capt. R. A. Rafferty.
O.C. "D" Company—Major D. A. Lane.

The rations were good, more especially when compared with those received on the Peninsula, but I think that which was most appreciated was the bread—arriving in an unbroken condition and comparatively fresh. The cooking arrangements reflected great credit on Sergeant-Cook Sam Salt. It was not long before a Sergeants' Mess was started, although many difficulties were raised, and overcome one at a time.

The weather had by now improved and although cold, there was a pleasant crispness in the air and the sun shone brightly, while the penetrating wind which was so dreaded had entirely died away.

Training was now commenced in the morning and the newly appointed N.C.O.'s were segregated for special instruction. In the afternoon recreational training was freely enjoyed, while some of the men roamed round the country visiting the adjacent villages of Athos, Porthianos and Ysophargo, purchasing coffee, cakes, chocolates, fruits and other luxuries, which had been unknown to us for some time.

Unfortunately, at this time some slight cases of diphtheria were reported from the Brigade camp, and in consequence we had to be isolated. This meant posting a cordon of sentries round the camp—known as the Perimeter Guard—at about twenty yards interval, with instructions to let no one in or out of the camp without a special pass. Although this precaution considerably reduced the traffic to and from the camp, it was no difficult matter to get out. If you had a particular friend on duty it was generally an easy task to make an exit through his post. Failing this a football was generally kicked outside the cordon, when a dozen or more diggers would rush out, and *some* would not return.

At this time I was Battalion Orderly Room Sergeant, and the work in the Orderly Room was very heavy. Corporal Bridger, who had been assisting me on the Peninsula, had been evacuated sick, and Corporal W. V. Keats, of "B" Company, was giving me a hand, but as his Company Commander wanted him to take charge of his section, he was also taken away. Peter F. O'Loughlin, of "C" Company, was then detailed, and for many weeks rendered valuable assistance during a strenuous period, until given his stripes and placed in charge of the Battalion Post Office.

The 2nd Brigade Units commenced to arrive at an adjacent camp about 12th December, and for some time we could not attribute a reason to their sudden return, for they had already had their spell. However, as soon as we were able to have a yarn with them, we were astounded to hear of the projected evacuation of the Peninsula. We could not—we would not—believe it! After our landing, defending and occupying Anzac for all those months, after our hardships and sufferings there, it was hard to conceive that our almost sacred strip of land was to be given up voluntarily. Of course, to account for the presence of the 2nd Brigade, numerous rumours circulated through the Battalion, each of which was eagerly received in the hopes that it might be more authentic than the suggested evacuation. One of the most prominent of these rumours referred to Canadians relieving the Aussies on the Peninsula to allow the latter to go on to the Salonica front. But alas! it was only a "furphy," and, as all the world knows, the actual evacuation of Anzac did take place, on the night of 19th-20th December, without a casualty.

While we were at Sarpi Camp, the Brigade held its first combined sports meeting. It was a great success, and each event was keenly contested by the competitors of the various Battalions. The 12th Battalion gained a fair share of the honours, the Sheffield Handicap (the event of the day) being won by Coomer.

Every effort was made to ensure that our second Christmas away from Australia should be as enjoyable as possible. The chief feature, of course, was the issue of Christmas billies, packed to the brim by our generous folks in Australia. They were issued on Christmas Eve, and great excitement prevailed as the contents were exhibited and the names and addresses of the donors disclosed. It has always been a mystery to us how so many presents could have been packed into so small a space. Most of the billies came from Melbourne and suburbs, but a few of our fellows were fortunate enough to receive some sent by our own North-West Coast residents. It would be impossible to record the many things that came in these billies, ranging from a Kodak camera to a proposal of marriage; but, generally speaking, they contained mittens, scarves, socks, chocolate, dried fruits, biscuits, soap, writing paper, pencils and Keating's powder. The latter was, of course, very acceptable and useful, but when the lid came off it did not always improve the cake of "Old Gold" chocolate which came with it. The illustrated label on the billies was ironically humorous, for it represented a kangaroo wearing an Australian hat, well established on the Gallipoli Peninsula, and a disconsolate

Turk slinking away in the distance, while underneath was the quotation, "This bit of world belongs to us!" To supplement our Christmas dinner, we also had an issue of Christmas puddings.

During the day, services were held in the Y.M.C.A. tent, and there was a splendid muster of men in the evening for the singing of Christmas carols. At this time there was a Brigade Choir, led by a man of the 10th Battalion, which used to do good work at the Brigade church parades—at least, it was generally thought that they did good work, until on a certain Sunday a Digger went up to one of them and said, "What's crawlin' on youse blokes? You spoilt the singin' to-day."

As soon as Christmas was over, it began to be known that we were to return to Egypt, and accordingly, on the afternoon of 1st January, 1916, we embarked on H.M.T. "Lake Michigan." We remained on board for a couple of days and finally left Lemnos about 3 a.m. on 4th January, and found ourselves well out to sea at daybreak. The 12th Battalion was the only large unit on the boat, but there was a crowd of smaller units and details in addition. Lieut.-Col. Gellibrand was C.O. Troopship, and Capt. Margetts, Ship's Adjutant. There was a multitudinous number of disembarkation returns to prepare for the M.L.O. (Military Landing Officer) at Alexandria, and the work of compiling them was not easy. It was not until the second day at sea that we obtained a complete and correct nominal roll from some of the units, and in consequence the Orderly Room Staff had to work well into the early hours of the morning completing the returns, as we arrived at Alexandria at 11 a.m. on January 6th. The congratulatory remarks passed by the M.L.O. regarding the correctness of our figures fully compensated us for the time and trouble taken in preparing them.

We did not disembark until late in the afternoon, when a train came on to the wharf, into which the officers and men were soon packed. This was our first experience of travelling in open trucks (for there were only a few carriages), and we knew all about it before we arrived at our destination. Before starting, most of the men went to the engine, got boiling water in their Christmas billies—they were already proving their usefulness—proceeded to make tea, and supplemented their rations by the purchase of fruit. The train pulled out at 5 p.m. Travelling at night in an open truck soon dispels the illusions that Egypt is a land of burning sands, for we "perished" from the cold before we had gone far. However, the longest journey under these conditions must sooner or later come to an end, and at 11 p.m. we came to Tel-el-Kebir siding, adjacent to the camp site. Our troubles were not yet over, for no tents had been erected, and there was nothing for it but to open up our waterproof sheets and blankets and finish the night in the open. Our transport had already arrived from Alexandria (where they had been stationed at Mex Camp during our occupation of Anzac) and a number of us went down to their lines and bivouaced under the G.S. limbered wagons.

We were busy the next morning laying out the camp, drawing tents from ordnance and erecting them. During the morning a large number of officers, N.C.O.'s and men returning from hospital reported to Battalion Headquarters and were reposted to their various companies.

As soon as we had time to look around us, we

discovered that the camp was quite close to the famous battlefield of 1882, and a continuous line of troops could be seen wending their way to Arabi Pasha's trenches. They were in a wonderful state of preservation, for the trenches and parapets could easily be discerned, and were a formidable obstacle for transport when moving to our parade ground. Skulls and bones lay exposed, and souvenir hunters added yet another "item" to their collection.

Training, reorganising and refitting again continued, and for the first time since our return from the Peninsula, we really began to look respectable. The Quartermaster was now able to get an appreciable quantity of clothing and equipment from ordnance, and in consequence each company had a fairly liberal issue. Leave to visit Cairo for a few days was given to all officers, N.C.O.'s and men who had spent all, or a greater portion of the time, on Gallipoli, and as most of them had a good substantial credit balance in their pay books, due to their inability to spend money, they had a good time.

While at Tel-el-Kebir Camp, a Brigade equitation class was started, and I feel certain that every member of the Battalion who kept a diary has noted the fact that on 13th January Major Elliott and Captain Tozer (the R.M.O.) attended the class —at least, I mean that they made every effort to attend, and it was not for the want of urging, coaxing and persuading their respective mounts that they failed to report there. As soon as the horses felt the hard, solid gravel under their feet, they went mad with delight, and, detaching themselves from the rest of the party, made straight for the horizon. Major Elliott was observed to disappear over one rise, and as he made his reappearance he came a terrible "cropper," and everyone who was looking on (that is, the whole Battalion) feared that he had hurt himself. But not so, he quickly got up and was bent on recapturing his mount and proving his superiority over it. The horse, however, entered into the joke; he allowed himself to be caught and beguiled the Major into mounting again. Before he could get his feet into the stirrups, the old game was restarted, and off went the horse in an ever-widening semicircle, to complete his tour of the desert. Field glasses were now brought into use and in the far distance Major Elliott was again seen to fall. Realising that an order once given must be obeyed, the spirit of discipline prevailed, and the Major once more caught the horse and mounted; it was now that the lessons learnt during the afternoon's class of instruction proved their usefulness, for he was able to ride straight back to camp and thus once more uphold the First Australian Divisional motto, "What we have we hold."

The M.O.'s experiences were somewhat different, as he left the saddle only once, and under different circumstances. His horse was more of a stay-at-home, and delighted in galloping up and down the whole length of the Brigade lines. Intuition seemed to tell him that the Doc. was not a Light Horseman and he took advantage of the fact. Having passed Brigade Headquarters a couple of times, he determined to make for home, and as he went by the head of the Battalion line, the M.O. made a valiant effort to keep his seat. Hatless, with clenched teeth, grasping the reins with one hand and the pummel of his saddle with the other, his stirrups flying, and clinging to the horse with knees and legs, the Doc. passed like a flash. Round the corner and straight for the horse lines went the pair, when we knew that their wild career must cease. The horse, however, had never approached the transport lines from this direction, and knew nothing of the greasy pit which was in the way, but seeing it in the nick of time, and without intimating his intention in any way to his rider, he stopped dead. The Doc., as everyone knows, was the best of sportsmen, and, playing the game, went straight on, taking a graceful header into the placid, though slimy, water of his favourite greasetrap. This particular pit was a hobby of the M.O.'s and he used to inspect it daily, but, I venture to suggest, never so thoroughly as on this day.

On Saturday, 15th January, the First Australian Division was reviewed by General Sir Archibald Murray, when a wonderful spectacle was presented. The Infantry Battalions marched past in column of platoons, and proved conclusively that they were as good on a ceremonial parade as they were on the battlefield. Our own Battalion surpassed itself on this occasion, and compared more than favourably with any regular British regiment of pre-war days. In commenting on the review, General Murray expressed himself in very eulogistic terms. There are two points deserving of note in connection with this parade. First, that it took the twelve Infantry Battalions fifty-five minutes to pass the saluting-base; and, second, that this was the first and only occasion on which the First Australian Division was reviewed as a complete unit, disregarding the Divisional route march carried out at Mena.

On the same day, I was instructed to report to the Divisional Pay Office in Cairo with all the pay books of the Battalion, in order that they might be audited. It was a laborious task, but with the assistance of Cpl. M. Dunkin, of "B" Company, I completed the job in a week. The books were found to be in a very creditable state, some of the early promotions on the Peninsula had not been recorded in the pay office, and one of the acquittance rolls embodying a Peninsula pay must have been sunk or lost in transit, and did not appear in the pay office books.

Training continued in the camp, and efforts were made to improve the conditions of living for the men. Mess sheds and baths were erected and the sergeants were given a tent in which to re-establish their mess. During our stay at Tel-el-Kebir Camp we received a huge accumulated mail numbering over fifty bags, and the orderly room staff, who mostly dealt with mail matters in those days, were working well after "Lights Out" for several nights before it was ultimately disposed of.

Our sojourn at Tel-el-Kebir was brought to a close on 24th January, and all the afternoon the whole Battalion was at work striking tents and returning them with other camp equipment back to ordnance. The military custom was carried out as usual on this instance, for the work of striking and cleaning up the camp was completed about 6 p.m., after which, there was nothing to do and nowhere to go, and it was not until about 9 p.m. that we were told that the troop train would leave at 2 a.m.

Some men started a game of cards, some formed a "two-up" school under one of the arc lamps, others found wood somewhere and, lighting a huge fire, sang songs around it; but the majority took out their greatcoats and attempted to get a few hours sleep (our blankets being rolled in bundles and stacked at the Q.M. Store).

JANUARY, 1916

We entrained at 2 a.m. and started at 2.40 a.m.—once again in open trucks. If it had been cold on our journey from Alexandria it was freezing now. The air was biting, and as we travelled fairly rapidly it was impossible to keep it out. We were blue with the cold when we arrived at Serapeum, on the western bank of the Suez Canal, at 7 a.m. A march of some 300 to 400 yards in the loose sand helped to warm us, when we came to the pontoon bridge across the Canal, over which we passed to the eastern bank, and pitched our camp about 400 yards inland from the bank. It was on this short march that Pvt. Chopping fell out and was taken to the hospital at Ishmalia, when he died of cerebro-spinal meningitis on 29th January.

When we arrived at Serapeum the staging camp was fairly well established, as it already formed a base for mounted patrols who penetrated many miles into the desert. There was a field ambulance established under the trees on the western bank, and a large A.S.C. depot on the opposite side. The pontoon bridge represented a wonderful piece of engineering work and was the means of a constant stream of traffic—both mounted and unmounted—being able to pass backwards and forwards across the canal. The control of the traffic was in the hands of officers, who carried on continuous duty in reliefs. Whenever a boat came through the canal, one end of the bridge was detached and a gang of natives hauled it across the canal and thus kept this international waterway open for allied and neutral shipping.

The Battalion at this time (as a unit of the First Australian Division) was forming a part of the Canal defence line, which consisted of garrisoned posts situated at intervals right along the eastern bank of the Canal. In 1915, when the Turkish force attacked and attempted to cross the Canal, the defensive line was situated on the western or African bank of the Canal, and any detached posts or patrols were withdrawn from the Asiatic side before the attack eventuated.

This invasion proved to be a miserable fiasco, but it was also realised what an important factor the Suez Canal was in our lines of communication. When Lord Kitchener made his inspection of the Eastern theatre of war, during the autumn of 1915, he inspected the Canal defences and embodied his report, more or less, in one question, namely, "Are you defending the Canal, or is the Canal defending you?" The outcome of this criticism was that the garrisons were transferred to the Asiatic side and a strong defence system was projected, about 10 miles east of the Canal itself. This was how the position stood when the First Australian Division arrived at Serapeum, and thus, the camp at which the 3rd Brigade first rested on its arrival on the Canal was known as Staging Camp, through which it was to pass on its way out to the sector of the defence line in the desert, which we had to construct and subsequently occupy, ready for the strong Turkish force which was believed to be pushing its way across the desert from the direction of Palestine.

On our arrival, the Quartermaster issued a Maconochie ration for breakfast (which was always appreciated), after which parties were detailed to draw tents and we proceeded to erect them. The issue proved to be somewhat inadequate, and since the Commanding Officer's efforts to obtain more were fruitless, space had to be economised in every conceivable way.

The Battalion Orderly Room was established in a corner of the officers' mess tent, the Regimental Quartermaster improvised a store out of ammunition boxes and tarpaulins, tents for Headquarters details and Company Quartermasters' stores were consolidated and reduced to a minimum, and even after these efforts the men had to sleep 12 to 14 in a tent.

Rations were again unsatisfactory during this period, for biscuits once more took the place of bread and the issue of meat was very light indeed. The only method of supplementing our rations was to obtain a special pass and cross the Canal, where a small canteen was established. It carried only a small stock, however, and if you did not get in early, it was a case of "sold out." Water was almost rationed, too, and was generally handed over to the cookhouse for culinary purposes. The use of fresh water for washing was discouraged, owing to the shortage and the obvious need for economy, but as a substitute we were granted permission to bathe in the Canal, and between the hours of 12 noon and 2 p.m. practically the whole Battalion could be seen wending its way, with towels over shoulders, to the Canal. It was humorous to see the rush for cover that took place when a boat passed through the Canal, possibly with women aboard.

The Australian Camel Corps was formed just about this time and Capt. E. Y. Butler had already left the Battalion to take a command in the unit, followed on January 29th by Sgt. Watt and 17 men. While we were at Serapeum our strength was further depleted by the formation of the 1st Pioneer Battalion, when Capt. T. Holland and from 70 to 80 tradesmen left our ranks to assist in forming the nucleus of this unit, which was to render us such valuable service in France.

The means of communication from the Staging Camp to the proposed defence line in the desert were road and rail as far as Railhead, and then by camel or afoot. A light railway had been constructed and was gradually being pushed farther and farther into the desert. When we first arrived on the Canal it penetrated only about two and a half miles, but when we left, at the end of March, Railhead was six miles from the Canal bank. Every morning and every afternoon a loaded train of about twelve trucks went out, hauled by a little, but powerful, motor engine. Trucks generally were laden with rails and sleepers for the railway extension, big iron pipes for the water main, horse and camel fodder, rations and engineering material. The road was gradually pushing its way into the sandy waste, too, and a large gang of natives was continually working on it. The foundation of the road consisted of chalky rock, brought down the Canal in native dhows and transported to that portion of the road under construction on a light tram-track, the trams being pushed by the natives.

Railhead was now becoming a centre of activity, and the stores accumulating there, as well as the ammunition supply and the 1,200 camels (used for transporting rations, water and R.E. material out to the defence line) needed a garrison for protection. This was supplied by the 12th Battalion on the 30th January, when "B" Company, under the command of Capt. H. A. MacPherson, moved out to Railhead for that purpose.

In view of the fact that an enemy force was known to be advancing on to the Canal, even though it was still a long way off, and the possibility of hostile mounted patrols, every night an outpost line was thrown round the camp, at a distance of from 600 to 800 yards, by each Battalion of the Brigade in turn, and the same duty was imposed on the garrison at Railhead. Each sentry was instructed to challenge everyone approaching his post. One man of "C" Company took this command so literally that when his Company Commander was inspecting the posts he challenged him by saying, "Halt, Major Rafferty! Who goes there?"

The 11th Battalion left Serapeum on 31st January to occupy their sector in the frontage of the defence line allotted to the First Australian Division, known as Gabel Habeita. They were followed on 2nd February by the 10th Battalion, and on the same day "C" Company of our own Battalion, under the command of Major R. A. Rafferty, moved out to Railhead, together with Major C. H. Elliott, who assumed command of the garrison.

During this period, the training of the Battalion continued steadily and every member realised how fortunate we were in being commanded by Lieut.-Col. J. Gellibrand, who not only possessed a thorough knowledge of infantry training, but was gifted with a wonderful understanding of human nature, and was thus able to get the maximum amount of work out of his Battalion without apparent effort.

Officers were sent to an Infantry Training School at Zeitoun, near Cairo, while Lieut. Harry Webber, Sgt. F. H. Ripper and L.-Cpl. E. T. Domeney attended the first Lewis Machine Gun School at Ishmailia. Training otherwise was mostly carried on under Company arrangements, the newly appointed N.C.O.'s receiving special instruction from officers and senior N.C.O.'s. At times the Commanding Officer would co-ordinate the day's work by organising an attack on the Railhead garrison. The latter would probably march halfway to the Staging Camp and take up a defensive position by a pre-arranged time, at which moment the attacking force would send out an advance guard from the Staging Camp, which would ultimately develop into an attack. This exercise was both reversed and otherwise varied on many occasions, and in this manner the Battalion maintained the high standard it always held in open warfare training.

We lost the services of Major J. L. Whitham on 4th February, when he was appointed D.A.A. and Q.M.G. of the Second Australian Division and left for Ferry Post (which was farther north on the Canal) with his batman and groom, Pvts. Dennis and James respectively.

The Staging Camp was a little more than a quarter of a mile from the spot where the Turks made one of their attempts to cross the Canal in February, 1915, and it was customary for bathing parties to take their cameras with them, and after their swim, to go to the spot in question and take snapshots. There were numerous graves of unknown Turkish soldiers, marked by improvised crosses, and one, also, of a German officer, Major Von dem Hagen. Most of the equipment and military gear left behind in the rapid retreat had been salvaged long ago, but groups of men would scour the country in the hope of finding souvenirs. One of them found a clip of Turkish cartridges, with unexploded caps, but the bullets were made of *wood* and painted with a nickel-coloured paint. The deception would not have been noticed but for the fact that the wood had shrunk through exposure to the sun and weather and fitted loosely into the cartridge-case, while the paint was wearing off in places.

About the middle of February, we first heard of the projected formation of the 4th and 5th Divisions. The explanatory order took the following form:—

A.I.F.

Diagram showing details of five Divisions and method of completing same.

(Infantry)

Division Nos.	1			2			3			4			5			
Brigade Nos.	1	2	3	5	6	7	9	10	11	4	12	13	8	14	15	
Battalion Nos.	1	5	9	17	21	25	33	37	41	13	45	49	29	53	57	(a) The new Battalions to be formed in Egypt are 16, numbered 45 to 60 inclusive.
	2	6	10	18	22	26	34	38	42	14	46	50	30	54	58	
	3	7	11	19	23	27	35	39	43	15	47	51	31	55	59	(b) These will be formed by splitting existing Battalions 1 to 16 and making up with reinforcements.
	4	8	12	20	24	28	36	40	44	16	48	52	32	56	60	
Battalions formed from existing Units or existing Units forming new Battalions	53	57	49							45	13	9	1	5		Explanation: Each existing Battalion, 1 to 16, is in the same relative position on the diagram as the Battalion formed from it; thus, 11th Battalion forms the 51st; the 59th Battalion is formed from the 7th.
	54	58	50							46	14	10	2	6		
	55	59	51							47	15	11	3	7		
	56	60	52							48	16	12	4	8		

(Remains Unchanged)

The object, of course, was obvious; while on the

Peninsula the First and Second Australian Divisions required a considerable number of reinforcements regularly, to keep the various units up to fighting strength, and these were arriving in a steady stream from the camps in Australia. Now that the Australians had been withdrawn temporarily from the fighting zone, the need for these reinforcements ceased, and in consequence, the number of men in the Training Battalion camps around Cairo (which included reinforcements and an ever-increasing number of men returning to their units, recovered from sickness or wounds) became considerable. It was estimated by the General Staff that there was a sufficient number of men in the training camps surplus to the establishment of the two existing Divisions, to form two new Divisions. However, it was deemed inadvisable to form these from untried troops, and so it was decided to take 50 per cent. of the First Australian Division and the 4th Australian Brigade to form the nucleus, and to build all three Divisions up to strength with the men in the camps.

This news gave all ranks, both commissioned and non-commissioned, much to talk about and conjectures were numerous as to the probable methods of dividing the Battalion. This was actually done on 17th February, 1916, when two platoons of each Company, with an equal proportion of officers and senior N.C.O.'s, were drafted to "A" wing of the Battalion and the remaining two platoons, with officers and senior N.C.O.'s, formed "B" wing. The same was done with Headquarters specialists and the Transport Section. The whole arrangement was a very fine example of our Commanding Officer's tact and impartiality, for it was not until within a few days of the actual "split" that anyone knew which wing was to remain with the parent Battalion and which was to go to our offspring, the 52nd Battalion. It was finally decided one night in the officers' mess by the toss of a coin.

After this decision had been arrived at, the 12th Battalion wing was concentrated at Railhead, and the 52nd Battalion quota at Staging Camp. On 25th February, "A" Company 12th Battalion went out to Railhead (leaving "A" Company 52nd Battalion behind at Staging Camp) and exchanged places with "B" Company 52nd Battalion, which returned to Staging Camp. Similarly, on the next day, "D" Company 12th Battalion went out to Railhead, and "C" Company 52nd Battalion completed the concentration by returning to the camp on the Canal bank.

The Battalion suffered a severe blow on 27th February, when our Commanding Officer, Lieut.-Col. J. Gellibrand was transferred to command the 6th Australian Infantry Brigade. Of course, everyone was glad to hear of his promotion and proud to think that the 12th Battalion had been the stepping stone by which he had attained his appointment, but, at the same time, we were sincerely sorry to lose such a popular commander, who had brought the Battalion to a high pitch of proficiency in such a brief period. Major C. H. Elliott at once assumed command and subsequently received his substantive promotion and appointment on March 1st, 1916, which he held without a break until the cessation of hostilities in 1918. Lieut. W. Kennedy and R.S.M. F. Herbert also left us on this day as prospective Adjutant and Quartermaster of the 52nd Battalion respectively.

The actual "split" occurred on 1st March. It

was a particularly hot day, and the morning was occupied in striking tents, packing the gear and equipment, and carefully checking the 52nd Battalion's nominal rolls. The Brigadier addressed them at 10 a.m. and delivered a very impressive farewell speech. He told them that they were taking the traditions of their parent Battalion with them, and yet they had to win their own battle honours and set the same high standard in their new Division that had been maintained by the First Australian Division at Anzac, particularly the 3rd Brigade. They must always remember that the eyes of the 12th Battalion would be on them, and that their career would be closely watched.

They paraded for the last time at 1 p.m., when Major D. A. Lane, the senior Major of the 52nd Battalion, took command of the draft. I stood and watched them march out, and felt as though I were having a limb amputated without any anaesthetic. With keen regret we saw them go, these men with whom we had trained under varying conditions, shared joys and sorrows and, more than all, with whom we had faced death.

At 3 p.m. a draft of 500 reinforcements arrived, which were to bring the Battalion up to strength again. They had left Australia as reinforcements to the 26th Battalion and were largely composed of Queenslanders, with a percentage of Tasmanians, but owing to the reorganisation of the Divisions, they had been diverted to the 12th Battalion. They were accompanied by Lieuts. Potter, Shepherd, Sellick, Burnaby, Chapman and Lawrence.

With my Orderly Room Staff and gear, we waited for the afternoon "Desert Express," which for

3rd BRIGADE TROOPS WAITING TO CROSS PONTOON BRIDGE OVER SUEZ CANAL AT SERAPEUM, JANUARY, 1915

(*Photo. loaned by Lieut.-Col. C. H. Elliott, C.M.G., D.S.O.*)

some reason was delayed, and in consequence we got aboard about 8.30 p.m. and arrived at Railhead at 9 p.m.

During the next few days a terrific gale and sandstorm raged, and living conditions became very objectionable. Sand penetrated the tents and cookhouses and rendered our rations even less palatable than usual. Lieut. Holyman had to procure a fatigue party, which comprised nearly half the Battalion, in order to erect the officers' mess tent.

Our camp life took rather a monotonous turn while we were out in the desert. We had been able to play football down at the Staging Camp, where the ground was of a hard, gravelly nature, but football in loose sand soon looses its allurements. We therefore contented ourselves—when off parade—with watching the arrival, departure and unloading of the train, and the despatch of the caravan of heavily laden camels on their way out to the defence line at Gabel Habeita, still some three to four miles farther out on a ridge of low-lying hills.

The Battalion did eventually receive its orders to go to the defence line, and actually set out, but just before we arrived a mounted despatch rider overtook us with orders to return to Staging Camp. This was done without any hesitation, although everyone was at a loss to ascribe a reason for this sudden reversal of orders. However, before long it was obvious that the whole of the First Australian Division was once again concentrating on the Canal Bank.

On March 12th, R.Q.M.S. Claude Lyne, Cpl. E. W. D. Laing and myself received commissions, these being the first granted since the Battalion had recovered from the Lone Pine engagement.

While at Staging Camp, on this occasion, a Brigade church parade was held, at which H.R.H. the Prince of Wales was present with his own personal staff, in addition to that of our own Division and Army Corps. The display of "red tabs" is said to have impaired the eyesight of half the Brigade! Everything went well until after the parade, when the Prince, in stepping backwards, fell over a form and measured his length in the sand. An obvious titter of suppressed laughter from the Diggers agitated the staff considerably. The Prince, however, was a first-class sport, and entered fully into the joke against himself, and looked round with a broad grin at the assembled men.

It soon became obvious that a big move was once again before us. The officers of the 12th Battalion were detailed for traffic control duty on the pontoon bridge, and in consequence got all the "right oil." On 25th March the 2nd Brigade crossed the Canal, bound for an unknown destination, but generally believed to be Alexandria *en route* for France. Our own surplus blankets were also handed in to the Q.M. Store, and black kit bags were stacked at the railway siding on the other side of the Canal.

Next day the Pioneer Battalion, our own Brigade Headquarters, together with the 9th and 10th Battalions, entrained at Serapeum, and still no rumour leaked out as to their destination.

On 27th March, the 11th Battalion moved out and left us alone, so the Medical Officer, in order to cheer us up, decided to inoculate us. It was either for typhoid, diphtheria, para-typhoid, or something—they seemed to inoculate us for everything except gun-shot wounds.

We saw the last of the Staging Camp at 5 p.m. on the next day, and crossing the canal bivouaced at Serapeum railway siding. Just before leaving we saw the first of the 4th and 5th Divisional stragglers arrive in groups of six to twelve men from their much condemned march from Tel-el-Kebir to the Canal. They were in various stages of exhaustion, and all appeared very footsore and weary.

"A" Company entrained at 10 p.m. and left in advance as a loading party, whilst the remainder of the Battalion followed about midnight. Alexandria was reached about 7 a.m. after an uneventful train journey, and we at once embarked on H.M.T. "Corsican," depositing our gear on the troop deck, and proceeded to transfer all the military stores and equipment from the quay on to the troopship, whilst a party was specially detailed to stack it in the hold. Much amusement was caused during the morning by an Arab urchin, who was wearing a miniature uniform of the Australian pattern, correct in every detail, including a broad-brimmed hat, tunic and puttees. He carried a small rifle, and the boys delighted in putting him through his rifle exercises, which he carried out to perfection, including many obsolete and ceremonial movements such as "Shoulder arms," "Secure arms," and "Reverse arms." Some of the boys tried to trick him by giving complicated words of command ("Ground arms" from the "Slope") and incorrect orders ("Trail arms" with fixed bayonets); but not once was he caught napping—in the one instance he would go through the double movement by coming to the "order" first, and in the latter order he "stood fast." After the exhibition was over he reaped a little harvest of piastres which the onlookers showered upon him.

We eventually passed through the hands of the

Embarkation Staff Officer, and, together with the 11th Battalion, 1st Australian Casualty Clearing Station, a Butchery Unit, some 3rd Echelon Clerks, and one or two other weird and miniature units unheard of any other time, were packed aboard the troopship and left Alexandria at 9 a.m. on 30th March, *en route* for Marseilles.

Lieut.-Col. S. R. Roberts, commanding officer of the 11th Battalion, was O.C. Troops, and Capt. Hemingway, of the same unit, Ship's Adjutant.

Owing to the congestion on the boat and the shortness of the trip there was very little parade work—it consisted mostly of roll calls, inspection of arms, boat drill, and lectures on the new conditions of warfare which we would be likely to experience in France.

We arrived outside Valetta Harbour, at Malta, about 2 p.m. on 2nd April, but merely received our orders without going inside and then proceeded on our way. During our passage from Malta to the Straits of Bonnefacio, we were told that an enemy submarine had torpedoed a ship two hours' run ahead of us, and, later on, that another boat was being chased astern of us, so that it is quite within the bounds of possibility that we had a narrow escape.

Chapter IX.

ARRIVAL IN FRANCE

WE sighted the shores of France at daybreak on 5th April, and passing the historic Chateau d'If, arrived beside the quay at 7 a.m. Everyone was excited and in the best of spirits; we were all thinking that we had at last arrived in the country that was foremost in our minds when we enlisted. For us, the war was in France and Belgium, and although Gallipoli did, and always would, mean much to us, yet all other campaigns, whether big or small, were of a subsidiary nature to that in the great Western theatre.

During our voyage across, Lieut. C. H. Lyne became very ill with pneumonia, and he was removed as soon as we arrived, to one of the Australian hospitals which had already been established at Marseilles. It was with great regret that we afterwards learned of his death there, his loss being the first that the Battalion sustained on arriving in France.

The 12th Battalion was once again the last unit to leave the troopship, and a short march along the cobbled streets near the wharves brought us to the entraining point. All ranks were settled, more or less comfortably, in quick time, and we steamed out of the station at 4.20 p.m., with plenty of cheers from the Diggers, which were responded to by the crowd of civilians which had gathered on the platform and in the station yard.

During the three or four remaining hours of daylight, we passed through some very delightful scenery—olive groves, vineyards, fruit trees in blossom, and a general rural picturesqueness. All along the line the children shouted a welcome in broad *"patois,"* which was unintelligible to even our most accomplished French scholar, while the housewife came to her door and waved a handkerchief or apron and wished us *"bon chance."* Even the workman in the field ceased work while we were passing to give us a wave and a smile.

Every six or nine hours the train would stop at some wayside station or shunt into a siding, when hot tea would be awaiting us. The administrative arrangements on this long train journey were very well conducted, for our halts were so regulated that the troop train was withdrawn from the main line when various expresses were due to pass. The Quartermaster's store was situated in the rear truck, and it was from here that the dry rations were issued. A line of sentries was invariably supplied by the duty Company at each stopping place and posted on either side of the train to prevent the Diggers—as far as it was possible—from indulging in their favourite pastime of strolling off to purchase bread, cigarettes and a stray bottle of *"vin rouge."*

During the next day, 6th April, we passed through some of the most beautiful country imaginable; the grassy slopes and the wooded *"chateaux,"* situated in the valleys of the Rhone and Saone, almost defy description. At times we would be running along the banks of the river, with its verdant green pasture banks, whilst later on we would view the river rushing over a pebbly bed from some overhanging bank. The quaint architecture of the wayside cottages and grand *"chateaux"* was exclusively French, and the delicate green tint in all the spring foliage and surrounding meadows, made us think that *this* was indeed a country worth fighting for.

We passed through the larger towns of Lyons, with the river running through its midst, spanned with beautiful bridges, Challon-sur-Saone and Dijon with their beautiful church spires. At all these towns, an excited crowd soon congregated about our train and engaged in a desperate conversation with the boys. The latter very soon learnt two essential things; first, that *"bakshee,"* *"saieda"* and *"bint"* were not much good in France; and secondly, that a sentence in English with a few demonstrative actions goes a long way, and a *"compris"* tacked on the end ensures a complete understanding. However, before we steamed out of the station, addresses had been exchanged with *"mademoiselles"* (in spite of the censor), and rash promises entered into to write regularly, at least once a week.

The second night was passed in the train, and during the early hours of the morning we passed through the environments of Paris, much to everyone's disappointment, for we had all hoped to have a sight of the gay city, even from a distance. Amiens was passed at 3 p.m., Bolougne at 7 p.m., and Calais at 11 p.m. The country was proving itself to be far less interesting in the north, and not nearly so picturesque. The countryside was flatter, the cottages of meaner appearance, and the peasantry evidently poorer. If at any time we slowed up and stopped near a township or large village, an army corps of young children would appear from apparently nowhere, and eagerly hold out their hands for *"bisquit"* and *"bullee boeuf,"* and, in spite of issued orders, tins of bully beef and a shower of army biscuits would narrowly miss the kiddies' heads. At one time (when, I think, we were passing somewhere near the rear of the Champagne district) we actually saw barbed wire! and a devastated bridge across a dirty creek! It was our first "whiff" of the war in France, and all eyes were glued to the windows in the hope of seeing more indications of the campaign, but in vain.

During the day and the following night we discovered for the first time what travelling in troop trains in France really meant. The wonderful administrative arrangements previously referred to, became less and less apparent as we neared the battle area, and finally disappeared completely. It was soon evident that we had left the main line of the Paris, Lyons and Mediterranean Railway and were now on the lesser used rails of the Chemin de Fer du Nord. We were stopped and side-tracked for no apparent reason; we would remain stationary (*always* in some vile and uninteresting vicinity) for any period up to four or six hours, and then, without any warning, and once again without any apparent reason, the engine would give a consumptive snort, angrily jerk every carriage and truck in the train, and continue its crawling movement across Flanders.

We arrived at our journey's end at 3.30 a.m. on 8th April and detrained in the darkness at Godewaersvelde (God's Fair Field), after having spent three days and nights in the train. We sat down by the side of the cobbled road and on the doorsteps of the houses and waited for dawn to break. This eventually happened and we were formed up and set out for our billeting area. We marched with light hearts round the foot of Mont des Cats (where the first engagement between British and German cavalry took place in 1914) with the quaint old monastry balanced on its summit, but hard, cobbled roads, soft feet, cramped legs and a heavy pack soon made us feel tired. Although the march was not long, it showed how soon one can grow soft if training is relaxed. Soon after passing through Fletre, we were met by Major L. M. Mullen, who had left us in Egypt and come on in advance as Billetting Officer. He guided each company to its respective billetting area and indicated which billets were available for occupation.

The Battalion's first billet area in France was on the North of the village of Strazeele, and, although out of place at this juncture, it is interesting to know that, in 1918, when the Bosch broke through the Portuguese lines in front of Laventie and endeavoured to reach the railway centre of Hazebrouck, the 3rd Brigade stopped his advance at this spot, and the 12th Battalion assisted successfully in defending the village of Strazeele and prevented its capture.

The area was scattered (as we afterwards came to judge billetting areas), some companies being two to three kilometres from Battalion headquarters. Most of the Company billets were of a stereotyped kind, seen all over the northern part of France, and generally owned or occupied by the successful middle-class farmer. It was usually a brick or plaster farm-house, with an adjoining vegetable garden on one side and the indispensable *"middean"* just outside the back door, on the other side, surrounded by the farm buildings. These latter buildings were invariably allotted to the troops for billets whilst the officers were accommodated in the farm-house itself. The word "billet" (to the uninitiated) is always suggestive of a cottage or some disused granary or hall, and although the boys hardly knew what to expect, the sight of the barns and stables and the knowledge that they had to feed and sleep there came as a slight shock. A member of one of the companies was heard to say, "Do they think we're a lot of blooming sheep?" and from the noise that started one would have thought that they were either sheep, cows, horses, chickens, dogs, or any other kind of farmyard animal. But it was a good sign! All at once someone discovered a loft of straw, and before many minutes had passed every member of that company was assured a soft bed for the night. Of course, *"madame"* stormed and raved, and said it was *"pas bon"* and the men were *"brigands,"* but after she had stated her price and was paid, she was apparently quite satisfied.

During the day we could distinctly hear the sound of artillery in the distance, and also see aeroplanes being fired upon by German anti-aircraft guns, and everyone was anxious to enquire how far we were away from the firing line. Knowing that I had a slight schoolboy's knowledge of French, I was persuaded to ask the *"madame"* at our billet. While she was being found, I racked my brains to form a coherent sentence, but was confident that "firing line" or "front line" were not included in my school vocabulary. The only thing to do was to improvise. A brain wave seized me as a "*mademoiselle*," with a mass of flaxen hair half hanging down her back, enquired, "*Comment, messieurs?*" I cleared my throat, knowing that my reputation as a linguist was at stake, and asked how far "*la ligne de bataille*" was from Strazeele; she said, "*Oui, monsieur*," and disappeared. I knew that something was wrong and felt uncomfortable, but she returned a few moments later carrying a broom which she handed to me amidst a roar of laughter from the other members of the mess, led by Captain Margetts himself. I then realised that she had mistaken "*bataille*"—battle—for "*balai*"—broom. However, I assured them that it was only their "*patois*" in the north.

It was not long before the men wended their way into the village and were sampling "*biere*," "*vin rouge*" and "*cafe noir*," and making themselves generally popular with the "*mademoiselles*" in the various "*estaminets*" and shops.

Next day the whole Battalion attended a lecture on "Gas," very ably delivered by a British gas officer. Then we all had to put on our P.H. helmets and march through a demonstration trench, full of gas. This, of course, was to impress upon the men the safety the helmet conferred and the absolute immunity from ill consequences if correctly worn. After this, we passed over a shell-hole containing the contents of a lachrymatory or "tear" shell, which made our eyes water very freely and caused a violent irritation which was extremely disagreeable. We were then told that this latter gas had no harmful effect if inhaled, but was merely used by the enemy to cause discomfort and generally used just prior to an attack, so that we could not use our rifles to stop his advance. However, we were issued with a pair of ordinary goggles, which safeguarded the eyes from any deterrent effect of the fumes.

The weather during the next few days was very cold and wet, and we experienced a fairly heavy fall of snow, so that much of our training took the form of lectures to the men in their billets. Whenever possible, route marches were carried out under company arrangements to the adjacent villages of Borre, Pradelles, Caestre and Merris, but the hard roads were very injurious to the men's feet after their recent sojourn in Egypt, so the marches were necessarily very short at first and gradually increased. The boots themselves also began to crack in the wet and the Quartermaster and Bootmaker Sergeant were kept extremely busy.

On 17th April, in the Y.M.C.A. tent, a British Major gave us a very fine lecture on "Bayonet Fighting," which was demonstrated by a Sergeant-Major. Shortly afterwards, several of our officers and N.C.O.'s attended a school of instruction in physical training and bayonet fighting, which was organised by the lecturer and held in the upper story of a factory at Erquinghem.

Soon after this the First Australian Division moved into the line in the Fleurbaix sector, and the 3rd Brigade occupied the role of Reserve Brigade, being billeted at Sailly-sur-la-Lys, to which place the 12th Battalion marched on 20th April. The march was from 16 to 18 kilometres, through the villages of Vieux Berquin, Neuf Berquin and Estaires, and on a hard cobble road the whole way. While on the march, we passed an English "Bantam" Battalion on its way out to a training area, and these miniature specimens of the British Army carrying their heavy packs with bright, smiling faces, were the subject of much good-natured chaff from our fellows. Cpl. Billy Atkins, of "B" Company, and many other of our own midgets, were urged by their platoon comrades to apply immediately for a transfer. By the time the Battalion reached Sailly many of the men were suffering from blisters and tender feet, and the M.O. (Capt. Tozer) was busy giving them relief soon after the Battalion's arrival.

All four companies, together with Battalion Headquarter details, were concentrated in the centre of the township, the men being billetted in barns, stables, lofts, military hutments and an empty granary. It was not long before they made themselves known to the residents and became very popular, particularly with pretty Marie Louise, who served drinks at an *estaminet* in one of "A" Company's billets, as well as others matrons with their hard-working daughters, who catered for the soldiers by providing meals of fried eggs and chipped potatoes and omelettes.

Sailly was only about three miles from the front line trenches, and it was a source of wonder to us for a long time as to why the Germans never shelled it, knowing well that there were troops there. We afterwards surmised that by a mutual understanding it had become the custom for both sides to refrain from shelling villages and billets in the rear areas. It is almost superfluous to say that this "mutual understanding" was observed to a much lesser extent when the Australian batteries occupied this sector.

It was found very difficult to impress on the men the danger they incurred by congregating in the streets or anywhere in the open. Enemy aeroplanes were constantly flying over the village for the purpose of aerial reconnaissance, and it eventually became necessary for the Provost Sergeant to organise a squad of men to patrol the streets during daylight and after parade hours, to disperse large groups of men and endeavour to keep them off the main Armentieres road. To many of the men the aeroplane was entirely new and a source of wonder. In consequence, all eyes were turned to the sky as soon as one was fired at. Needless to say, every effort was made to prevent this "sight seeing" from becoming a habit. To impress upon the men its seriousness, they were shown two aerial photographs—one of a crowd of men in a village, hardly distinguishable from their surroundings, the other the same men with their faces turned to the sky, and easily discernible by the numerous white dots which showed distinctly in the photograph.

Having moved into fairly close proximity to the line, it was now necessary for each company to provide a billet guard over each billet or group of buildings used as billets. The sentries were generally posted at the entrance of the billet on to the road, and in consequence, much attention was paid to the quality of their ceremonial drill, for when a staff officer passed through a village it became customary to more or less judge a unit by the smartness or otherwise of its billet guards. The sentries were also supplied with a gas alarm (generally an empty 18-pounder cartridge case suspended on a wire) and were responsible for raising the alarm in the event of the gongs ringing in the front line or adjacent areas.

Training was of a more difficult nature now owing to our restricted movements. It generally took the form of individual platoon training in the paddocks immediately in rear of the various company billets. Lectures and musketry instruction were carried on under trees and behind cover of hedges, and all movement would cease when enemy aeroplanes were reported overhead by men detailed for that purpose. Short route marches were carried out to Estaires and Bac St. Maur by companies in turn, movement being by sections at 50 or 100 yards distance.

It was at this time that the Bombing and Intelligence Platoons first came into existence. The former was under the command of Lieut. I. N. Holyman and was between 20 to 30 strong, the men being detached from their companies and rationed as a separate unit with Headquarters' details. It was always a cause of much murmuring among the rest of the men of the Battalion that the bombers, like the stretcher-bearers, considered themselves "specialists," and consequently exempt from fatigue. When warned for guard or fatigue duty, the reply was invariably, "I'm a bomber; I don't do fatigue." Their O.C. was inclined to support them in this idea, but if a ruling was asked for from the Colonel, he always said, "There are *no* 'specialists' in the Battalion as far as fatigue work is concerned." Lieut. Holyman deserved great credit for the manner in which he trained his men at Sailly, for he was placed at a great disadvantage. Bombing work, as carried out in France, was something which was quite new to us; text books on the subject were hardly yet in circulation in the Division, and schools of instruction only in their infancy. With these difficulties to surmount, Holyman instructed his bombers at the rear of the Y.M.C.A. shed in the art of throwing bombs, clearing and advancing along a trench and firing various kinds of rifle grenades.

The Intelligence Platoon consisted of a sergeant, corporal and 24 men under the command of Lieut. B. J. Andrew, with Sgt. R. Lapthorne and Cpl. Sully as his first N.C.O.'s. This unit had also been an unknown quantity during the Gallipoli campaign and while training in Egypt, so that here, again, much uphill work was required to fully train these men ready to go into the line in a comparatively short time. Each company commander had been instructed to detail six "intelligent" men to form the nucleus of this platoon, but on the first roll call they could very easily be grouped into "good," "bad" and "indifferent," and a certain amount of weeding out had to take place.

Their duties, and incidentally their training, proved to be fairly comprehensive, and included observation, reconnaissance, scouting and patrol work, writing of comprehensive reports, map-reading, signalling, carrying of messages, etc., and our subsequent experiences proved how useful and valuable a well-trained member of the Intelligence Platoon can make himself.

Great excitement prevailed among the men when the Company Orderly Corporals went round preparing a roster for English leave, which was started on 27th April. In those days it only consisted of seven days leave, from the time one left Boulogne to the day the crossing was made again from Folkestone. Preference was given to the 1914 officers and men, and those who had seen seven months or considerable service on the Peninsula were placed on the top of the list.

Church parade was always held in a spacious building not far from the ruined church, and just adjacent to the A.S.C. ration dump. The padre, in conjunction with Mr. Beaurepaire, the Y.M.C.A.

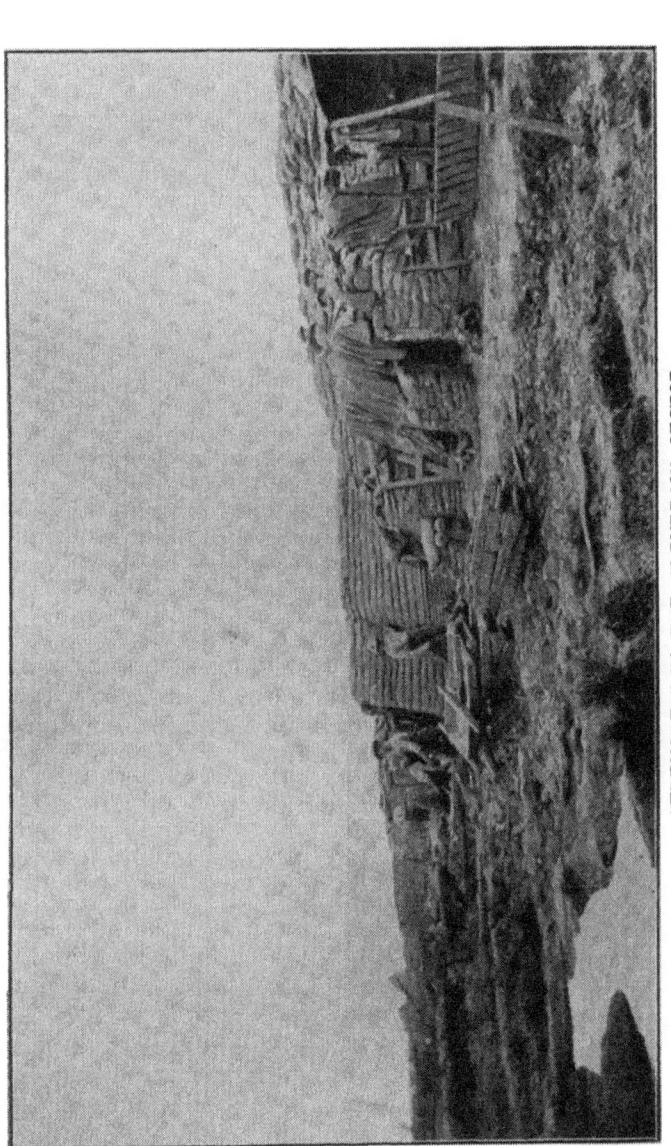

"TRENCHES" IN THE FLEURBAIX SECTOR

(Photo. loaned by Capt. K. M. W. Thirkell, M.B.E.)

representative attached to the Brigade, also organised one or two good concerts, which were given in the same hall and always well attended.

The Battalion had to supply some very large working parties at this time, to go out at night to dig trenches for the Divisional Signallers in which to bury cables. Large parties of perhaps four to six officers, with about 300 men, would set out soon after 8 p.m. when it began to get dark and march to the appointed spot about a mile and a half behind the line. Each man was given a task, namely, to dig six feet of trench to a depth of 4 to 5 feet, and when the cable had been laid, to fill it in again. The object of this, of course, was to sink the cable to such a depth that would protect it from shell fire. It may be gratifying to any men who were on this work to know that in 1918, when the Germans broke through this sector of the line and captured Sailly, Estaires and other villages, thus forming a huge salient, communication was maintained between Armentieres and Merville by means of these sunken cables, until eventually the former town had to be evacuated. On one particular evening we had been working hard and had almost finished our task, but were oblivious of the fact that an 18-pounder battery was situated in an orchard less than 100 yards away. Suddenly, without warning, the four guns fired at once, with a blinding flash and a deafening roar. It was so unexpected that the working party thought that a shell had landed, and immediately proceeded to take cover. Those in the trench dropped flat, those on top jumped into the trench, but Pvt. Balmer, of "A" Company, took a flying leap into an adjacent ditch and discovered, only too late, that it was full of water. On being rescued, he was more cheery than might have been expected, and when asked what it was like merely replied, "Not bad! A bit froggy!"

Every effort was made to impress upon the men the need for secrecy as regards information of a military nature, both on this sector and in any other part of the line to which we might be transferred—it was just as much part of our training as firing a rifle or throwing a bomb. Although the local peasants were known to be loyal allied subjects, yet in their midst were spies who collected information and transmitted it to the enemy, and in consequence every man was told that it was his duty to report any occurrence of a suspicious nature. The effect of this order was to turn every member of the Battalion into an amateur Sherlock Holmes, and acts of a most innocent kind were at once misconstrued into the worse kind of espionage and reported through the official channel. For a while the Intelligence Officer, whose duty it was to investigate these reports, was a much over-worked man. One of the companies reported that a pedlar, selling chocolate, post-cards, cigarettes, etc., was constantly walking past their billet, looking in as often as possible, as though estimating the number of troops there. He was afterwards seen to write something on a piece of paper, drop it on the ground and walk away. This was reported by the sentry on duty, and one of the men commandeered the paper and discovered on it one or two letters and figures conveying no apparent meaning. However, it was considered in the light of a cryptic message and reported to Battalion Headquarters, who communicated with the A.P.M. (Assistant Provost-Marshall). This important personage ordered the arrest of the supposed spy, which was immediately effected, and the services of the interpreter attached to the Brigade were utilised for the purpose of interrogating him. He was searched from head to foot for concealed messages, and his basket of goods was turned upside down, without effect. In answer to questions, he said that he resided in an adjacent village and supported an invalid wife, statements which were substantiated by some of the villagers, who had congregated since the news of the "arrest" had become known. When asked for his passport (which every civilian has to carry when leaving their village) he admitted leaving it at home, and was fined 20 francs by the local *"gendarme"* for the offence.

On another occasion, men were seen measuring distances with a tape, from point to point along the the river bank, in the twilight, just as the visibility was becoming poor, and the assistance of the provost-sergeant was requested. But the "spies" proved to be merely members of a local company of Royal Engineers completing a section of survey before dark, in connection with a big drainage scheme which was to be put into effect before the next winter.

The most popular report, however, was that regarding the flashing of coloured lights from the top of Sailly church tower. Unfortunately, it was never possible to get any corroborative evidence, and two members of the Intelligence Platoon spent a very profitless night sitting in the knave of this draughty ruin in their efforts to capture a real, live spy.

However, although the lighter and more humorous side of this subject has been detailed here, every man was in earnest about the whole matter and thus demonstrated, in a most practical manner, the seriousness with which he regarded his entry into the new mode of warfare on the Western Front.

It was while at Sailly that many of us—in fact, most of us—saw Field Marshall Sir Douglas Haig for the first and only time. On 27th April, the 11th and 12th Battalions were formed up in review order in a paddock just out of the village, when the Commander-in-Chief, accompanied by a small staff and our own Divisional Commander, arrived and was given the "general salute." He inspected the two Battalions and spoke to several of the officers who had served on Gallipoli, after which he took up a position at the saluting base and we marched past in column of route.

The monotony of training was broken on several occasions during our sojourn at Sailly by alarms—both genuine and fictitious. Several gas alarms were started in the front line and the ringing of gongs could be heard all over the adjacent countryside, and although they could never be disregarded, they invariably proved to be a scare and generally traceable to evening and morning mists, which strongly resembled a gas cloud to the sentries on duty in the line. On 1st May, however, an order was received from Brigade at 9 p.m. for the whole Battalion to assemble in fighting order. This seemed more reliable, and within ten minutes the Battalion was roused, dressed and fallen in on their respective alarm posts and marched off in perfect silence. We proceeded for about a mile and a half to two miles by platoons at fifty yards distance, along unfamiliar roads, wondering where our destination was to be, when lights could be seen flashing in the distance and voices giving and countermanding orders. Then, out of the darkness an electric torch would flash, and you would find

MAY, 1916

yourself nearly run down by a restive horse, then more torches and another horse, followed by a string of questions issued by voices which were easily recognisable as those of C.O., Major Mullen and Capt. Newland, the Adjutant—"Who are you? 'C' Company? Which platoon? Where's your Company Commander? Pass the word for Major Rafferty. Where the —— has 'B' Company got to? What's this, the Bombing Platoon? You ought to be at the head of the column. Put that light out! Why don't you keep to the side of the road? Fall in. About turn. Quick march." Then we knew that it was only another "stunt"! It was merely a night operation to familiarise us with the approach to our assembly position in case the Brigade was called upon to reinforce the front line. We reached out billets again at 12.30 a.m. and the movement was generally considered to be highly satisfactory, but to the rank and file it is always referred to as the "torchlight procession."

It was now obvious that our time to commence a tour of duty in the front line was rapidly approaching, for officers and N.C.O's were warned daily to proceed on reconnaissance work up to the trenches in different sectors of our front. It was usual to borrow bicycles from the Signalling Section and to proceed in this manner (thanks to the flat country, trees and hedges) to within a mile of the line. The bike was then "planted" in an adjacent ditch and further progress was made on foot up the communication trench, either V.C. Avenue or Cellar Farm Avenue.

Another indication that we would shortly be moving into the forward area was the fact that steel helmets were issued to us by the Quartermaster (Lieut. G. P. Potter) on 18th May. These were very strange to us for a while, and were the cause of much amusement, but this soon wore off, and we learnt to value them as a means of protection, whilst many of the men found them to be indispensable for wash-basins, and even for heating shaving water.

Chapter X.

FLEURBAIX SECTOR

THE same evening, 18th May, the 3rd Brigade moved into that portion of the line known officially as Petillon Sector. Two battalions were in the line, the 9th Battalion on the right and the 11th Battalion on the left, while the 10th and 12th Battalions occupied similar positions in support. Battalion Headquarters, with the details attached, were billeted in Jerry Villa, Rue de Quesney, while Capt. Margetts and "A" Company were in billets about 100 yards down the same road, towards Fleurbaix. Major Rafferty and "C" Company were in Barlette Farm (situated in the road in rear) and Capt. Foster and "B" Company were in a farm-house and outbuildings which did not boast of a name, about 300 yards away. Capt. Vowles and "D" Company were nearest to the line, being billeted in a farmhouse at the crossroads, known as Croix Blanche, with one platoon detached to garrison Dee Post in Rue de Petillon, and one to guard a bomb store in a billet in the Rue du Bois. "C" Company also had a platoon detached, under the command of Lieut. C. N. Richardson, and billeted at Croix Blanche, on the opposite corner to "D" Company's farm-house.

During our three weeks of duty in the support area we experienced some delightful summer weather—the countryside was ablaze with wild flowers and the sun shone almost every day. Under these idyllic conditions, it was almost criminal to keep the men in their billets during the daytime, and yet this restriction had to be more or less enforced to the letter, as our close proximity to the line rendered any movement visible to the enemy observation balloons, which were up on our front continuously during the hours of daylight. In fact, a sentry was placed at the estaminet corner (Croix Lescornez) just near Battalion Headquarters, with orders not to allow more than two persons to advance together forward of that spot.

Our work, from now onwards, was done at night and engineers' fatigues took the place of platoon and company drill. Parties, varying from a platoon to a company, were detailed every afternoon and invariably set off in the twilight to report to an engineer sapper at a given map-reading. The *"rendezvous"* was reached, but there would be no sign of the sapper, and after about an hour's wait an effort would be made to find him, which might take place after another hour's search. Explanations would then follow, when it would probably be found that your map-reading was quite different from the one given to the sapper. This fact would ultimately be communicated to the Staff Captain on Brigade Headquarters, who would promise that a repetition would not occur. It did *not*, for on the next night, the map-readings would be reversed and you would have your party waiting where the sapper had been and he would be cooling his heels at the cross-roads where the party had wasted their two hours on the previous night.

The work of these parties varied in detail, but

generally consisted of improving and repairing communication, supoprt and front line trenches, constructing strong posts and laying duck-boards. Other parties were detailed for carrying work, and assisted a section of a tunnelling company who were operating on this sector, by carrying mining timber, sandbags and other material from the trench tramway to the mine shaft. By the time the various parties had got on to their jobs and received their instructions, there remained generally only about two or three hours of darkness in which to complete the task allotted before it was time to vacate the front line in order to reach our billets before daylight. The work, therefore, was not tremendously strenuous while the weather was fine, but on one or two occasions we experienced some wet nights, which made the work difficult and tiring in the extreme. Only those who have attempted to carry a duck-board, an "A" frame or a load of sandbags along a slippery, greasy trench track broken by shell-fire and littered with trench paraphernalia, know how tiring and exhausting this class of work proves to be.

Lieuts. A. A. Heritage, R. Sherwin, S. L. Hughes, G. T. Gandy and O. J. Roper reported to the Battalion on 25th May, the two former officers being posted to "A" Company, Gandy and Hughes to "B" Company, and Roper to "D" Company.

Although there was not a great deal of shelling in the support area, certain localities received their daily quota and were avoided whenever possible. The cross-roads at Croix Blanche were apparently a source of annoyance to the enemy, for he never missed a day without paying it some little attention. At times it was only a salvo, while at other times it took the form of a half-hour *"strafe."* "C" Company's platoon and "D" Company therefore had a very restless existence, for the men were only sleeping in the rooms of the house and in the outbuildings, which afforded no protection from shell-fire, and in consequence had to vacate the billet and occupy the "funk holes" whenever the shelling commenced. The "funk holes" were a small system of trenches, about 4 feet deep, situated about fifty yards in rear of the billet, in which the men were distributed as soon as the billet was shelled, in order to minimise the number of casualties that might occur. The village of Fleurbaix was shelled more or less continuously in a desultory manner, and "A" Company's billet in Rue de Quesney, little more than 150 yards from the village, sometimes came in for its share. On the morning of 4th June, "B" Company's billet was heavily shelled from 6.30 a.m. to 7 a.m., when Pvt. Harry Thomas was killed and five others wounded. Capt. Foster quickly got the men out into the "funk holes," with the smart assistance of C.S.M. Fisher, who was also wounded, and thus was able to obviate a heavy list of casualties which must otherwise have happened. In this instance, however, the "funk holes" themselves had to be abandoned and the men distributed behind the hedges in the adjacent fields, for the enemy seemed to concentrate on the trenches, as it was surmised that he mistook them for some new gun emplacement.

There were still a few peasants living even as close to the line as this, and they employed their time in cultivating as much of their farm lands as possible. The fact was firmly planted in the imaginative minds of our Diggers that many of them were secret agents and communicated with the enemy. One of the means employed was the ploughing of fields with a white horse, and a distinctive furrow across the field would indicate the direction of a good target which would justify a *"strafe,"* and in consequence the boys were convinced that a locality in which a white horse had been ploughing would be shelled within a few hours.

In order, more or less, to equalise the amount of nerve strain to which the men were subjected, orders were issued for "A" and "D" Companies to change over billets, the transfer being effected on the evening of 26th May.

It was about this time that the Commanding Officer of the 11th Battalion asked the G.O.C. 3rd Brigade for an additional platoon in the support line every night—not for duty in the front line, but merely for garrison work, and to have them handy in case of attack. "A" Company was detailed for this duty and it became customary for me to take Nos. 3 and 4 platoons on alternate nights up to the support line. The "possies" in this line were not in the best of condition, and we utilised the first night in improving them, knowing that we would benefit thereby. Our only other duty was to "stand to" an hour before dawn, and after daylight was fully established, permission was asked from the officer in charge of the support line to withdraw. After we had been going up for a few nights, we were told by the platoon of the 11th Battalion, which formed the permanent garrison of this support line, that every night at dusk the Bosche had been in the habit of firing a trench mortar which had the exact range of this support trench and had carried out some effective, though disastrous, shoots. One evening a man had been killed; another time two men were wounded, while on one occasion we arrived just as they were clearing away the *debris* of the very dug-out I had been in the habit of occupying. We generally heard the bursting of these mortars as we entered the communication trench, and on our arrival were congratulated on our discretion in judging the time so well.

On 30th May, we entered the communication trench at the Rue Petillon at 8.15 p.m., when the sound of firing was heard. "Don't hurry, sir," one of the men said. "There's the evening *'strafe'* which we're just in time to miss again." But on this occasion the firing continued and increased in volume, until a heavy bombardment was in progress. I hurried the men forward and reported to the 11th Battalion Headquarters, which was being heavily shelled, so I quickly urged the men to take cover of some kind which would protect them, before reporting to Lt.-Col. Roberts. He was at the 'phone at the time, and was eagerly awaiting our arrival. Telephonic communication to his two right companies was broken, and he told me to stand by close at hand until he could gain some information as to what had happened and what was required. At this moment a gas alarm was raised and a pungent smell penetrated into Headquarters. I rushed out and quickly roused the N.C.O.'s of No. 4 Platoon, and, with their assistance, saw that every man put on his gas helmet. The shelling was still heavy and we seemed to be enveloped in a thick cloud when the 11th Battalion Medical Officer came along and told us that we could take our helmets off, as it wasn't a gas cloud, but only lyddite and phosphorous fumes from the bombardment—which will convey some idea of its intensity. The C.O. 11th Battalion then called me in and said that the enemy was raiding a local salient, held by his right centre company, and that the parapet had been blown up and an entrance made by the enemy. The two right flank companies had lost touch and he wanted me to take my platoon up into the line and fill the gap, and thus re-establish communication between the two companies. Warning was passed to the men, and we proceeded along Mine Avenue, which was the quickest approach to the right flank of the Battalion front and which was not being shelled so much as Cellar Farm Avenue—the main communication trench. As we neared the line, the trench became very congested and progress was slow, owing to the sides having been blown in and stretcher-bearers and walking wounded making their way out. Just after passing the support line, I discovered that half the platoon, including most of the N.C.O.'s, had gone astray, and so had to go back and find them.

Eventually, we arrived in the line and found everything in great disorder. I reported to the O.C. "A" Company, 11th Battalion, in passing and proceeded to carry out the task allotted to us, for by this time the shelling had decreased considerably and the machine guns were traversing the parapets and playing on the breaches in the line. At the head of the salient a mine had been fired, making a huge crater, fully twelve feet deep, *inside* our line and destroying about twenty yards of parapet. I detailed a party of men under two N.C.O.'s to man the gap in the trench, whilst the remainder of the platoon worked like Trojans in recovering any of the sandbags which were still serviceable and building up the parapet once again. The officers of the 11th Battalion were now able to confer together and take stock of things in general. It was discovered that the bombardment had been concentrated on a frontage of 200 yards and although the enemy had effected an entrance, they had apparently been ejected almost immediately.

The 11th Battalion then re-organised the line and established posts in the gap and thereby relieved the 12th Battalion men and thus enabled them all to continue with the repair work. When day broke we were able to see the awful wreckage which had taken place. The dead were still lying in various unnatural positions along the trench, with waterproof sheets thrown lightly over them, whilst many of the wounded were still waiting for the much overworked, though ever ready, stretchers-bearers to take them out. Hardly a dug-out was left standing; they were mostly wrecked, and represented by a few twisted sheets of corrugated iron, or some splintered wood sticking out of a heap of broken sandbags. On looking over the parapet, into a white morning mist, one could see many dead Germans lying alongside and across the white tape lines they had used to guide them over No Man's Land.

Inside our trenches they had left dozens of "stick bombs," as well as packets of explosives tied together, with a fuse attached, which were intended for demolition work. It was afterwards ascertained by the 11th Battalion that their casualties during this raid were 26 killed, 16 missing and 58 wounded. During the morning, other platoons of the 12th Battalion came up to assist in the repair work and about noon, Major Denton (second in command 11th Battalion) thanked and congratulated No. 4 Platoon for the great assistance they had rendered during the night and gave them permission to return to their unit, which they were only too pleased to do, being very tired, but at the same time very thankful that they had sustained no casualties.

On the evening of the same day, "A" Company's billet at Croix Blanche was shelled without warning, and Stuart, who was on sentry duty at the doorway, was killed by the first shell, while Heawood, Fraser and Balmer were wounded. Pvt. "Tiny" Cairnduff did good work at this time, assisting the wounded to a place of safety, whilst the billet was still being heavily shelled.

Lieut. B. J. Andrew was detached for duty with Brigade Headquarters on 3rd June and I was detailed to take over the command of the Intelligence Platoon.

On the night of 7th June the Battalion moved into the line and relieved the 11th Battalion and took over the role of the left Battalion of the Petillon Sector, the relief being complete at 10 p.m. Just before the 11th Battalion moved out, we heard of the sinking of the "Hampshire" and of the tragic death of Lord Kitchener, which, when it became generally known, cast a gloom over the Battalion. The technical units, such as the Intelligence and Bombing Platoons, Signalling Section and Lewis Gunners, had moved up during the previous twenty-four hours, in order to receive technical details regarding the sector by daylight, from the outgoing unit. One officer per company and one N.C.O. per platoon also formed part of the advance party to take over the numerous trench stores, such as periscopes, braziers, gas alarms, ammunition, bombs and verey lights, maps and other trench equipment which is transferable and remains the property of the garrison unit.

The trenches in this particular sector were not trenches—if I may be permitted to use this figure of speech—for the simple reason that the parapet was built up to a height of about seven feet from

the ground level. This was due to the fact that
the country in this part was very low and wet, and
would have been almost untenable in winter if
trenches had been dug in the ordinary way. We
had a fair indication of what it could be like after
a couple of days' rain. Before the Australians
occupied this sector, an English "Bantam" Division
had held this part of the line, and in consequence,
our first job was to continue the work started by
our immediate predecessors, by heightening the
parapet and at the same time making it wider.

The Battalion occupied just over 1,000 yards of
frontage, which was held by four companies, each
having three platoons in the line and one in support. Capt. Margetts and "A" Company were on
the right flank; Capt. Foster with "B" Company,
right centre company; Major Rafferty and "C"
Company, left centre company; and Capt. Vowles
and "D" Company on the left flank.

Owing to the heavy bombardment sustained by
the 11th Battalion, the original "possies" occupied
by the men had been entirely demolished on a
large frontage, and consequently new ones had
been erected; on these our men were still working.
These "possies" were very good, and the men,
although somewhat cramped, were moderately
comfortable. The dug-outs were built of sandbags,
and in rear of the parapet, thus forming the parados
of the trench. The support line, sometimes called
"the 300 yard line," from its distance from the
front line, was in good condition, and there was
plenty of room for the men garrisoning it.

Battalion Headquarters was situated in some
camouflaged dug-outs hidden under some trees,
from 600 to 800 yards down Cellar Farm Avenue.
The Commanding Officer, Senior Major, R.M.O.,

AERIAL PHOTO: FLEURBAIX SECTOR

(Photo. loaned by Lieut. L. M. Newton, M.C.)

Signalling and Intelligence Officers and the Regimental Aid Post were situated here, and telephone wires connected them to Brigade Headquarters in the rear, and to the four companies in the line.

This was our first tour in the line since the Battalion had been issued with Lewis guns, and without doubt, the gunners made full use of them. It would have been hard to find a keener body of men than the Lewis Gun Section, commanded by Lieut. H. Webber. During the day this officer would visit all company commanders and ask them for targets on their sector, and together with his sergeant, Sergeant F. H. Ripper, he would there and then make out his range card for use that night. He also kept in close touch with the Intelligence Officer regarding movements and breaches in the enemy's line, and without doubt his work must have worried and harassed the enemy to a great extent in addition to inflicting casualties. As soon as darkness fell, his crews would be out with their guns and, mounting the parapet, would discharge a magazine into the enemy, either traversing the parapet or dispersing wiring or working parties. Indeed, I often heard company commanders commiserating among themselves over the section's zeal, for it was often the means of bringing a *"strafe"* on the particular company's sector.

Lieut. Holyman and his Bombing Platoon were quartered in the support line, and were not long in making their presence known, both to the enemy and to the front line troops of the 12th Battalion. The bombers were distinctly unpopular in the trenches, because they used to carry out their *"strafe"* in daylight, with a visible means of torment, namely, the rifle grenade, and consequently the Bosche was accustomed to retaliate somewhat freely on the sector from whence the grenades were being fired, with either 12lb. bombs or even *"minenwerfers."* The consequence was that Holyman and his bombers were pushed from pillar to post, each company commander assuring him that there was a much better "possie" to fire from a little farther down the trench.

One rather sad mishap occurred during our tour in the line, when Holyman tried to work the "shanghai." He had it one afternoon in "A" Company's sector (much against Capt. Margett's wish) and was trying some new elastic thongs. They were working well, but the range was rather short, so Holyman was instructing the bomber to increase it. The bomber seemed to hesitate, casting a queer glance at the elastic, so Holyman said, "Let me have a go," and proceeded to increase the range another 50 yards; but it was more than the "shanghai" could stand, for with a loud report it snapped and the elastic recoiled, bringing half the "shanghai" with it, and struck Holyman in the mouth. He spat a few teeth out and then relapsed into semi-unconsciousness and was conveyed into "A" Company Headquarters, where he was revived with a tot of rum. The R.M.O. was sent for and first aid rendered, but Holyman was off duty for one or two days, and carries the mark of the "shanghai" to this day.

The only other incident which marred the triumph of the bombers was a premature burst, which occurred when the "battery" was firing one day in "D" Company's sector. "Bunga" Timothy was wounded, and was unable to sit down with comfort for a week or so, while "D" Company's cook was also temporarily put out of action—that was all.

The Intelligence Platoon were accommodated in the dug-outs around Battalion Headquarters, and in carrying out their newly acquired duties, suffered much ridicule and abuse from the companies. They were generally referred to as the "Intellectual Platoon" and, in fact, one morning on coming out of my dug-out I found a notice, "High Velocity Officer," nailed to the doorway. Their duties were to observe, snipe, report on enemy shell-fire and also trench mortar and *"minenwerfer"* fire, observe the effect of our own shelling, patrolling at night, and, in fact, be prepared to answer any question the Brigade Intelligence Officer, the Staff Captain, the Brigade Major, the Brigadier, or anyone else might put to them. I think they got most chaff from the fact that it was one of the platoon's duties to count the shells which came over from the enemy in various defined areas. Of course, in theory this is excellent and discloses a lot of information, but when the shelling is pretty willing and the "whizz-bangs" are coming at a good pace and narrowly missing your observation post, it is easy to see that it affords a very excellent subject for the wit of the commissioned and non-commissioned rank.

Observation was carried out from both the front and support lines. Sniping and observation "possies" were built right into the parapet, which was anything up to ten to twelve feet thick in parts, and supplied with an iron plate with a small aperture and shutter. Naturally, these were placed in position at night and carefully camouflaged, so that they were invisible to the enemy; but, even so, the latter was known to locate them at times, for Kerrigan, one of the snipers, was shot in the hand by a bullet passing through the loophole when it was open. Observation from the support line was done by means of long periscopes, from ten to twelve feet long, secreted in the foliage of pollard willow trees, and also from seats fixed in the high elm trees around Headquarters. This latter means of observation was not utilised to any great extent, however, for it was necessary for the observer to take up a position before dawn and remain in the tree until dusk, while equally good information was obtained from more accessible posts in the rear.

It was believed at this time that the Bosche was mining under trenches, or, at any rate, under No Man's Land, in order to make a series of mine craters which could be connected and made into an advanced or jumping off trench, from which to attack our sector of the line. About 6 a.m. one day, an earth tremor was felt, and soon after "B" Company rang up to say that a small mine had been fired on their front, but that no crater was visible. I at once forwarded the information to Brigade before going up to the line to make a personal report, and forwarded it in writing to the Brigade Intelligence Officer. Nothing could have caused greater consternation at Brigade, at this particular time, than this piece of information, and the fact that there was *no* crater did not coincide with their theory, and consequently did not satisfy them. In their opinion, there *ought* to have been a crater, and in half an hour the front line was alive with "brass hats" of various ranks, who, after much periscope work, begrudgingly agreed that the mine was craterless.

That was all right, but, unfortunately, "Fritz" exploded another mine next day, and there *was* a small crater. Brigade promptly communicated the news to Division. Instructions were issued for a patrol to go out that night, and Lieut. Gould took three or four men and came back with the information that there were several small craters already linked up into a trench. Things began to look serious, so to keep up the reputation of the Intelligence Platoon, I went out next night, taking Sgt. Ede with me (who had accompanied Gould), together with two other men. Ede showed me the "connected craters," but on closer investigation they proved to be nothing more than an old ditch with various shell-craters, which probably had the appearance of craters. To substantiate our statements we brought back some of the water weeds and growth that were stagnating in the ditch. Needless to say, I heard no more of craters after this, and no attack by the enemy eventuated on this front at this period of the war.

It was the duty of each company commander to forward an Intelligence Report to Headquarters every morning at dawn, giving a *precis* of everything that had happened on his frontage during the preceding twenty-four hours. To illustrate the seriousness with which these reports were regarded at this time, it will be necessary only to state that Capt. Margetts, on one occasion, reported that no shelling had taken place on his company's front during the night, and alliterated his opinion by stating that "such stony silence surely suggested something strangely suspicious."

The 3rd Australian Light Trench Mortar Battery (better known as the Stokes Trench Mortar) and the Medium Trench Mortar Battery (always referred to as the "Plum Pudding" Battery, from the suggestive shape of its missile) used to fire almost every afternoon from some portion of our front. The former is a very mobile gun and can be brought into action and dismantled in a very few moments. It was customary at this period for the battery to fire a couple of dozen rounds, then dismantle the gun and leave the particular sector of the trench just as the enemy started to retaliate, leaving the infantryman to suffer it alone. This was not considered "cricket" by the company men, who, after all, were the permanent occupiers of the trench in question, and consequently they gave the Stokes gunners the name, "Imshee" Battery.

The "Plum Pudding" fellows were commanded by a cheery Western Australian officer named Shenton, who was as popular with our unit as he was with his own artillerymen. On many occasions I used to observe for him. He put in some fine shooting on the enemy's lines, either making big breaches in his wire or in his parapet, which, of course, would need to be repaired during the night, and which were consequently given to the Lewis gun officer as good targets.

"Plum Pudding" shoots were generally quickly followed by a retaliatory fire from *"minenwerfers."* These were much dreaded, not so much from the casualties inflicted, but from the demoralising effect they had on the men. The mortar fired was sausage-shaped, and from the fragments I found on several occasions, I should imagine that they were about 2 feet in length. They could be seen after they had been fired, as soon as they cleared the parapet, and it was possible to follow them in their parabolic flight until they reached their zenith of about 200 feet. Then, as they commenced to descend, it was necessary to judge which firing bay they were going to fall into and quickly dodge into the next one. They struck the ground with a dull, heavy thud, and sometimes for fully fifteen seconds there would be a deadly silence, until someone would say, "Dud." But not so, for there would be a loud tearing report and a shower of clods and dirt would be thrown high into the air, often injuring a man as they descended. The crater made by the *"minenwerfer"* was of huge dimensions, sometimes being as much as ten and twelve feet across and five to six feet deep. Everyone agreed that the *"minenwerfer"* was *"no bon."* The Bosche sometimes fired them at night, in which case it was possible to follow their flight through the air by a trail of sparks, but it was not so easy accurately to dodge them as in the daytime. However, his range was never very good, and in consequence nearly all of them fell in a paddock at the rear of the lines, and during the whole of our tour in the line in this sector we lost only about three men as casualties from *"minenwerfer"* fire, and two of them were slight cases of shell-shock. The 12lb. bomb, although a much smaller missile, was responsible for more casualties — although even these did not amount to a great number, the most important being a very capable N.C.O., namely, Sergeant Venus, who was killed whilst taking cover behind a traverse, on June 22nd. The only other death sustained by the Battalion in the Fleurbaix sector was Pvt. Hean, a very popular lad amongst his comrades. Both were buried in the Rue de Petillon Cemetery by Padre Douglas.

The 18-pounder batteries which supported us were consistent in their efforts to harass the enemy and fired at intervals throughout the day and night at his front line, communication trenches, tracks, roads and rear areas. The most favoured targets were the village of Fromelles, Ferme Delangre, Ferme de Mouquet (both within 100 yards of his front line) and the Tadpole, the latter being a small system of trenches opposite "D" Company's sector of the line. Great consternation was caused one afternoon by a single gun, of a very large calibre, consistently firing short into the right company. Capt. Margetts rang up Headquarters and reported it, and the Artillery Liaison Officer promptly got into touch with his battery and brigade, who assured him that no gun of that size was firing in the divisional area at that time. But still the gun persisted to fire regularly every three minutes, gradually increasing its range until, eventually, having commenced at our support line, it ultimately landed one right into our parapet. This apparently satisfied the gunner, for the firing promptly ceased, much to "A" Company's relief.

A word may be said regarding the code messages that were sent over the telephone. To report this incident it was necessary for Capt. Margetts to tell the Adjutant (Capt. J. E. Newland) that someone was planting cabbages in his back garden, but that the stalks were not long enough. This indicated that a heavy gun (code word, "cabbage") was firing into his rear ("back garden") and that its range ("stalk") was too short. In the same way, a company commander would tell the Adjutant that "Tom had just called and he might get Dick to come and have a yarn to him." This meant that the enemy was firing (Tom) and retaliation was necessary (Dick). This used to amuse us at first, but I think after we had had more experience, we saw that it was rather ridiculous.

Aeroplanes did not cross over into the enemy's lines very much in this sector, for the simple reason that there was not much need. They were used mostly in connection with artillery contact work, for the country was so flat that most of the observation for movement was carried out by observation balloons. On the evening of 26th June, one of my observers noticed that an enemy balloon was coming down in a trail of smoke on the left of our sector, near Armentieres, and a moment later another and yet another were observed to be on fire, whilst one of our 'planes could be seen darting along the line, making an effort to bring more down, but the Bosche, apparently, had had enough and was pulling all the remaining balloons down in double quick time, and simultaneously brought heavy fire to bear on the aeroplane, which casually made for home after having completed a very satisfactory evening's work.

A slight diversion was caused one day by one of the companies exhibiting a board over the top of the parapet (quite contrary to orders), asking the Germans when their fleet intended coming out of Kiel Harbour. About an hour afterwards the Germans responded by putting up a notice bearing the names of all the boats we had lost in the Battle of Jutland, together with their respective tonnage, and at the bottom, in large letters, "H.M.S. HAMPSHIRE." This latter name caused many of the men to remark on the rapidity with which the Germans had obtained the news of the calamity. On another occasion, the Germans put a notice on a board in No Man's Land on the 10th Battalion's sector, on our right, which, when recovered by a patrol at night, was found to be an announcement to the effect that General Townsend had surrendered Kut-el-Amara, with the number of prisoners stated. We did not receive this information ourselves until some days later.

During our tour in the line the Transport Section was billeted at Bac St. Maur, where the Quartermaster also had his store. The only event of any consequence which happened to them whilst we were in the line was the tail end of a gas cloud which had been liberated by the enemy in the salient north of Armentieres and which the wind carried along the main road. The horses were at once liberated and taken by the drivers as far away from the contaminated atmosphere as possible. Garney Rundle was seen trying to break the local steeplechase record and, as far as is known, is "still going strong," not having yet reported back to the Battalion.

It was the duty of the Transport Section to bring the rations up in limbers at night to a dump in the Rue du Bois, from whence a fatigue party would push them up a light tram-track to Battalion Headquarters, where the Company Quartermaster Sergeants would take charge of them and take them right on into the line. All the company cooking was done in the front line and hot meals were given to the men twice a day, and tea at every meal. The cooks used charcoal for fuel, with the object of preventing smoke issuing from the trench and thus exposing the position of the cook-house and making it a vulnerable target for trench mortars.

After a three weeks' tour of duty, we were relieved by the 52nd Battalion on the evening of 26th June, this being their first appearance in the line in France. It was decided to relieve one company every other night, owing to the fact that a large number of the men had never been in the line before. It afterwards transpired that it was a wise precaution, because the meeting of the two sister battalions meant that brothers, cousins, and bosom companions were seeing one another again after the lapse of some months, and the buzz of conversation which followed was far from desirable in a front line trench. In order to drown the noise, Lieut. Webber and his Lewis gunners were instructed to fire from the sector of the company being relieved, until the last man had gone and things again became normal. In this manner "D" Company was relieved on 23rd June, "B" Company on the 25th, Battalion Headquarters and details on the following night, "C" Company on 27th June, and "A" Company on 29th June. On relief the Battalion marched back once again to our old billets at Sailly.

Chapter XI.

THE ROAD TO THE SOMME

OUR recent tour of duty could not in any way be called strenuous (as we afterwards got to know front line work) and the men had had good food and a fair amount of sleep, yet we had taken the work very seriously, and in consequence were glad to be back in billets again. The first thing to be done was to get the men bathed, and next morning we were allotted the baths at Bac St. Maur. They were situated in an old civilian laundry and were about the best baths we ever experienced in France, with almost an unlimited amount of hot water, and last, but by no means least, the men were also issued with a good clean set of underclothing.

The C.O. next informed us that the 12th Battalion had been detailed to carry out a raid on "The Tadpole," on the front we had just vacated, during out next tour of duty in the line. The raiding party was forthwith selected from men who had volunteered for the job from each company, together with a percentage of Lewis gunners, bombers and Intelligence men. Capt. P. D. Nicholas was given charge of the raiding party, while Holyman and I were detailed as his subalterns. It was intended to segregate the raiding party, and to billet, ration and train them as a sparate unit; but our enthusiasm was short-lived, as the next day, 2nd July, we were warned to be ready to move within 12 hours.

The only other thing worthy of note during our second brief stay at Sailly was a most interesting lecture given to the officers and N.C.O.'s in the Y.M.C.A. hut, by Professor Atkins, M.A. (Camb.) on "Why we are here. How the war was brought about."

At 8 p.m. on Sunday, 2nd July, we left Sailly and proceeded to billets at Outtersteene, about eight to ten miles away. It was pleasant marching in the summer evening, although the road we had to take was very intricate with its many windings and corners, and in consequence was not easy to follow after darkness fell. However, the Hazebrouck 5A maps proved their accuracy on this occasion and we turned on to the Bailleul road soon after 11 p.m., and finally got the Battalion settled in billets by midnight. With the exception of "A" Company, which was self-contained in a farm-house and outbuildings half a mile along the Bailleul road, the Battalion was concentrated, in varying states of comfort, in the few billets which were available in this small village.

We spent a week of delightful weather here. The parade hours were conveniently short and the work generally consisted of route marches, three to five miles in length, either to Bailleul, Meteren or Merris. One of the companies organised a very fine paper chase as a form of recreational training, in which all the company participated. The hares took them for a good three-and-a-half miles course, and when the chase was completed all the survivors had a shower bath at the baths near Merris, prior to the mile sprint home. During this sprint Brig-Gen. Gellibrand passed at the head of the 6th Brigade, and as soon as he recognised some of the men of his old Battalion, cheered them as they passed.

Before leaving Outtersteene, I relinquished the command of the Intelligence Platoon to Capt. J. A. W. Kayser, who had returned to the Battalion, whilst I re-assumed command on my old No. 4 Platoon.

We once again kept up our reputation by moving on Sunday, 9th July, to billets in the Fontaine Houcke area, where the Battalion was very scattered, some of the companies being as much as two miles apart. After staying here for two days, we left at 8 a.m. on 11th July and marched about seven miles to Godewaersvelde, where we entrained soon after 10 a.m. We were well aware where our destination would be, although we had not been warned, for the "Big Push" had been started on the Somme on 1st July, and it was a foregone conclusion that we were on our way to participate in it.

We proceeded via Lillers, St. Pol and Frevent, finally arriving at Doullens, where we detrained at 4.30 p.m. A billeting party of officers and N.C.O.'s were detailed to push on ahead to make the necessary arrangements before the Battalion arrived. This was no small order, for they were carrying full packs and blankets, and it was a sweltering day. In addition, this party had to maintain a sufficiently fast pace that would allow them to gain enough time to scour the village and allot billets to the various companies and details before the Battalion arrived. It so happened that they arrived at their destination, the village of Halloy, just as dusk was falling and found most of the villagers in bed and particularly adverse to billetting troops. After repeatedly knocking at the door, an upper window would be opened and a voice moan that someone was *"malade"* in the house. This excuse became monotonous after a while and was not helping with the billetting, while the officers knew that the Battalion must be fast approaching. In view of the fact that the village was so small and there was need to utilise every barn and outhouse as a billet, the party had to force its way into many of the places and had barely finished the allotted task when the head of the column was reported to be nearing the village.

In the meantime, the Battalion having detrained, we found our way, with some difficulty, through the winding streets of this old-world town until, finally, following round the ramparts of the citadel, we discovered ourselves once more outside the town. We soon noticed the changed contour of the country; we were now in the rolling country of Picardy, with fewer trees and a distinct absence of isolated houses, these being grouped together in compact villages and, as we surmised, the result of a bygone age when bands of robbers used to harass this part of the country.

As stated previously, the day was extremely hot and it was not long before the men started to show symptoms of fatigue. We have since considered this as one of the worst marches we experienced in France, and, without doubt, it was very tiring even to the most hardened soldier—a seven mile march in Flanders, a long, fatiguing train journey, and now another march of at least fourteen miles in the hot afternoon sun. About 6.30 p.m. the C.O.

halted and the Battalion rested by the roadside for the best part of an hour, during which time tea was made in the cookers and a haversack ration meal was partaken. Major Mullen, the Senior Major, and Capt. Tozer, R.M.O., had an unenviable job at the rear of the column urging and persuading the sore-footed stragglers to keep up with the column, and as many horses as possible were utilised to give the worst cases a lift on the way.

Eventually, Halloy was reached about 11 p.m. and very few of the men commented upon the dinginess of their billets, a complaint which would have been justifiable in this instance. Guides were posted along the road to direct the limping stragglers to their billets, whilst the rest of the Battalion was very soon in a heavy sleep.

Our respite, however, was of short duration, for at 7.30 a.m. the Adjutant was around rousing the officers and conveying the news that the Battalion had to move again at 8.30 a.m. The officers were just about as tired as the men, and were very reluctant to leave their blankets; in consequence, the company cooks were late in being warned. This, of course, meant that breakfast was delayed, and it was not until 10 a.m. that a very tenderfooted battalion set out once again, many men carrying half-consumed rations in their pocket. Just as we were passing a magnificent *chateau* near Canaples, we discovered that the Brigadier had taken up a position on the other side of the railway bridge. He complained bitterly and forcibly of our straggling and lack of march discipline as we passed by.

Once again it was distressingly hot, and the roads were particularly dusty. After skirting the village or Havernas, with its church and convent on the hill, and passing through Wargnies, surrounded by

ALBERT CATHEDRAL
(Copyright by Australian War Museum)

beautiful, shady trees, we eventually arrived at Naours, where our billetting party informed us that it had once again experienced a chilly reception from the peasants. After dinner, the men proceeded to explore the village and endeavoured to make purchases of bread, eggs and fruit. The villagers were loathe to do any trading at all, but apparently rightly assumed that if they did not make a legitimate, but at the same time extortionate, bargain, much of their produce would disappear as soon as darkness fell. We remained at Naours for four days, and during that time carried out short route marches and company training in very inconvenient paddocks. We also received instruction in the new means of attacking by "waves," and the principles involved in village fighting (although there was nothing left of the villages when we did actually get there).

A large percentage of the Battalion failed to discover that there were some very wonderful caves at Naours, known as *"Les Souterrains,"* with their entrance almost in the village itself. They had been excavated and occupied by the French peasantry of this district during the middle ages, when the bands of robbers previously referred to were accustomed to ravage the countryside. The caves and underground passages were hewn out of the chalk, and capable of accommodating fully 300 refugees; they were entirely self-contained and provided with an underground water supply, and even a chapel, and generally consisted of single chambers, and larger ones for families. We were conducted along miles of corridors by an old Frenchman, who talked very rapidly in his own dialect. I am afraid few of us who accompanied him were able to understand much of what he said. At one point I understood him to say that a certain chimney, which he indicated, went right through the solid chalk and made its exit through a disused windmill, now in ruins.

We made another forward move on 16th July (Sunday) and journeyed as far as Rubempre, where everyone was billetted much more comfortably than at the two previous villages—a sure indication, from the Diggers' point of view, that we were not staying long.

Interest was aroused the next day when it became known that the C.O. and company commanders had proceeded up to the line on a forward reconnaissance, and on their return we learned of the wonderful artillery duels which were taking place and of the shell-torn condition of the battlefield.

On 18th July we left at 9.15 a.m. and, marching through Herissart and Toutencourt, arrived at Hedauville, where we bivouaced in a paddock in front of a beautiful *chateau*; at this time of year it was really delightful. At 9 a.m. next morning there was a meeting of all officers at Battalion Headquarters, when we were told of the operations that the First Australian Division had to carry out, and the part that the 3rd Brigade, and our own Battalion in particular, would have to play. We were told that we had to capture the village of Fozieres, which held a commanding position on the ridge in front of the present front line, and which was holding up the advance. It had already been attempted two or three times without success, and as it was held in strength by the enemy it was no small task that was being asked of the Australians. The Colonel also told us that in view of the number of casualties that must be expected, including officers, a percentage of the latter would be left out of the operation, so that if the worst happened the Battalion would not be altogether devoid of officers when it was relieved from the line. During the remaining part of the morning, we were issued with a pink coloured material; this was cut into six-inch squares and one square issued to each man to sew on to the back of his tunic. This was to enable us to distinguish friend from foe in the attack, during the hours of darkness, and also to assist the observers in the contact aeroplanes to pick up our front line after consolidation was effected.

While at Hedauville, we first came in contact with a Divisional or Corps Concert Party, which was "playing to crowded houses twice daily" in a local barn. A crowd of "Tommies" formed the talented company, and kindly issued an invitation to the 12th Battalion to attend a *"matinee."*

We stayed at Hedauville only for one day, and left at 2 p.m. on 19th July and proceeded via Bouzincourt to Albert. All along the road we noticed the tremendous amount of artillery, ammunition and transport of all kinds, until it became apparent that the operations in progress were on a larger scale than any we had yet experienced. The amount of traffic on the road made our pace very slow, and it was after 7 p.m. before we actually arrived at Albert. The town had been only about two miles behind the front line on 1st July, before the advance began, and had been shelled considerably. As we passed beneath the spire of the cathedral we saw its ruinous condition, with the leaning statue of the Madonna and Child on top. The base of this statue had been hit by a shell in the early days of the war, and it was hanging down in, apparently, a very dangerous way, but we were told that French engineers had made it quite secure, while there was a belief amongst the French peasantry that when the Madonna fell the war would end. These events did not actually happen simultaneously, but the Armistice was signed within six months of the statue falling, when the cathedral was reduced to a heap of ruins.

The Battalion was billetted in houses along and adjacent to the Bapaume road, and while here were subjected to periodical bursts of shelling—particularly at night time—from a gun of large calibre, which was apparently searching for one of our own heavy guns which fired from the railway. It was necessary for the officers and N.C.O.'s to rouse the men during the night and make them take shelter in the cellars of the houses, and even with this precaution "B" Company was unfortunate enough to suffer four casualties.

We discovered next day that there were still a few fugitive Frenchwomen residing in Albert, in spite of the shell-fire, and who sold post-cards, souvenirs of Albert, and eatables at very advanced prices; they did a fairly good trade, however, with our fellows, who, I think bought, in most cases, out of sympathy. Lieut. Heritage (who, since his sojourn at Fleurbaix had become known by the name of "Big Stuff") discovered a woman living near to our billets, who still had a few fowls left and was selling eggs at the exorbitant price of a franc each.

We formed up by platoons at 1 p.m. the next day (20th July) ready to move off, when the big gun opened fire and landed a shell which detonated on the tile roof of a house, near to where "B" Company was falling in, and which caused Sgt. Loudon Macleod to be slightly wounded by flying tile splinters. The next shell landed within twenty yards of "A" Company, and although no casualties resulted the men began to get very jumpy. So Capt. Margetts took the initiative and ordered the companies to move off by half platoons at fifty yards distance. As we proceeded along the Bapaume road it became very interesting, for we could plainly distinguish the old reserve and support lines and thus estimate the extent of the advance. Then we crossed the old front line and No Man's Land and realised that we were on territory which only three weeks ago had been occupied by the Germans, but we were also able to realise the tremendous artillery bombardment to which they had been subjected before being dislodged. The C.O. then led us through a maze of obliterated trenches, where the chalky spoil on either side was a mass of war litter, which is always left behind after every major operation. Everyone was keenly interested, for this was the first time that we had experienced warfare in such a gigantic and terrible form; on all sides could be seen the unburied dead (where the German field-grey uniform predominated) hopelessly mixed up with rifles, equipment, ammunition, bombs and many other weapons, implements and contrivances which we had not a chance yet of investigating. The route we were taking led us into a gully in front of Becourt, known as Sausage Valley, where Battalion Headquarters was situated, while the companies were disposed in the adjacent trenches, near to the village once known as La Boiselle.

Needless to say, the men immediately commenced to explore the neighbourhood, and found much to occupy their attention in the system of deep dugouts with which the village was honeycombed. It soon became obvious why the La Boiselle salient had always been considered impregnable, for the Germans had constructed an inside wall of solid concrete in all suitable houses in the village, before the British guns had demolished the brickwork and which now stood out gaunt and bare as if still defying the men and guns which had passed beyond them. In the village itself there was a Brigade Headquarters with dug-outs fully thirty feet deep, one of which led down to a system of corridors and rooms and which was labelled *"Wilhelmstrasse."*

Most of the fellows went down here, and everything they saw astounded them; double beds and bedding (doubtless salvaged from the village before it was destroyed); many of the rooms or cubicles had wall paper and carpets on the floor, full-sized mirrors, coke-heaters, whilst electric light was installed throughout. Of course, we appreciated the fact that the Germans considered that they were there to stay and catered for their own comfort accordingly, while we had taken the offensive and were expecting to make an early advance, in which case it would have been bad policy to have wasted stores and money in elaborating a system of trenches such as we had just seen. At the same time, I think it made many of the men a little envious, and it came as a slight shock to them when they had to admit that the Germans—in this part of the line, at any rate—had been living under better conditions than they had themselves.

At night, officers from various companies were detailed for duty with carrying parties, in most cases taking ammunition and R.E. material up to the front line units. This generally resulted in wandering over the countryside in pitch darkness, being led by a "guide" who knew still less about the geography of the Brigade sector than the officer himself. After falling into every available shell-hole and trench and running into numerous batteries of 18-pounders, the party finally reached the point from which it had started, just as day was breaking, and meekly put the ammunition and R. E. material back on the dumps from which they had been taken earlier in the night.

During the day time the men worked on salvaging the tons of derelict stores in the immediate vicinity, as well as the British and German rifles and ammunition of all kinds, which lay everywhere. This was the first occasion upon which we had come into actual contact with the Mills bomb, and consequently someone had to try one and see how it went off. Corporal Killalea took this duty upon himself for the benefit of his bosom companions, and pulling the pin out, threw it into the next shell-hole and ducked. It seemed to be a long time in going off, so he looked over the top to see if it was still there, and was just in time to see it explode—in fact, he was able to give first hand knowledge as to its effectiveness, for he was wounded—fortunately not seriously—in the head and arm and evacuated to the Casualty Clearing Station.

At 6 a.m. on the morning of 22nd July, Ray Sherwin and I, together with one N.C.O. per platoon of "A" Company, proceeded up to the forward area to view the situation. (Other companies either had done or were doing the same). It was a thick misty morning and we could barely see fifty yards in front of us and although we undoubtedly started out in the right direction, we soon became hopelessly lost in the fog. We thought we were making in the direction of Contalmaison and Black Watch Gully, but eventually came across a Vickers machine-gun team posted on the main Bapaume road. After the officer in charge had shown us his map and indicated the position of his post, we set out again and very soon picked up a shell-shattered railway line which was shown on our trench map and followed it until we reached a point where it had literally been shelled off the face of the earth, and once more we were left to our own devices. The fog seemed to thicken for a while and we proceeded onwards, hoping to strike a reserve or support trench before long, from which we could again pick up our bearing. Just as we appeared to be gaining some high ground, a breeze sprang up and within a few moments the fog had temporarily dispersed and we were astounded to find that we were walking straight towards the village of Pozieres, which was not more than 600 yards from us. By moving over to our left we found "D" Company of 11th Battalion, who supplied us with some excellent information regarding the ground in front.

The Battalion was restless all day. No one could settle down to do work, for we knew that the attack was to take place some time during the night. During the afternoon each officer inspected his platoon and made sure that every man had his full compliment of ammunition and also his gas helmet. He also made certain that the special gear, such as wire cutters and flares for signalling to the aeroplanes, were being carried by the men detailed for that purpose. There was only a limited number of bombs in these days, and they were carried exclusively by the Bombing Platoon. After a late tea, twenty-four hours' rations were issued to every man, while all water-bottles were filled with tea.

At 10 p.m. the companies silently concentrated at Battalion Headquarters and proceeded on by sections with the necessary interval, during which time the silence was almost uncanny, for not a gun was firing on the whole of the divisional front.

As soon as the last man had gone, a small party consisting of Majors Mullen and Rafferty, Captains Connell and Love, Lieutenants Moore, Gould, Sellick and myself, with our respective batmen, reluctantly turned our backs on the line where many of the men in our temporarily-relinquished commands had gone to face the Great Unknown. Silently we returned to Divisional Headquarters at Albert, to form the nucleus of a new battalion should the old one be too badly shattered in the operation before it.

Chapter XII.

POZIERES AND MOUQUET FARM

NARRATIVE CONTINUED BY LIEUT.-COL. C. H. ELLIOTT
C.M.G., D.S.O., V.D.

POZIERES is, or rather was, a small village on the main road running in an absolutely straight line for over eleven miles from Albert to Bapaume. It was situated about three miles from Albert and extended for nearly half-a-mile along the road, which rises gradually to a point about 280 feet higher than Albert four miles from that town. It will easily be seen, therefore, that the place was of great tactical importance, and it is no wonder that the Germans made such strenuous efforts to retain it.

Their original front line, whence they were driven by the offensive which started on 1st July, crossed the main road near La Boiselle, about a mile-and-a-half from Albert, and their second line of defence, consisting of two well-prepared trenches, known to us at the time as O.G. 1 and O.G. 2 (*i.e.*, Old German Trench No. 1 and Old German Trench No. 2), crossed it a couple of hundred yards above Pozieres, midway between the village and the top of the hill. These formed such an excellent assembly point for counter-attacks that it was perhaps only to be expected that the village should have been recaptured by the Huns several times after it had been carried by assault.

The front line crossed the main road from north to south, but at Fricourt, two-and-a-quarter miles south, a pronounced salient was formed where the line took a sharp bend to the west. By 20th July the offensive had progressed in an easterly direction along the main road almost to Pozieres, and in a northerly direction along the O.G. trenches to within about 1,000 yards of the main road.

The First Australian Division was detailed to attack the village of Pozieres, and the 3rd Brigade was allotted the right sector, that is, they attacked from the south at right angles to the road. The 9th and 11th Battalions took over the line on the night of 20th July, the former being on the right in O.G. 1 and 2 and the latter on their left. The 9th had a particularly strenuous tour of duty, being kept busy fighting to hold their own and work along the German trench lines, chiefly by bombing attacks, during the whole time they were in the line. Their excellent work made the task of the 10th and 12th Battalions a much easier one, as regards the opposition we received from rifle, machine-gun and bomb, though we suffered far more from the intense artillery bombardment of 25th July.

On the morning of the 21st, accompanied by the Adjutant, Captain Newland, and Medical Officer, Major Tozer, I went forward to reconnoitre the ground over which we were to make the attack, and also inspected the site of our Headquarters, which were in a short trench about 1,400 yards south of Pozieres, and containing two fair-sized, deep dug-outs. One was used for the H.Q. officers, signallers, runners, etc., and the other as the aid post. It had evidently been started as a battery position, and the site, being well-known, received plenty of attention from the hostile artillery, a considerable number of casualties resulting therefrom.

In the afternoon, the four battalion commanders were summoned to Brigade Headquarters at Contalmaison to discuss the attack of Pozieres. Three objectives were allotted:—*(a)* a line of enemy trenches about six hundred yards south of the village, *(b)* the outskirts of the village, including a small copse and several hedges about three hundred yards from the road (a small trench tramway ran partly through this objective), and *(c)* the southern edge of the main road. The orders provided that the attack was to be made in eight "waves," each of two lines of skirmishers, numbers one to four being provided by the 9th and 11th Battalions, and numbers five to eight by the 10th and 12th Battalions. Our front line consisted of three rather roughly-dug lines of trenches, in rear of which was a communication trench called "Black Watch Alley," running from Contalmaison to O.G. 1. By midnight 22nd-23rd July, the first wave was to be lying in the open 150 yards from the enemy trench which formed the first objective, second in our front line, third and fourth in our second trench, fifth in our third trench, sixth in Black Watch Alley, seventh and eighth to be furnished if needed by the support companies of the 10th and 12th Battalions.

At 10 p.m. we moved from Sausage Valley along the road to Contalmaison, two companies of the 10th Battalion leading, then "A" and "D" Companies 12th Battalion (under Captains Margetts and Vowles), then the other two companies 10th Battalion. "B" and "C" Companies 12th Battalion (under Captains Foster and Nicholas) remained in the sunken road near Contalmaison as part of the Brigade reserve, near to the spot where Black Watch Alley leads off to the left. The guides of the 10th Battalion, unfortunately, missed this turn-off, and by the time they had discovered their error and retraced their steps, sufficient time was not available for the fifth and sixth waves to be in position at midnight. Zero hour, the time at which the attack was to commence, was fixed for half-an-hour later, and, of course, could not be delayed on account of the artillery support. However, the advance of the 11th Battalion met with but slight resistance, and by 1.15 a.m. they had captured the second objective, taking several prisoners and capturing five howitzers and a machine-gun. The 9th Battalion met with more resistance in the O.G. trenches, and did not make as great an advance, with the result that our right flank was left exposed later.

At 2 a.m. Capt. Margetts came to Headquarters and reported being held up by 10th Battalion, but that "A" and "D" Companies were then in Black Watch Alley. Owing to the delay and the broken nature of the country, which was a mass of trenches and shell-holes, touch with the 11th Battalion had been lost. Captain Kayser, who was acting Intelligence Officer, guided the companies forward, and they dug in on the right of the 11th Battalion, roughly along the line of the tramway. (We had not then acquired that skill in finding our direction and location by the detailed maps issued to us, which in later engagements rendered the work of Divisional and Brigade staffs so much easier). A number of casualties were sustained both from artillery and machine-gun fire, Capt. Kayser receiving a severe flesh wound in the thigh. As soon as Brigade received word that the first and second objective had been captured, they ordered "B" and "C" Companies forward, and they occupied trenches just forward of Battalion Headquarters. The only casualty these companies had suffered up to this time was Lieut. A. Green, who was evacuated "gassed."

At daybreak, Lieut. A. T. Brine, with a couple of men, went into the village to reconnoitre. Brine got out of touch and did not return, being later posted as "missing." He told us after the Armistice that he had been stunned by a piece of shell and taken prisoner.

During the morning I inspected the new line and found that a good trench four feet deep had been dug, but, as the men were too crowded, ordered a platoon from each company back to the support line. The front line was not being shelled, but several casualties had been caused by the snipers in the O.G. trench on the right. Lieut. Thirkell and Major Tozer were wounded at Headquarters, the latter being replaced by Major J. Sprent as R.M.O.

During the afternoon a message was received that the Air Force had reported that the enemy had evacuated Pozieres, and we were ordered to occupy the village. (How we used to love the Air Force when they sent messages of this sort!). Patrols of an officer and thirty men were ordered to be sent forward from each company. Captains Margetts and Vowles themselves went forward later, and, finding all clear, Vowles went back for the companies while Margetts waited and chose the site for the new trenches. While thus engaged, Capt. Margetts was killed at about 10 p.m. by shrapnel shell, his death being a great blow to the Battalion. He was universally liked, and whilst holding the appointment of Adjutant had become well-known to the men of all companies. He had had a splendid record on Gallipoli and was the only officer of the 3rd Brigade who was on the Peninsula as an officer for the whole seven months. Lieut. Ray Sherwin assumed command of "A" Company, and the new line in front (N.E.) of Pozieres was consolidated. The order stated that *all* battalions would conform to this movement, but those on our right were still held up in the O.G. trenches, so that our flank was still more exposed in that direction, while neither the 11th Battalion nor the 1st Brigade on our left appeared to have moved. A large dug-out was discovered and an officer and nineteen men taken prisoners. The officer said, in good English, to Captain Vowles, "My name is Ponsonby Lyons; I am the Commandant of Pozieres." "You mean that you *were*," replied Vowles.

The 24th was occupied in strengthening the new position, "A" and "D" Companies being across the road north-east of Pozieres and "B" and "C" in the trenches vacated by "A" and "D" near the tramway. Heavy shelling of our support lines and back area took place intermittently all day, causing many casualties. Captain H. Z. Stephens relieved Major Sprent as Regimental Medical Officer.

In the evening orders were received to advance our line about one hundred yards north of Pozieres on the left flank, and to swing the right flank back to form a defensive line facing O.G. 1. Lieut. Laing and a patrol of thirty men were sent forward to protect the working parties, but were driven back by heavy machine-gun fire. Nevertheless, by the morning of the 25th the trenches were dug, connecting up with the 2nd Brigade in the cemetery.

The 25th July was a fateful day for the 12th Battalion. The enemy had now definitely withdrawn from Pozieres and subjected the village to an intense bombardment with 5.9 howitzers from about 4 a.m. to 6 p.m. Later, we experienced many hurricane bombardments, lasting half-an-hour or more, of far greater intensity, but I do not remember any other so severe for such a long time. The enemy brought fire to bear from the directions of High Wood and Thiepval, which with Pozieres make almost a straight line, so great was the salient we had made. The ground was very soft, and each shell sent a great cloud of dust into the air, often coloured red with brick dust. Whenever a shell burst in or near a trench, the latter would be obliterated for yards and the men of the Battalion had to work hard digging out unfortunate comrades who had been buried in the *debris*. The great majority of the 375 casualties of this engagement were suffered on this day. One unfortunate shell landed in "C" Company Headquarters and killed Capt. P. D. Nicholas, a most conscientious and able officer, Lieut. C. D. Lucas, who had joined as a reinforcement just before we left Egypt, and Company Sgt.-Major Small. On the 24th it was the support lines which were so badly *strafed*, but on the 25th it was the village which suffered. In the evening, when I went up to arrange for our relief by the 19th Battalion, I could hardly find a trace of the trenches that had been so well dug the previous day, though their site was easily determined by the remains of hedges, etc. Capt. Vowles and about eighty men were all that were left in the front line, and most of these had taken shelter in the deep dug-out captured the previous day. Lieut. Moore was severely

GIBRALTAR STRONG-POST, POZIERES

(Copyright by Australian War Museum)

wounded, five other officers shell-shocked, but only Capt. Foster and Lieut. S. L. Hughes were evacuated.

That so little fighting is detailed in the above account may occasion surprise to those who have been accustomed to regard Pozieres as one of the landmarks in the fighting record of the 12th Battalion. As far as I know, from my own experience of the battle and from what I have learned from others present (and this engagement is one we have seldom discussed), there was very little hand-to-hand fighting with bayonet or bomb. Nevertheless, the battle rightly ranks among our chief engagements, and was certainly one of our greatest achievements. It was the extreme strategical importance of the locality that caused its capture to be given such prominence at the time by the "High Commands," while to the humble "Digger" it was the fact that his initiation to the horrors of heavy shell-fire was such a fierce and intense one (in my opinion the worst we ever suffered), as to sear the remembrance of it for ever on his mind.

I cannot speak too highly of the wonderful grit, plucky determination, willingness and cheerfulness of each and every N.C.O. and private of the Battalion in the trying ordeal. For each of the three short summer nights (it was dark for about six hours only) they were fully occupied in the strenuous task of digging new trenches, in accordance with our orders to keep pushing the line forward, and on two of the three long summer days, when, under normal circumstances, a little broken rest could have been obtained, they were kept still harder at it, improving, deepening and strengthening the lines, or more often in digging out comrades who were continually being buried by the concussion of the shells bursting in the dry, broken ground.

226 THE STORY OF THE TWELFTH

The stretcher-bearers, as in any engagement of any size, had a tremendous task in evacuating the wounded, and no class of men carried out their duties more conscientiously and with less thought of self, and as the lines of communication were continuously shelled they had one of the most dangerous, as well as the most strenuous, of tasks.

It was about 4 a.m. on the 26th before the last of the Battalion reached the brickfields near Albert, where we were to bivouac. The officers who had been left out of the line awaited our arrival, and Lieut. E. L. A. Butler joined as a reinforcement. Breakfast was served between nine and ten, and all hands rested the remainder of the day. Quite a number of officers of higher commands called and congratulated us on the success of the Brigade.

The following are the names of those whose work was specially commended:—

Capt. A. S. Vowles	L.-Cpl. H. E. Holtum
Lieut. E. W. D. Laing	,, W. J. Kelly
,, R. Sherwin	Pvte. M. G. Blackman
R.S.M. E. Heurtley	,, T. E. C. Bridger
Sgt. F. J. Shore	,, A. McKenzie
,, J. Sandeman	,, M. Gould
Cpl. D. Clark,	,, A. A. Mears
,, F. E. Priddey	,, R. R. O'Connor
,, F. R. Miller	,, J. O'Neill
,, A. J. Goodwin	,, T. Evans
,, R. Burrell	,, E. Harding
Pvte. W. G. Podger	,, W. Stone
,, H. O. Weighill	,, A. Reading
,, C. C. Arnold	,, V. Chilcott
,, L. Bird	,, W. G. Copcutt
,, A. Waddington	,, A. G. Towers
,, E. J. Franks	,, A. Temple

At 4 p.m. a very small and subdued Brigade fell in and marched in the cool of the evening by back roads and across country to billets at Warloy.

On the 27th July we moved at 1 p.m., had our evening meal by the roadside at Val-de-Maison, and finally bivouaced for the night in the open in a grassy orchard at La Vicogne.

The following day we left at 11.30 a.m. and marched into comfortable billets at Berteaucourt, the principal industry of which is the manufacture of jute, and a large factory was an item of great interest to the troops. Just before reaching the town, we marched through the billets of our sister battalion, the 52nd, who lined the road and welcomed us with a rousing cheer.

The 29th July was a Saturday, and no parades were held. Company officers were busy getting particulars of acts of gallantry with a view to recommendations for the award of honours. Two hundred reinforcements arrived, making the strength of the Battalion 23 officers and 836 other ranks.

On Sunday we had a church parade, at the conclusion of which the Brigadier, General MacLagan, thanked the troops for their excellent work in capturing Pozieres. He said that no troops in the world could have done better.

Up to the 8th August, vigorous company training, musketry on a thirty yards range, and route marching were carried out, the weather being fine and hot. Reinforcements were allotted to companies, platoons and sections, and the Battalion generally reorganised. Capt. J. E. Newland was transferred from Adjutant to command "A" Company, and Lieut. L. M. Newton was appointed acting Adjutant; Capt. W. A. Connell was appointed O.C. "B" Company.

Orders were received for ten new officers to be appointed, but only nine were recommended, and on 5th August the following were promoted 2nd.-Lieutenants:—

J. A. Campbell, E. Heurtley (who later re-assumed his correct name, E. Heurtley Reed), W. H. E. Hale, George Vaughan, K. S. Field, B. W. Mitchell, A. J. Hearps, A. D. Tynan and S. W. Dobson. This was the greatest number promoted at the one time in the Battalion, and they proved themselves one of the best lots, too.

On the 9th August we moved to Bonneville, where Capt. W. W. S. Johnston joined as Medical Officer, vice Capt. Stephens, who returned to 3rd Field Ambulance.

On the 11th we had a demonstration of how to make an attack under cover of smoke, and also how to keep contact with aeroplanes. General Birdwood was present.

Capt. B. J. Andrew rejoined the Battalion on the 12th, and was appointed Adjutant vice Lieut. Newton; Lieut. H. Webber was promoted Captain.

We marched to Herissart on August 14th, and on to Vadencourt Wood the next day, where we were billetted in huts. General Birdwood presented ribbons to a number of N.C.O.'s and men who had been awarded Military Medals.

On the 16th we marched to Albert and bivouaced on the Brickfields, and two days later moved to Sausage Valley. General Birdwood informed us that Capt. Vowles had been awarded the D.S.O.

and Lieut. Sherwin the M.C., and presented these officers with the ribbons of their respective decorations.

About 4 a.m. on the 19th, accompanied by Capt. Connell and Lieuts. Newton and Leo. Butler, I went forward through a dense fog, to reconnoitre the new line we were take over. During the four weeks we had been out of the line heavy fighting had taken place, and the enemy had been driven about 1,200 yards north of Pozieres. In the sector we were to occupy the ground was fairly level for about 800 yards, and then fell away suddenly down a 40ft. bank, starting almost at once to rise again to the heights of Thiepval. Near the foot of this slope ran our front line, whilst 600 yards beyond stood the ruins of Mouquet Farm, a large building surrounded by stone walls and with large cellars, which were connected by tunnels and trenches to other strong points forming the defences of Thiepval. This had proved a veritable thorn in the side of the British, being taken and recaptured several times, and it was not until the attack of the 26th-27th September, resulting in the capture of Thiepval itself, that the position was finally made good to us.

We made for Pozieres, and passed a deep dug-out with a concrete top, built after the style of the pill-boxes later so familiar in the Ypres sector, which the Australians had named "Gibraltar." We went along Ration Trench and found the Headquarters of the 4th Battalion, whom we were to relieve, in dug-outs near the gates of the cemetery, on the northern edge of Pozieres, and Major Stacey offered to show us round. The fog now cleared and the sun shone out strongly, disclosing some gruesome sights—bodies of both Australians and

Germans killed in the recent action and not yet buried, in varying stages of decomposition.

We proceeded along Ration Trench till we reached the edge of the bank referred to above, and on attempting to descend in order to visit the front line, came under heavy fire from snipers, so as we had a good view of all the ground in front, we decided not to proceed further. We returned "overland," getting into trenches again near the cemetery, where there were also a lot of dead. As a large proportion of the Battalion were recent reinforcements who had not yet been under fire, it was decided to take the two companies who were to garrison the front line by the overland route to minimise the possibility of their being demoralised by the revolting sights they would necessarily pass in going up by the trenches.

"B" and "C" Companies, under Capt. Connell and Major Rafferty, left at 4 p.m. and relieved the 4th Battalion, with a few casualties from shell-fire. "A" and "D" Companies remained at the head of Sausage Valley and supplied fatigues and carrying parties, taking forward rifle and trench mortar ammunition, bombs, etc.

Hostile artillery was active all night and throughout the 20th, which was occupied by the front line companies in improving and strengthening the trenches. A deep German dug-out was found there, which made an invaluable forward Headquarters. Patrols located a number of enemy strong-posts in close proximity to our line.

During the evening orders were received for an attack next day to increase our hold on the ground in front of Mouquet Farm. It was not intended to attack the Farm itself, but to work round its right flank. The 9th Battalion on the left of the 3rd

Brigade sector did not participate in the operation, but lent platoons to aid the other battalions. The 12th had to advance from about forty yards on the left to about 120 yards on the right. The 11th Battalion had a small sector including the O.G. trenches, and the 10th Battalion had to work well round the right of the Farm.

The 11th Battalion had been detailed as Brigade reserve, and employed in carrying supplies, water and ammunition (over 100,000 rounds of S.A.A. alone were taken up to the front line, while the long hot summer days made an ample supply of water a necessity), and were relieved too late for them to get into position by zero hour. The 10th Battalion came under an intense bombardment and lost 350 out of 620 men in the front line within half-an-hour of the attack, and were unable to make good their ground. When the 12th went forward, therefore, their right flank was left exposed and had to be protected by manning the O.G. 1 trench, which ran towards our original line.

Our orders provided that "B" and "C" Companies were to remain in the original front line, and "A" and "D" Companies, under Capts. Newland and Love, were to pass through them to the attack. The attacking companies were to move forward during the day, "A" Company leaving Sausage Valley at 11 a.m. and "D" Company at 2 p.m. They proceeded along a trench called "Centre Way," which had been dug through the centre of Pozieres, connecting with Ration Trench. As the latter was the only communication trench for two battalions, it was very congested, especially with stretcher-bearers bringing back casualties. Capt. Newland therefore led his men along the top and descended into the trench again before crossing the ridge, but as the trench was not much more than waist-deep, the Company was undoubtedly observed at this juncture by the numerous enemy observation balloons, and on reaching a point where Ration Trench overlooked the gully which separated them from the front line, they suffered a heavy hostile barrage for about an hour, causing a number of casualties. Just as it eased off the appearance of "D" Company caused a further bombardment with renewed vigor. The trench being a poor one and being now doubled-banked, the casualties were mounting up and the men tended to become somewhat demoralised, so Capt. Newland suggested that he and Lieut. Newton should double across the gully in order to pick up Major Rafferty's Headquarters and find out what arrangements he could make to accommodate them in the front line. The time now was between 4 p.m. and 4.30 p.m. He was found with Capt. Connell in his headquarters. The latter was very shaky having been badly blown up by a shell earlier in the day. Rafferty appreciated the situation and could see how they were being shelled on the other side of the gully, so arranged to distribute his own men and "B" Company in shell holes, immediately in rear of the line, so that the trench itself would be available for "A" and "D" Companies to occupy. Newland and Newton left the line, being sniped at on the way, and crossing the gully reached the two companies in Ration Trench, the shelling having eased off somewhat. Capt. Newland told Capt. Love what he intended doing, and the N.C.O.'s and men were advised accordingly. Between 5.15 and 5.30 p.m. the whole line jumped the parapet and plunged headlong into the gully in extended order. This was dead ground and they were enabled to go slowly, but as soon as they came to the crest of the next ridge where the firing line was situated, they had to do the fifty yards in double quick time, and fairly fell into the trench. This left them about half-an-hour only in which to organise the attack. Whilst Newland was learning the lay of the country and picking up our flanking boundaries, the other officers commenced organising the men by sending "D" Company to the left and concentrating "A" Company on the right. The next thing to do was to tell them off into waves. Nos. 2 and 4 Platoons constituted the first wave of "A" Company (with two platoons of "D" Company) and Nos. 1 and 3 the second, with the other two platoons of "D" Company. "B" and "C" Companies likewise formed the third and fourth waves. They had barely finished telling the men off and explaining their objective, when our barrage opened up at 6 p.m. It was a wonderful barrage, and too much praise cannot be given to the 18-pounders on this occasion. There was a wall of shrapnel bursting about 150 yards in front of them, in which it was almost impossible for a man to expose himself. At 6.2 p.m., Capt. Newland gave the signal and the first wave mounted the parapet and advanced as one man, "A" Company being guided on the right by the wire of the O.G. 1 trench. This was the first daylight attack carried out by the 1st Australian Division in France, and officers of both flanking battalions, the 9th and 11th Battalions, said that the whole thing was like a model attack carried out on the parade ground. The barrage went forward as the attackers advanced, and the latter kept in a line that would have done credit to a company on parade. About 150 yards from our line they came across an enemy trench running obliquely across the front, and as they approached it the garrison of Huns ran for their lives, leaving much ammunition and equipment behind them. The enemy rifle and machine-gun fire was now increasing in volume, much of it coming from the rising ground in front and from our right flank.

It was at this moment that Lieut. Newton was wounded, though he at once organised the digging of a communication trench back to the old front line before evacuating himself.

At 6.5 p.m. the second wave of "A" Company, under command of Lieut. Heurtley, advanced and soon joined their comrades. The men over-ran the objective in their eagerness to get to grips with the retreating enemy, but Capt. Newland called them back, and organised the digging of a new line, in which task they were helped by finding a four feet high bank, which served as a ready-made parapet.

Things were lively on the extreme right, where a machine-gun was causing casualties, and a party of Germans were standing exposed from the waist, firing point-blank at our men. Our Lewis guns came into action and Cpl. A. Adams led a party out, which, after a short, sharp encounter, drove the enemy off. At the same time Cpl. Manser, with another party, attacked a strong-point in the O.G. 1 trench, which was quickly captured, the two parties between them dispatching about twenty Germans with the bayonet. A machine-gun was captured and turned on to the retreating enemy, causing them several casualties. Sgt. L. K. Ford was also responsible for some particularly good work, leading his men with great dash.

On the left, the two waves of "D" Company, under Lieuts. O. J. Roper and A. J. Hearps, went forward simultaneously, without meeting much opposition, as the trench they had to capture had been almost obliterated by our artillery.

It was estimated that the dead bodies of over one hundred Germans were found in the vicinity. Capt. A. Love, acting Company Commander, received a severe wound in the left hand, and after evacuation did not again join the Battalion.

Seeing Mouquet Farm so close, less than two hundred yards away, a section of the Battalion Bombing Platoon, under L-Cpl. H. E. Lord, advanced through our barrage, losing two men in doing so, and threw more than twenty bombs into the cellars of the farm, killing a number of the enemy. Lieut. Hearps followed with some of his platoon and was severely wounded in the neck. His batman was also wounded, and both were left in a dug-out with some wounded Germans. We afterwards learned that Hearps died soon after. He had had an excellent record as an N.C.O. on Gallipoli, and it was most unfortunate that he should have lost his life just as he had got his commission.

Two platoons of "B" Company, forming part of the third wave, reinforced "D" Company and helped to dig the new line, which they did by linking up shell-holes.

Similarly, two platoons of "C" Company, under Lieut. K. Field, reinforced "A" Company.

The fourth wave, two platoons each of "B" and "C" Companies, under Lieuts. G. F. Gould and Leo Butler respectively, remained in the original front line and dug communication trenches forward to the new line.

The whole of the 22nd was employed in improving and strengthening the new line and the communication trenches. Early in the morning a deep dug-out was discovered in the O.G. 1 trench, and fifteen Germans who had been lying low there were taken prisoners.

The enemy artillery was very active during this engagement. Evidently judging from having seen "A" and "D" Companies moving forward that an attack was imminent, they put down a severe barrage just before dusk which resulted so disastrously for the 10th Battalion. All that night and through the 22nd they kept firing, many of the shells falling on our old front line, though the new one, which had evidently not yet been located, almost completely escaped. Perhaps the Huns hoped to occupy it themselves as they made two severe counter-attacks, which our rifle and Lewis gun fire completely overwhelmed.

Their artillery paid much atention to our lines of communication through the village of Pozieres, where the 3rd Brigade "forward-report centre" was established in the "Gibraltar" dug-out. The telephone wires were continually being cut and messages had to be sent by hand. Two runners were usually employed, and one message was taken by the Headquarters runners, "Skinny" Mears and "Scottie" Widdop. They reached "Gibraltar" just as a section of the Signal Company returned there with a coil of wire, saying the shelling was too intense for them to lay it as a new line to the Battalion. Mears and Widdop said they had just come through it and were going straight back and would lay the line. This offer was accepted, and they brought the wire through, when it was joined up by the Battalion Signallers and held for about four hours during a critical period of the battle before it received its first cut from a shell. (Sometimes a couple of signallers would have a dozen or more breaks to mend in a short line during a few hours heavy shelling).

We were relieved by the 19th Battalion on the evening of the 22nd. Divisional Headquarters evidently had a wrong idea of the visibility of our lines of communication, for they sent the incoming Battalion in about 4 p.m., in broad daylight. This at once brought down a heavy barrage, causing losses to both the 12th and 19th Battalions. Major Rafferty, who was senior officer in the front line, ordered them to scatter into shell holes, where they stayed till dusk, when the work of relieving the various posts was commenced. Several barrages during the evening sent the 12th to cover, and it was after 3 a.m. on the 23rd before the Battalion got clear of Pozieres.

Just about dusk, Lieut. Leo Butler sustained a severe wound in the left foot, necessitating amputation. Word of this was received at Headquarters just as Captain Johnston had been relieved by the R.M.O. of the 19th. The "Doc.," who should then have gone back to Albert, volunteered to go forward to the front line to render first aid. He had to pass through a heavy barrage, but arrived safely and remained till the last squad of the Battalion had left, tending not only Butler but a number of other wounded. Unfortunately, Butler died a few days later of shock and loss of blood. Although he had only been with the Battalion a short month, his manly qualities and strict sense of justice had won the hearts of the men of the platoon, while with the officers he had become a first favourite.

We bivouaced on the Brickfields on the 23rd, and were visited and congratulated on our work by General Birdwood and other officers. Our casualties were: 2 officers died of wounds and 2 wounded; 45 other ranks killed, 137 wounded, 41 missing; total, 227. Eighty-four reinforcements were waiting us at the Brickfields and were taken on the strength.

At 3 p.m. we moved to Warloy and marched into fairly comfortable billets at 6 p.m.

An early start was made at 8 a.m. on the 24th, and, after a long, hot march of twelve miles, we were billetted at Beauval, "marching past" General Walker, our Divisional Commander, *en route*.

We rested all day on the 25th, and marched at 7 a.m. on the 26th for Doullens, where we entrained once more for the north, a very different Battalion from that which detrained at this station on 11th July to take its share in the Somme offensive. Our strength at this time was 28 officers and 679 other ranks.

We left at 10 a.m., and in the afternoon entered Belgium for the first time, detraining at Proven at 6 p.m., and marched four miles to billets at Poperinghe, a fair-sized town eight miles west of Ypres.

On the 28th, company training was carried out, and the following day we moved to "Ontario" Camp, which consisted of wooden huts.

After a couple of days training and cleaning up, we moved on 2nd September to another camp called "Scottish Lines."

From the 4th to the 12th September, the Battalion was put through a thorough course of platoon and company training each morning, and held sports, inter-company football matches, etc., each afternoon. Lieut. L. Dadson held a class of instruction for non-commissioned officers. All ranks were shut up for a short period in a "gas" chamber to give them confidence in the efficiency of their gas-masks. Competitions were held between the several Lewis gun teams.

On the 12th September, the 3rd Brigade took over part of the front line in front of Ypres, opposite the famous Hill 60, and on the 13th the 12th Battalion, as Brigade reserve, moved to Halifax Huts.

The war diary entry for the 14th reads: "Intercompany football match in morning. Rain in afternoon. Lecturettes in huts by platoon commanders. Concert in evening." This was typical of the succeeding week—half the day devoted to training and half to sports, with rain nearly every day.

On the 19th we moved to Chateau Belge, and were billetted, not in the Chateau, but in dug-outs among the trees in the grounds.

On the 20th, General Birdwood presented the ribbon of Military Medal to C.Q.M.S. Sheedy, Sgt. Miller, and Pvts. Mears and Manser, they having been awarded this decoration for work done in the attack at Mouquet Farm. Sir Newton Moore, Agent-General for West Australia, inspected the men of that State serving in the Battalion.

During the next four days some of the men were sent as working parties to improve the front line, and some worked at the dug-outs in which we were billetted. Officers and senior N.C.O.'s went forward daily or nightly to become acquainted with the front line.

On the evening of the 24th we were moved into the "Railway Dug-outs," and became Brigade close support Battalion.

About one-and-a-half miles out of Ypres the railway to Menin passed over a long embankment about twenty feet high. This had been hollowed out to form dug-outs sufficient for a battalion, Brigade Headquarters, and a number of other small units. They were quite dry, and with the ballasted sleepers on top were considered fairly safe.

Our tour of duty at Chateau Belge and Railway Dug-outs was marked by the large number of working parties supplied nightly by the Battalion. Many of these were small, consisting of an N.C.O. and six or more men, while some consisted of a whole company. All had different destinations, often only a map reading (that is, a spot located by its position on the map), and varying tasks, and it is to the credit of the Adjutant, Capt. B. J. Andrew, and R.S.M. J. Cooper, as well as the leaders of the parties, that not one failed to perform its allotted task.

On the 26th September, owing to the Brigade frontage being increased, "A" Company (Captain Newland) took over part of the front line from the railway to Verbranden Road.

On the 1st October we relieved the 10th Battalion in the line, "B" and "D" Companies in the trenches, "C" Company in support in Larch Wood, and "A" Company, which was relieved by a company of the 9th Battalion, in reserve at Battersea Farm. Our right rested on the Ypres-Comines Canal, which here ran through a cutting, the spoil from which was piled on the northern bank, thereby forming Hill 60. This was the crest of a long slope from both sides, and the holder had the advantage of having the lines of communication of the opposing forces well under observation. It had been won and lost many times early in the war and was now held by the Germans. Vigorous mining operations had been carried out, and there were a number of small craters in the vicinity. While we were in the line, a Canadian Tunnelling Company was hard at work driving a tunnel under the enemy lines, and it was confidently thought that he had mines under ours.

The opposing trenches near the canal were much closer together than any we had hitherto experienced, so much so that orders had been given that no one was to speak above a whisper. On the left they widened out, and on our side ended in a morass where it was impossible to dig trenches, and a gap between us and the unit on our left had to be patrolled quarter-hourly every night. The front line trenches were very poorly constructed, and it was not felt that they could be held in the case of attack. In addition, the long, even slope made it ideal for an enemy gas attack (this being the locality where gas had first been used by the Huns), so that all ranks had to wear their masks "at the alert"—that is, with the box respirator on the chest so that the mask could be adjusted in a few seconds. In these circumstances, all ranks "had the wind up," well and truly. The defence scheme was very elaborate, containing instructions for action to be taken in case the enemy blew up a mine under our lines, or we under his, in addition to the details common to all sectors.

The 2nd, 3rd and 4th October were very wet, not only causing much discomfort, but also making the sides of the trenches slide in.

From the 5th to the 8th the weather was fine, and good progress was made in improving the trenches. The whole tour of duty was very quiet as regards the artillery, though snipers were very active. Many rolls of barbed wire were put out in "No

Man's Land" by working parties to render the position more secure against sudden raids.

On the evening of the 8th a strong patrol under Lieuts. Holyman and Vaughan went out towards a small salient in the enemy lines, called by us "The Snout," to try to capture one of the enemy to identify the regiment opposite us, but without success.

On the evening of the 9th we were relieved by the 8th Battalion and entrained at Ypres at 10.30 p.m., arriving at Scottish Lines at 3 a.m. on the 10th, where we rested all day.

Just before we were relieved, Pvte. F. A. Chapman, who was on sentry duty in a trench in the support line, was killed by the shock of the explosion of a large shell, not a trace of a wound being found on his body. This was our only fatal casualty during this tour of duty.

On 11th October we provided all Divisional duties, held an inspection of arms and equipment, and made out requisitions for new clothing, etc. Capt. Andrew left the Battalion to take up Staff duties at Corps Headquarters. Lieut. Ray Sherwin was appointed acting Adjutant. Capt. Appleby joined the Battalion.

From the 12th to the 15th, the 3rd Brigade route marched a distance of about thirty miles in delightful weather, and through very interesting country, passing Mont des Cats, Cassell, Arneke (a rich pastoral district), Watton (with an ancient castle overlooking the town), and a number of smaller towns and villages. The 12th Battalion finished the march by getting into very good billets at Nordasques, a picturesque village on the St. Omer-Calais road, about 12 miles from the latter town.

Until the 20th, company training, with route marches and musketry on a thirty yards range in a chalk-pit, was carried out. Rain fell on a couple of days.

On the 18th October a Field General Court Martial was held at the 11th Battalion Headquarters, when a member of the Battalion was being tried for some offence against a civilian. A French witness said he knew the accused was an Australian "because he used words which were not in the English language."

On the 19th the referendum on "Conscription in Australia" was taken. Without attempting to influence their opinion, I asked a number of the men what they thought of it, and found that the majority seemed to be opposed to the idea, chiefly on personal grounds, such as not wanting a younger brother sent. Quite a number expressed the opinion that they, who had volunteered, did not wish to have to fight alongside conscripts. Our strength at this time was 30 officers and 952 other ranks.

On the 21st, after a very early "Reveille" on a cold, frosty morning, we marched out at 7.30 a.m., and after a four miles march entrained at Ardruicq at 10 a.m., and after passing through Boulogne, Etaples and Abbeville, detrained at Pont-Remy, on the Somme about ten miles below Amiens. The transport of the Brigade proceeded by road and joined up a couple of days later.

On the 23rd, after a march of about six miles, we were picked up by motor 'buses and conveyed to Buire-sur-Ancre, three miles from Albert, arriving at 6.30 p.m.

The following day we left at 9 a.m., and marching with intervals of two hundred yards between companies, reached a camp near Fricourt by noon. It was an open, wind-swept area, with very poor accommodation. Rain commenced to fall soon after our arrival and the place soon became a quagmire, one company cooker becoming completely bogged.

During the next few weeks rain fell repeatedly, rendering the conditions of living most deplorable, and effectually holding up the Allied offensive. The traffic on the roads was very heavy and congested, and the Battalion was employed chiefly on road repair work during the week's stay at Fricourt. Large pits would be dug by the road-side, the earth being thrown well back, and then the mud and slush on the roads would be swept into the pits.

On 30th October we moved at 9 a.m. for Bernafay Wood, about four miles distant. We were supposed to move with intervals between platoons, but there was so much traffic on the road that a solid mass on either side of the road moving in opposite directions was formed. First there would be a platoon of infantry, then a few vehicles, then more infantry, then a battery of 18-pounders, and so on. Progress was so slow, the column moving a few paces and then having to halt, that I ordered the Battalion to break down into single file and thread its way through the gaps in the traffic as best it could. In this way we reached Bernafay Wood in time for lunch, but it was 11 p.m. before our transport got through, having taken fourteen hours to go four miles.

During our tour of duty in Belgium, the offensive on the Somme had been carried on with vigour and we were now bivouaced well in advance of Pozieres. The method usually employed at this time in conducting the offensive was to put down an intense artillery barrage on an area two hundred to four hundred yards in depth, the infantry following this and digging in. A small advance of this nature was made about once a week, as after each push time was required to consolidate and bring forward fresh supplies of bombs, rifle ammunition, etc., for the infantry, and, more important still, fresh ammunition for the artillery.

On the 15th September a new method had been tried, "tanks" being used for the first time. They preceded the attacking infantry, giving the Germans an unpleasant surprise and contributing largely to the success of the offensive. With the assistance of these "tanks," High Wood, a very important and strongly fortified position, and the villages of Flers, Martinpuich and Courcelette were carried by assault, an advance of about a mile on a ten-mile frontage being made and over 4,000 prisoners captured in the one day. During the latter half of September and October, very little further progress was made on the front which we were to take over, the heaviest fighting having been on our left flank nearer the River Ancre.

Chapter XIII.

THE WINTER OF 1916

NARRATIVE CONTINUED BY LIEUT. L. M. NEWTON, M.C.

TO adequately describe the conditions under which the Battalion was living when I returned on 3rd November would require the pen of an Ashmead-Bartlett or Phillip Gibbs.

They were bivouaced in a depression on the northern fringe of Bernafay Wood and lived in extreme discomfort in a sea of mud. The camp site was about 300 to 400 yards from Trones Wood, in and around which there was so much fighting during the latter summer months, and thus the whole area consisted entirely of half-obliterated trenches and shell holes, all more or less full of water. The men actually lived in "possies" and dug-outs, which they excavated for themselves in the slopes of the hill and endeavoured to make weatherproof by covering them with their waterproof sheets. It was a hopeless task, however, for the bottom of the dug-out soon became a slimy mud, while the rain penetrated down the sides, which invariably commenced to fret, and in many instances fell in altogether. Thus it would often happen that some three or four men who shared a "possie" would find themselves shelterless in the middle of a cold, dark night, with rain falling steadily. Some of the men had managed to obtain a few tarpaulins (known at later periods as "trench shelters") whilst one or two isolated sheets of corrugated iron were visible, concerning which the Company Commanders did not ask too many searching questions.

During these early days of the winter campaign we were not receiving regular consignments of socks from our Comforts Funds in Australia, and in consequence, many of the men remained wet footed for a week or ten days at a time.

All battalions in the Brigade were furnishing very large working parties at this time, averaging from 600 to 700 men per battalion, for constructional and repair work on the roads, carrying material for engineers' parties and furnishing general fatigues in connection with the broad gauge railway which was pushing its way along our valley from the direction of Bazentin. It was customary for these parties to be out in the wet and cold all day, taking a mid-day haversack ration with them, while every effort was made to have a hot stew and tea, prepared in the company field-cookers, awaiting their return.

The only other outstanding feature connected with our uncomfortable stay at Bernafay Wood was the presence of two guns of fairly large calibre, which used to fire at almost extreme range from a position situated right in our very midst. These guns were nick-named "Booming Bertie" and "Barking Bessie" respectively, from the terrific detonation which took place when they fired. The atmospheric vibration, as a result of the discharge, was so great that every candle in the camp was blown out each time a gun fired, and it may well be imagined that it became very monotonous relighting them when the battery was firing at intervals throughout the whole evening. We got to know the artillery gun drill fairly well in those days—"No. 1 Gun ready?" "No. 1 Gun ready, sir." (Pause). "No. 1 Gun, fire!" followed immediately by a tremendous report, the extinguishing of all lights, and the superfluous reply, "No. 1 Gun fired, sir."

November 7th was a particularly raw, cold day, and rain did not cease from daylight to dark. It was a day that will ever be remembered by all who were with the Battalion at the time, for at 3.30 p.m. we started for the notorious Switch and Gap Trenches, *via* Longueval and Delville Wood. The road to Longueval had been badly damaged by shell-fire during the summer fighting, but had since been made passable for traffic by the laying of a corduroy track. As we traversed this road it was a sea of mud and water varying in depth from two to fifteen inches, whilst the logs which had worked loose from the corduroy and floated about, were very dangerous in the failing light. A spice of adventure was created by the fact that one never knew whether the next step taken was to be on the solid track or in a gap or shell-hole, knee-deep in water.

Delville Wood itself, with the duckboard track winding its way round trees and between shell holes, was a depressing place. The wet, bare tree trunks, many of which were mangled and hanging in unnatural positions as a result of shell fire, gave the place the appearance of a deserted nether-world. Although the battle *debris* had mostly been salvaged, yet the multitudinous shell holes and the hopelessly twisted tangle of barbed wire gave ample evidence of the tremendous artillery duel which had taken place in this vicinity.

It was almost dark when we emerged from the northern side of the wood, with the rain beating full in our face. Our route soon took us off the duckboard track, and the "going" on the slippery muddy ground was extremely heavy, especially for the Lewis Gunners, with their guns and panniers of ammunition. Lieut. "Soss" Heritage expressed the thoughts of many a man in the Battalion when he measured his length into a shell-hole and remarked in lurid language that "he'd been in every blanky hole in France."

At last we reached a trench, which, after consulting the map, we were grudgingly compelled to agree was Switch Trench, whilst some fifty to one hundred yards farther on was another, which must be Gap Trench. But what trenches! And what a howl of dismay went up from the men when they saw their night's resting place! Even the officers failed to discover a small ray of comfort upon which to enlarge, and thus wisely commiserated with them in silence.

The trenches themselves were from four to six feet deep and wide at the top, without any attempt having been made by the Germans in their retirement to revet them. The mud and water in the bottom came well over the boot tops before any traffic had taken place in the trench and rapidly became worse as our occupation was prolonged. With the exception of two unfinished dug-outs, there were no shelters or "possies" of any kind, and the nature of the wet ground afforded little prospect of any being made without R.E. material. The top of the trench was infinitely preferable to the inside, and it was here that the majority of the men passed what is unanimously considered as the worst night in the whole Battalion's existence.

The rain ceased during the early hours of the morning, and when dawn broke we discovered that we were on the crest of a rise, whilst a couple of shells landing in our near vicinity proved conclusively that we were under enemy observation, which made it necessary for all men to get down into the trench.

The sick parade was somewhat inflated next morning, colds, general debility and rheumatic pains being the predominant ailments. The Commanding Officer's groom and batman, "Bill" Russell, regarded the night as his Waterloo, and after evacuation, saw the remainder of the war on the Blighty front.

The First Australian Division was administered in rather a peculiar manner at this period, for the 10th and 12th Battalions occupied positions in the right sector of the Divisional front and received orders direct from the G.O.C. 2nd Infantry Brigade, whilst the 9th and 11th Battalions operated in the left sector under the command of the 1st Infantry Brigade. The 3rd Brigade occupied the *role* of Reserve Brigade, with its headquarters in the quarry adjacent to Bernafay Wood, and for purposes of command was composed of 1st, 2nd, 5th and 7th Battalions, 3rd M.G. Coy., and 3rd L.T.M. Battery.

The next day, November 8th, was somewhat better as regards weather, the rain having ceased temporarily, but at the same time it was very raw, cold and bleak. During the day, "A" and "C" Companies furnished large working parties, whose task it was to provide better accommodation for the support battalion in trenches known as Cocoa Lane and Bull Trench, while orders were received for "B" and "D" Companies to move into the line the same night. Relief was effected during the early hours of the evening without any casualties; "B" Company was on the right of the sector in Grease Trench, and "D" Company on the left in Biscuit Trench, being in front and to the left of the village of Gueudecourt.

The next morning, Battalion Headquarters (in which I was now included, having taken over the duties of Adjutant on my return, from Lieut. Ray Sherwin, who had been acting in that capacity) moved down to a small dug-out in Pilgrim's Way, in order to be in closer touch with the line companies, after which, the C.O. went up in daylight and inspected the front, and found the trenches in a deplorable condition and almost defying description. The trenches were half full of a thick, viscous mud, which made traffic almost an impossibility. There was literally nowhere for the men to sit down, and many of them spent the whole twenty-four hours in a standing position with this wet, cold and clammy mud up to, and in some cases over, their knees. At night time, the officers and N.C.O.'s organised the line and supervised the improvements being made by walking along the parados of the trench, while the men were urged to do likewise (when not working or on sentry duty) in order to keep the blood in circulation. Under these conditions, it will readily be perceived that sleep in the front line was almost an impossibility.

"D" Company had a particularly wet sector of the line to hold, in many cases the water being well over the boot tops. Empty ammunition boxes and duck-boards were given to the men to stand on, but these disappeared into the quagmire of mud before they had been in use many hours. In consequence of these conditions of life, "D" Company evacuated twenty-seven cases of trench-feet during its forty-eight hours of duty in the line. This complaint, as everyone must know, was particularly disagreeable and painful, the more important symptoms being that the feet swelled considerably and went blue-black in colour, while the unfortunate victim suffered excruciating pain, particularly in the instep, which made walking extremely difficult and painful; many of the men were carried out of the line on stretchers.

On the night of 10th-11th November, an inter-company relief was effected, when "A" Company went into the right sector and "C" Company to the left, and on relief "B" and "D" Companies went into more comfortable quarters in Pioneer Trench, immediately in rear of Pilgrim's Way.

During this tour in the line, the front line trenches were not subjected to very much shelling, many of them being situated on a reverse slope, but the village of Gueudecourt itself was shelled incessantly from morning till night. We were at a loss to ascribe a reason for this bombardment, knowing that no troops were quartered in the ruins of the village, but a persistent rumour was in currency that the Germans had buried or hidden some 15-inch guns in the village before retiring and were using this method of ensuring their destruction. One morning, during a lull in the shelling, Lieut. G. Vaughan (Battalion Intelligence Officer) and myself, crossed an intervening mangold field and made a thorough inspection of the village, but did not find any sign of guns, large or small, nor could we find any apparent cause for the shelling. At a later period, however, the reason was made obvious to us and will be referred to in its proper sequence.

The rations were brought up to Headquarters on pack mules, after dark, by the transport section, under the direction of Transport Officer, Lieut. E. A. Shepherd. This was by no means an easy or enviable task, for the road between Longueval and Flers, which was the only available track for transport, was continuously shelled and consequently full of craters. It was then necessary to take a cross-country track to strike Battalion Headquarters, with no distinctive landmarks as a guide. During our first night in the line in this sector, only half the rations arrived, owing to a very thick mist; the convoy of mules got into a bad patch of barbed wire, and whilst endeavouring to find a safe passage, half the drivers got astray, and, after wandering round a strange area in a thick fog during half the night, eventually struck the road and turned back. This was our first experience of having hot tea brought up to the line in petrol tins, and, although the Quartermaster had thoroughly rinsed the tins out with boiling soda water, the tea was almost undrinkable owing to the flavour of petrol which still lingered. The only way in which we could make the tea at all palatable was for each man to empty in his rum ration, and thus to a large extent drown the oily flavour. It was afterwards discovered that the best method of cleansing the tins was to drop a lighted match in and thus burn out all the petrol before treating the tin with hot soda and water.

We were relieved on the night of 12th-13th November by the 46th and 47th Battalions, the former unit relieving Headquarters and "A" Company and the latter unit, "C" Company. The 46th Battalion arrived about 7 p.m. and proceeded into the line by an overland track, but apparently they were sighted by the enemy, for they were subjected to a heavy shrapnel barrage and suffered a few casualties, although "A" Company moved with more caution in coming out and escaped all danger. The 47th Battalion got hopelessly lost on their way to the forward area and did not make an appearance until midnight, when our guides, who were awaiting them, showed them the best passages through the ocean of mud in Cheese Road and eventually guided them to the various posts in the front line in front of the village.

We reported "Relief complete" to 2nd Brigade Headquarters at 1.30 a.m. and started a long tramp home through Delville Wood and Longueval, back to our bivouac in Bernafay Wood. Just as we were emerging from Delville Wood, we saw, on the left of the track, a newly erected shanty with "Australian Comforts Fund" painted on a linen sheet. It was surrounded by Diggers who had removed their saturated equipment, while the fellows in charge were dispensing steaming hot cocoa in old jam tins, with the lids bent back as handles. There was no officers' mess here; majors and privates rubbed elbows in their efforts to get the next "plum-and-apple-jam-tin" cup filled full of ambrosia—the drink of the gods. This Comforts Fund stall remained in Delville Wood, under shell fire, during the whole of the winter, and supplied a hot drink to every man who passed through the Wood (either way) during the long nights; probably more than a thousand cups were provided nightly. The value of this stall to the Diggers throughout the 1916 winter cannot be over-estimated.

A steaming hot stew was awaiting our arrival at 3.30 a.m., after which we took off as many of our wet clothes as possible and indulged in a much-needed rest, some of the men not having slept for over forty-eight hours.

Orders were received early in the morning for another move back to Fricourt Camp, and on this occasion transport was made available for all packs and blankets to be carried. The road was congested with traffic, and progress was possible only by moving forward in single file and individually threading a way through the mud, in between limbered wagons and under horses' noses. We looked a very bedraggled unit marching along in this irregular formation and caked with mud from head to foot. Capt. Sid Houghton looked no better than the rest, and was hardly distinguishable from any N.C.O. or private in his company, except for the fact that he led them and was mounted on a horse. Just as they were nearing Montauban, a young English officer came along, also mounted, with a breast of ribbons and—scrupulously clean. Sid Houghton gave him the time of day by saying, "How are you, Dig?" The young officer smiled and said, in a sedate manner, "Good morning." It was learned afterwards that he was the Prince of Wales. A little farther along the road we passed the 52nd Battalion moving in, and were thus able to give a hurried greeting to many old comrades in passing.

On arriving at Sydney Camp, Fricourt, we discovered that we were to be quartered for the first time in Nissen huts. These huts were constructed of corrugated iron and were semi-circular in shape, like a baker's oven. They were about fifteen feet wide and eight feet high in the centre, and generally about forty feet long, although, as they were built in sections, it was possible for the length to vary. They undoubtedly proved a great boon during the winter months, and were considered a great success. The camp site was a quagmire and we at once requisitioned for some duckboards, which we fixed on to piles, and thus made communication between the huts and the cookhouses and other camp buildings.

Next day, November 14th, found us on the road again, and, marching *via* Meaulte, we proceeded to uninviting billets at Dernancourt, and once again joined up our own Brigade. We spent three days in this village and endeavoured to clean the Battalion up as much as possible. The weather was extremely cold and the billets very dingy, for a poor type of peasant seemed to occupy the village. Our short stay there was neither particularly comfortable nor enjoyable.

On November 17th, we marched to the next village—Buire—only a matter of a mile-and-a-half to two miles, and stayed there for forty-eight hours. During the night there was a fall of snow; it lay quite thick in the morning, but thawed rapidly during the day. The only other incident worthy of note during our sojourn at Buire was a stack of wood which mysteriously disappeared during the night. Unfortunately, the tracks it made in "disappearing" were so obvious that the company into whose billets it "disappeared" was detailed to pay the bill submitted by the owner.

We moved from Buire on Sunday, November 19th, at 12.45 p.m., by motor 'buses, which were waiting for us in a long queue outside the village, and proceeded along the main Albert-Amiens road, through the villages of Pont Noyelles and Querrieu

SWITCH TRENCH
Occupied by 12th Battalion, Nov. 7th, 1916
(Copyright by Australian War Museum)

(where Army Headquarters were situated). We avoided the town of Amiens by merely passing through the suburbs, and at 4 p.m. arrived at our destination, which was the village of Rainneville, situated from five to six miles from the afore-mentioned town.

During our ten days of rest and training in this village, we experienced some very cold, raw, damp weather, which did not tend to convey a favourable impression of the place. It did not appear to be used much for billetting purposes, and the sheds and outhouses were in a state of disrepair. A considerable amount of regimental funds was expended in purchasing straw in order to make the billets more comfortable for the men.

During our stay at Rainneville, a percentage of men were granted leave into Amiens each day, and most of them found the town very interesting. The time was usually spent in having a haircut, shave and bath, after which a search was made for a suitable restaurant in which to enjoy a meal of anything which varied the monotony of army rations. The cathedral was also of absorbing interest and received a visit from most of the boys, who were quick to appreciate the grandeur of its architecture, magnificent carving, and the solemn beauty of the richly-coloured stained glass windows. We were unable to inspect many of the carvings, both inside and out, as they were protected by a barricade of sandbags to prevent any damage from air raids.

The R.M.O. had a fairly busy time during our period of rest, for many of the men were feeling the effects of the exposure and damp experienced in the line, and Capt. Johnston was tireless in his efforts to coax his patients back to health without evacuating them. He was also popular with the civilian population, a sick and sorry crowd, who freely requisitioned his services, for on one day alone he was called out to attend a woman, three children and a cow.

The inclement weather did not lend itself to training, and as a substitute every effort was made to smarten up the Battalion. The men's clothing, particularly the puttees and greatcoats, were literally caked with mud, which proved very difficult to remove. Many of the men have lively recollections of an entry which the Commanding Officer caused to be made in their pay books for "wilfully mutilating" Government property, namely, cutting off about twelve inches of their greatcoats where the mud was thickest.

The only other incident connected with our stay at Rainneville worthy of note was the fact that under the supervision of the Padre, Capt. W. K. Douglas, we first started a modest regimental canteen. Our regimental funds were not extensive, and in consequence the stock carried in the canteen was not excessive and required continual replenishing. Nevertheless, the biscuits, cake, tinned fruits, cigarettes, etc., were much appreciated by the men and found a ready sale on the days immediately following a pay. In these early days, the O.C. canteen also had strict instructions to keep his stock low, on account of the limited amount of transport at our disposal, for it was not possible to requisition the services of an extra motor lorry as in the later days of our campaigning in France.

On November 30th, we once again made a move towards the line, leaving at 8.15 a.m. for billets at Franvillers. The R.M.O. brought much censure upon himself by evacuating 63 men with sore feet (as a result of our last tour of duty in the line) on the morning of the march. We proceeded *via* Cardonette, Allonville, Querrieu, Pont Noyelles, and La Houssoye, and were met by our billeting party on the outskirts of the village of Franvillers, where we merely spent the night and continued on to our old billets at Dernancourt, passing large parties of German prisoners on the way, working on the roads.

A diversion was caused while we were here by one of "D" Company's billets catching fire during the evening of December 2nd. A slight breeze caused the fire to spread quickly through the old buildings, and ere long half the Battalion was at work preventing the owner's house from becoming ignited. The Frenchman himself adopted a peculiar attitude, for he did all in his power to dissuade the men from salvaging his threshing machine, and then removed the handle of the well, which was the only means of obtaining water. Apparently he preferred the heavy compensation which he would claim, and which would enable him to build a complete set of outbuildings.

The next day we again moved to Sydney Camp, Fricourt, when our Brigade Commander, Brig.-Gen. E. G. Sinclair-MacLagan, came to bid us good-bye, prior to his departure for special duty in England, accompanied by his successor, Lieut.-Col. H. G. Bennett, of the 6th Battalion, who commanded us until the cessation of hostilities.

Our progress towards the line was continued the following day by moving to New Carlton Camp (afterwards re-named Launceston Camp) at Bazentin-le-Grand, where we were crowded into camouflaged tents. We also first encountered a new kind of hut (which we utilised as the Battalion

Orderly Room) made of brown canvas and stretched over a framework, which was composed of sections, and thus easily erected and pulled to pieces. But one member of the Battalion did not have a high opinion of it in the forward area, for, as he put it, "It wouldn't stop an expended flare."

On December 5th, we left Bazentin at 2 p.m. and moved into the Flers sector, "A" and "C" Companies garrisoning the line in front of Gird Support ("A" Company on the right) whilst "B" and "D" Companies were in support in Grass Lane, and Battalion Headquarters occupied a chalky tunnel in Bull's Run, about two hundred yards east of the village of Flers.

The trenches in this sector were a decided improvement on those we occupied during our previous tour of duty in front of Gueudecourt, although the left company's sector left much to be desired. They were duckboarded and revetted in most parts, and "A" Company's sector also contained two deep dug-outs, one of which was used as a regimental aid post.

There was a gap of nearly two hundred yards between the two companies, which had to be covered in double-quick time by runners and other persons, who had cause to visit the left company during the hours of daylight, for the enemy snipers were well aware of the fact and generally had a couple of shots whilst the gap was being traversed.

In taking over the left sector the Compay Commander had been informed that it was a "secret trench," and that the enemy was not aware of its existence. As a result, Major Rafferty would not allow any firing to take place during the daytime and *strafed* unmercifully whenever a runner or other venturesome person ran the gauntlet by sprinting across the gap and approaching the trench in daylight. However, in view of the fact that the trench showed plainly on all aerial photographs and, in addition, received its full share of the shellfire which was distributed along the front, the idea was not encouraged by the Commanding Officer, and died a natural death before we vacated the line.

The support companies occupied a trench and some dug-outs built into a bank in a valley running from Headquarters to the front line, known as Grass Lane. Being hidden from observation (except from the high ground near Bapaume), and an obvious approach to the front line, the valley received a fair amount of searching fire, but the companies located there were not worried much from concentrated or aimed shooting. Their duties comprised carrying rations to the front line companies at night, and also R.E. material for improving the front line. They also supplied working parties for improving the communication trench which led from Grass Lane into the front line. In parts, this trench was was almost impassable, the mud coming well above the knees, and in order to make progress, it was necessary to jump up on top and run some twenty or thirty yards and again enter the trench where the mud was not so deep.

The R.M.O. did wonderful work in his aid post during this tour in the line. The casualties were few, and so he concentrated on keeping the men as fit as possible. The dug-out which he occupied soon developed into a small hospital, where men were kept for twenty hours or more off duty and given the few medical comforts which he had at his disposal. He also had two primus stoves, upon which he made hot cocoa and milk (supplied by the Comforts Fund) and which he supplied to every man in the front line throughout the night, they being allowed to come along in pairs for a quarter of an hour each. He was ably assisted in this work by Cpl. Johnson, Hedley Gillard, Sid Kershaw, and many of the stretcher-bearers. The latter men were also detailed by him to inspect the men in the front line daily, to see that no one was wearing puttees (which tended to stop the circulation and encourage trench feet) and to examine every man's feet to see that no symptons of this complaint were appearing. It was also the duty of the platoon commanders to see that every man rubbed his feet daily with a special white powder which was now being issued instead of whale oil.

On December 5th, Capt. Burt returned to the Battalion together with 2nd-Lieuts. L. T. Butler and A. S. Webb and 94 reinforcements, which brought our strength up to 32 officers and 806 other ranks.

An inter-company relief was effected on the night of 7th-8th December without incident, when "B" and "D" Companies changed places with "A" and "C" Companies respectively.

Major L. M. Mullen left us on December 8th to command the 9th Battalion, with the rank of Lieutenant-Colonel, as from 1st December.

We were experiencing some very wet weather at this period, and orders were received from Brigade that the men were not to do more than forty-eight hours duty at a time in the line. In consequence, the two line companies were again relieved on the nights of 9th-10th and 11th-12th December.

The cooking arrangements were supervised by Sgt.-Cook Geo. Storey and were carried out in the cellars of the houses in the village of Flers. Drying rooms to which the men in the line could send their wet socks and gum-boots were established and dry sets were received in exchange when the rations were sent up. Hot meals were sent into the line twice during the night—just after dusk and just before dawn. The evening meal generally consisted of a hot stew or curry and tea, while the morning meal was usually bacon (and sometimes porridge) with tea. The dry rations were sent up in sandbags containing five men's rations and had to last the whole day, whilst the hot meal was conveyed in a "hot food container." This latter receptacle was a tin about two feet six inches in height, with an outer covering. The intervening space was packed with a non-conductive material, which gave to the container many of the properties of a thermos flask, and thus kept food hot for a number of hours. The containers were fitted with straps and were shaped to fit on to a man's back, and usually held rations for forty men.

An unfortunate occurrence happened on 11th December, when a party of fourteen men, under the command of Cpl. Nicholson, proceeded up to the line with the morning rations. As already stated, the communication trench leading to the front line was almost impassable in parts, and even in daytime it was customary to proceed along the top in order to make headway. It will be understood, therefore, that a heavily-laden carrying party would ignore the trench altogether and take an overland track to the line with comparative safety. The right boundary of the Battalion's sector was where the continuation of Grass Lane crossed the front line, and the ground here was of such a low-lying nature that it was nothing less than a quagmire, and quite untenable, and in consequence there was a gap of 150 to 200 yards between us and the 2nd Brigade unit on our right, which was patrolled at regular intervals during the night. Cpl. Nicholson had been on ration fatigue on more than one preceding occasion and always made for the line in the vicinity of the right flank. On this particular morning, however, he must have kept too far down the slope, and instead of striking the right flank, he and his party walked right through the gap and were not aware of the fact until they were fired upon by the Germans, within a few yards of their parapet. They immediately withdrew, and in so doing two men were wounded. Cpl. Nicholson very gallantly went back for one of them, and was killed. The remainder literally fell into our own lines, in great disorder, and on mustering them it was discovered that, in addition to the three casualties already mentioned, Pvts. Knight, Nightingale and Boultbee were missing.

By this time it was daylight. A patrol was sent out after darkness had fallen again, to endeavour to find the missing men in the hope that they were wounded and unable to move. But a strong German fighting patrol was already out, and, bringing superior fire to bear on our patrol, caused the latter to retire. Pvt. Boultbee eventually turned up forty-eight hours later. He had dug a place of concealment in a shell-hole with his hands within a few yards of the German barbed wire, where he had to stay for over two days and a night, before he had a chance of escaping. Pvts. Nightingale and Knight were afterwards reported "killed," their bodies being identified at a later period, when our line was advanced. Needless to say, after this incident a tight strand of wire was stretched across the gap to prevent a repetition.

We were relieved by the 10th Battalion on the evening of December 12th ("relief complete" being reported at 8.25 p.m.) and proceeded back along the old duckboard track through Delville Wood, past the Australian Comforts Fund stall, to a tented camp ("C" Camp) at Bazentin-le-Grand. The men were extremely tired and required a lot of urging to complete the long march, many of them wanting to sleep on the wet roadside, but those of the officers and N.C.O.'s who were not too heavily laden themselves carried the rifles and packs of the worst cases, and by coaxing some and ordering others, the remnants finally arrived at the camp just after midnight.

On inspecting the camp site next morning, the Commanding Officer discovered that the tents had been pitched on almost the worst place on the whole of the surrounding countryside, and he took the opportunity of pointing out its disadvantages to the Divisional Commander, Major-General Sir H. B. Walker, who visited us that day. The latter could plainly see the men drawing their mid-day meal from the field cookers, and floundering about knee-deep in mud. He quickly appreciated the deterrent effect these conditions would have upon the men, and promised to see what he could do. As a result, we moved into the adjacent camp ("B' Camp), composed of Nissen huts, on the next day. At this time, the Battalion occupied the role of "D" Battalion of the Brigade (Divisional Reserve).

The weather was wet and cold while we were in this camp, snow falling on more than one occasion. Lt. G. T. Gandy (Battalion Lewis Machine-Gun Officer) drew up a very comprehensive syllabus of Lewis Gun instruction, which would give every company its full complement of gunners, with a large number of semi-trained men as a reserve to fall back upon. With the instructors at his disposal, this syllabus was largely put into operation. The remainder of the Battalion were sent out in large parties, some of which were utilised in burying cables; some did duty as unloading parties at the railhead, which was near by; while others were also employed in building the Decauville light railway, which was pushing its way along the valley in rear of Flers. A certain number of men were always kept in camp to drive in piles on which to fix the duckboards, and thus give us dry communications throughout the camp.

The R.M.O. was much concerned at this period over the health of the Battalion, and the melancholia with which it seemed to be suffering. He discussed it on many occasions with the Commanding Officer and other members of Headquarters, and pointed out the apathy with which the men carried out all their duties. He emphasised the fact that one never heard singing in the huts, and a distinct absence of practical joking among the men—at other times so pronounced and typical —was noticeable. With a view to improving things, officers were urged to visit the men's huts more after working hours and encourage them to liven up and, in a diplomatic manner, ask for suggestions to rouse the camp in view of the approaching festive season. The results, however, were disappointing, and the Padre's efforts to organise a concert were equally futile. The Somme winter, with its mud, wet, and depressing atmosphere, had the Battalion in its grip, and did not release it until trench warfare temporarily ceased, at the end of February, 1917, when the exhilarating effects of an advance roused the unit from its lethargy. Now that the war is over and we can view the whole period from a proper perspective, it can be said, without fear of contradiction, that the morale of the 12th Battalion was never so low as during the month of December, 1916.

During all this period the Quartermaster's store and transport lines were situated at Pommiers Redoubt at Montauban, where the men and horses existed under deplorable conditions. Having read a description of the trenches in the front line, it should not be difficult to imagine transport lines under similar conditions, with the constant in and out traffic of G.S. wagons, water-carts and pack mules. The horses and mules had constantly to be moved, as, owing to their natural shiftiness when on the lines, the mud became deeper and deeper, until it was well nigh up to their bellies, and to prevent them from being entirely bogged a new site was picked for the location of the lines at frequent intervals. Most of the Divisional transport lines were situated within this vicinity, and it was by no means an uncommon occurrence for a horse or mule to be bogged in the mud, as a result of which it had to be shot.

The life of the transport drivers at this time was not to be envied, and they must all look back on it as a kind of nightmare. Long hours, heavy work, irregular meals, comfortless surroundings, with little sleep, and an element of danger at times, comprised their cheerless existence. They had to be up long before daylight feeding their horses and grooming them as much as possible, after which they took them to water. During the morning practically a full team went to Railhead with the Quartermaster to draw rations and fodder for a whole Battalion. Then came the loading of pack mules, and an early start would be made for the

line in order to cover as much ground as possible
in daylight, when the convoy was invariably
accompanied by both the Transport Officer and
Quartermaster. A limber for the Battalion mail, a
water-cart for water, the mess-cart for Ordnance, a
half-dozen trips detailed by the Brigade Transport
Officer, in addition to the usual routine and an
occasional tour of piquet duty, will serve to illustrate the strenuous life these men led during the
Somme winter of 1916. And as a reward, the A.A.
and Q.M.G. would inspect the lines and *strafe*
to some order because the harness was not oiled
and the steel-work burnished!

On December 21st, without shifting its location
in any way, the Battalion took over the duties of
"C" Battalion (Brigade Reserve). The change did
not affect the men in any way, who still carried on
with their working parties, but was merely promulgated to the officers; it chiefly concerned the
Commanding Officer, whose orders in case of attack
on the Divisional front were somewhat altered.

As soon as it was known that the Battalion was
to stay in this camp for more than a fortnight, it
was suggested that an officers' mess should be
formed in a spare Nissen hut, and, for the first time
in France, the officers messed together.

There was very little to distinguish Christmas
Day, 1916, from any of the 359 days which had
preceded, from a point of view of routine, for the
working parties went out just the same as usual,
although perhaps the officers in charge of same
were unofficially told not to work the men too hard
and that no questions would be asked if they
returned a little earlier than usual.

The Quartermaster (Lieut. O. J. Roper, who had
a few days previous relieved Lieut. G. P. Potter, who

DECEMBER, 1916

was evacuated sick) did his best to put on a nice, appetising meal, but the possibilities were very limited. The usual rations were once again supplemented by an issue of Swallow and Ariel's Christmas pudding, whilst tinned fruit and cake were purchased with regimental funds. The Christmas Billy of 1915 was replaced this year by a Christmas parcel issued by the Australian Comforts Fund, and which was fully appreciated by all the recipients.

Our functions were again altered on December 30th, when we became "B" Battalion (Brigade Support), being relieved by the 9th Battalion, whilst we, in our turn, relieved the 11th Battalion. "A" and "C" Companies were situated in Launceston Camp, Bazentin-le-Grand, whilst "B" and "D" Companies were in Switch and Gap Trenches (not to be recognised as the same trenches occupied by us early in November, however, owing to the many alterations and improvements which had been effected). Battalion Headquarters were situated in a ruined house, opposite the church, in the village of Flers, with a cellar beneath. This meant that some companies were no less than three miles from Headquarters, and the promulgation of orders and general administration was made very difficult.

Capt. Johnston, the R.M.O., was evacuated with the mumps on the day of the move, and his place was filled during his absence by Capt. O. A. Field.

The Battalion was fully employed in supplying working parties to carry on the various works in progress on the Brigade front. Generally speaking, these consisted (as far as our particular unit was concerned) in laying a track for the Decauville railway by carrying bricks and rubble from the ruined houses in the village, and building a good support line in rear of the front line, known as Hay Reserve. A Battalion Works Officer was appointed for the first time at this period, Lieut. C. N. Richardson being the first officer to carry out the duties. It was his responsibility to divide the men placed at his disposal into parties and allot them to specific tasks to carry out during their working hours; he also requisitioned for R.E. material and arranged for it to be ready waiting on the job when the working party arrived; he advised the Adjutant when he considered that too many men were employed on a job, and suggested means by which they could be more suitably employed, and last, but not least, he compiled the daily "Works Report" and "Return of Material Used" and forwarded them to Brigade Headquarters. Too much praise cannot be given to Lieut. Richardson for the manner in which he tackled the job, as I, personally, as Adjutant, know the volume of work and worry he saved me. He was also largely responsible for the congratulatory remarks made by the Brigadier concerning the quantity and quality of the work carried out by the Battalion in this sector.

It is pleasing to know that the value of the work performed by the Battalion during the fighting in the summer months, together with the sterling qualities of its Commanding Officer, were recognised. Lieut.-Col. C. H. Elliott was awarded the Distinguished Service Order in the New Year's list of Honours and Awards. Lieut. E. W. D. Laing was at the same time awarded the Military Cross.

A well-known and original member of the Battalion, Pvt. C. B. Thorne, of "B" Company, was killed by shell-fire on January 6th, 1917, and was buried by the Padre, Capt. W. K. Douglas, on the outskirts of the village, and his death caused a gloom in the company to which he belonged.

JANUARY, 1917

The Battalion was relieved on the night 8th-9th January by its sister Battalion, the 52nd, and on relief "A" and "C" Companies moved back by train direct to Dernancourt, whilst Headquarters, "B" and "D" Companies spent the night at Perth Camp, on the opposite side of the Montauban-Longueval road to Bernafay Wood. As some of the Headquarters details were leaving Flers, a shell burst close to one party and killed Bootmaker-Sergeant Z. Poultney, while the Gas N.C.O., Sgt. Les. Brill, was wounded.

The 11th and remaining portion of the 12th Battalions entrained at Quarry Siding, in trucks, at 12.30 p.m. on January 9th, and proceeded to Meaulte, from which place we marched *via* Vivier Mill to our old billets at Dernancourt. The next day, 2nd-Lieut. F. Marriott reported to the Battalion with twenty-nine men returning to the Battalion from wounds and sickness, and also forty-one partially-trained men. These latter men were inspected by the Commanding Officer, who was well pleased with their appearance and general bearing. Before allotting them to companies, he explained to them that they must consider it a privilege to have been allowed to join their unit in the field before their training was fully completed, but it was considered that a week's training in company with seasoned N.C.O.'s and men would be as beneficial as a month's training in the Bull Ring at Etaples, and he hoped that they would make every effort to prove the statement to be true.

The weather was still cold, rain and sleet falling almost every day, unceasingly. Training was well nigh impossible under these conditions, and in order to allow the men to recover from their strenuous period in the forward area, the Divisional Commander authorised a rest of three days, the only duties being internal fatigues, roll calls and general cleaning up. We were also allotted a day for bathing the Battalion at the baths at Vivier Mill. There was a good supply of hot showers, and the men were given a clean set of underclothing and towels. A certain amount of humour was introduced into the bathing parade, owing to the fact that everything was done on the blast of the whistle. You first undressed and stood waiting, in a somewhat chilly atmosphere, for the water to be turned on; if you were slow in undressing, you missed a certain amount of time under the shower, and consequently it often happened that a man was well covered with a good lather of soap when the last whistle went and the water was turned off; he had to make room for the next batch of men, without having a chance of rinsing the soap off.

On Sunday, January 14th, we moved our billets to the village of Bresle, situated about four miles away on the other side of the Albert-Amiens road, and two days later the Commanding Officer went on Blighty leave, when Major F. G. Giles, of the 10th Battalion, commanded us during his absence. Bresle was the usual peasant type of village found throughout the Somme cantonment, and situated in a natural shaped basin, with low hills all round it. The billets were considerably better than those we had left at Dernancourt, but the roads passing through the village contained an even bigger quantity of mud. "A" Company were fortunate in being self-contained in an immense billet, which could only be described as a stadium. There were tier upon tier of bunks all the way round, which provided ample accommodation for the whole company, whilst the space in the centre was nearly big enough for a platoon to drill. Efforts were made by

JANUARY, 1917

Brigade to commandeer it for concerts during the evenings, but we protested, although the Padre promoted a boxing tournament, at which Chapman, Bill Fisher and other Battalion "pugs" gave some truly marvellous exhibitions of the art. A round of blindfold boxing was also given, but the Padre, who was acting as referee, got such a rough time that he began to suspect it was a put-up job and that the competitors could see beneath their bandages, and declared the fight "off."

During the latter portion of our stay at Bresle, the weather became exceedingly cold and a heavy fall of snow covered the ground, followed immediately by a prolonged frost. Training continued both in billets and on parade grounds, and on one occasion the Divisional Commander came over to inspect the Battalion in attack. At the conclusion of the practise, arms were piled, and "A" and "B" Companies and "C" and "D" Companies respectively entered into a lively snow fight. It resulted in a win for "B" and "D" Companies, and every man in the Battalion thoroughly enjoyed himself, and it was indeed gratifying to see them once more regain their natural high spirits, which had been so sadly lacking during the preceding months.

Orders were again received for another move, and on January 24th the Battalion relieved the 1st Cameron Highlanders in a Nissen hut camp at Fricourt Farm. We were timed to leave Bresle at 9.45 a.m., but the transport of the 11th Battalion, which was immediately in front of us, delayed us considerably owing to the fact that their horses had not been fitted with frost cogs and consequently experienced great difficulty in getting their transport up the frosty and slippery hill out of Bresle. We marched through Henencourt, Millencourt and

R

Albert with one hundred yards distance between companies and two hundred yards between transport and marching troops. As we were emerging from the outskirts of Albert, a German Taube flew over and dropped a bomb in the vicinity of one of the companies; one man was wounded slightly from a flying splinter.

We remained at this camp for four days, during which time the snow still lay thick on the ground and the frost showed no signs of abating. Parties were detailed for road repair work, and a certain amount of camp improvement was effected. The men were also given Lewis machine-gun and musketry instruction in the huts, and physical training and supervised recreational training.

On Sunday, January 28th, we were relieved by the 5th Durham Light Infantry and proceeded, with intervals of one hundred yards between platoons, to a camp at Bazentin-le-Petit. The camp was adjacent to a wood, which had suffered badly in the preceding summer's fighting, and in consequence provided an almost unlimited source of firewood, which was freely used by the men in their efforts to keep warm during the cold evenings and nights. The cold at this time was so intense that, although good fires were maintained in the huts until well after 10 p.m., in the morning everything containing any moisture was frozen hard, including tins of "Ideal" milk, eggs, and the boots themselves. Even the ice in the bread used to crackle as it was being cut.

Every day the Battalion supplied a large party, consisting of six officers and from 400 to 450 men, for work on the Anzac Corps Railway, while the men remaining were utilised in improving and cleaning up the camp generally. A great deal of interest was aroused in the daily inspection of huts, when the competition between companies and platoons became so keen that the cleanliness and tidy manner in which bedding, rifles and equipment and mess utensils were arranged was almost brought to perfection, for which great praise was received from the Brigadier.

Two officers and one hundred men from "B" Company were detached for duty with Lieut. Dentry (detached for duty from one of the other Battalions in the Division) at Clarke's Dump, in the vicinity of Highwood, and were utilised in unloading stores for the dump and supervising their distribution to authorised persons. Lieut. Heritage was also detailed as O.C. Bazentin Baths, but he merely had to wait for the water in the pipes to thaw, with the full conviction that they would leak badly when this did happen, and which, consequently, would mean a further delay pending their repair.

During the end of the first week of February, it became known to us that we were shortly to relieve the 4th Battalion in the Eaucourt L'Abbaye sector, and it then became customary for forward reconnaissance parties of officers and N.C.O.'s to proceed up to the support areas in order to learn the geography of our new sector. The approach to the line was *via* Highwood, where the New Zealanders put up such a gallant fight, and thence by the Decauville railway line, past Elm Siding to a point somewhat more than a thousand yards this side of the Butte de Warlencourt.

The actual relief took place on the evening of February 11th and was complete at 8.30 p.m., when "A" Company occupied the right sector of the line and "B" Company that on the left. "C" and "D"

Companies were in support in the cellars under the ruins of the old *abbaye* or monastery, which, although substantially built and proof against shell-fire, were hardly commodious enough for two companies, and in consequence the men were rather crowded. Headquarters were situated in some dug-outs built into a bank along Hexham Road, just at the spot where the communication trench (Pioneer Avenue) started, while the Q.M. store and cookers were located at Pioneer Camp, at Bazentin-le-Petit.

The front line in this sector was wretched, and afforded very little shelter in parts. In many places it merely consisted of a line of posts connected by a shallow trench which was so pitted with shell-holes that it was difficult to differentiate it from the surrounding area. The posts were formed by deepening and enlarging the shell-holes sufficiently to hold an N.C.O. and three men, whilst in some cases shell-holes were connected to form a larger post of six men. The front line was respectable in parts and was even duckboarded, but the frozen state of the ground at present prevented this work from being continued. On this occasion the German trenches were nearer than we had yet experienced them in France, the width of No Man's Land being a shade under a hundred yards in parts. It often happened that enemy flares would fall right into our front line posts and burn brightly for some time before going out, and although the German flare was superior to our Verey light in both brilliancy and range, yet it was generally supposed that the enemy posted his "flare kings" in shell-holes in front of his line.

The barbed wire on this sector was conspicuous by its weakness rather than from the protection it gave, for the whole of the Battalion front was covered by one strand only! It certainly prevented parties and individuals from losing their way in moving from post to post and thus wandering out into No Man's Land, but the garrison placed no faith in it in case of an attack.

On the right of our sector there was a small local salient, occupied by the enemy and known as The Maze, which the 9th Battalion had been detailed to capture in a minor operation in the near future, and for which purpose they were at present training hard at Albert. In the meantime, the heavy artillery would pound away at the trenches in the hope of entirely obliterating, or at any rate demoralising, the garrison. This worried the Hun considerably, and in retaliation he peppered our line at night with "pineapple" bombs (a light trench mortar projectile, ribbed like a Mills bomb and shaped like a pineapple, and therefore very much resembling that fruit). The range suited the mortar well, and the firing was so accurate that many of the bombs fell right into our line, and on February 15th actually wiped out one of "D" Company's Lewis machine-gun posts, Pvt. Rice being killed and four others wounded.

Earlier the same day, we had been warned that the "heavies" were going to register on the The Maze and carry out a concentrated shoot, and in view of the inaccuracy of their initial shots, before correct ranges had been discovered and errors adjusted, we were told to withdraw our front line troops before daybreak and put them into the support line. It was just as well that we did, for our front line was a total wreck and hardly distinguishable when we re-occupied it at night. Owing to the frozen nature of the ground, the detonating power of the shells was increased considerably, and our right company's line was freely pitted with shell-holes varying from four to eight feet in depth and porportionately wide, whilst huge boulders of frozen earth weighing anything up to half-a-ton littered the countryside. If our own guns had played havoc with our front line in this manner, we only hoped that the enemy fared still worse.

"C" and "D" Companies relieved "A" and "B" Companies on the night of 15th-16th February, and the frost which had held so hard for the last five weeks commenced to relax and the thaw set in very rapidly.

Just in rear of our support line, a section of the Heavy Trench Mortar Battery had a position from which they used to fire on to the Butte de Warlencourt, on our left flank. This trench mortar used to fire a huge projectile, and was always referred to by the boys as "The Flying Pig." The mortar, weighing several hundredweights, must have caused the enemy much annoyance, and it is generally believed that a "pineapple" barrage launched against our right company on the night of February 16th was their method of retaliation. The whole thing was so intense, and so sudden, that concerted action was almost impossible, and individual commanders—whether officers or N.C.O.'s—had to act quickly on their own initiative. The sound of the bombardment was plainly heard at Battalion Headquarters, but before the cause or location could be discovered and the artillery advised, the tornado had ceased. For some ten or fifteen minutes the sky literally rained "pineapple" bombs, and the darkness was illuminated with the trail of sparks which followed in the wake of each bomb. The range was so accurate and the bombardment so sudden and intense, but for one brief moment it looked as if the garrison would stampede.

It is at such critical moments that the instinct of leadership asserts itself, and "C" Company proved that it had its full quota of officers and N.C.O.'s with this quality. The only thing possible under the circumstances was to rally the men and push them *forward* into No Man's Land, and this was quickly done by Lieuts. Sellick, Dobson and Radford and Sgts. "Cock" Russell and Cole. Together they formed a strong line of skirmishers about fifty yards in front of our line, and quite immune from any "pineapple" bombs. Too much praise cannot be given to Sgt. Russell for the excellent manner in which he handled his men and the wonderful example he set them. Lieut. Radford's work, also, was highly commendable, more specially owing to the fact that this was his first tour of duty in the line. Cpl. Cummings handled his Lewis machine-gun team with skill and coolness, and although wounded before the bombardment ceased, refused to leave the line until things again became normal. Lieut. Cyril Richardson became a casualty very early in the "stunt," and although suffering from a painful wound in the thigh, he crawled a considerable distance down the trench to a 'phone and apprised Headquarters of what was happening. The saddest event of all, however, was the death of the Company Commander, Capt. J. A. W. Kayser; almost the first bomb that exploded wounded him severely and he crawled into a cupola dug-out, which was used as a forward Company Headquarters, to await the stretcher-bearers, but almost immediately another bomb struck the top of the dug-out and penetrated before exploding, and in doing so ignited a large stock of coloured Verey pistol ammunition and killed Capt. Kayser. In his death the Battalion suffered a great loss, for, apart from his thoroughness in training and administrative work, he had proved his bravery both at Anzac and Pozieres. The incident was made more pathetic a few days later when his promotion to Major, dated a few days before his death, was promulgated. In addition to the casualties mentioned, L.-Cpl. Miles, Pvts. Stemp, Davidson and Pennefather were killed and six others wounded.

Capt. L. E. Burt supplied the only humorous incident which occurred in this sector, when he and an artillery officer were observing the effect of one of the "heavy's" shoots. The 'phone at Headquarters was buzzed frantically and I was requested to speak. "There's a Hun coming down Blue Cut Road in broad daylight," says Burt. I wanted to know why our fellows didn't shoot him, but was informed that he was right inside our lines. I at once roused R.S.M. Joe Cooper and the Orderly Room Staff (Cpl. Freddie Green and Norman Powell), and with loaded rifles they advanced along Blue Cut Road like sleuth-hounds without seeing anyone, when suddenly a head bobbed up, and the Hun patrol turned out to be nothing more alarming than one of the "Flying Pig" merchants looking for a few bits of firewood.

The method of raising the gas alarm in the forward area was by sounding a Klaxon horn, which was situated at Battalion Headquarters and under the control of a gas guard. One evening, about 7 p.m., the horn started to blow with a penetrating sound, and before many seconds had elapsed the horns for miles to right and left were sounding freely. I rushed out of the dug-out and shook the frightened sentry and asked him what was the matter. He muttered that he only wanted to "see how the thing worked," and the result had so frightened him that he hadn't the presence of mind to turn it off.

On the night of February 17th, "C" Company was again subjected to fire from the German light mortars, and one bomb landed on the parapet of a post and killed Pvt. Woods, one of the garrison.

At 4 a.m. during the same night, a wonderful spectacle was presented, some two to three miles on our left, when the Naval Division attacked and captured the villages of Irles and Miraumont, together with ten officers and six hundred other ranks prisoners. The German method of signalling by coloured lights was well illustrated, although I am inclined to think that every available message must have been signalled, as every kind of flare was used, including white, red, green, golden clusters, "bunches of grapes," and many others which have not been given names.

We were relieved on the night of 19th-20th February by the 10th Battalion, and were then disposed of as follows:—Headquarters in Yarra Reserve, three platoons of "A" Company in Hexham Road, three platoons of "B" and "D" Companies in Flers Switch Trench, and "C" Company with the remaining platoon of "A," "B" and "D" Companies in Pioneer Camp at Bazentin-le-Petit.

Chapter XIV.

THE GERMAN WITHDRAWAL — SPRING, 1917

FOR the next few days we furnished working parties for improving the support and communication trenches (Yarra Reserve, Gaby Glide, Yarra Bank and Pioneer Avenue), and also carrying parties. A party from "A" Company repeatedly received orders to report to a certain "Turk's Dump" for carrying duties, and although the location and map reference were given, and although search was made for it by daylight, it was never discovered by the 12th Battalion. I am certain that the officers detailed for the job doubted whether the dump ever existed.

The time was now drawing near for the 9th Battalion to carry out their operation on The Maze, and they commenced sending out patrols to locate enemy posts and machine-guns and to investigate the condition of the enemy's wire. A sensation was therefore caused on February 24th, when a daylight patrol went out at 5 p.m. and discovered that the enemy's front line was empty! This, of course, may have been due to the intense bombardment which had recently been brought to bear on this

FEBRUARY, 1917

locality, but the abnormal quietness and absence of flares during the evening aroused the suspicions of Brigade Headquarters, and the Brigadier took the initiative of issuing an order announcing to all units that the enemy was believed to have evacuated his front line, *and that the whole line would advance!* The effect was electrical, and any remaining signs of the winter lethargy were shaken off like an old garment. The men were at once obsessed with the idea that the Hun was at last on the move and that he must be kept moving.

Two companies were at once detailed for carrying duties with the 9th and 10th Battalions and were at their entire disposal. Encouraging news was received at 10 p.m. that the 9th Battalion had occupied Bank Trench and had found it empty (but containing several good, deep dug-outs) and that they were continuing the advance. At 10.30 p.m. the 10th Battalion occupied Gird Trench and discovered one poor, unfortunate German who could barely walk, as a result of trench feet in a very bad form.

During the morning of the next day, the enemy commenced to shell his vacated trenches, but in a very spasmodic and erratic manner, which proved fairly conclusively that, as yet, he had no idea of our new dispositions.

The Brigadier came up to our Battalion Headquarters just before noon and said that he would like the advance on the left sector to proceed more rapidly, and issued orders for the 12th Battalion to relieve the 10th Battalion as soon as possible. An operation order was at once despatched, instructing "C" and "D" Companies to relieve in the line, and "A" and "B" to take up support positions. The Commanding Officer and I then proceeded to the 10th Battalion's sector and arrived in the front line at 1 p.m., just as they were "hopping over the top" to occupy Wheat Trench. The enemy, in his retirement, had withdrawn almost the whole of his garrison and left a comparatively small rearguard of picked men, armed with a considerable number of machine-guns. As the 10th Battalion advanced over the open country in daylight they were subjected to very heavy machine-gun fire and suffered a considerable number of casualties, but after traversing from 800 to 1,000 yards they appeared to occupy the trench without a great deal of protracted opposition.

Our own companies commenced to arrive in artillery formation about 4 p.m., and came under fairly heavy artillery fire as they passed the vicinity of our old front line. Their approach to the line was opposed by heavy machine-gun fire, which necessitated advancing in skirmishing order by short rushes. A considerable number of casualties were suffered in this advance, more particularly amongst the officers, for Capt. L. E. Burt and Lieut. S. W. Dobson were wounded, whilst Lieuts. E. W. D. Laing, Frank Priddey and Frank Marriott were all wounded by the same sniper within a few moments of one another as they advanced along Blue Cut Road. Priddey received a serious wound in the shoulder and collar-bone, and Laing a painful and disfiguring facial wound, while Frank Marriott's distressing disability resulting from his wound is so well known that it scarcely requires mention. He ranks among Tasmania's few blinded soldiers, and yet manfully carries his disablement by occupying a seat in the Tasmanian House of Assembly.

It was afterwards recalled that practically every

officer who was wounded during this advance into the line was carrying a stick, or could in some manner be distinguished as an officer, proving (1) that it was aimed shooting, and (2) the necessity for officers to wear uniform and equipment similar to that worn by the N.C.O.'s and men.

The relief was not complete until about 10 p.m., when "C" and "D" Companies were in the front line in Wheat Trench, "A" and "B" Companies (together with the Regimental Aid Post) were in support in the old German trench, Gird Support, while Battalion Headquarters were in Turk Support in a dug-out previously occupied by "B" Company (when in the line) as a Company Headquarters. Later in the night, "B" Company was also ordered into the line.

Orders were at once issued for patrols to be sent out to gain touch with the enemy, and more particularly to ascertain if Malt Trench was occupied. This latter trench was about 300 yards in front, and fringing the village of Le Barque, extended well over to the left beyond the main Albert-Bapaume road. Lieut. Lines and about fifteen men volunteered for this duty, and after being out for nearly an hour were fired upon by the enemy from both Malt Trench and guns situated in the wooded outskirts of the village itself.

The next day, February 26th, the Commanding Officer went around to the companies and gained first-hand knowledge of the situation. All around Battalion Headquarters the bodies of 1st Brigade troops, as well as of a kilted Scottish Regiment, gave silent evidence of the effort that was made, as far back as November, to gain the high ground around Bapaume for winter occupation. The recently vacated front and support lines of the enemy were in a far worse condition than our own, and were well over the boot-tops in mud.

As the Colonel proceeded along the line, he stopped at a Lewis gun post and, pointing to some Germans who were plainly visible some distance away, asked the men to estimate the range. "About 600 yards, sir," was the average opinion, when the C.O. said, "Then why the devil don't you fire at them?" "They are too far away, sir," said the Corporal. "Get that idea out of your head," replied the C.O. "You've been so used to trench warfare that you think the rifle and machine-guns are not to be fired at targets more than 200 to 300 yards away. You must quickly realise, now that we are once again engaged in semi-open warfare, that the rifle will kill at over 3,000 yards, and that individual fire is considered effective up to 600 yards."

During the night, advice was received from the 18th Battalion, our our left, that they intended to advance and capture Malt Trench (on their frontage) together with an enemy post at Battery Copse at 1.30 p.m. on the 26th February.

Considerable sniping was carried out during the morning of February 26th, and our companies in the line eagerly awaited the advance of the 18th Battalion in order to give them plenty of covering fire, but zero hour passed without any movement taking place. Orders were then received for the 12th Battalion to advance, in conjunction with the 9th Battalion, on the right of Blue Cut Road and occupy Malt Trench, which was accordingly done at 4.30 p.m.

"B" Company made the initial advance and the

method adopted was by a patrol of thirty-three men, consisting mainly of Lewis gunners, bombers, and a few riflemen, under Lieut. G. H. C. Hart, which moved cautiously under cover of a bank in Blue Cut Road, and then bombed its way along Malt Trench. The Trench was only held lightly by the enemy and the garrison did not put up a very vigorous defence, only three of the patrol being wounded. "A" and "C" Companies then advanced, and in doing so encountered considerable machine-gun fire from Battery Copse.

As soon as darkness fell, patrols were sent out to the front and to the flank to gain touch with the enemy and with our flanking unit. Although one patrol went fully 300 yards to the left, almost half-way to the main road, no sign of the 18th Battalion was seen, and a message was subsequently sent to them conveying the information that Malt Trench was now ready for occupation. Sgt. Reg. Lapthorne also led a patrol into the village of Le Barque and discovered that it was still lightly held by the rearguard. The enemy fired a considerable number of "tear gas" shells during the early part of the night, which, although unpleasant, did no damage.

In the meantime, the Quartermaster had prepared and brought up a hot meal, which was carried up to the line. Blue Cut Road, the line of approach, was in a shocking state, especially for about 200 yards on either side of the old front line, and the carrying parties found it a very arduous task ploughing through the deep mud, tripping over barbed wire and avoiding deep shell-holes, with heavy hot-food containers on their backs. The road was almost obliterated in one spot and it became necessary to lay a white tape-line to prevent parties and individuals from losing their way.

I should like to mention, at this stage, that during the many tours of duty in the line which interspersed our two-and-a-half years of campaigning in France, there was never one night that Battalion Headquarters staff failed to send a hot meal (at least once) into the line. The credit of this is largely due to the Quartermasters—Lieut. Potter and Lieut. (afterwards Captain) H. E. Spotswood—with their competent staffs, and R.S.M. Joe Cooper and his successors, and to the Transport Officers, Lieuts. E. A. Shepherd and E. A. Potts. Of course, at times during the stress of fighting, a party was often delayed to such an extent that the food was comparatively cold when it arrived, while at other times casualties occurred amongst the carrying parties which resulted in a shortage in the hot ration. It sometimes happened that it was not possible to distribute food at isolated posts, and at other times when fighting was actually in progress the meal was not issued for a considerable period after its arrival, but the fact remains, nevertheless, that a genuine effort was made on all occasions to provide adequately for the comforts of the men in the line as far as hot meals were concerned.

During the evening the Commanding Officer again went up to the line and conferred with company commanders regarding the capture of the villages of Le Barque and Ligny-Thilloy, and Bark Trench on the left flank. The plan finally agreed upon was for "A" Company, under Capt. Newland, to advance up the left side of the village and to clear and occupy Bark Trench. "D" Company, under Capt. Harry Webber, were detailed to advance on the right flank of the village and to establish a strong post in a quarry about 150 yards along one of the roads of exit leading from Ligny-Thilloy. "C" Company (Capt. J. R. Jorgensen) were instructed to clear the village thoroughly by seeing that none of the enemy were lurking in the woods, or occupying the cellars under the houses, etc. They were then to withdraw to Wheat Trench and act as a Battalion Reserve, with the exception of an officer and twenty men detailed to establish a post on one of the roads leading from Le Barque to the main road. "B" Company (Capt. S. R. Houghton) were also instructed to remain in Wheat Trench and act as a forward report centre, with the exception of an officer and twenty-five men detailed to establish a post on the Le Barque—Bapaume road, just clear of the village. It was suggested that the attack should take place at dawn, thus preventing the enemy from launching a counter-attack during the hours of darkness, to which the C.O. agreed.

Between 3 a.m. and 4 a.m. the companies commenced to move out and take up their battle positions. "A" Company found it necessary to move through the woody outskirts of the village in file, and at a convenient spot came into the open on the left flank and adopted the formation line of platoons in file, with Lieut. Heritage on the left, then Sgt. Jack Whittle, Lieut. Leicester Butler and Lieut. Bensley on the right.

The signal for the advance—a pistol shot—was given just before dawn, and the companies moved forward without any artillery support. The companies moving through the village and on the right flank did not meet with a great deal of opposition, and force of numbers induced the enemy to retire without putting up much of a fight, and before very long each platoon had established a well-sited post at, or in the vicinity of, the spot laid down in the operation order. "A" Company, on the left of the village, advanced silently and cautiously, platoons keeping touch one with the other. Owing partly to the silent manner in which the advance was made, and partly to the undergrowth through which they were passing, the attack was almost on top of the enemy before being detected, the alarm being raised by some of the men tripping over a tension wire, which was held up by a stunted hedge immediately in front of the enemy position. A verbal challenge was at once given, followed by the firing of a red flare. This was responded to by considerable machine-gun fire from the left front, which caused a number of casualties. The men at once took whatever shelter they could obtain, the majority in shell-holes, and others merely lying flat on the ground. Word was passed along to be ready to storm the post when the command was given, and on the command "Rush," every man responded vigorously. Lieut. Butler and Sgt. Whittle were the first on the scene, and threw some bombs into the midst of the enemy with very deadly effect, three of the enemy being killed in the post and about eight more being wounded, as they retreated, by a Lewis machine-gun which was rapidly brought into action. The whole encounter was short and sharp, and, owing to the determined manner in which the men attacked, the resistance of the enemy was of short duration. While this had been happening, Lieut. Heritage, with his platoon on the left, had successfully dislodged the machine-gun, which had previously caused trouble, from a position at the junction of Misty Way and Warlencourt Road. In the dull light he continued his advance, but in some way slightly mistook his direction. Seeing an occupied post in front, he carefully stalked the position and finally called upon the commander to surrender by threatening him with the point of the revolver. He was somewhat astonished, therefore, when he was assured that "that would be alright," and recognised the voice of his company commander, Capt. Newland. The advance continued in accordance with the operation order, and at 6 a.m. Battalion Headquarters were able to advise Brigade that the villages of Le Barque and Ligny Thilloy were in our possession.

During the fighting, Capt. Newland and Lieut. Bensley were both slightly wounded, whilst Capt. Webber was also wounded about 9 a.m., when passing through the village, and in consequence Capt. Houghton was sent forward to take charge of the front line.

During the day, 27th, our only trouble was a little scattered shelling in and around the captured villages, but insufficient in volume to cause any worry. During the latter part of the afternoon, companies were again ordered to advance the line in conjunction with the 11th Battalion on the right, in order to envelop and capture the village of Thilloy. Under the command of Capt. Houghton, posts were successfully established some 400 to 500 yards in front, and in the absence of the 11th Battalion, Lieut. P. F. Heurtley-Reed threw out a light screen of men around the left front of the village, all of which was effected without opposition or casualties. The 11th Battalion came up shortly afterwards and took over their proper frontage.

During these operations, which had lasted three days only, the Battalion had been responsible for advancing the line some 2,000 yards, capturing three villages together with one solitary prisoner. As a result of the advance our casualties consisted of eight officers wounded, sixteen other ranks killed and forty-eight wounded.

Singularly good work was done by Sgt. Hillman in bringing the Lewis gun rapidly in action and inflicting heavy casualties on the retiring enemy on the morning of the capture of the village. Pvte. T. H. Magrath was also responsible for good work with his gun, but, unfortunately, he received a serious wound in his right arm, which ultimately resulted in amputation. He arrived at the Aid Post in Gird Trench with his lacerated wound caked with mud, and, in spite of the pain he must have been suffering, insisted on a message being sent back to his company telling them where he had left his bag of spare parts, which was afterwards found.

Pvte. Taylor, of "B" Company, also did excellent work as a runner and guide, and through his wonderful sense of direction at night time, he was able to guide his company successfully into Wheat Trench on the night of the relief.

Stretcher-bearers do good work at all times and it is hard to differentiate between them, but Pvts. O'Neill and Sam Clark on this occasion not only showed great bravery in rescuing their wounded comrades under heavy machine-gun fire, but were also untiring in their duties, which consisted in some exceptionally long carries over difficult country.

On the evening of the 27th February, we were relieved by the 4th Battalion, who commenced to arrive at 8 p.m., but for some unknown reason they failed to bring their machine-guns with them, and so our Lewis gunners, together with a couple of officers and N.C.O.'s, were not able to leave the line until well after midnight, and consequently preferred to spend the night in a dug-out in Wheat Trench and continue the journey in the morning.

Relief was reported complete at 11.40 p.m., and

after a long, weary tramp we arrived at No. 3 Camp, Bazentin-le-Petit, at 2 a.m., where a hot meal and warm blankets awaited us, and every man went to sleep with the firm conviction that the Battalion had fully maintained its high reputation, and with an inward feeling that perhaps we had materially assisted in bringing the end of the war somewhat nearer.

As a result of the operation, the following officer, N.C.O.'s and men received decorations: —

Military Cross.—Capt. S. R. Houghton.
Distinguished Conduct Medal.—Sgt. J. Whittle.
Military Medal.—Sgt. Possingham; Pvts. S. Clarke, J. O'Neill, L. Hassen, K. Driscoll, G. Taylor.

The next day the majority of the men slept in and enjoyed a well-earned rest, after which a parade was called, when a complete and correct casualty list was forwarded to Headquarters and lists of shortages taken. The men were also given every facility to clean themselves and scrape off some of mud with which they were still covered.

At 9.30 a.m. the following day (March 1st) the Battalion marched back to its old, familiar billets at Dernancourt, arriving at 1 p.m.

We expected to stay here for about five days, but it was eventually three weeks before we made another move. A syllabus of training was drawn up and regular parades commenced. It is deserving of note that at this period, owing to three company commanders having been wounded at Le Barque, Major Rafferty being on leave and Capt. Houghton evacuated sick, the only senior officers with the Battalion were the Commanding Officer and Capt.

Jorgensen, and, although the other companies were commanded by subalterns, yet the discipline and efficiency of the Battalion were seldom better.

Lieut. W. J. Kelly at this time had just returned from a school of instruction, where he had learnt the "model platoon" organisation, which he explained to the officers in a very capable and interesting lecture, to enable them to carry it into practice during the present period of training. In this organisation, "every man had a special task, being a rifleman, Lewis gunner, bomber, rifle grenadier or 'mopper-up.' The duty of the last named was to go over with the last line of the attackers, when the objective was an enemy trench, and on no account to pass the trench when it was captured, but to make an exhaustive search for any deep dug-outs and account (by capture or otherwise) for any enemy lurking therein. The necessity for these men had been learned in the Somme offensive, when repeatedly the first of a series of enemy trenches had been taken without opposition and passed over by our troops, who later on were shot in the back by the Huns, who emerged from deep dug-outs where they had been sheltering from our artillery fire."

The recent release from trench warfare seemed to put new life into the men and all signs of the winter melancholia passed away, and they carried out their drill and training with a keenness which had not been seen for some months. With the rattling of kerosene tins to represent a protective barrage, whistle blasts to represent enemy machine-guns, and heaps of stable manure (which littered the parade ground) to represent trenches, we practised attacks with two, three and four objectives.

Most of the men will also remember that Sgts.

Hillman and Ripper went on "Blighty leave" about this time, and on their return appeared on parade with Horseferry Road tailor-made tunics, "Lotus" trench boots and—gloves. They caused a stir for a while, until called aside and given a gentle hint that as there had been no mention of their commissions in orders, it would be better if they went off parade for a short while and returned looking more like N.C.O.'s.

The only other incidents worthy of note during our sojourn at Dernancourt are the facts that the weather was still wet and cold, snow falling on some occasions; the men were again able to have good baths and clean clothing from Vivier Mill at Meaulte; news was received that the 5th Australian Division was continuing the advance in the forward area and occupied Bapaume on 17th March; several lectures were delivered by Divisional Staff officers in the Church Army Hut to officers, and in some cases to N.C.O.'s.

We left Dernancourt on March 23rd and marched *via* Lavieville to billets at Baizieux. A slight diversion was caused when we were passing an aerodrome near the former village. A 'plane, in its efforts to land, crossed right over the road just as the Battalion was passing, and in doing so seemed to miss our heads by a matter of inches (but really by some thirty to forty feet) and caused a stampede in the column.

The day of the move was beautifully sunny, and as we had our lunch on the roadside the warmth of the sun could be distinctly felt, and it would have required very little persuasion to make us believe that spring had actually commenced, but the usual cold and inclement weather which followed proved that this was too good to be true.

The outstanding feature of Baizieux was its beautiful *chateau*, which accommodated the Divisional Commander and his staff.

No unit is ever anxious to be billetted in the same village as Divisional Headquarters, because, being under the eye of the Divisional Commander and his staff, it is expected to be exemplary in conduct and manner, and to some extent live under a cloud of restraint. Although no definite course of action was adopted by the Battalion to enforce "Sunday behaviour" during our ten days of rest and training, beyond the usual caution, it is gratifying to know that during unofficial conversations with the Divisional Commander and other Divisional Staff officers, the C.O. received some very congratulatory remarks regarding the smartness of our billet guards, the general behaviour of the troops, and the cleanliness of the billets and village.

Companies continued to train their men in musketry, bayonet fighting, bombing and Lewis gunnery, while signallers and the Intelligence Platoon also received instruction from their commanders.

Major R. A. Rafferty went to command the 11th Battalion, temporarily, on March 28th, and on the same day Major H. James, of the 1st Pioneer Battalion, joined us as temporary second-in-command.

The country around Baizieux was particularly suitable for training in open warfare, and it became customary to take a mid-day meal with us and spend the whole day in more advanced training when the weather permitted. A comprehensive "advance guard" scheme was successfully carried out under Brigade supervision on March 29th, when everything was more or less of a stereotyped nature, with the exception of a rabbit which was disturbed by the advancing troops, a half a company of whom chased and ultimately caught it.

The next day the whole Brigade carried out an attack practice under Divisional supervision, but the 12th Battalion were only used as supports and spent most of the time under cover of a high bank, enjoying the spring sun, which was shining all the morning.

On March 31st the Battalion carried out its first sports meeting in France, and, although modest when compared with others that we had at later dates, everyone entered into the spirit of the day and made it an unqualified success. In addition to the usual athletic events, for the first time we had competitions of a military nature, such as bomb throwing, bayonet fighting and Lewis gun drill.

The Divisional Commander, Major-Gen. Walker, reviewed the Brigade at Bresle on April 2nd, which proved to be a particularly cold day. The parade ground was on the top of a high slope and entirely exposed to the piercing wind which was blowing and which culminated in a snow storm before we had left the ground. The "march past" was anything but good, for the men had been kept waiting a long time in the cold, and in consequence their hands were so numbed that they could hardly hold their rifles. The Brigade marched in column of companies, and the flags for directing the march were so badly placed that after "changing direction," instead of approaching the saluting base at right angles it was inecessary to advance obliquely, and in consequence the left flank of each company at it passed was very ragged. The men, however, could not be blamed on this occasion.

The strength of the Battalion was now 40 officers and 977 other ranks, Lieuts. R. D. Newitt and J. H.

Snaden having joined us at Dernancourt, and Lieut. H. S. Uren at Baizieux, each bringing a draft of reinforcements. News was now received of the formation of the 6th Australian Division in England, and each Battalion was detailed to send a certain number of officers, with experience in the field, to form the nucleus of the new battalions. For this purpose Lieuts. Hart, Jacob, Gandy and Lines left the Battalion on April 4th and the days immediately preceding.

We left Baizieux on April 4th and marched to a hutted camp at Montauban. The day was particularly cold and a driving rain was beating in our face the whole time; it was one of the few occasions that we carried out a long march under these conditions. Almost everyone commented on the different appearance the area had now, compared with November, 1916, when we first passed through it. The roads were now in a fair state of repair, but the heaps of caked mud on either side gave evidence of the unceasing work of the Labour Battalions, whose duty it had been to keep them clean. All traffic now proceeded along the main Albert-Bapaume road, and in consequence the area in general appeared devoid of military occupation and it was hard to believe that only five weeks ago it had been a seething mass of transport lines and military organisations generally. As soon as the cookers arrived and were in position, a meal was prepared and the men attempted to dry their clothing.

The next day was a complete contrast, the sun shining brightly out of a clear sky, and the interesting country over which we marched made the men forget the length of the journey and the bodily fatigue which accompanied it. We set out along the old familiar road until we came to Bernafay Wood, when we took to a new duckboard track which led us to Delville Wood and the valley beyond. The men's spirits began to rise as we passed close to Gueudecourt village and then actually passed over the notorious Grease Trench, where "A" and "B" Companies had been initiated into the conditions of a Somme winter. Familiar landmarks were sighted and commented upon, and a tragic period of the Battalion's existence was made a subject of joke and laughter by the very men who had suffered so much at the time.

At last we realised that we were actually on captured territory and an estimate could be made of the extent of the advance. Every minor detail of military interest was quickly spotted by the men and freely commented upon, such as the condition of enemy trenches, barbed wire, gun positions, discarded equipment and ammunition, tracks, "possies" and the general cleanliness of the ground, both from shell-fire and from a sanitary point of view.

In view of the fact that the whole Brigade was marching along the duckboard track in single file (and we were at the tail of the column), the pace became very erratic and caused the men to "concertina" a good deal, which is very tiring, and everyone was pleased when we halted about a mile short of the Bapaume-Peronne road for lunch. Having finished the meal, we proceeded onwards and turned on to the main road at the village of Beaulencourt, when many of us, for the first time, looked back over the country we had traversed. And what a panorama lay spread out before us! The main Bapaume-Peronne road appeared to run along the crest of a moderately high ridge, and, looking towards Albert, the country receded in a gradual slope, whilst the villages and roads showed out surprisingly distinct and clear. Everyone was spellbound for a while, and inwardly wondered why the Germans had allowed us to pass such a comparatively quiet winter, as far as shell-fire was concerned, for all our tracks, paths, roads, light railways and broad gauge railways had been made and used in front of his very eyes. When we remembered the congested state of the roads and the large parties employed at Railhead and other forward dumps we marvelled at his apathy in not employing his guns more freely. The road we were traversing was lined on either side with beautiful trees, many of which were fitted with elaborate and comfortable observation posts in the branches.

It was now possible to understand the statements made by a prisoner, who said that when on observation duty in rear of the lines, he had seen our working-parties constructing the hutted camps at Bazentin-le-Petit. We could also realise now why Gueudecourt had been shelled so consistently whilst we occupied that sector, for the village, surrounded by trees, stood out particularly clear and was a distinct landmark in the surrounding countryside, and it was very obvious that such a target would be used by all artillery units upon which to register their guns.

After a while, we left the main road once again, and passed through the villages of Riencourt and Bancourt, and for the first time began to realise what a systematic retirement actually means. All churches were blown up and lay in a heap of mangled masonry, in order to prevent the towers being used as vantage points and means of observing the movements of retiring troops. Houses were more or less demolished in every case, or, if time did not permit of their total destruction, the roofs were blown off with explosives to render them useless as billets. In many instances farmhouses with the outbuildings attached had been destroyed by fire for similar reasons. Fruit trees had all been cut down level to the ground and growing crops destroyed. Even the smaller crops such as currant and gooseberry bushes had been uprooted and lay withering in heaps. The trees had been sawn off close to the ground and felled across the roads which they had lined, as an obstruction to traffic, for it took large working parties many hours to clear the roads again sufficiently for vehicles to pass. For similar reasons all cross-roads had been mined, and huge craters from thirty to forty feet in diameter, and proportionately deep, marked the intersection, and proved a serious obstacle to transport. As soon as we became more fully acquainted with the evacuated area, we discovered that the enemy had destroyed the majority of the wells and had thus made the supply of water a serious question.

Our destination, the village of Fremicourt, was now visible a mile or so away, and the unbroken nature of the country enabled us to take a short cut across the fields, threading our way through one or two belts of barbed wire, which had doubtless served as a means orf protecting the village in the retirement. Fremicourt was a somewhat bigger village than those through which we had passed, but closely resembled them in every other way. The central building had apparently been the church, which was now represented by a huge heap of white stone, surmounted by a pole with a white flag on it. Billets were almost unobtainable and the men improvised shelters from the mass of *debris*, which was lying everywhere. Battalion Headquarters, with the Orderly Room Staff, discovered a stable which had not been destroyed, and established the Regimental Office there, endeavouring to ignore the stench which arose from the accumulated manure.

As soon as the Battalion was fairly settled, the Commanding Officer sent for all company commanders with their horses, and together we all proceeded at a canter along the main Bapaume-Cambrai road, through the village of Beugny, in order to learn the geography of our new sector in case we were called upon to move up to the line at short notice. A group of six or seven mounted officers consulting maps within 2,000 yards of the front line was too good a target to be missed by the German gunner, and before long two "Jack Johnsons" burst fairly close overhead, which had the required result of breaking up the deliberation and frightening the horses into the bargain. The horses took the bits between their teeth and galloped towards home, followed by several more short-ranged shrapnel bursts, and those of us who were not expert horsemen found it somewhat difficult to handle our frightened mounts, especially when a belt of barbed wire appeared in front, which required careful navigation. On arriving back at Fremicourt, we found that orders had been received from Brigade Headquarters that we should relieve the 29th Battalion in the front line around Louverval and in sunken roads on the opposite side of the main road to Beaumetz, on the following day.

The actual relief took place in heavy rain, and the men found the long, hard march through Beugny on the hard, cobbled road very tiring. "A," "C" and "D" Companies relieved the 29th Battalion in the line in front of Louverval, "A" Company holding the village and main road (inclusive), "C" Company a position on their left and in front of the wood, and "D" Company on the left of the sector. "B" Company relieved elements of the 54th Battalion and were in reserve, being accommodated in "possies" in rear of the *chateau* grounds.

Orders were received from Brigade Headquarters on the morning of 7th April, apprising us of the fact that the 1st Australian Infantry Brigade were detailed to attack and capture Hermies, a large village of importance about two miles on our right flank. In order to divert attention from the major operation, the 3rd Brigade was ordered to capture the smaller village of Boursies on the main Bapaume-Cambrai road, and the task was allotted to the 12th Battalion. It may here be said that this operation is of particular interest to the Battalion, because it is the only occasion on which we carried out an attack (of any size) without the assistance or co-operation of other units of the Brigade.

The Brigade Order provided for the attack to be carried out in two phases. The first phase consisted of advancing the line and establishing posts on either flank of the village, while during the second phase, to be carried out twenty-four hours later, posts were to be pushed out in front, after which the village was to be "mopped up" and cleared of the enemy. The whole attack was carried out without artillery support, and the only assistance we were to receive was from the 10th Battalion on our left, who were detailed to secure the high ground on that flank and thus protect us from machine-gun fire.

During the early part of the night of 7th-8th April, "C" and "D" Companies were relieved by the 10th Battalion. The former company then assembled in rear of the wood, while "D" Company relieved "A" Company in the line to enable the latter to withdraw to a sunken road near Louverval and organise for the attack.

The actual assault on the village, situated nearly 900 yards in front, was entrusted to Capt. J. E. Newland and "A" Company, with a platoon of "B" Company, under Lieut. R. D. Newitt, to assist. The task of advancing the posts on the left flank was shared by "C" and "D" Companies with the remaining platoons of "B" Company.

At 4 a.m. (April 8th) "A" Company advanced over the bank of the sunken road in lines of sections in file, after which they extended and organised into two waves on a four platoon frontage, Lieut. A. A. Heritage being on the right, Lieut. W. J. Kelly right centre, Lieut. R. Sherwin left centre, and Sgt. J. W. Whittle on the left flank.

Lieut. Newitt and "B" Company's platoon had been ordered to occupy a position on the right of the road for purposes of demonstration, and at zero hour they opened fire with Lewis guns and rifles and did everything possible to draw the enemy's attention and fire to their portion of the front. The ruse was entirely satisfactory and reflected great credit on Newitt and his men, and in view of the fact that the ground receded in a convex slope, they were enabled to obtain ample cover from fire, and thus sustained no casualties.

While this was happening, "A" Company had sent a bombing section up the left side of the main road with the object of dislodging the enemy from the ruined mill, about 400 yards short of the village, which was the extent of the advance in the first phase. At the same time, the waves commenced advancing and, as a result of Newitt's effort on the

THE VILLAGE OF BOURSIES, CAPTURED BY 12th BATTALION
April 6th-10th, 1917

(*Copyright by Australian War Museum*)

right of the road, were able to cover a considerable portion of the open country in front of them before being detected by the enemy. The alarm was given by several of the men encountering a trip-wire, which the enemy had stretched across the front, and immediately heavy rifle and machine-gun fire was brought to bear on the advancing troops, during which Sherwin was killed as he led his men. He was one of our most valued officers, his work at all times, both in and out of the line, being of the highest order, and, above all, he had the entire confidence and respect of his platoon.

The second wave followed closely, and, to the accompaniment of cheers, yells and fiery language, the attack was successfully pushed home and the enemy retired in haste. Kelly had also been wounded in the advance, and in consequence Heritage was the only officer in "A" Company left in the line. Posts were quickly established in advantageous positions, one of extreme importance being on the right flank, near an old sugar refinery, on the left of the main road, of which Sgt. L. G. Scott was in charge, together with Cpls. E. T. Domeney, I. C. Whitelaw, L.-Cpl. "Pick" Wickins and Pvte. Rogers. Domeney rapidly brought his gun to bear on the retiring enemy, but his fire in one particular quarter was masked by the nature of the ground, so Rogers quickly picked the gun up and put it on his shoulder, from which position it was fired with good results.

Another post was established on the left flank with Cpl. P. O. Hay in charge with a Lewis gun, and Pvte. "Andy" McHugh acting as his No. 2 gunner, while Cpl. F. Dalgleish occupied a position nearby. The gun was in constant demand from several quarters and Hay was able to get in some excellent firing.

T

Pvte. J. M. Finlayson, a very popular member of "A" Company and an efficient No. 1 gunner, became a casualty at this time, and within a few moments succumbed to his wounds. Excellent work was also performed by Pvte. C. J. Allen, who directed the fire of his gun to such advantage that many dead Germans were afterwards found in front of his position. Domeney's post on the main road appeared to be a thorn in the side of the enemy, for several efforts were made to dislodge the garrison, and the cover of a bank permitted parties of the enemy to approach within bombing distance before being discovered, but dawn eventually broke without the Hun's object being effected.

Newitt's platoon on the right of the road had, meanwhile, joined in the attack, and occupied a German trench in front without any protracted opposition.

On the left of the position, "C" Company had advanced in two waves, Lieut. G. F. Gould on the left and Lieut. R. D. Radford on the right of the first wave, and Lieut. J. R. Taylor and Sgt. Gurr in charge of the second wave. It was almost daylight when they started, and in crossing the valley in front of them they were subjected to intense machine-gun fire from the high ground on the left which the 10th Battalion had failed to make good. This prevented the advance being made as far as it was intended, and Radford had to dig in on the rear of the slope, but was able to connect up with "A" Company on his right. During this advance, excellent work was performed by Cpls. Lamont and Bruce, while Pvte. S. Lee proved himself invaluable as a runner.

Simultaneously, several parties from "B" Company, detailed by Lieut. I. N. Holyman, had done excellent work in carrying ammunition, bombs, entrenching tools, etc., up to the front line, particularly good work being done by Sgt. Jack Fisher. Pvts. F. O. Gherkie and J. Wilson also did good work as runners.

The front line was subjected to a considerable amount of shell-fire during the day, when Sgt. Scott was unfortunately killed. Before this calamity occurred, however, about 8 a.m. the enemy once again essayed to occupy the post on the roadside, by creeping up under cover of the bank before mentioned. Stick bombs were showered into the post, causing everyone but Domeney (with his gun) to seek better shelter in the building in rear. Domeney kept his gun in action until a bomb fell right alongside his leg and almost blew his foot off. Fortunately, the Hun did not follow up his temporary success and the garrison were able to return. An effort was made to carry Domeney to the rear, but the fire from snipers was too severe and he was left in a shell-hole to await the arrival of stretcher-bearers after dark. A little later in the morning, "Pick" Wickins jumped out of the trench and ran along the parados, and while doing so became the victim of a German machine-gun, thus making another of the original members of the Battalion to pay the price of this operation. This left Cpl. Whitelaw in command of the post, together with Allen and Moore, and although the shelling became more intense, he refused to evacuate until receiving orders from Capt. Newland, but, fortunately, after midday the hostile fire eased off until dusk.

In the meantime, Battalion Headquarters were having a somewhat worrying time, for the lines of communication were long and the telephone lines were constantly being cut by shell splinters. While endeavouring to locate and mend one of these breaks, the Signalling Section lost a conscientious worker in Pvte. C. R. Willing, who was killed by shell-fire. The Commanding Officer was apprehensive regarding the situation on the left flank, for the attack from this quarter not having taken place until just on daylight, the only reports received at Headquarters concerned the heavy fire encountered and the checking of the advance, and the actual position taken up by "C" Company could only be approximately determined.

At 3 p.m. an exceptionally heavy bombardment commenced some miles on our left flank towards Arras, and the "drum-fire" increased to such an extent that it grew into a continuous rumble. This afterwards proved to be the preliminary bombardment to the attack on Vimy Ridge by the Third Army.

The enemy delivered a hurricane bombardment of "pineapple" bombs at 10 p.m. and appeared to concentrate on the ruins of the old mill, around which there was afterwards some very heavy fighting.

The bombardment was quickly followed by a violent counter-attack from the left front and along the main road, when bombs were used lavishly by the enemy and our forward posts around the mill were driven in until checked and organised by Sgt. Whittle. Capt. Newland now came up and took an active part in the attack and personally set a magnificent example of bravery to everyone concerned. He quickly saw the urgent need of reinforcements and at his request Lieut. R. Harrison and a platoon of "D" Company came to his assistance. Lack of retaliatory bombs (the only effective weapon in close range fighting) and the force of enemy numbers drove our line still further back until many of the men reached the road from which the attack had originally started. Cpl. H. G. Kelly performed some good work at this juncture by reorganising the men and forming them into fire units along the bank of the sunken road. Cpl. Hay and Pvte. Montgomery also remained at their individual posts until surrounded by Germans, when, by taking considerable risks, they broke through the German attackers and regained our own lines, fortunately without becoming casualties from our own gunners. Capt. Newland's example and organising powers saved the situation, however, for he appeared to be at every point of the line at almost the same moment, leading men here, urging men there, arranging for ammunition, directing reinforcements to weak spots in the line and, above all, instilling confidence into all ranks by his tenacity and utter disregard of his own personal safety.

On the right of the road, Newitt's platoon had also been attacked, but fire was judiciously held until the enemy was almost on them, when a sweeping fire from Pvte. Butler's Lewis gun, together with rapid fire from the rest of the platoon, completely broke the force of the attack and the Huns retired in great haste and disorder. Newitt quickly followed up his advantage and counter-attacked, capturing the German trench and a machine-gun. After daylight, the number of German dead found in front of his post was considerable. His platoon was naturally weakened, and he was reinforced by Lieut. O. J. Roper and a platoon from "D" Company.

At 4 a.m. the remainder of the Battalion, together with two platoons of the 11th Batatlion, attacked on the left and endeavoured to reach the cemetery on the left of the village. Various platoons were led by Lieuts. L. Dadson, R. Harrison, H. F. Uren, Sgts. R. Lapthorne, Fisher, Talbot, and Polinelli. Once again they were subjected to heavy machine-gun fire from the high ground on the left, which seriously wounded Uren, resulting in his death. Dadson led his men with exceptional skill and was able to capture two enemy trenches without sustaining casualties. His men also captured two enemy machine-guns and fired them at the retreating Germans. The enemy's desire to retire soon became general, and by dawn we had entirely re-occupied the position from which we had been temporarily dislodged.

"A" Company was now withdrawn from the line, and as Capt. Newland was beginning to feel the effect of the heavy nerve strain, the Commanding Officer sent me into the line to relieve him. I took over the posts on the right of the line and, patrols having been sent into the village and having discovered it empty, Roper and I established a large platoon post on the farther extremity of the village. During the counter-attack, Lieut. Heritage sustained a severe wound in the leg, and it was also discovered that Domeney had remained in the shell-hole during the whole of the attack and for a considerable period was behind the German line until rescued after the enemy was pressed back. Sgt. Trevor Young was also found in a very forward position, having been killed in the advance on the first morning.

The Commanding Officer once again lived up to his already high reputation and handled the critical situation in a capable manner. The absence of reliable information and, in one or two instances, the more or less unavoidable delay in effecting counter-attacks at the allotted times, caused him a considerable amount of anxiety. However, his good generalship and the prompt and gallant action of Capt. Newland and other officers in the line brought the operation to a successful issue and much kudos to the unit.

The non-combatant members of the Battalion, in the persons of Major W. W. S. Johnston and his A.M.C. Staff, and the Padre, Capt. W. K. Douglas, did wonderful work at the R.A.P. in rear of Louverval *Chateau*. Under continuous shell-fire, the R.M.O. and his staff tended the wounded unceasingly, whilst Douglas maintained a constant supply of hot cocoa and administered other medical comforts as needed. He, afterwards, took a burial party out and read the burial service over every member of the Battalion who had joined the ranks of "The Deathless Army" on this Eastertide.

It snowed heavily on Tuesday, April 10th, and continued cold throughout the day, therefore we were not at all sorry to be relieved by the 11th and 1st Battalions after nightfall. After relief we moved back to "possies" in the sunken roads around Morchies, well pleased with our work, which had enabled us to wrest the last village in the Somme Cantonment from the hands of the enemy.

Our casualties during the four days of fighting were as follows:—

2 officers killed, 5 wounded;

5 sergeants killed, 9 wounded, 1 missing;

55 other ranks killed, 170 wounded, 9 missing; these casualties, exclusive of officers, being distri-

buted as under:—

	Killed & Missing	Wounded
"A" Company	30	73
"B" Company	15	37
"C" Company	10	27
"D" Company	15	42
Total	70	179

After a spell of four days, we moved into the line in front of Lagnicourt on the evening ot April 14th and relieved the 9th Battalion. This was supposed to be a quiet sector of the line, and the Battalion held a frontage of 3,000 yards by small posts varying from fifty to one hundred yards apart.

All four companies were in the line, in order from the left, "D" Company (Capt. A. S. Vowles), "A" Company (Capt. J. E. Newland), "B" Company (Lieut. I. N. Holyman) and "C" Company (Capt. A. H. Appleby), while Battalion Headquarters was situated in the bank of a sunken road in the rear of Lagnicourt.

"Relief complete" was reported at 11.30 p.m. and the night was occupied by reorganising the line and strengthening the piquets and sentry groups. It was particularly dark and everyone remarked on the lack of artillery and rifle fire, while flares were noticeably absent.

About an hour before dawn, the Commanding Officer was called to the 'phone and Capt. Newland conveyed the astounding news that the enemy had attacked on his front and to his left, where they had broken through and were now threatening his rear. The Colonel, for a moment, was inclined to think that Newland had the "wind up," for the situation up to this time had been abnormally quiet, but as the telephonic conversation was in progress the distinctive crackle of rifle fire could be heard from the line, while the syncopated bursts of machine-gun fire kept up a continuous rattle.

On ringing up "B" and "C" Companies, similar reports were received, but all efforts to raise "D" Company, on the left (where the attack was reported to have been first launched), proved fruitless. The seriousness of the situation was now realised and Headquarters' garrison were roused, when a number of men were seen coming down the Lagnicourt Road, who stated that they belonged to "D" Company, and that the enemy had attacked in considerable force, overwhelming the front line, and were now in possession of the village and were still advancing. This was confirmed by some artillery gunners, who had received orders to withdraw the breach-blocks and abandon their guns in rear of the village, and had even now left them in the hands of the enemy.

Capt. Vowles and Lieut. Roper now arrived and stated that the enemy had attacked at 4 a.m. in considerable numbers. The "stunt" was a silent one, delivered in an oblique direction from the vicinity of Queant. The 20th Battalion, on our left, had received the first impact of the attack, and by sheer weight of numbers their line was forced back, taking with them the two left posts of "D" Company. This now exposed our flank, and, in addition to meeting a frontal attack, "D" Company discovered the enemy pouring into their rear from the left of the position. The attack had been so silent and sudden that there was not sufficient time to arouse the whole of the support platoon and Company Headquarters' garrison before the enemy was on top of them (for, as this was a new sector, many of the "possies" were yet unknown to the N.C.O.'s), and in consequence some of the men were killed before they had time to get out and defend themselves.

Vowles now saw the hopelessness of the situation and ordered the men to fight their way back through the increasing number of Germans who were pouring into his rear. Two officers and about fifty men, together with three Lewis guns, were able to do this, but Lieut. Harrison was badly wounded in the fray. He remained in German hands for nearly two hours and was rescued in the counter-attack, but, unfortunately, succumbed to his wounds nearly a month later.

"A" Company, meanwhile, were putting up a magnificent stand. The silent manner in which the attack had been carried out had surprised them almost as much as "D" Company, while the enemy advance obliquely from the left made it still more confusing.

The numerical strength of the enemy soon forced the sentry groups back to the piquet line, although even this was done regularly and systematically, the Lewis gunners giving covering fire to the garrison as they retired. Capt. Newland was now faced with a difficult problem, for the Hun was rapidly filtering through to his rear, and sniping and directed fire from this quarter steadily increased. In summing up the situation, he discovered that he was being attacked from three sides by a force which was afterwards estimated to outnumber our front line garrison by ten to one. He therefore withdrew his line still farther, to the sunken road leading to Lagnicourt, where his Company Headquarters were situated, and, lining the bank on either side, his men fought back to back and put up a wonderful resistance. The enemy was now seen to attempt to mount a gun in a position along the road, which would have enfiladed the whole position and made it untenable. Without daring to stop and think, Sgt. Jack Whittle rushed out over the intervening ground, which was subjected to extremely heavy fire, and before the crew could mount the gun and get it into action, he attacked them with bombs, single-handed, and after killing the whole of the crew, brought the gun back to our lines.

Every man in "A" Company did good work that day, although special mention must of necessity be made of Sgt. L. Ford for bravery and personal example; Pvte. Clem Keen, for keeping Lewis guns supplied with ammunition; L.-Cpl. C. J. Allen, for first-class Lewis gunnery and devotion to duty; Sgt. S. Hillman, for accepting the risk of firing No. 23 rifle grenades without a cup attachment; Pvte. F. Craig, for loading magazines and keeping the Lewis guns supplied, etc.

"B" and "C" Companies on the right, although they did not receive the full force of the attack, were called upon to exert their full energies in repelling the fringe of the attacking force, and, above all, to give covering fire to the companies on their left. In the course of the fighting, excellent work was done by both Lieuts. R. D. Radford and G. F. Gould, the latter being wounded. Once again Pvte. S. Lee proved himself an invaluable runner, and Sgts. Joslin and Lee also did good work. A good stretcher-bearer was temporarily lost in Pvte. McFarlane, who was wounded and evacuated.

It is not often that one has to carry the scene of fighting back to Battalion Headquarters, but it is necessary to do so on this occasion.

As soon as the seriousness of the situation was realised, the whole garrison of cooks, runners, signallers, batmen, intelligence men and pioneers were roused and lined the high bank facing Lagnicourt. The Commanding Officer, personally, organised the line and utilised the services of R.S.M. Joe Cooper, C.Q.M.S. Ernie Potts and Sgt. F. Ripper in taking charge of hastily-appointed sections.

Day was just beginning to break, and in the half light a thick, black line of advancing Huns could be seen on the left of Lagnicourt and about halfway between us and the village.

Lieut.-Col. Elliott had already sent two urgent messages by 'phone to the 9th Battalion to reinforce "A" Company, on the right, and now despatched Sgt. Ripper for the same purpose and to expedite their arrival. He instructed Lieut. Jack Webster to take a handful of pioneers, stretcher-bearers and intelligence men, and occupy a position on the right of the road, to protect that flank if the enemy advance continued. Webster, however, misunderstood the C.O.'s intention, and, instead of establishing a post, he actually made an advance from the right flank towards the village of Lagnicourt. He handled his men so well, that his party actually effected an entry into the village before Webster himself was wounded and many of the men became casualties. This necessitated the others retiring, and Webster was left in the hands of the enemy, who dressed his wounds and cared for him, until he was eventually rescued in the counter-attack. The results of this daring piece of work were undoubtedly far-reaching, and prevented the enemy from occupying a sunken road in rear of "A" Company, which would have been a distinct menace.

In the meantime, the Commanding Officer had commandeered the services of a Vickers anti-aircraft gun, which he had mounted at the crossroads near Headquarters, and even the small amount of fire we were able to bring to bear on the enemy caused a temporary check to the advance, and the appearance of the 9th Battalion approaching in an artillery formation definitely stopped the Hun. A counter-attack was now launched from the sunken road by 9th and 12th Battalion men, and in a very short time the Germans commenced to waver and ultimately to retire. The withdrawal was quickly followed up and soon became chaotic and disorderly, whilst "A" Company took advantage of the turning of the tables by participating in the counter-attack, re-establishing themselves in their original position, and enjoying a quarter of an hour's sniping and sanguinary machine-gun fire.

We very soon re-occupied the whole of the line from which we had been temporarily dislodged and the number of German dead on the Battalion front, especially in front of "A" Company, was enormous and estimated at several hundred. As the enemy retired, the artillery was advised and concentrated fire was brought to bear on the gaps in the belts of wire through which he had to pass, and many additional casualties were inflicted.

The situation was reported to be normal once again at 11 a.m., and half-an-hour later the Commanding Officer was wounded in the head by a shell-splinter while inspecting the line, and the command was transferred to Major H. James.

Our total casualties in the attack were:—

Killed	29 other ranks
Wounded	4 officers, 55 other ranks
Missing	37 other ranks

while in addition to the numerous enemy dead

which lay on our front, 155 prisoners passed through our Headquarters *en route* for P.O.W. cages.

Battalion Headquarters were at once moved up to the sunken road occupied by "A" Company, in order to be in closer touch with the depleted companies. After passing a quiet night and day, we were relieved by the 7th and 8th Battalions in rain and inky darkness, and after reporting "Relief complete" at 2.15 a.m. we returned to billets at Fremicourt, where, for the next few days, the men were allowed to rest themselves thoroughly and smarten up generally.

Two platoons of "C" Company, under Lieut. R. D. Radford, were detached on 21st April to act as an escort to the heavy batteries in and around the village of Morchies. In the event of an attack or a "break through," like the one recently experienced, it was their duty to form a defensive flank, or to delay the enemy sufficiently long to enable the batteries to withdraw.

The weather was particularly fine during this week in Fremicourt, spring having come in almost a day. The Corps Commander, General Birdwood, visited the Battalion almost every other day and conversed freely with the men, who, after his visits, were in high spirits in anticipation of the long spell the Corps was to get in a few days, as soon as an attack to be carried out by the 3rd Army, 62nd British Division and 2nd Australian Division was effected.

It was rather a surprise, therefore, that orders were received on 24th April for us to relieve the 6th Border Regiment in the Beugny-Ytres* line—

---
*Ytres must not be confused with Ypres.

this being the Corps line of defence. We were relieved in Fremicourt by the 8th Northumberland Fusiliers and thus enabled us to complete our move by noon. The accommodation in the Beugny-Ytres line was fairly good, some platoons being accommodated in deep dug-outs and others in improvised shelters in the trench and in banks, while one company was billetted in the outbuildings of Delsaux Farm. All companies were able to utilise their field cookers and thus get hot meals regularly.

The Battalion once more became complete on April 25th, when Radford and his party were relieved by the Northumberland Fusiliers and reported back to the unit.

The fine weather continued during the whole of our tour of duty in the Beugny-Ytres line, which was extremely fortunate, as after events proved, for the men were able to rest themselves thoroughly. During the next five or six days a very heavy bombardment was carried on in the sector immediately to our north, and aerial reconnaissance was particularly keen.

The expected attack took place at 3 a.m. on 3rd May, when the 3rd Army, assisted by the two left flank divisions of the 4th Army (*i.e.*, 62nd British Division and 2nd Australian Division) attacked the Hindenburg Line. Strong opposition was encountered on the right flank of the attack and fierce fighting ensued in the vicinity of the village of Bullecourt. Orders were received from Brigade Headquarters at 3 p.m. to "stand to" and prepare for an early move, which took place at 11 p.m. when we occupied 1,000 yards of the Beugny-Ytres line, between Beugnatre and Vaulx, to the north of the sector vacated.

The next day, at 4 a.m., we were again ordered to move, with instructions to relieve the remnants of the 26th and 28th Battalions in the Noreuil-Longatte road. The Battalion moved off in small parties from 7 a.m. onwards, and, being under observation, were subjected to a great deal of shelling *en route,* but managed to complete the relief by noon without sustaining any casualties. The Noreuil-Longatte road was situated on high ground and was only partially sunken; moreover, it was very little more than 2,000 yards from the front line and the village of Bullecourt itself.

All communication to the forward area was effected by cross-country routes, and consequently this road was a seething mass of 12th Battalion men, making themselves temporary homes in the "front line" side of the bank of the road, ration and ammunition carrying parties, stretcher-bearers and walking wounded, and as a natural result of this abnormal amount of movement the road was subjected to heavy shelling throughout the day.

During the afternoon, I accompanied advance parties from each of the companies and proceeded to reconnoitre the forward area and to make arrangements for the relief of the 2nd Battalion in the line during the evening.

This was effected without any hitch or casualty by 1.30 a.m., with "A," "B" and "C" Companies in the line (in that order from the right) and "D" Company in support with Battalion Headquarters in a sunken road about 800 yards behind the line.

On taking over the line, we discovered that we had penetrated the Hindenburg Line and were holding the enemy's first system of trenches, known as O.G. 1 and O.G. 2. Our right post, however, rested on the Riencourt road, and the unit on our right formed a protective flank, as the line fell back in this direction to Lagnicourt.

The 2nd Australian Division, in making their attack, pierced the Hindenburg line, and in spite of fierce counter-attacks and intense shelling, retained their hold. The 1st Brigade, on relieving them, had exploited the success by systematically bombing their way to the right, and had thus won 500 to 600 yards of trench from the enemy.

This was the situation when the 12th Battalion took over. During May 5th we continued these tactics and crossed the Riencourt road, and, by bombing their way along, "A" Company was able to capture about 100 yards of trench, ably led by Lieut. P. F. Heurtley-Reed, assisted in a most fearless manner by L.-Cpl. L. W. Marriner, who lost his life in so doing. Concentrated shelling during the afternoon, however, forced them to evacuate this part of the trench, which the enemy re-occupied.

At 6 a.m. on May 6th, the enemy concentrated his forces on our front and launched a violent counter-attack, using bombs, grenades and *flammenwerfer*. The effect of the last-named hellish invention was most demoralising, and, combined with the strength of the attack, forced our line back and the enemy occupied O.G. 2 and parts of O.G. 1. A wonderful rally was made by Captains J. A. Foster and J. E. Newland, and after nearly three hours of hand-to-hand fighting—some of the severest the Battalion ever experienced—the enemy was driven out and we again occupied O.G. 1 and 2.

During the attack, the Company Signallers of "A" Company, with a power buzzer unit complete, and several wounded men, were down a deep dugout and remained there during the whole of the attack without being molested, fortunately, and were afterwards relieved by their own men on the re-establishment of the line.

It would be difficult to enumerate the many acts of gallantry which were performed during this fighting, but in addition to the wonderful leadership displayed by Foster and Newland, invaluable work was performed by Lieuts. R. D. Radford, A. L. Wardlaw, Heurtley-Reed, and 2nd-Lieuts. W. K. Gill, R. G. Walduck and J. Youl.

Of the N.C.O.'s and men, Sgts. T. Henty, Joslin, E. J. C. Barwick, A. L. S. Davey, Ruthmuller, Cpls. T. W. Fordham, Doyle, Waye, L.-Cpls. F. H. Williams, G. W. Turner, and Pvts. A. O'Loughlin, G. W. Taylor, F. O. Gherkie, P. A. O'Neill, L. T. Simpson, R. W. Morris, "Darky" James, Bracken, Bowden and Seymour were all magnificent in their various duties as platoon and section leaders, Lewis gunners, bombers, runners, stretcher-bearers, signallers, etc.

The casualties sustained by the front line companies during this period were heavy and expensive, for many of our good officers and N.C.O.'s were killed and wounded. Capt. A. H. Appleby was badly wounded by shell-fire and died a short while afterwards in the front line; 2nd-Lieut. R. Adams, a newly-arrived reinforcement officer, was also killed in his first tour of duty in the line; while 2nd-Lieut. J. Youl, who had proved himself so valuable to the R.Q.M. for such a long and difficult period, and who had only recently received his commission, also "went west." He was an original member of the Battalion, and although quiet and unostentatious in manner he had the happy knack of handling men and getting things done, and his actions immediately prior to his death proved that he was equally as good in the line as an officer as he was in the Q.M. store as a lance-corporal.

Meanwhile, "D" Company and Battalion Headquarters had suffered heavy casualties in the sunken road in rear. This was under direct observation and enfilade fire from Inchy and Pronville, and was heavily bombarded all day. One shell landed near a group of "D" Company officers and wounded Capt. Houghton, Lieut. D. McLeod (who had recently rejoined the Battalion *with an artificial arm*, after being wounded at Lone Pine, August, 1915), Lieut. O. J. Roper and 2nd-Lieut. M. Crawford.

"D" Company was used exclusively as a carrying party and did good work in keeping up a somewhat meagre supply of bombs and ammunition to the front line. After the counter-attack and re-occupation of the line, it was necessary to send "D" Company up to strengthen the garrison, and the carrying was done by all and sundry details at Headquarters, under the supervision of R.S.M. Joe Cooper (until wounded) and Sgt. F. H. Ripper.

During the night the Battalion was relieved in the line by the 10th Battalion. It is doubtful whether the relief was advantageous, as the companies were withdrawn to the sunken road at Headquarters, where the accommodation was totally inadequate. The nerve strain was certainly relieved, but the shelling in this road was even more intense than in the front line itself, and our casualties were consequently heavy. Hot meals were brought up from the cookers at Noreuil, and the men rested—or at least did not fight, for it could hardly be called rest under conditions such as these.

On 7th May, much to our surprise and disgust, we were again ordered into the line, and owing to our depleted numbers the Commanding Officer organised the whole Battalion into one company, each company forming a platoon. The officers had had a very nerve-racking time, and in order to give them a longer spell, he himself took the "company" into the line, while the platoons were commanded by Lieuts. Tynan and L. T. Butler (just returned fresh from schools of instruction), myself and Lieut. R. D. Radford, the latter being the only officer to serve the whole time in the front line.

Capt. A. S. Vowles acted as Commanding Officer by receiving messages from Brigade Headquarters and transmitting them to Major James in the line, while Lieut. I. N. Holyman assisted him as Adjutant.

During the night and the following day the shelling was intense at intervals, but no attacks or bomb fighting occurred on the Battalion sector. Rain fell in the early morning and made the white clay trenches very uncomfortable and repulsive, and efforts were at once made to bury and dispose of the Germans, who were lying everywhere.

The Battalion was relieved during the latter part of the night of May 8th-9th by the 53rd Battalion, but just before midnight the shelling became so terrific that it was feared an attack was impending. The S.O.S. was fired and the magnitude of the bombardment was trebled. This lasted for fully an hour-and-a-half, when it gradually quietened without any attack taking place.

Relief was completed at 3 a.m., when the Battalion moved out to a bivouac near Vaulx, where a steaming hot stew awaited them. About 9 a.m. we again moved and marched in easy stages *via* Beugnatre and Favreuil to a camp in the vicinity of Biefvillers, where Lieut. H. E. Spotswood, R.Q.M., had tents erected and blankets waiting for the men, who were soon asleep.

The next day we marched on to Bapaume, where the Battalion was billeted in the hospital and buildings adjacent thereto.

The casualties sustained by the Battalion from its entry into the line on April 6th to May 9th may be summarised as follows:—

	Boursies	Lagnicourt	Bullecourt	Total
Killed—				
Officers	2	—	3	5
Other ranks	60	29	31	120
Wounded—				
Officers	5	4	12	21
Other ranks	179	55	213	447
Missing—				
Officers	—	—	—	—
Other ranks	10	37	25	72
Total—				
Officers	7	4	15	26
Other ranks	249	121	269	639

During the operations covered by these casualties, the following decorations were awarded by H.M. the King, the Commander-in-Chief and the Corps Commander respectively:—

Victoria Cross.—Capt. J. E. Newland and Sgt. J. W. Whittle, D.C.M.

Bar to D.S.O.—Lieut.-Col. C. H. Elliott, D.S.O.

Bar to M.C.—Lieut. L. Dadson, M.C.

Military Cross.—Lieuts. L. Dadson, G. F. Gould, A. A. Heritage, P. F. Heurtley-Reed, 2nd-Lieuts. R. D. Newitt, W. K. Gill.

D.C.M.—Sgts. S. Hillman, P. S. Stott, G. C. Lukin, Cpl. M. G. Blackman, Pvts. A. J. Hubble, L. M. Courtney, W. T. Young.

Bar to M.M.—L.-Cpl. M. G. Blackman, Pvts. A. Long, A. O'Loughlin, G. W. Taylor, F. O. Gherkie, J. B. McCulloch, F. Hamilton.

Military Medal.—Sgts. E. W. Huxley, N. Ransom, T. Henty, H. E. George, E. J. C. Barwick, A. L. S. Davey; Cpls. J. Bruce, P. O. Hay, T. W. Fordham; L.-Cpls. W. L. Higgins, E. T. Domeney, F. H. Williams, G. W. Turner, I. C. Whitelaw; Pvts. F. N. Craig, R. P. Bugg, D. McFarlane, J. E. Johns, F. F. Townsend, A. S. Butler, G. R. Gillam, C. J. Allen, F. O. Gherkie, F. Hamilton, P. A. O'Neill, R. W. Morris, J. A. Wilson, A. Reader, A. E. Jones, S. A. Lee, A. Long, V. T. Stone, J. McCulloch, B. Sutton, L. T. Simpson, A. S. Harris.

2nd-Lieut. J. Webster was awarded the French Croix de Guerre.

Chapter XV.

THE SUMMER OF 1917

THE strength of the Battalion when leaving the line after the recent operations was 14 officers and 489 other ranks, which will in itself indicate the strenuous time we had passed through, and the fierceness of the fighting. It is scarcely necessary to state that every member of the unit experienced a distinct feeling of relief when the long-promised rest came and we left Bapaume for the training area. During the winter "stalemate" and the spring fighting, we had seen war under some of the worst conditions possible, but now we were going to enjoy a well-earned rest and recuperate generally (for the nerves of the majority of the men had suffered considerably) to fit ourselves for the next task we were called upon to perform. None of us, however, had any idea that the period of rest and training was to be prolonged, through force of circumstances, into a spell of four months duration.

Lt.-Col. Elliott assumed command of the Brigade on the 20th May, whilst the Brigadier relieved the Divisional Commander, who had proceeded on English leave.

On the 23rd May, the Brigade left Bapaume and marched to Bazentin-le-Petit, where they stayed one night only, and then marched on to billets at Ribemont, on the River Ancre. This latter journey was a long and tiring one, for, starting at 8.25 a.m., we marched through a desolate, war-pocked area and did not arrive at our destination until 3.15 p.m.

The whole Brigade was billetted at Ribemont, and I am certain that all who were members of the Battalion at that time, will always have very pleasant memories of their sojourn there. The weather was particularly good, the billets were better than any we had had during the whole winter, and last, but by no means least, the peasants of the village did everything they could to make our stay enjoyable.

The Commanding Officer returned to the Battalion on the 1st June, taking over from Major A. Steele, of the 3rd Machine-Gun Company, who had commanded us during his absence.

As soon as we were settled in our billets, a comprehensive syllabus of training was drawn up and put into operation forthwith. All officers and N.C.O.'s were impressed with the immediate necessity of smartening up the men both on and off parade, and many suggestions were made and adopted to induce the men to become more regimental in their bearing. The Australian was already recognised as "a 100 per cent. front line soldier," but a considerable amount of criticism was levelled against his behaviour and discipline in "rest areas," and we, who knew his temperament and character so well, resented this very much, and were now determined, in our own small Battalion and Brigade, to create a different impression founded on facts and results.

Every morning the Battalion paraded as a unit on the Battalion parade ground and carried out a few rifle exercises and battalion drill movements before training was continued under company arrangements. During the winter, officers and N.C.O.'s had been extensively sent to Corps and Divisional schools of instruction, and in consequence almost every company had a specialist instructor for Lewis gunnery, bombing, musketry and bayonet fighting. A Brigade school for infantry training was also commenced, and as many of the newly appointed N.C.O.'s as could be spared were detailed to attend and received special instruction.

The weather at this time was so hot that it was not possible to carry out training of a strenuous nature during the middle of the day, and in consequence the hours of the morning parade were altered to 7 a.m.-11 a.m. Afternoons were invariably given up to sports, organised pastimes and competitions. Inter-company competitions were held in each battalion throughout the Division early in June, to decide, after a series of Brigade heats, which was the best company in the Division. The competition was of a purely military nature and comprised tests in company drill, bayonet fighting, musketry, Lewis gun drill, bombing and grenade firing, signalling and wiring. Each company keenly entered into the contest, which was ultimately won by "B" Company, who represented the Battalion in the Brigade heat on 7th June, but, unfortunately, attained only second place. Battalions in the Brigade also carried out a local contest comprising battalion drill, transport inspection, etc., but the undermentioned results will show that we, as a unit, did not uphold our reputation as well as "B" Company.

Result of Brigade competitions:—

	Battalion	Company
1	9th Battalion	10th Battalion
2	10th „	12th „
3	12th „	9th „
4	11th „	11th „

During the hot weather the men used to avail themselves of every opportunity of bathing in the River Ancre, which, although only a narrow stream in this vicinity, was beautifully cool and delightfully picturesque.

The Quartermaster, Capt. Spotswood, worked hard during this period, for he had not only to feed the Battalion, but also to make a complete inventory of the equipment and gear, and indent for fresh supplies to replace the serious losses we had sustained in the forward area. In many instances he had to rack his brains for a feasible excuse to explain some particular shortage, for although "lost by shell-fire" will cover most of the discrepancies, yet it is hardly applicable to the loss of a "watch, signaller's, luminous," or a "knife, butcher's," which normally do not take front-line risks and yet have an unfortunate habit of becoming irrecoverably lost. The rations, drawn from the Brigade dump outside Ribemont Church, were particularly good, and every effort was made to vary the meals as much as possible. Regimental funds were freely expended to purchase vegetables and other condiments to supplement the rations, whilst a monthly order (which had been placed during the winter months) for curry powder was still being received from the Army and Navy Stores, London.

The officers' mess was once again constituted in one of the large billets, under the supervision of Capt. I. N. Holyman, and proved a great success. One night every week was reserved as a "visitors' night," when members of Brigade Staff, Commanding Officers of other units and friends of various officers were invited to dine with us.

The health of the Battalion was very good during our stay at Ribemont, as undoubtedly it should have been, living, as we were, under such favourable conditions. With small sick parades, the R.M.O. discovered that he had a certain amount of time on his hands and promptly requested me to arrange an inoculation parade, much to everyone's disgust. He still ran a small "rest home" in the Battalion, where he coaxed a few of his patients back to health under his own treatment, rather than that they should be evacuated and perhaps lost to the Battalion for several weeks. The rest of his time was spent in training stretcher-bearers, rousing up Sgt. Ray Clark and his pioneer squad, inspecting billets, cook-houses, latrines and incinerators, and bringing the sanitation of the unit generally to a degree of perfection which had not been attained for many days. He also made a determined effort to eliminate the presence of lice amongst the men, and present conditions were most favourable for this purpose. Bathing was encouraged, the Quartermaster was urged to obtained clean sets of underclothing at frequent intervals, while the R.M.O. himself made arrangements for the use of the Foden engine, in which to fumigate all blankets. This "engine" consisted of a cylinder or boiler, into which the blankets were loosely packed and enveloped in steam. The trouble always was to get clean underclothes and the use of the Foden engine simultaneously, for, obviously, unless they could be used together the usefulness of either was to a large extent neutralised.

Meanwhile, training was progressing well and giving complete satisfaction to the Commanding Officer as well as the Brigade Staff. Route marches were carried out periodically to the adjacent villages of Mericourt, Heilly and Bonnay, while the rifle range near Buire was also made available to us for musketry on various days. The smartening up of the battalions in the Brigade had been carried into effect so thoroughly that the changing over of Brigade duties outside Ribemont Church at 5 p.m. daily became one of the events of the day and was the cause of much rivalry amongst units. The inspection which the guards and fatigues had to go through was very severe, for, first of all, the N.C.O. in charge scrutinised his own command, then the Company-Sergeant-Major criticised before the Company Orderly Officer actually inspected them. After this, they paraded to the Battalion Orderly Room, where the Battalion Orderly Officer discovered grease spots on tunics, missing chin-straps, bulging pockets, puttees incorrectly rolled, or—biggest fault of all—an uncleaned rifle. The smartness of the guard affected the reputation of the Battalion so closely at this juncture that even this overhauling was not considered sufficient, but necessitated another microscopic inspection by the Adjutant, who, apparently, thought it his bounden duty to discover some apparent or imaginary fault in the "turn-out" of the guard. In order to obtain the best results possible and to engender the individual competitive spirit, I used to pick out the best dressed man in the guard and grant him some concession — either preference on the leave roster or a period of exemption from all fatigues. By this time the Brigade band had arrived and the Battalion Orderly Officer marched the duties off for a final inspection by the Brigade Captain of the day, after which, in front of a crowd of interested "Diggers" of all units, as well as civilians, the "compliments" were exchanged by the new and the old guards in a manner which compared very favourably with any of the British regular regiments, the Guards, perhaps, excluded.

A Divisional sports meeting was held at Henencourt Wood on 12th June, and reflected great credit on everyone who was in any way responsible for the arrangements. The spot chosen for the carnival was admirably suited for this purpose and can only be described as a natural Stadium. The events were contested on a flat stretch of country, whilst the spectators, comprising some thousands of troops, were accommodated on terraces, one above the other, which made it possible for everyone to have an uninterrupted view of the races as they proceeded. The usual athletic events, novelty races and tug-o'-war comprised the programme, whilst a troupe of comedians provided the necessary amount of humour. We had taken the field cookers with us and gave the men a mid-day meal, which they supplemented with canteen purchases, and when we finally left about 4 p.m. to return home, everyone agreed that the day had been most enjoyable and the sports meeting a huge success, and our only regret was that no prizes had been won by our own members. The next day the meeting was continued, when several mounted events were contested, transports inspected, and the finals of many of the preceding day's events run.

Sport in its various forms was having such a

beneficial effect on the men, both physically and morally, that every effort was made to encourage and vary it. With this end in view, a small committee of officers and men conducted a miniature aquatic carnival on the River Ancre on June 16th, which, being the first of its kind, was much appreciated and very popular.

Leave was also granted daily to five per cent. of the unit to visit Amiens, and generally resulted in an average of thirty men catching the morning train at 8 a.m. from Mericourt station.

It will thus be seen that summer weather, comfortable billets, pleasant surroundings, good food, congenial villagers, regular fortnightly pay-days, leave passes, early morning parades and a maximum of sport had the combined result of keeping the Battalion in excellent health, increasing their physical fitness, inculcating a wonderful *esprit de corps* in the unit, and, above all, raised their morale to a standard equal to that experienced at Mena Camp and on our first arrival in France.

A steady influx of officers returning from hospital and detached duties, together with rank and file, as well as reinforcements, brought our strength, approximately, up to 30 officers and 700 other ranks by the middle of June. Each draft of reinforcements was inspected, and before being allotted to companies was given a brief *resume* of the Battalion's career—battles we had fought and won, and the decorations gained by its members, including the two Victoria Crosses—and it was thus impressed upon them that they should consider it as an honour to be drafted to the 12th Battalion, and that we relied on them to assist us in maintaining our good name both in and out of the line.

Our training took a fresh turn on Sunday, June

24th, when we moved to the Mailly-Maillet area to carry out extensive field training to prepare us once again for open warfare in the event of a "break through" during the next offensive. We made an early start at 7.30 a.m., in order to cover as much of the journey as possible before the sun got too hot, and proceeded *via* Lavieville, Millencourt and Senlis to billets at Beaussart, Brigade Headquarters, and the other units being quartered at Mailly-Maillet itself.

The area allotted to us was in the vicinity of the old front line at Beaumont-Hamel prior to the "Big Push" in July, 1916, and included the villages of Englebelmer, Martinsart, Mesnil, Auchonvillers, Serre and Beaumont-Hamel, as well as a portion of Aveluy Wood. Soon after our arrival, Battalion Headquarters Staff and company commanders proceeded on their horses to inspect the area and found it not only very suitable, but also extremely interesting. Being very close to the old front line the ground had not been under cultivation for some two or three years, and during the last twelve months had become overgrown with long grass and weeds. Considering the amount of artillery fire which took place on the Somme during 1916, the area was particularly free from any great number of shell holes, and, with the exception of a few trenches and tangled barbed wire in places, formed an excellent training ground.

The first day after our arrival was spent quietly in the billets, the troops having been warned of impending night operations, and in accordance with this programme we set out soon after darkness had fallen to carry out an outpost scheme in the vicinity of Englebelmer. Unfortunately, we had barely taken up our dispositions, posted our sentries, and commenced preparing a picquet line, when it started to rain steadily, and, as there was every indication of it continuing, we had no option but to withdraw, which we did, arriving home at 11.30 p.m.

On Tuesday, June 26th, we carried out an attack practice, our objective being to dislodge the 11th Battalion from the village of Auchonvillers and the ridge upon which it was situated. The next day we did not set out until 7.30 p.m., when we carried out a night advance, which culminated in an attack at dawn. Once again it rained very hard as we were returning, and everyone was wet through to the skin on arriving back at billets at 5 a.m.

Thursday was again spent in the billets, but on Friday, the 29th, we were roused at 4 a.m., breakfasted at 4.30 a.m. and moved off at 5.30 a.m. for Aveluy Wood, which we reached at 7.30 a.m. From here we moved off as a main-guard, until an imaginary message was received from the advance guard notifying contact with the enemy, when we adopted "battle formations" and continued the advance until becoming enveloped into the attack, which once again was in the vicinity of Auchonvillers.

A trench-to-trench attack was to have been carried out on the Saturday, but a heavy rain-storm drove us back before we had got many yards along the road.

While awaiting a night attack on July 2nd, a quiet day was again spent in billets, after which we set out at midnight, together with the other units of the Brigade, to carry out a scheme under Divisional arrangements, which was an exact replica of the attack on the village of Serre as originally carried out on July 1st, 1916. We arrived at the

OUR TWO V.C.'s

CAPT. J. E. NEWLAND, V.C.

SGT. J. W. WHITTLE, V.C., D.C.M.

trenches at 3.15 a.m. and zero hour was timed for 5 a.m. The whole operation was carried out in a perfect manner and brought forth much praise from the staff officers who witnessed it. The attack was practised under "front line" conditions and normal happenings were improvised to make it appear as real as possible. The various objectives were indicated by sheets of corrugated iron (salvaged from the battlefield) stood on end at intervals, while our own artillery barrage was represented by fatigue men, who waved blue and white signalling flags and advanced in accordance with a barrage time-table. Messages to and from the front line were sent by runners, whilst a telephone line was laid to Brigade Headquarters. Various officers and N.C.O's. were detailed as "casualties" and were evacuated through the R.A.P. by the stretcher-bearers.

Another four days' training on similar lines to that recorded above brought our stay at Beaussart to an end. Everyone was of the opinion that our standard of training had been materially advanced during the ten days spent in the area. Although the men had had a fairly easy time, it had been very strenuous for the officers, particularly Headquarters Staff, as it was always usual to reconnoitre the ground over which a practice was to be carried out, and in many instances the N.C.O's. had been taken out and the operation rehearsed without troops. In addition to this, operation orders were always issued prior to an exercise, giving a full narrative to illustrate the action and detailed instructions regarding the operation set out in the prescribed form. This, necessarily, gave much additional work to the Commanding Officer, the Adjutant and Orderly Room staff, particularly Ken Brockett, the typist.

On July 6th we left Beaussart at 6.30 a.m. and returned by the same route to Ribemont, arriving at 11 a.m.

A ceremony, which will live long in the minds of those who witnessed it, was performed on July 8th, when General Birdwood unveiled a memorial at Pozieres erected in memory of all men of the 1st Australian Division who were killed during July and August, 1916, near that spot. Each battalion in the Division sent a representative platoon of one officer and forty men to attend the unveiling ceremony, and I always appreciated the honour of being selected to command the 12th Battalion's representatives. The parade consisted of staff officers from Corps Headquarters, our own and sister divisions, our three Brigade staffs and all senior officers, in addition to the parade of N.C.O.'s and men. The simple service was conducted jointly by Church of England, Roman Catholic, Presbyterian and Salvation Army padres, after which an address was given by General Birdwood, followed by the unveiling of the memorial, when the troops presented arms and the "Last Post" sounded.

On returning to our unit, we discovered that Major H. A. MacPherson had arrived, having been transferred from the 52nd Battalion, and everyone was very pleased to see him.

Corporal D. Bishton (Orderly Room Corporal) and I proceeded to Rouen on July 9th and inspected our Battalion Records and found them kept in a very creditable manner by our Orderly Room Sergeant, who was stationed there for that purpose. He was an incapacitated soldier transferred from some other unit and was not generally known to anyone in the Battalion. We studied their methods and came away with much useful information, which would assist us in compiling our returns and thus bring about a closer co-operation between the unit in the field and the Records section at the Base.

While there, I was confidentially given the following figures representing the total casualties of the 12th Battalion from the time of its arrival in France to 30th June, 1917, on condition that I did not make them known during the war period:—

	Officers	Other Ranks
Killed	9	355
Died of Wounds	2	73
Died of Disease	1	7
Missing	—	40
Wounded	43	999
Gas Poisoning	1	3
Prisoners of War	1	17
Total	57	1494

On returning four days later, I took over my duties as Adjutant once again from Lieut. L. T. Butler, who had been relieving me in my absence, and discovered that on July 12th the Brigade had been "inspected" by H.M. the King. In order to be inspected, the Brigade marched on to the Albert-Amiens road, which they lined on either side, with instructions to cheer as the King passed in his motor car. After waiting some time, a car approached, without any warning, and passed the column at the rate of something over thirty miles an hour, before anyone had time to realise that the King himself was in it. This car was followed by several others containing Staff officers, and as their rank decreased, so the cheering appeared to increase, until the ovation received by some mounted military policemen, who brought up the rear, seemed to lift the clouds.

A word might be said at this stage regarding the discipline of the Battalion, which was distinctly good. Crime of a civil nature was most unusual and only happened on very rare occasions during our four-and-a-half years of service. Military offences were generally of a minor variety and capable of being dealt with by the Company Commander, but sometimes it was necessary for the soldier to be paraded before the Commanding Officer, who, everyone in the Battalion agreed, gave the escorted soldier a "fair burl." Before awarding a sentence of field punishment (when the option rested with him) he asked the prescribed question, "Will you accept my punishment, or do you elect to be tried by Field General Court Martial?" and in nine cases out of ten received the usual reply, "By you, sir."

The principal crimes in the Brigade which necessitated a F.G.C.M. during this period were:—

(1) When on active service, absent without leave;

(2) When on active service, failing to comply with an order given by an N.C.O.;

(3) When on active service, conduct to the prejudice of good order and military discipline.

A Field General Court Martial entailed much work for everyone concerned, but was generally considered a very fair method of trial. Capt. Eric Johnson (of Hobart) attended all Courts Martial as an additional member and advised the president on legal points and procedure, and by means of tact and suggestion usually assisted the court to such an extent that a considerable amount of time was saved.

The sentences passed were either field punishment or imprisonment with hard labour, although in a number of cases the latter punishment was suspended or commuted to field punishment by the Lieut.-General commanding the Army Corps. Field punishment was dreaded, more particularly for the reason that an entry appeared in the paybook and pay was stopped for the period in question. As a punishment, it practically lapsed if it was not possible for the prisoner to be sent to the Divisional F.P. Compound, as the facilities for providing a guard room within the Battalion were very poor, either because billets were too scarce to spare one for this purpose, or of too flimsy a nature to expect the N.C.O. in charge of the guard to keep prisoners in custody.

During our stay at Ribemont, I was told one evening by the R.S.M. that someone had told him (having received the information from a third person) that there was a spy in the adjacent village of Mericourt. The information was conveyed in this roundabout manner owing to the fact that Mericourt was "out of bounds." Our informants told us that he was wearing an Australian uniform with 1st Brigade colours, was staying at an *estaminet*, and yet could not speak a word of English. The Brigade interpreter could not be found, so the Provost Sergeant went and got him and I proceeded to question him in crude French. He stated that he belonged to one of the 1st Brigade battalions, but could not remember the name of his commanding officer or any of his officers. I next asked him for his paybook, which he could not produce. He stated that he arrived in Sydney just prior to enlistment and had not learnt much English. The circumstances were suspicious, and I detained him for the night, pending enquiries from his unit, but next morning brought the news that he was "dinkum," and had been detached (with a number of other men from the Division) to assist some of the civilians to gather in their harvest.

The strength of the Battalion was 42 officers and 956 other ranks when we left Ribemont on July 16th, for during the latter part of our stay there we had received a steady flow of men returning to the unit from wounds and sickness, and also 2nd-Lieuts. P. T. Miller, A. N. M. Greensill and J. B. Catterall from the Cadet Corps, W. Lambert from 4th Battalion (originally a 12th Battalion N.C.O.), and Bovell from 5th Div. Artillery, in addition to many of our own officers returning to duty.

The men had made themselves very popular with the villagers, who appeared to be genuinely sorry to see us going. We marched *via* Treux, Ville-sur-Ancre and Meaulte to a hutted camp at Bronfay Farm, on the Bray-Carnoy road. The day of the march was extremely hot and a considerable number of the men fell out, giving the M.O. and the second-in-command an unenviable job in consequence, urging them to keep up with the column.

The huts in the camp were originally built by a French unit and were of a different type to any we had seen or occupied. They were almost double the size of a Nissen hut in length and height, and almost in width, also. They had straight sides, with a distinct bulge at the bottom, where the men used to stack their bedding, equipment and mess utensils.

We stayed at this camp for a week, during which time we practised attacks on villages, model platoon organisation, and carried out route marches to Bray and to our old familiar area around Mametz.

The Y.M.C.A. had converted a barn, which was adjacent to the camp, into a picture theatre, and thus gave considerable pleasure to the troops. "Bronfay Cinema" did not uphold the dignity of such a flash name, from either the outside or the inside of the building, but the quality of the pictures was good, and the establishment of a cinema within the Brigade was a distinct improvement.

We now knew that within a few days the 1st Australian Division would be moving back north to the 2nd Army area once again, and therefore, on the evening of July 24th, we moved into Forked Tree Camp, on the Albert-Bray road (only a matter of a mile or a mile-and-a-half), in order to reduce the march into Albert when entraining.

"Reveille" was at 3 a.m. on July 27th, the day upon which we moved, for there was a considerable amount to be done in loading the transport and gear, cleaning up the camp and afterwards loading at the station. Capt. I. N. Holyman was detailed as Brigade Entraining Officer, "C" Company was responsible for loading the transport and gear, while "D" Company came on by a later train with the 3rd Field Ambulance.

Brigade Orders stated "that the transport and one company will arrive at the entraining station three hours before the time of the departure of the train" and that "the entraining of all units must be completed half-an-hour before the time of departure of the train," thus giving two-and-a-half hours clear for the actual work. In our case everything went of smoothly. "C" Company and the transport arrived at Albert station, the limbers were parked, horses unharnessed and watered, transport and gear loaded on to the train and secured, and "C" Company reported to the R.T.O. within the hour. He congratulated and thanked Capt. Richardson and Lieut. E. A. Potts (Transport Officer) for the way in which the men had worked, and, although he had never kept count at any time, thought that they must have broken all records.

The train left at 9.15 a.m. and everyone kept a close look-out as we passed many familiar scenes at Dernancourt, Buire and Ribemont, on our way to Amiens. Our detraining station was Steenbecque, near Hazebrouck, where we arrived at 5.15 p.m. and found hot cocoa provided for us in the station yard by the Australian Comforts Fund, which proved very refreshing after the long train journey.

A two hours march brought us to our billets at Longue Croix, in the Staple area, and, being very tired, everyone turned in early.

"D" Company arrived the next morning at 9 a.m., and during the day the Battalion was settling down generally. The billets were very scattered and not particularly roomy, the Battalion Orderly Room and Staff having to be accommodated in a leaky bell tent.

Sunday, 29th July, was a pouring wet day and a combined church parade for the 11th and 12th Battalions had to be abandoned.

During the evening there was a conference of commanding officers at Brigade Headquarters, and at 10 p.m. the C.O. arrived back with the astounding news that we were to move again at 6 a.m. in the morning for a training area some distance the other

side of St. Omer, and would proceed by motor
'buses. It took us some few moments to assimilate
this startling and unexpected piece of news, but
quickly pulling ourselves together, the Quartermaster, Transport Officer and I held a "council of
war" regarding transportation of gear, and a movement order was at once issued. We have often
since compared this move, with eight hours' notice,
to the one we had from Mena, which was rehearsed
many times, and several others in France which
required more than one trip of the transport to
make complete. Just as we were turning in, Capt.
Don McLeod and 26 reinforcements arrived, who
had to be given a shake-down for the few hours
sleep which would be at their disposal.

"Reveille" was timed for 3.15 a.m. and breakfast
at 4 a.m., and the transport section left at about
6.30 a.m. The Battalion formed up on the road
outside Headquarters at 8.30 a.m. (leaving a small
guard of men selected by the R.M.O. to look after
some of the surplus gear left behind), and moved
off to the "embussing" point on the Wallon-Cappel
road. Unfortunately, it turned into a wet day as the
journey proceeded, and the beautiful country we
passed through near St. Omer lost a lot of its
charm in consequence. We "debussed" at 2.30 p.m.
at Bayenghem and marched about four miles in a
rainy drizzle to our billets at Nielle-les-Blequin.
Our billetting officer, Lieut. B. W. Mitchell, had
only arrived about three-quarters of an hour before
us, and as a result some of the Battalion had to sit
by the roadside for a while until the area was
allotted.

Everyone in the unit will agree, I think, that the
billets at Nielle-les-Blequin were the best we ever
occupied in France prior to the Armistice. For

almost the first time in our experience, the people encouraged billetting and were anxious to have troops not only in the barns and outhouses, but in their house itself. Officers were provided with beds—with feather mattresses and eiderdown quilts —warrant officers and sergeants were also provided with billets and beds, whilst many of the men made their own arrangements and fared similarly. Even the men in the sheds and buildings were infinitely more comfortable than usual, plenty of straw being provided voluntarily by the villagers. The only trouble about the whole thing was that it was very difficult to leave such a comfortable bed in the morning, after the hard floors and wire-netting mattresses we had been used to lately.

The next morning, 31st July, we marched to our training area, which was nearly five miles away, on the main St. Omer-Boulogne road. We selected the slope of a steep hill, facing the road, where the rest of the morning was occupied in digging a shallow system of trenches upon which to operate during our period of training in the area.

On arriving back at our billets, we received news that a new offensive had been launched during the early hours of the morning east of Ypres, but the advance made had not come up to expectations owing to the wet and muddy condition of the country.

The next four days, August 1st-4th, were all wet, rain falling continuously all day. For the first two of them, the men carried out training in billets with plenty of gas drill, but this became so monotonous that, at their own request, we carried out route marches in the rain on the last two days to the adjoining villages of Seninghem and Wismes. All ranks expressed their regrets (in lurid language) at the deterrent effect the weather would have on the new offensive.

Sunday, August 5th, turned out to be fine, and so church parades were cancelled and the training syllabus was put into operation in order to prevent the *whole* of our period in this area being wasted, as orders had been received for our return to-morrow.

The 3rd A.L.T.M.B. then fired some dummy Stokes trench mortars as a preliminary bombardment, and the Battalion carried out a very satisfactory attack practice on the trenches. The members of the Intelligence Platoon had been detailed to represent tanks by carrying canvas stretched on a framework, and continued to perambulate over the "battlefield" in a most conscientious manner long after the attack had been concluded and the troops withdrawn.

We afterwards concentrated on the road and the 3rd M.G. Coy. and the 3rd A.L.T.M.B. gave us a very realistic demonstration of firing with live ammunition, after which we filled in the trenches and returned to our billets.

Two new officers had joined us during our stay at Nielle-les-Blequin, namely, 2nd-Lieut. A. D. Anderson (commissioned) and P. C. Thompson (reinforcement).

The transport section left at 7 a.m. in the morning, but the remainder of the Battalion killed time in one way and another until 1.45 p.m., and as we moved out on one side of the village the 54th Battalion moved in on the other. We got into the 'buses on the main road, which conveyed us once again to Wallon-Cappel, where we arrived at 5.30 p.m. and marched back to our scattered area at Longue Croix. "C" Company discovered that most of their billets were full of refugees from Hazebrouck, which had been shelled considerably during our absence by longe range guns.

Our next move was on August 9th, when the Brigade moved to the Vieux-Berquin area, which was situated very much nearer to the line, and thus made us more accessible when we should be wanted.

We left Longue Croix at 10 a.m., and Hazebrouck, which had been bombarded fairly consistently during the night, was still being shelled. All along the road we met refugees—mostly in motor lorries—being conveyed to places of safety. It was very sad to see women with babies in their arms and young children, all dressed in their best clothes, leaving house and home in this manner. Some were on the road pushing barrows and perambulators laden with household treasures, whilst carts were also seen full of cradles, bedclothes and children, the latter not being able to comprehend fully what was happening.

The route—as mentioned in the Brigade Order—would have taken us through Hazebrouck, but, in view of the shelling, a messenger met us on the road, instructing us to avoid the town by taking the roads on the S.W. side of it, which was accordingly done.

As we left the town behind us, the shelling seemed to cease, and many of the civilians commenced to return to their homes and take the risk of further bombardment.

It was a pleasant day for marching, the atmosphere being very fresh after the recent rains, and the sun was not too hot. We passed through the village of La Motte and had lunch on the roadside, just as we were merging from the Forest of Nieppe. At

Vieux-Berquin we were met by a guide, who conducted us over another four miles of winding roads to our billets at Noote Boom and Steent-Je. We had thus completed a fifteen mile march without a single man falling out—one, however, being evacuated on the march with appendicitis.

The Brigade was very much scattered in this area, our own Battalion being between four and five miles from Brigade Headquarters, which made heavy work for the Battalion messengers, Widdop and Mears, as there was no telephone communication.

Training in this area was restricted to a great extent, as most of the country was under cultivation, and therefore was reduced to parades under company arrangements, according to a Battalion syllabus, at which Lewis gunners, bombers and grenadiers received specialists' training, interspersed with musketry and bayonet fighting instruction.

Route marches were carried out by the whole unit to neighbouring localities, including Bailleul (from which we were only from two to three miles distant), Meteren, Outtersteene and Steenwerck, and on one occasion a fifteen mile march to the top of Mont Des Cats.

The unsatisfactory advance (due to bad weather) being made on the Ypres front caused us to remain at Steent-Je for nearly six weeks, and to prevent the men getting stale on their training, we once again resorted to giving them as much healthy sport as possible.

Very successful sports meetings were held by each individual battalion in the Brigade on 18th August, whilst Brigade sports were held on the 22nd, prior to which General Birdwood inspected a composite battalion from the Brigade in a "march past." "D" Company represented our Battalion and were commented upon very favourably, the only complaint being that the officers were wearing caps instead of hats on a ceremonial parade.

Almost every night enemy aeroplanes used to fly over the neighbourhood dropping bombs, and although none fell in our immediate vicinity they frequently burst within a radius of a mile of our billets. On one occasion, a bomb was dropped on one of the 11th Battalion's billets at Le Verrier, wounding two men, one of whom afterwards died of wounds. Numerous searchlights endeavoured to locate the 'planes, and sometimes caught them in the beam of light, when they appeared like luminous moths. Anti-aircraft guns fired a considerable amount of ammunition at them but did not succeed in bringing one down. Owing to our own proximity to the line, each company had an anti-aircraft gun team on duty during the day, which brought fire to bear on any enemy 'planes which ventured over in daylight.

Our strength was further increased by small drafts of reinforcements and old hands returning to the unit, while 2nd-Lieuts. W. C. B. Daly, M. W. Blacklow and A. R. MacDonald joined us from cadet battalions. Our strength was now 53 officers and 1,064 other ranks.

A very useful Brigade school for junior officers and N.C.O.'s was organised at Vieux Berquin, and each battalion sent a liberal number of both to attend.

The health of the Battalion was still very good, and every opportunity was given for the men to utilise the baths at Outtersteene. One of the dreams of the R.M.O. was realised on 13th August,

AUGUST, 1917

when the men were bathed, received a change of underclothing and had their blankets fumigated in the Foden engine, *all in the one day*. All day long the Doctor went about with a smile on his face, and carried his offensive one step further by arranging for each company to have the use of a set of flat-irons, which, when heated, were utilised in ironing the seams of the men's trousers, which always harboured the vermin. I am certain he went to bed that night in a satisfied frame of mind, well knowing that he had a comparatively clean Battalion under his medical command.

It did not take us long to discover that our sister Tasmanian battalion, the 40th, was only about eight miles or so away, at a camp near Dranoutre, and many of the men obtained passes to visit their relations and friends in that unit, when the colours of the 40th Battalion, for the first time, mingled with those of the 12th. The 1st Australian Casualty Clearing Station was also situated nearby at Outtersteene, only a mile away, and many old friends were discovered, including Sisters King and Radcliff, who had left Tasmania with us in 1914 on the S.S. "Geelong."

On August 28th, two composite battalions from the Brigade marched past the Army Commander, General Sir Herbert Plumer. The 12th Battalion was represented by Battalion Headquarters and "B" and "C" Companies, and although it was a very windy day, which made it difficult to hear the band, yet the marching was very good and our appearance generally was favourably commented on by the General.

During this period a Brigade concert party was formed, which gave gratuitous vaudeville shows to the Brigade units in turn in the Y.M.C.A. tent, which was situated in a fairly central position in the area and from two to three miles from our village. September 6th was reserved as a 12th Battalion night, and every company was previously warned of the fact and asked to promulgate it to the men. During the morning of this day, however, a competition in battalion drill was conducted by the Brigadier, with a silver cup trophy for the winner. We arrived at 10.30 a.m. in drill order and looking very smart, but extremely hot after our march, it being a particularly warm day. I do not ever remember the Battalion drilling worse than on this occasion—the Commanding Officer himself, company commanders, the Adjutant, N.C.O.'s and men were all bad. The C.O. on one occasion gave a wrong order (a thing I had never known him do before) and if it was possible for a movement to be carried out incorrectly, the leading Company Commander was bound to do so. Altogether, we felt very disgusted with ourselves, in addition to being hot and tired, as we marched home, well knowing that we would be at the bottom of the list. The actual scores were:—

   10th Battalion .... 83 points
   11th " .... 68 "
   9th " .... 58 "
   12th " .... 51 "

About 5 p.m. the same afternoon, Capt. E. Y. Butler, of "A" Company, rang me up and said, "About this Brigade concert. Only one of my men want to go, so will it be necessary for an officer to accompany him as specified in the Order?" I was very annoyed at this and accused "A" Company officers of not having taken the trouble to inform the men of the concert. On my reporting the fact to the C.O., he told me to find out how many men were going from the other companies, and on doing so I discovered that no one wished to go from "C" Company and "B" Company had forgotten to tell their men, so I didn't bother about "D" Company. The C.O. then detailed one platoon per company to attend the concert compulsorily, and as they marched past Battalion Headquarters I could hear them singing "Bolshevik" songs and passing rude remarks about the war in general. Thinking that there might be some trouble brewing, I decided to go myself, and as I passed the platoons, loud remarks were made for my benefit to the effect that "the —— on Headquarters could make them march to the —— concert tent, but they could not —— —— —— make them go inside." On approaching our destination, I could see big thunder clouds appearing on the horizon, and as we arrived big drops of rain commenced to fall. One platoon had already arrived and were forming themselves into a "two-up" school, when it commenced to pour with rain and everyone had to take shelter in the tent. For a while, the heavy rain on the tent prevented conversation of any kind being heard, but as it eased off I went to the leader of the concert party and told him how things were and urged him to commence before the rain stopped, otherwise he would lose his audience. The first item was received in silence. The second item appeared to amuse them, but was accorded no applause. At the third item they laughed. The fourth item was distinctly good, and from then onwards the artists were applauded according to merit, many *encores* being demanded, and on leaving three cheers were called for the concert party. In such a manner a shower of rain relieved an awkward situation and gave a hundred men an evening's pleasure.

W

On one occasion a 'plane was seen to be flying extremely high over our area, and all at once a lot of shiny specks which sparkled in the sun were seen to drop from it. It took fully half-an-hour for these to reach the ground, some of them falling around Steen-Je, and on procuring one or two we discovered them to be a French newspaper — "Gazette des Ardennes"— published behind the German lines at Charleville. By means of illustrations and photographs, they strongly condemned the English method of warfare, and showed ruins of churches and public buildings in occupied portions of France damaged by the British artillery. This was one method of German propaganda designed to create discord between the French civilians and the British Army in France.

It was now definitely known that the 1st Anzac Corps would shortly be called upon to participate in the operations east of Ypres, and on September 7th the Brigadier held a conference of commanding officers and informed them that the task of the 1st Australian Division was to capture Polygon Wood, east of Westhoek. Two days later, all the officers of the Battalion, and a considerable number of N.C.O.'s, proceeded by motor lorry to Devonshire Lines, near Busseboom, and viewed a large-sized model of the country on the Divisional front, over which we would have to advance. This model was quite thirty yards square and constructed accurately to scale, including contours. Small notice-boards were freely used on the model, and indicated the names of trenches and tracks (corresponding with the maps which we were using), while others pointed out the positions of woods, marshes, machine-gun positions, strong posts, etc. It was thus possible to have an intimate knowledge of the ground over which we would have to advance, before the attack was even made, and proved to be invaluable to the officers and men on the actual day of the operation.

The only other incident of importance which happened during our sojourn in the Vieux-Berquin area was a Brigade attack which was practised in the presence of the 2nd Army Commander, General Sir Herbert Plumer, on September 11th. The order for the attack was issued in great detail, and the manner in which it was carried out by all units must have caused the Brigadier to feel proud of his command. A conference of officers was afterwards held, at which the Divisional Commander criticised the practice, although in reality no really serious fault was found. At the conclusion of these remarks, the Army Commander gave a most interesting and instructive lecture on "British Offensive and German Defensive Tactics," which gave us some small insight into the deliberations which affected the higher commands when making their dispositions and framing their methods of attack.

Our summer rest and prolonged period of training was brought to a close on September 13th, when we marched *via* Outtersteene, Merris, Strazeele and Caestre to billets in the Thieushouk area. As we passed the 1st Australian Casualty Clearing Station, almost the whole staff lined the side of the road and wished us the best of luck in the forthcoming attack as we passed. A percentage of officers, N.C.O.'s and men (mainly specialists), who were being left out of the line during the "stunt" (always referred to from this time onwards as the "Nucleus"), were detached from the column *en route* and proceeded to the Brigade Wing of the Divisional Reinforcement Camp at Rouge Croix to await our return.

Chapter XVI.

THE BATTLE OF THE RIDGES—AUTUMN, 1917

IN these words the Divisional Commander circularised all units of the 1st Australian Division as soon as we commenced our move forward to the line, thereby impressing on them the importance of the impending operations:—

"FIRST AUSTRALIAN DIVISION"

"After a lengthy period of rest and training we are being called upon to participate in an operation, the success of which will have the most important results for not only the British armies, but all the Allies. The part this Division has to play is the most important of all. The position we are to attack is the keystone of the whole. If we fail the tasks of the Divisions on our right and left will be rendered extremely difficult. I am full of confidence that the 1st Australian Division will achieve success and add to its already enviable record, and that, having carried our objectives, we shall hold them against all counter-attacks, living up to our Divisional motto—'What we gain, we hold.'

"Last year we took Pozieres under much more difficult circumstances and with little preliminary preparation or reconnaissance. In the impending operations we shall have the best of artillery support and everything is in our favour. Each Australian soldier is equal to any two Germans. Let every officer and man know where he starts from, the direction of the attack, what everyone has to do, and all be determined to succeed in spite of diffculties."

"H. B. WALKER, Major-General."

As soon as the Battalion had settled down into their billets at Thieushouk, the Commanding Officer and I went round to each company in turn and showed them a huge calico map (10ft. x 10ft.), illustrating the forthcoming attack, after which the Commanding Officer lectured them, pointing out the "jumping-off" trenches, the various objectives, known strong points and marshy ground, which was more or less impassable, at the same time carefully explaining the method of attack.

The next day we marched to Patricia Camp, in the Wippenhoek area, where we remained for two days and were comfortably billetted once again in huts.

Capt. Holyman, Lieut. J. J. Keen, 2nd-Lieut. V. L. Bovell and I, together with some N.C.O.'s, proceeded up to the line at 4 a.m. on the 15th September, for reconnaissance purpose. Motor lorries took us *via* Poperinghe to Ypres, where we alighted at the Lille Gate, and after walking along Warrington Road as far as Hooge, we kept to the track through Chateau Wood, by which the

Battalion would proceed when moving into the line. The road through the wood was quite distinguishable, but forward of this it became practically obliterated by shell-fire, and we took a cross-country track over to the Menin Road, passing a captured anti-tank gun in a concrete conning-tower on the way, and reported ourselves to the Headquarters of the 7th London Regiment. They were situated in an old German dug-out underneath the road, which was re-named Clapham Junction. A guide was provided for us and we proceeded to the front line and carried out a most successful reconnaissance being able to approximate the position of our jumping-off tapes, and obtaining a good view of the enemy country for some 500 to 600 yards in front. We had been warned to return to Clapham Junction by 9 a.m. as our artillery was timed to carry out a "shoot" at that hour which, in all probability, would be the cause of a retaliatory barrage from the enemy. The whole of the artillery on the Corps front opened fire almost simultaneously on the tick of 9 o'clock, and the noise created made conversation almost an impossibility. It was quite the biggest concentration of artillery that any of us had experienced, and the smile of satisfaction and confidence which passed over every face, was quite sufficient to indicate the thoughts passing through their minds. Before long, the enemy barrage commenced to fall around our dug-out, and one of our allotted tasks was to discover and accurately plot the enemy "barrage line" on our maps, so as to avoid casualties on the night of the operation. Bovell, who was an ex-artilleryman, showed considerable interest in the whole of the *strafe* and displayed great bravery and daring in exposing himself in order to gain a more accurate observation of the barrage line. We urged him not to take unnecessary risks, but he seemed to be almost devoid of fear as he sat on the side of the trench and explained to us in technical language various faults in the barrage. After about an hour, the shelling eased off somewhat, and we decided to "run the gauntlet" and get out before another hornet's nest was stirred up. We had barely got 100 yards along the track when the shelling recommenced, so I turned round and called out to the others to scatter, but discovered that Holyman and Keen had already turned back and only Bovell was following me. As we continued, the shelling increased considerably, and in desperation we took shelter in two shallow shell-holes. "It's no good squatting here like a couple of partridges," said Bovell, so we started off again, until at one spot the 5.9's, with instantaneous fuses ("daisy-cutters"), were bursting all around us, and I could not conceive how we could hope to get through the belt of shelling without a calamity happening. However, we eventually did do so, and I suggested that we should have a spell—for sprinting across a stretch of country full of shell-holes is tiring in the extreme —but Bovell said, "No, we must keep going, for they will lengthen their range in a minute." We then made for the Menin road once again and continued to run for all we were worth, but had not gone far before heavy howitzer shells commenced to fall ahead and behind us. Just as we thought we were out of the danger zone, I heard the distinctive sound of an approaching howitzer, followed by a blinding flash and a deafening explosion, the force of which knocked me down. On getting to my feet, I discovered Bovell lying on the ground with a wound in his neck and shoulder, so quickly ran back some hundred yards to where I remembered seeing some English stretcher-bearers. The shelling was still severe, but I persuaded a sergeant to accompany me with a stretcher, only to find on arrival that Bovell had "gone West." I enquired from the sergeant where his officers were and arranged for them to bury him when the shelling ceased and to put a cross on his grave. I then proceeded back *via* Warrington Road to the Lille Gate, where I awaited the return of the other members of the party, who were very shocked at the news I had to give them, and in return informed me that Pvte. Gladman, of the Intelligence Platoon, had also been wounded. We were a very subdued party returning to camp, with most useful information, but bad news.

The next day, 16th September, we proceeded to the Ouderdom area, where we remained for two days. We left Patricia Camp at 9.30 a.m. and found the roads extremely dusty and full of traffic. A somewhat humorous incident occurred when we were passing a paddock where a Chinese Labour Corps were busily engaged in laying a pipe line. Just at this time a squadron of fourteen big Hun 'planes was flying overhead, and "Archies" (anti-aircraft guns) were pounding away at them from all directions. Before long, the empty shell-cases commenced to fall with an ever increasing "swish," followed by a dull thud. Finally, one fell in the paddock with the "Chows," who promptly dropped their tools and made for every point of the compass in their efforts to find cover.

We were eventually met on the road and guided into Micmac Camp, where I was to be initiated into the administrative work connected with a well organised offensive. The Battalion Orderly Room was a hive of industry during the next forty-eight hours receiving Brigade Orders, supplements, appendices, amendments and addenda to Brigade Orders; instructions to draw battle stores; intelligence summaries from Division, Corps and Army; and orders for individuals and parties to report to Brigade Headquarters for special duty in connection with the forthcoming operations. The promulgation of these orders and the carrying out of instructions entailed an enormous amount of work, and Brockett and his typewriter were in constant demand.

The intelligence summaries were very wonderful and conveyed most useful information obtained by the Air Force, front line troops, and from prisoners and captured documents. These reports were eagerly read by all officers and promulgated to the men on parade whenever possible, for they contained reports of patrols, observers, front line units, artillery activity, in addition to information of the following nature:—

> "Captured orders indicate that the enemy lays great stress on the wiring of hedges, trees and woods generally. Battery positions are also to be wired."

"An officer and a N.C.O. of a field battery captured on the 16th August, east of Westhoek, made the following statement:

(a) A battery has, as a rule, three alternative positions.

(b) In quiet sectors, inaccurate guns are kept in use for considerable periods.

(c) A balloon remains up throughout the night, in order to pick up barrage signals.

> (d) The practice of moving guns forward during the night is confirmed."

"An order issued by General Von Unger, Commanding 49th Res. Div. (Yser) gave precise instructions for the front trench to be held very lightly both by men and machine guns, the front line system being held by at most one-third of the effective strength of the troops."

"A captured order of the 235th Division states that in order to avoid observation by hostile aircraft, movements in relief were to be undertaken in the early morning."

"(From a secret order of 23rd Res. Div. dated 31st July) 2-200 'Yellow Cross' shell for field guns will be issued to the 23rd Res. Div. This 'Yellow Cross' ammunition (together with H.E. shell in the proportion of three to one) will be employed in firing at railway stations, dumps, camps, billets, ammunition depots, and other specially important targets."

(Note.—"Yellow Cross" ammunition was the new mustard gas shell).

The Quartermaster was also kept very busy drawing stores from Ordnance, including white tape for the jumping-off trenches; extra cup attachments for No. 23 Mills grenades; special S.O.S. rifle grenade parachute rockets (red over green over yellow); paint, for painting the steel helmets prior to dusting them with fine sand to prevent them shining; ground sheets and signalling apparatus, for signalling to contact aeroplanes; special wire cutters, for attachment to the bayonet; and in addition to this was constantly receiving lists of shortages from company commanders.

On Tuesday, 18th September, we moved another step nearer the line and bivouaced in a paddock adjacent to Chateau Belge and just off the Ypres-Dickebusch road. While at this camp, we had to forward a certificate to Brigade Headquarters certifying that all stores had been drawn and issued and that all ranks in the Battalion were now fully equipped. This was a distinct indication that the actual operation was fast drawing near, for in all orders up to the present it had always been stated that the 1st Australian Division, in conjunction with other Divisions on right and left, would capture the enemy defended area Nonne Bosschen-Polygoneveld "at zero hour on 'E' day," and it was not until now that we were informed that "E" day was to be 20th September, and that "zero hour would be notified later."

During the next morning we moved by small parties *via* Shrapnel Corner to Half-way House Dug-outs near Hooge. Three companies arrived by 11 a.m., when our artillery started a practice barrage which drew a considerable amount of counter-battery fire, and so "C" Company took cover until it ceased and finally arrived at 11.55 a.m. The whole Battalion was accommodated in the dug-out, which was very deep and safe, but at the same time very damp and gloomy. The soakage of water was so considerable that it was necessary to have a party working continuously in reliefs on the pumps, otherwise the water would very soon rise ankle high, and in some manner used to put all the electric lights out and leave the whole place in darkness.

The men were urged to rest as much as possible during the day, as it was known that the following twenty-four hours would be very strenuous for everyone. During the evening advice was received in code from Brigade Headquarters that zero hour would be 5.40 a.m.

The task of the 3rd Brigade was to advance through Nonne Boschen and the northern fringe of Glencorse Wood and to establish a line about halfway through Polygon Wood and just short of the old racecourse. Nonne Boschen was a thinly wooded area of very swampy nature, and at this time was almost impassable. The attack was to be delivered in three stages on the leap-frog principle, the first objective (known and represented on the map as the "Red Line") being approximately the eastern boundary of Nonne Boschen, and allotted to the 11th Battalion for capture and consolidation. The second objective (the "Blue Line") was about 500 yards farther on, and more or less coincided with the western edge of Polygon Wood, and was given to the 12th Battalion. The 9th and 10th Battalions shared the third objective (the "Green Line"), which was to be the limit of the advance—a matter of about a mile.

During the evening, the Intelligence Officer, Lieut. J. J. Keen, with Pvte. F. R. Fox, went up to the line, and, together with the Brigade Intelligence Officer, laid out the jumping-off tapes, which afterwards proved to be invaluable in assembling the troops.

At 10 p.m. it started to rain heavily, and it looked as if the new advance was to take place in the same inclement weather as had doomed the previous attempts earlier in the summer. The rain ceased, however, soon after midnight, and the Battalion moved off in single file at 1 a.m., companies being commanded as follows:—

"A" Company .... Capt. E. Y. Butler
"B" Company .... Capt. I. N. Holyman
"C" Company .... Capt. D. McLeod
"D" Company .... Major H. A. MacPherson

The paths and duckboard tracks were very muddy and slippery, and progress in consequence was difficult, especially for Lewis gunners, stretcher-bearers and carrying parties, all of whom were heavily laden.

We were scheduled to pass Hooge Crater at 1.30 a.m., but the 28th Battalion blocked our progress, by marching across our track, and delayed us more than half-an-hour, so that we actually passed at 2.5 a.m.

"C" Company had been detailed exclusively for carrying duties, and stopped at a large dump near Hooge Crater to pick up entrenching tools, barbed wire, screw pickets, bombs, and other material necessary for consolidation.

The remainder of the Battalion proceeded through Chateau Wood, until the road became almost impassable, when Lieut. Keen and I led the way cross-country, taking a derelict tank on the skyline as a landmark, and were successful in marching straight on to the tape line. "A" Company were then led round to the right and "D" Company to the left, whilst "B" Company occupied a position in rear. It was then reported that Lieut. W. C. B. Daly, of "A" Company, with his platoon, was lost, and runners were sent back to endeavour to find him. They discovered that through a big gap occurring in the column, he had not noticed us leave the road after passing through Chateau Wood, and consequently had proceeded straight on and was now trying to locate us.

Touch was gained with the 11th Battalion in front and the unit on our right, but no troops could be discovered on our left flank. In the meantime, both "A" and "D" Companies complained about being congested, and on investigation it was discovered that we were only occupying half of our correct frontage, and Major MacPherson consequently took his company over to the left. The enemy, during these happenings, appeared to be very jumpy and nervy, and kept firing short machine-gun bursts, which were extremely disconcerting. It must be remembered that the enemy was considerably less than 200 yards away, and the occurrences recorded above could not be carried out without a certain amount of noise occasioned by subdued (more or less) words of command, rattling of equipment, and a few of the inevitable Australian swear-words involuntarily uttered as some "Digger" discovered himself precipitated knee-deep in a shell-hole full of water.

The code message indicating that troops were assembled on the tape line was represented by the words "Rations arrived," and this was accordingly sent to Brigade Headquarters at 4.10 a.m., "C" Company, a carrying party, not being required on the tape line, within the meaning of this message.

The Germans, at this time, were firing a considerable number of inflammatory shells into our rear areas, in the hopes of igniting an ammunition or R.E. dump. Sometimes they were successful, but at all times the flare occasioned by the bursting of these shells illuminated the country for a radius of fully half-a-mile. At about 4.30 a.m. one of these shells was fired, and, on looking back, I could see our "C" Company and a company of the 11th Battalion just coming over a skyline and plainly silhouetted against the glare in the sky. The enemy also saw it and promptly fired his S.O.S. signal, which was responded to by heavy artillery fire.

The whole Brigade had now assembled and were lying in open shell-holes, and entirely devoid of

any other cover, on a frontage of 400 yards with a
depth of 200 yards. As far as the 12th Battalion
was concerned, more than fifty per cent. of the men
had never been under shell-fire before, and the fire
discipline displayed by all ranks during this intense
barrage, which was of three-quarters of an hour's
duration, compared more than favourably with any
of the Battalion's' previous front-line records. To
suffer shell-fire, but at the same time to repel an
advancing enemy, is one thing, but to sit tight with
shells bursting all around you during a period of
enforced inactivity is quite another matter. The
troops of the 9th and 10th Battalion seemed to be
suffering more from the barrage, and pushed their
way forward with our men and those of the 11th
Battalion in front, thus making the congestion very
much worse and disorganising companies and battalions.
The effect of the explosion of the shells
was considerably lessened by the wet nature of the
ground, which allowed them to penetrate before
bursting, and, more often than not, the burst
resulted merely in a shower of mud and water.
However, the long period of nerve strain was not
improving the morale of the men, and it was with
a feeling of distinct relief that the bombardment
appeared to ease off about 5.15 a.m. Those of us
who had luminous watches eagerly watched the big
hand move round towards zero hour. The cessation
of shelling was only of short duration, however,
for the enemy soon re-commenced to shell us
with lesser intensity until zero hour, at 5.40 a.m.
At 5.30 a.m. we first noticed a grey dawn breaking
in the east, which gradually developed into a dark
twilight, until, with a deafening crash of artillery
and rattle of Vickers machine-guns, our barrage
opened on the very tick of the prescribed time, to
everyone's intense relief. The whole Brigade

moved forward as one man, the majority of them advancing casually with fixed bayonets slung over their shoulders, while many were seen to take out a cigarette or pipe and light it before continuing the advance. There was a thick morning mist enveloping the battlefield, and the attacking troops had a very ghostly appearance as they moved about in the half light. I had long since been separated from the C.O. and very much feared that he had become a casualty. During the period of shelling, I had been with Lieut. Mort. Allan, but as soon as the advance commenced he left to locate his own men, and I collected three or four detached men near me and moved forward. The mist was so thick that I could barely distinguish the line of advance and before long found myself well over the knees in water and at once knew it was the marshy swamp in Nonne Boschen. A few yards away, Capt. Butler was in the same predicament, and by consulting a compass we eventually got out of the swamp and found the 11th Battalion already consolidating the "Red Line." The advance to this point had not been difficult, the only opposition being from a "pill-box" in Glencourse Wood. These "pill-boxes," which were scattered freely over the countryside, were really very substantial concrete block-houses, and usually strongly defended by machine-guns. The one referred to threatened to hold up the attack, but Lieut. G. Vaughan and No. 4 Platoon joined with the 11th Battalion in rushing it, and as soon as the garrison of some thirty Germans discovered that they were surrounded and liable to be fired at and bombed from the rear, they surrendered without any more ado. The advance to the "Red Line" had been covered by a "creeping" artillery barrage, which moved at the rate of 100 yards in six minutes, and all ranks implicitly carried

TYPICAL COUNTRY OF SECTOR IN FRONT OF YPRES, AUTUMN, 1917
Showing pill-boxes occupied by 12th Battalion H.Q., Oct. 1st-2nd, 1917

(Copyright by Australian War Museum)

out instructions by keeping close up to the wall of smoke which indicated the line of bursting shells. Indeed, many officers afterwards reported that the men were too eager to push forward and were apt to advance quicker than the barrage, and thus became casualties from our own shells, and had to be ordered back accordingly. The artillery were to be highly congratulated on the splendid protection they gave us, a very small number of short-falling shells being recorded.

A protective barrage of forty-five minutes duration covered the work of consolidation, during which time the companies of the 12th Battalion re-organised prior to the second advance to the "Blue Line."

The signal indicating that the barrage was moving forward was given by every gun firing one round of smoke shell, which was quite of an experimental nature and proved to be wonderfully effective.

The only serious opposition during this second advance was from a known strong post on the right flank, just outside our sector and near to Black Watch Corner. "A" Company had lost touch with our right flank unit and consequently had to tackle the "pill-box" on their own. This task fell upon Lieut. Vaughan and his platoon, which he divided into three parties. They crept as close to the barrage as they dared with safety, and almost before the shelling had passed the "pill-box," they rushed it from three different points, before the garrison could mount their machine-guns, and by this display of dash were enabled to capture the garrison of twenty Germans, together with three machine-guns. Cpl. Townsend displayed great gallantry on this occasion by out-running his section in the advance and, together with one other N.C.O., held the Germans at bay from the door of the "pill-box" until joined by the remainder of the platoon. He shortly after lost his life by attempting a similar act some fifty yards on the right without assistance of any kind. N.C.O.'s such as he are not to be found every day, and his loss was felt by the company for a long time, whilst many of his companions who had known him since the early days in Pontville Camp found it hard to realise that he would never call the section roll again.

The other companies had not been troubled with any protracted opposition and took up their positions on the objective without any further bother. In the meantime, I had been looking for a suitable "pill-box" to serve as a Battalion Headquarters, and discovered one which had not been destroyed by shell-fire, about seventy-five yards in rear of the front line. I marked "12th Battalion Headquarters" in chalk on the outside and went in to inspect it, in a somewhat preoccupied state of mind, for I was firmly convinced that the C.O. was a casualty and I was wondering where I could find Major MacPherson to ask him to take over command. It was almost pitch dark inside, and I nearly jumped out of my skin when I heard someone move in the far corner. I whipped out my revolver and covered the supposed German and ordered him to "come out," but a matter-of-fact voice told me to "put that away as he was only after a few souvenirs." On coming out into the sunlight, the first person I saw was the C.O., who was himself coming to claim the "pill-box" as a Headquarters, and reciprocated my views in thinking I was a casualty.

The objective, as laid down in the Brigade Order, was so congested with three stumps and roots that it was found impossible to dig a trench, so the C.O. directed the companies to take up a line some 50 yards in rear, where a good field of fire was obtained. This proved to be a very fine stretch of sandy soil and very different to the wet, muddy ground over which we had advanced, and by connecting up the various shell-holes, a good trench had been prepared to a depth of four feet by 10.30 a.m. The ground where we were was fairly high and commanded a wonderful view of the battle, both to right and left. The second Australian Division, on our left, were more noticeable and could be plainly seen behind the barrage, which appeared as a distinct line of smoke and dust for nearly two miles, and which gradually crept forward with the troops well in its wake.

Company commanders were now able to send in their initial reports, when it was discovered that Lieut. Allan, had been killed by a shell during the advance through Nonne Boschen. I must have been one of the last few to see him alive, and it will be always gratifying to me to know my last impressions are typical of the lad, who was so popular with us all — bright and cheery, always wanting to be with and looking after his men, who recognised fully his wonderful qualifications which made him "a leader of men."

Capt. Butler had been slightly wounded in the neck, while Lieuts. T. A. Lay and A. J. Atkinson were also reported as casualties. Lieut. Percy Thompson was reported "missing," and it was not until a couple of days later that his name appeared on one of the hospital lists amongst the wounded. Major MacPherson was wounded, but remained at duty.

The protective barrage remained in front of the

"Blue Line" for two hours, to cover the work of consolidation, after which the 9th and 10th Battalions passed over us to establish the "Green Line." A very quiet day was passed, during which the men improved their trench and made it quite presentable. The 10th Battalion gave us assistance in this work, as the front line was found to be too congested. Strong points were also established at each corner of the wood, each having a concrete "pill-box" as a Headquarters, with Lieuts. A. L. Wardlaw and G. Vaughan respectively in command.

Although the front line was fortunate in missing all the shell-fire (for not a single casualty was reported from the front line trench itself), the "pill-box" which formed Battalion Headquarters, and the adjoining one which served as an aid post, received more than their fair share and appeared to be right in the enemy's barrage line. Several direct hits were registered, two of which narrowly missed the open doorway and a loophole.

The signallers were unfortunate during the attack, for Sgt. Driscoll, of Headquarters Section, received a wound from a shell bursting inside the "pill-box" adjoining Headquarters, which resulted in a lengthy period of pain in hospital, after which he was called upon to make the supreme sacrifice. Signaller Locke, of "A" Company, was also seriously wounded at the conclusion of the advance to the "Blue Line" and suffered an amputation of his leg. I discovered him with an improvised *tourniquet* on his leg, and asked him if I could do anything more for him. He looked up with a smile and asked if I could get some stretcher-bearers to take him to the aid post. This was quickly arranged, and it was with regret that we afterwards heard that he had died of wounds at the advanced dressing station at Clapham Junction.

The part played by "C" Company during the attack is deserving of special mention, for, since they were not one of the three assaulting companies, the excellent work performed by them is sometimes apt to be forgotten. First of all, they had an exceptionally hard carry (as a matter of fact, the C.O. reported afterwards that it was altogether *too* hard), from the dump at Hooge Crater, over the muddy tracks to the assembly position. During the initial bombardment they became hopelessly disorganised and lost all their material, and actually advanced with the remainder of the Battalion to the "Red Line." Capt. McLeod then organised his company and carried out some wonderful work in getting tools, material and ammunition forward, almost as soon as we had established ourselves on the "Blue Line." Lieut. Tynan rendered valuable assistance in this work, and never failed to satisfy any request for ammunition or material originating from a front line company. Having completed their allotted task, they occupied a position with the front line garrison, and were only called upon to carry water and rations when the pack horses arrived with them, in the early part of the evening, in rear of Glencorse Wood.

At dusk, the S.O.S. signal was fired on our left flank, but no counter-attack appeared to develop, and, with this exception, we passed an abnormally quiet night, due, no doubt, to the fact that both sides were moving their artillery to new positions.

At dawn on 21st September, our artillery opened up another heavy bombardment, which the contact aeroplanes reported was the means of successfully breaking up an enemy counter-attack which was being organised on our front.

The remainder of the second day passed very

quietly, and only short artillery *strafes* reminded us of the fact that the war was still on. The sun shone out of a clear sky, and many of the men stretched themselves out on the parados of the trench and enjoyed a nap after their night's vigil.

It was with surprise that we learned during the afternoon that the 1st Brigade was to relieve us during the night, and arrangements were at once commenced upon regarding handing over.

The relieving units were the 1st and 2nd Battalions, who started to arrive at 10.50 p.m., although "Relief complete" was not reported until 2.25 a.m. On coming out of the line, we particularly noticed our assembly position prior to the attack and how exposed it was. It is marvellous that the enemy had not seen us concentrating long before the S.O.S. signal was fired.

The Battalion once again occupied Half-way House Dug-outs. On arrival, we discovered that no pumping party had been working for some time, and so had to wait about half-an-hour before the water subsided and the lights came on again.

The Padre then told us some distressing news about the R.M.O., Major W. W. S. Johnston. We had heard during the battle that he had been wounded, but now discovered that his injury was of a serious nature, and that he was in a very low state when passing through the advanced dressing Station. We also learned at the same time of his wonderful work during the initial bombardment and early stages of the attack, for he was dressing the wounds of the men in the open, without attempting to take cover of any kind, and carried on unceasingly and untiringly until about 10 a.m., when he was himself wounded.

We left the dug-outs at 9 p.m. and proceeded to a bivouac area near Dickebusch Huts, after having left a party of two officers and 100 other ranks behind for burial duties.

The attack and capture of Polygon Wood is always considered as one of the most successful "stunts" of the 12th Battalion, for a maximum result was obtained with a minimum number of casualties, while the nerve strain and privations suffered were practically negligible when compared with other of our operations.

The casualties sustained by the Battalion were as follows:—

	"A" Coy.	"B" Coy.	"C" Coy.	"D" Coy.	Total
Killed	3	5	5	3	16
Missing	6	4	4	2	16
Wounded	34	29	38	37	138
					170

together with 1 officer killed, 1 missing and 4 wounded. All the "missing" men were afterwards traced, the majority of them having been wounded prior to the advance.

To compensate these losses, we had captured 13 enemy machine-guns and prisoners estimated at 40, and recognition of the good work performed by various members of the Battalion was made by the award of the following decorations:—

Distinguished Service Order.—Major W. W. S. Johnston, M.C. (A.A.M.C.).

Military Cross.—Lieuts. G. Vaughan, A. D. Tynan.

Second Bar to Military Medal.—Cpl. M. G. Blackman, M.M.

Military Medal.—Sgts. N. A. Vallance, Taylor-Vernon, E. E. Terry, H. E. Holtum; Cpls. T. A. Evans, W. Hamilton, W. E. Phillips; Pvts. E. Butler, A. E. May, W. Barwick, J. H. Lewis, M. R. Archdall, W. T. Wiggins, J. J. S. Rogers, F. R. Fox, J. E. Neasey, T. Burgess, T. C. Hartland, G. H. Watts, S. H. Johnston.

On the afternoon of 23rd September, the whole Brigade was conveyed by motor 'buses to the Steenvoorde area, proceeding *via* Reninghelst and Abeele. It was indeed pleasing to be once again miles away behind the line, and to be amongst the hedges and paddocks instead of trenches and shell-holes, and the opinion of everyone in the Battalion was to the effect that if this was the result of their successful work as "shock troops," then *sturmtruppen* would do them!

The next few days were occupied in resting and cleaning up, while Battalion Headquarters staff were busily engaged in compiling "The Report on Operations," writing out recommendations for honours and awards, and dealing generally with the volume of paper work which had accumulated during our period in the forward area.

On 25th September, the details left at the Divisional Reinforcement Camp before going into action, joined us once again, together with Capt. Burt, Lieuts. Facy, Bridger, Priddey and Lay, and some few reinforcements. Training of an easy nature, together with plenty of organised games, were carried out until the last day of the month, when we returned by 'buses to a bivouac area near Chateau Segard, about a mile-and-a-half south-west of Ypres.

During our temporary absence from the forward area, the 4th and 5th Australian Divisions had successfully continued the advance, and it was once again the task of the 1st Australian Division to combine with other formations and carry on the offensive by capturing Broodseinde Ridge, although in this instance our Brigade occupied the *role* of Reserve Brigade only.

The Battalion had been issued with a small number of "trench shelters," and, with waterproof sheets in addition, had erected numerous bivouac shelters in an open paddock and were preparing to rest for the night. The enemy's bombing 'planes, however, became very active as soon as darkness fell, and bombed the rear areas very consistently. At 8.30 p.m. a 'plane was clearly heard overhead, and before long a bomb was dropped about a mile away, following in quick succession by another and yet another, when we discovered to our dismay, from the flash of the explosions, that our paddock was in the direct line of progress. The 'plane could not have taken more than thirty to forty-five seconds in covering the intervening distance, and yet it seemed more like thirty minutes to those of us who watched. With tragic regularity the bombs continued to fall, getting nearer every moment, until the majority of us stood rooted to the ground with fear and waited for the inevitable to happen. It was almost a relief when the tension was broken by the unmistakable sound of falling bombs and a terrific explosion, for we now knew that some action was necessary to relieve the distress of those who were wounded, as the cries for assistance could already be heard. The paddock was almost devoid of cover, with the exception of a tall elm tree, under which some of the men had sought shelter, and, strange, to relate, it was this particular spot where one of the bombs fell, killing three men.

It was afterwards discovered that four bombs fell in the bivouac area, and, in addition to the casualties already mentioned, eleven other men were wounded, including Cpls. I. Taylor and E. C. Briggs and Pvte. Saltmarsh. Lieut. Ernie Potts afterwards strolled up and casually remarked, "He dropped eighteen bombs altogether; I counted 'em."

Early next morning, 1st October, I roused my batman — Pvte. Erle Joseph — and we both proceeded up to the forward area on a tour of reconnaissance, proceeding by Ypres and Hooge, and passing over Belleward and Westhoek Ridges. The enemy artillery was particularly active, and the crest of each ridge was persistently being shelled, which necessitated rapid movement, and on several instances caused us to take shelter until the *strafe* eased off somewhat. The track over which we passed was of a substantial corduroy, and had been built by the engineers and pioneers, but was now littered with broken G.S. waggons, limbers, ammunition waggons, discarded stores and artillery ammunition of various calibre, and many dead horses and mules in more or less advanced stages of decomposition. Having located the area we were to occupy, we returned to Chateau Segard, only too glad to get out of such an unhealthy locality.

At 9 p.m. the Battalion left the bivouac area and went forward to relieve the 48th Battalion on Westhoek Ridge, the handing over being complete at 11.13 p.m., with only one slight casualty from "B" Company. Some platoons were able to find shelter in trenches and "possies" on the rear slope of Westhoek Ridge, where the ground was not too wet, although most of the Battalion was accommodated in "pill-boxes" on the forward slope of the ridge.

During the next day, the valley between Westhoek and Anzac Ridges was heavily barraged by 5.9 and 9.2 howitzers, apparently searching for battery positions, which were there in abundance. A large number of gas shells was also fired, which caused a considerable amount of inconvenience, as the deadly fumes remained in the low-lying ground for a long time and caused two evacuations. We were relieved during the evening by the 1st and 4th Battalions, who were moving up to participate in the forthcoming attack, while we returned once again to Chateau Segard, where four more men were evacuated from the effects of the gas.

The following evening, 3rd October, we left our bivouacs and went forward to relieve the 4th Battalion on Westhoek and Anzac Ridges in order to permit them to move into the front line trenches, as the attack was to take place early next morning. The corduroy track from the Menin road, through Chateau Wood to our present situation, was subjected to unceasing shell-fire, and it is wonderful to think that the whole Battalion traversed it four times in forty-eight hours, and only suffered one slight casualty from the shelling.

Zero hour was fixed for 6 a.m., and, apart from the roar of our own artillery and the counter-battery fire from the enemy, the first indication of the progress of the attack was noticed about 7 a.m., when a swarm of prisoners were seen being marshalled over the skyline, *en route* for the P.O.W. (Prisoner of War) Cage.

Carrying parties were furnished by the various companies for getting ammunition and R.E. material forward, whilst officers were detailed to reconnoitre the tracks to the new front line, in the course of which Lieuts. Field, Lambert and Anderson were wounded.

Rations, during this period, were brought up by the Transport Section on pack mules to the rear of Westhoek Ridge, where carrying parties conveyed them to their respective companies. The task of conducting the horses and mules backwards and forwards along the track twice every night, with guns firing on either side and shells bursting everywhere, was difficult in the extreme, and the drivers not only ran great risks themselves, but also had the unenviable job of keeping the animals under control and preventing them from stampeding, which would have meant the loss of the rations, and perhaps the mules, too.

A sad occurrence happened on the morning of 5th October, when a party from Headquarters were awaiting the arrival of the pack mules just before dawn, on the rear slope of Westhoek Ridge. They were all taking cover behind an old gun position, when a large shell landed in their midst, killing no less than sixteen of them, whilst an additional three were badly wounded.

Orders were received to move into the line that night and relieve the 1st and 4th Battalions. It was a particularly dark night, and a drizzly rain made it still more unpleasant. The duckboard track leading to the front line was badly damaged by shell-fire in front of Anzac Ridge, which caused several platoons to become hopelessly bogged in the morass. In many instances, men who were heavily laden with guns and ammunition sunk well over the knees in the mud and water, and only floundered deeper in their efforts to extricate themselves. Officers were eventually forced to detail men to take up positions on solid portions of ground and to lend a helping hand to pull their comrades out of the quagmire. It was during a period similar to this that a shell burst and killed Lieut. W. H. E. Hale and Cpls. Hamilton and Henderson.

The front line was in a very exposed position on the forward slope of Broodseinde Ridge, and about 300 yards in front of the Passchendaele-Becelaere road. This was the last ridge to be captured on this part of the front, although Passchendaele Ridge, on the left, was still in enemy hands. It was now possible to overlook the whole of the low-lying country in front, and all the German tracks and roads were exposed to our view. Our forty-eight hours of duty in the front line resulted in an unbroken period of shelling, and officers and N.C.O.'s of every company were tireless in their efforts to protect the men as much as possible and at the same time prevent them from getting too "windy."

Instructions were received from Brigade Headquarters for identification of the enemy to be obtained on the Brigade front, and accordingly a party of one officer and thirty other ranks from the 11th Battalion and a similar number from the 12th Battalion carried out a raid on Celtic Wood on the night of 6th-7th October. Lieut. P. Vowles, of the 11th Battalion, was in charge of the raiding party, and 2nd-Lieut. A. L. S. Davey was the officer who commanded the party from our unit. The raid was most successful, and can best be recorded by quoting the report forwarded to Brigade Headquarters by Davey on his return:—

"REPORT ON RAID ON CELTIC WOOD, 6th-7th OCTOBER, BY 2nd-LIEUT. A. L. S. DAVEY.

"My party consisted of Sgt. Cherry and 10

men of 'B' Company, and Cpl. Miller and 15 men of 'C' Company.

"We were formed up and started to advance out of the front line trench at 10.45 p.m., when word was received that the barrage did not start until midnight. We stayed in shell-holes until our 18-pounders opened, and then advanced. We went about 100 yards into the wood and came back when the two rockets were fired from our front line (signal for party to return).

"There was no wire, and no trenches. Three dug-outs were bombed; they were fairly deep underground, and had staircases. We captured a machine-gun and its crew of ten men, and brought them back prisoners, one man who was about to fire the gun being shot. The wood appeared to be lightly held, and there was very little resistance. We did not see any concrete pill-boxes.

"One man states that he saw a field gun fire from a concrete emplacement, concealed in an old building on the right of the wood. He saw the gun fire through the rafters. It was protected by two machine-guns.

"The ground was very wet and swampy, and the wood very much knocked about.

"Casualties, one other rank wounded.

"I did not see the 11th Battalion party after the advance commenced.

"(Signed) A. L. S. DAVEY, 2nd-Lieut.
" 'C' Company, 12th Battalion."

When the prisoners were brought into Battalion Headquarters, Pvt. T. Luhrs, of the Intelligence

Platoon, acted as interpreter and solicited from them the information that they belonged to the 448th I.R. of the 233rd Division, and had recently come from the St. Quentin front. They also stated that the wood was garrisoned by two officers and about 150 other ranks, with three machine-guns, and that the vigour with which our attack had been carried out completely surprised them and gave little chance to offer resistance.

Our R.M.O. during this tour of the line was Major C. J. Tozer, who had recovered from the serious wound received at Pozieres, and on hearing that Major Johnston was wounded, took the first opportunity of getting back as M.O. to his old unit. He had a rather strenuous tour of duty, for the task of holding the line proved to be very expensive and the Battalion suffered many casualties from shell-fire. Cpl. Albert Prentice was badly wounded and the M.O. found it necessary to amputate one of his legs in the Regimental Aid Post. We were shocked to hear at a later period that he had to lose his other leg, and, as far as is known, he holds the questionable honour of being the only surviving member of the 12th Battalion with a double amputation.

We were relieved in the line on 7th October by the 10th Battalion, and the companies moved back into a support position in rear of the ridge, although Battalion Headquarters remained in the same "pillbox." After occupying this position for forty-eight hours without incident (other than the usual shelling), a very satisfactory daylight relief was effected by the 29th Battalion (complete at 1.15 p.m.), when we moved out by Helles track to a hutted camp, near Belgian Battery Corner, on the Dickebusch road.

The following awards were made in connection with the raid on Celtic Wood, and to N.C.O.'s and men who showed conspicuous bravery and devotion to duty during a period of heavy shelling and nerve strain:—

Military Cross.—2nd-Lieut. A. L. S. Davey, M.M.
Bar to Military Medal.—Sgt. N. A. Vallance, M.M.
Military Medal.—Cpls. A. Prentice, J. H. Mumford; L.-Cpl. H. J. March; Pvts. K. Moles, W. H. Hammersley, W. C. H. Burr, H. L. Riggs, F. E. Kasehagen, P. V. Neilson, T. M. Dunbar.

The work of the Transport Section was recognised on this occasion, and the outstanding devotion to duty and bravery of the undermentioned N.C.O. and men whilst conducting pack horses during a period of intense shelling earned them the Military Medal:—

Cpl. W. E. Johnson; Pvte. W. J. Hart; Dvrs. W. J. Matthews, W. Tooley.

On 10th October we marched to Scottish Lines, about two-and-a-half miles south-east of Poperinghe, where the Battalion had once previously encamped when in the Ypres area after the summer fighting of 1916.

The fourteen days which were spent in this camp were mostly wet, and therefore prevented any great amount of training being carried out. The time was principally employed in resting and cleaning up generally, specialists' training in huts, close order drill, gas drill, appointing N.C.O.'s to replace casualties, while afternoons were invariably devoted to football, each company being supplied with a ball by the Australian Comforts Fund.

Capt. B. J. Andrew relinquished his appointment as Staff Captain, 3rd Infantry Brigade, on 11th

October, and resumed regimental duty, and three days later the C.O. went on fourteen days leave to England, when Capt. L. E. Burt commanded in his absence. The Padre, Capt. W. K. Douglas, also left us at this camp, being transferred to the 2nd Australian General Hospital at Boulogne.

The original band instruments which we had brought with us from Tasmania, but had left behind with the "surplus stores" in Egypt, before coming to France, arrived whilst we were at Scottish Lines, and the band was at once reformed and commenced practising.

2nd-Lieuts. A. T. Wertheimer and B. Vaughan, with 155 reinforcements, joined us on 15th October, who, together with another batch of 67 four days later, brought our strength up to 52 officers and 942 other ranks.

Attention was drawn to the fact that within a few days we would celebrate the third anniversary of leaving Tasmanian shores, and it was decided to mark the occasion by giving a dinner to all original members of the Battalion at present with the Brigade. The question of supplies was left in the hands of Capt. Holyman, who scoured the countryside for provisions, and in consequence provided a most excellent dinner for us on 18th October, comprising soup, fish, joint, sweets, and fruit. Of the 550 officers and men who left in the S.S. "Geelong" on 20th October, 1914, 14 officers and 75 other ranks celebrated the third anniversary with the unit in France. During the meal and the remainder of the evening, the Battalion band and the Brigade concert party rendered a very fine programme of instrumental and vocal items, whilst Lieut. W. B. Mitchell recited some of the experiences of "a gude guide, mister," in Egypt.

The enemy was most consistent in his night bombing, and very soon after dusk had fallen each evening, the three warning blasts on the whistle would be heard, followed by real and imaginary commands in many of the huts for someone to "put out that blanky light." On several instances bombs were dropped some 800 or 1,000 yards from the camp, while on one occasion, at dawn, one was dropped in the transport lines of the 9th Battalion, which just adjoined our camp.

We "embussed" on the Poperinghe-Ouderdom road on 24th October and proceeded to Ypres, where we were comfortably billeted in the old Belgian infantry barracks, which for three years had suffered an irregular bombardment, and showed many honourable scars in consequence, but at the same time still offered adequate protection to more than a battalion of men.

For the next six days we carried out specialists' training and supplied working and carrying parties, while officers and N.C.O.'s went forward and reconnoitred tracks to the Brigade's new sector in the line. The R.M.O., Major Tozer, was at this time evacuated sick.

At 9 a.m. on 30th October, we proceeded *via* the Menin road and relieved the 8th Battalion on Westhoek and Anzac Ridges and remained there during the midday hours to rest and have a hot meal, in order to break, what would otherwise have been, a long, tiring journey into the line. Although we only stayed here a short while, we suffered a considerable amount of shell-fire, in which Pvte. V. Collins was killed. This lad had only arrived with the last batch of reinforcements and was going into the line for the first time. He had come to the Battalion with an excellent record, having attended officers' training schools in England and obtained the best of results. After having proved himself as a front line soldier, he would undoubtedly have received an early commission. Sgt. Ken Scott, of the Signal Section, also received a nasty wound in the knee, which ultimately resulted in amputation.

We resumed the journey onwards at 4 p.m. and relieved the 5th Battalion in the line at the early hour of 6.45 p.m. The front line was situated on the forward slope of the Passchendaele-Broodseinde Ridge, and by day commanded a view of the enemy country extending more than half-way to Moorslede. "A" Company held the right half of the Battalion sector and "B" the left half, whilst "D" Company occupied a support position and lived in dug-outs and "possies" dug in a dry, sandy depression on the rear slope of the ridge. Battalion Headquarters were situated in a concrete "pill-box" (known as Moulin Farm) near to the old gasometer, and about 400 yards east of Zonnebeke village, whilst "C" Company were in reserve in the ruins of the old soda water factory on the outskirts of the village itself.

The posts in the front line were in a deplorable condition, being on the fringe of a swamp. In fact, a portion of "B" Company in Daisy Wood had to build barricades of tree trunks and branches behind which to take cover, as the country was altogether too wet to dig trenches of any kind. We did not know the exact location of the enemy, but patrol work carried on through the morass under great difficulties disclosed the fact that he was more than 400 yards from us. The front line was practically immune from artillery, machine-gun and rifle fire during the whole tour of duty, which in some measure compensated for the unenviable life the garrison led in their water-logged posts. "D" Company and Headquarters suffered considerably from gas shells, one bombardment lasting three-quarters of an hour. Although every precaution was taken, several men were evacuated and numerous others lost their voices, this being one of the after-effects of slight "gasing." "C" Company received the artillery fire of the whole sector, and many direct hits were registered on the old factory from guns of a large calibre, and it was by sheer luck that their casualty list was not large.

On the night of November 2nd-3rd, the 11th Battalion was relieved on our left by the 9th Battalion extending their line to the right, and the 12th Battalion acting similarly to their left. The code message notifying Brigade Headquarters that this "squeezing out" movement was complete, was "The moon is shining bright," but it so happened that the night was particularly dark, and I had to smile as I heard the signaller transmit the message (not knowing its full import) and afterwards turn to his companion and say, "What a —— of a message. Why, it's as dark as hell outside." The same night Lieut. W. C. Priest took a patrol of twenty men out to gain definite touch with the enemy, but unexpectedly encountered a machine-gun post situated in a crater on the Waterdamhoek road and was himself wounded, although the remainder of the patrol returned uninjured. Lieut. R. G. Walduck took a similar size patrol out the next night for the same reason, and on his way out met a patrol of the 18th Battalion (our right flank unit) returning. He persuaded them, however, to turn back again, and they joined forces and continued. Before long they met an enemy patrol and chased it back into the very machine-gun post which had fired on Priest's patrol the previous night. The fire of the machine-gun was badly masked by the enemy patrol rushing frantically for cover, and our patrol took advantage of this fact and stormed the post before they had time to recover their scattered wits and were successful in killing seven, capturing one wounded prisoner (which the 18th Battalion claimed as a souvenir), and dispersing the remainder, without sustaining any casualties themselves.

The conveyance of rations was still a difficult task, and the Frezenburg road, along which the pack horses had to come, was barraged incessantly all day. Sometimes the convoy would just fluke a trip by dodging the barrages, but more often than not they had some very nerve-racking experiences. On 2nd November, the pack train was coming up the road about 11 a.m., under the command of Capt. Spotswood (Q.M.) and Lieut. Potts (T.O.) when they became enveloped in a hurricane bombardment just before crossing the Ypres-Zonnebeke railway line. A "pill-box" was nearby and an effort was made to take cover, but before doing so a shell burst right in the middle of the road, badly wounding one horse and causing another to stampede and take to "the bush." Dvr. Matthews and an old fellow named Rowse did superhuman work in endeavouring to maintain control of some of the other frightened beasts, and, together with Lieut. Potts, set a wonderful example of coolness and bravery, which means so much in circumstances of this kind. It is superfluous to add that the Q.M. delivered his rations, although it is willingly admitted that there were a few short.

We were relieved by the 4th Battalion at 6.45 p.m. on 5th November, and proceeded *via* the Frezenburg road to our old billets in the Barracks at Ypres. Those of the men who managed to secure a ride in an empty ammunition lorry returning, got back in good time, but those who "padded the hoof" the whole way arrived in a very fatigued condition and barely waited for the stew which was prepared for them, before rolling into their blankets and were soon fast asleep.

As a result of this tour in the line, the following decorations were awarded by the Corps Commander and the Commander-in-Chief:—

Military Cross.—Lieut. R. G. Walduck.

Second Bar to Military Medal.—Sgt. N. A. Vallance.

Bar to Military Medal.—Dvr. W. J. Matthews.

Military Medal.—Cpl. W. Vickers; L.-Cpl. A. A. Flint.

This period of the Battalion's existence, which was spent in crossing and recrossing the ridges amidst a perfect hail of artillery fire, cannot be engineers, and gained a considerable amount of closed without mentioning the work of the Brigade Mining Company, one platoon of which was furnished by the 12th Battalion and commanded by Lieut. Radford. They spent the whole period in this unhealthy neighbourhood without going out for a spell, and worked unceasingly building corduroy tracks, light railways, aid posts, cupola dugouts, etc., under technical supervision from the praise from the Brigadier and Divisional Commander for both the quality of their work and their endurance of the adverse conditions under which they were living.

Chapter XVII.

THE WINTER OF 1917

THE usual cleaning up, reorganisation, and forwarding of "Reports on Operations," and recommendations for honours and awards occupied the next four days, and on 9th November we marched to the Halifax area and were billeted in Vancouver Camp. We were accommodated in huts, and would have been very comfortable but for the fact that the camp was rather small for our unit (51 officers, 941 other ranks) and the men had to be somewhat crowded, while the mud and slush which abounded everywhere did not tend to improve matters.

In the evening, practically the whole of the Battalion went to hear the Corps concert party (the "Anzac Coves"), which was performing to crowded houses in the local "theatre." The party displayed wonderful talent and received a full issue of applause, but the "star turn" of the evening was the lady impersonator, who carried "her" part through to perfection, and for which "she" was the recipient of numerous "glad eyes," and of many remarks from the boys that need not be repeated here.

On Sunday, 11th November, we left Vancouver Camp at 10.30 a.m. and proceeded to the Vlamertinghe road, where we "embussed" and proceeded *via* Poperinghe-Steenvoorde-Cassel to the Renescure area (a distance of nearly thirty miles), and after a march of about two miles, arrived at our billets at Campagne-lez-Wardrecques at 5 p.m. Lieuts. Sellick, Gill, Laing, Hart and Dobson, together with 25 reinforcements, joined the unit on arrival, and on the next day advantage was taken of the fact that an unusual number of officers were actually present with the Battalion, and the services of a *mademoiselle* at Headquarters' billet were commandeered to take several groups of photographs.

The 13th of November saw us on the march once again, and although our packs were conveyed by motor lorries, we carried out a twenty-two mile march, *via* Blendecques-Wizernes-Clety, to Campagne-lez-Boulonnais, with only six men falling out, one of whom was evacuated. Capt. L. E. Burt temporarily commanded the Battalion during the absence of the C.O. as acting Brigadier.

The next day was spent mainly in resting after the march, whilst the acting R.M.O. went round and inspected the men's feet. A few days of easy training followed, during which period the Corps Commander, General Birdwood, presented medals and ribbons to many members of the Brigade, the guard of honour being furnished on this occasion by the 12th Battalion.

Our next move was once more accomplished on a Sunday, when, on the 18th November, we marched *via* Bourthes-Gournay-Parenty to billets in the Hubersent area, a distance of from twelve to fourteen miles. The area was only of a second-class nature as far as billets were concerned, and the smallness of the villages necessitated the Battalion occupying a very scattered area, and companies were ultimately disposed of as follows:—

    H.Q. and "A" Company.—Hubersent.

    "B" Company.—Fassurne and Vertvoie (two miles away).

    "C" Company.—Rolet (one-and-a-half miles away).

    "D" Company.—Bout de Haut (one mile away).

It was afterwards learned that the area had previously been occupied by British cavalry regiments, who, apparently, had not created a good impression amongst the peasantry, a fact which, in some measure, explained our frigid reception.

The surrounding country was particularly suitable for training, as many acres of fallow land were available for parade and training grounds. Each company was provided with a miniature rifle range and several bayonet fighting gallows were scattered about the area, so that before long route marches, musketry and specialists' training were in full swing under company arrangements.

The Brigade school for officers and N.C.O.'s was once again opened at an adjacent village called Lacres, under the supervision of Capt. W. R. Jorgensen, while a special school for map reading and intelligence subjects was started at Thubeauville, with Lieut. G. Vaughan as chief instructor.

The C.O. returned to the Battalion on 29th November.

Every afternoon was given up to recreational training, when all ranks were expected to participate in exercise of some kind. The Australian Comforts Fund once again gave us a liberal supply of footballs, which meant that the companies, as well as Battalion Headquarters, had two footballs each. In addition to inter-company matches, the Battalion team played the 3rd Field Ambulance and the 10th Battalion, both being close and exciting games, the former being won and the latter lost.

Daily leave was granted for twenty-five men from each Battalion to go to Boulogne (less than twenty miles away), from 2 p.m. to 8 p.m., the men being conveyed both ways by motor lorries.

Military competitions were once again commenced, and the Battalion made up for its poor effort at Steent-Je by winning the Battalion drill competition and receiving a silver cup, while "B" Company won for themselves the honour of being accorded the best company in the Brigade. The actual scores of the Battalion drill competition were:—

12th Battalion	....	592
9th ,,	....	572
10th ,,	....	560
11th ,,	....	496

Training, meanwhile, proceeded progressively, until comprehensive orders were issued for Battalion advance guard and outpost schemes, while several trench-to-trench attacks were practised, the G.O.C. Brigade being present on more than one occasion.

Capt. J. M. Henderson joined the Battalion as R.M.O. soon after our arrival in the area, and quickly proved himself a worthy successor to Major Johnston, being most conscientious in his work. He not only looked after the health of the Battalion as a whole, but personally interested himself in each man's ailments. In addition, he was a great sportsman, and on many occasions participated in the Battalion football matches. Padre H. A. Hayden joined about the same time from the 38th Battalion, and before long had gained the confidence of all ranks. His cheery face and continual efforts, both in and out of the line, to break the monotony of army life and improve the conditions under which the men lived, caused him to be loved by all who had the privilege to come in contact with him.

During our rest in the Hubersent area, the Battalion enjoyed the very best of health, which was largely the result of plenty of training and exercise carried out in crisp, wintry weather. On two occasions the whole unit marched about eight miles to Etaples, where they enjoyed an excellent bath and received a fresh supply of clothes, and afterwards a cup of tea from the Y.M.C.A. hut, purchased with regimental funds.

Leave to Boulogne and increased leave to England, together with regular pay-days and deliveries of Australian mail, were jointly responsible for the high morale of the Battalion, which was so noticeable at this period.

Very few reinforcements joined us in this area, although the following officers reported for duty:— Major H. A. MacPherson, Capts. E. Y. Butler and H. Webber, Lieuts. P. T. Miller, C. H. McKay, J. B. Catterall and W. H. Boyce, whilst 2nd-Lieut. R. B. Goode arrived from the Cadet Battalion.

Our rest was brought to a close on 13th December, when the Transport Section was detached and proceeded in three stages to the forward area, while the Battalion marched to billets at Senlecques and continued the journey next day to the little village of Assinghem. Lt.-Col. C. H. Elliott left the unit here to enjoy thirty days' leave in England, and the command, in his absence, was assumed by Major MacPherson. The 15th of December saw the Battalion entraining at Wizernes at 11 a.m., without incident, whence we proceeded to De Kennebak Siding, on the Neuve Eglise-Kemmel road, and rested the night in Ramillies Camp, in the Kemmel area, and in rear of the Messines-Wytschaete Ridge.

We relieved the 10th Battalion after dark the next day as support battalion of the Brigade, and occupied huts and "possies" at Wulverghem, "B" and "D" Companies being in the main camp, and "A" and "C" Companies in a forward position at Bristol Castle. "A" Company were moved still farther forward the next day, 17th December, and occupied Bethlehem Farm and acted as a reserve company to the 10th Battalion in the line.

For the next week the weather was exceptionally fine, a sharp frost having set in, which made movement in the forward area very much easier. Large parties were supplied for work on the support line, carrying R. E. material for the 10th Battalion, and were also utilised for pushing the loaded trucks along the light tram-track.

On 21st December, while our parties were working in the forward area, a series of relay posts were tested for transmitting the S.O.S. signal during foggy weather, but this fact had not been promulgated to units and our parties were likewise unaware of the fact. The enemy evidently mistook it for some prearranged signal for an attack, and laid down a heavy barrage on the support line, which resulted in Lieuts. Gill and Boyce and several men being wounded.

We celebrated our fourth Christmas away from home by relieving the 10th Battalion in the line on the night of 24th-25th December, relief being complete at 5 a.m. "B" Company was the right company in the line, and "D" Company the left, whilst "A" Company occupied a support position near Battalion Headquarters, and "C" Company in reserve at Bethlehem Farm. The frontage held by the Battalion was about 1,000 yards, and consisted of a line of posts in fairly good condition. Those in the left sector were more or less connected, but on the right an overland track had to be taken in moving from post to post. The 11th Battalion was our left flank unit, while the River Douve served as a right boundary, with the 7th Australian Infantry Brigade on the southern bank.

During Christmas afternoon, the area around Battalion Headquarters was heavily shelled for more than an hour, and a direct hit was obtained on "A" Company Headquarter dug-out, which killed Capt. Cruickshank, of the 10th Battalion, who was sheltering there, and slightly wounded Lieut. Lines. Capt. Burt was also evacuated with shell-shock.

Snow fell heavily during the night and was fully three inches deep at daybreak. This had a tendency towards retarding the progress of the work in hand, as all new work had to be camouflaged and sprinkled with snow to prevent enemy aeroplanes from detecting the construction of the new posts in the support line. It also necessitated the issue of white duck patrol suits to allow the front line companies to continue their activities in this direction, and thus maintain the command of No Man's Land, which the Germans were apt to dispute at times.

Before we had been in the forward area long, the first symptoms of trench feet again made an appearance in the Brigade, and in order to check its progress as much as possible, the Brigadier ordered that inter-company reliefs should be carried out in the line every forty-eight hours. This was effected in the 12th Battalion on the night of 27th-28th December, but, as the men had to carry out their nightly task of constructing the new support line before going into the front line, relief was not complete until a short time before dawn. Indeed, the Company Headquarters staff did not change over until after breakfast, and in that short interval a dire calamity occurred. "B" Company Headquarters in the line consisted of a cupola dugout half-submerged in the ground and covered with earth. Shortly after 8 a.m., Capt. W. A. Connell, Lieuts. J. A. Campbell and P. T. Miller were occupying this dug-out when the enemy fired some "pineapple" bombs, one of which struck the dugout in a most vulnerable spot and penetrated almost before exploding, with the tragic result that Campbell and Miller were at once killed and "Wac" Connell sustained a fractured thigh. He was at once conveyed with difficulty by the stretcher-bearers down the knee-high communication trench, and as he passed Battalion Headquarters appeared to be bearing his painful injury with wonderful composure. We were all shocked to hear later in the day that he had succumbed to his wounds at the advanced dressing station (Kandahar Farm) at Wulverghem, about noon. His death affected the whole Battalion considerably, for it seemed to be taken as a foregone conclusion that "Wac" would see the war out. He, who had gone through the Landing and earned the only D.C.M. awarded to the Battalion on that occasion; he, who had gone through Pozieres and Mouquet Farm; he, who had seen so much actual fighting and normal front line work without being wounded, and then to be the victim of a miserable "pineapple" in a quiet sector! It was hard to believe! He was known throughout the Brigade and Division and was popular with everyone, but with none so much as the officers and men whom he actually commanded. No better epitaph could be selected for such a gallant comrade—to be read by all who knew him—than the words of Shakespeare—

"He was my friend, faithful and just to me."

Jack Campbell was also a favourite with his fellow officers and men, but, being more of a reserved nature, it was not everyone who was given the opportunity of becoming intimate with him. He had been a useful officer in the Battalion, both as a platoon commander and as Lewis machine-gun officer.

"Paddy" Miller was a comparatively new arrival, having been commissioned to the 12th Battalion from the 2nd Brigade during the preceding summer, but in the short time that we had known him we recognised his sterling qualities, and always enjoyed his jovial company.

During this tour of duty, "A" Company occupied the right sector of the line, while "C" Company were on the left; "D" Company carried out the duties of the support company and occupied "possies" in the S.P. (strong post) line and Pollard Support, and "B" Company were in reserve near Battalion Headquarters.

Another inter-company relief took place on the night of 29th-30th December, and two days later (night of 1st-2nd January, 1918), the whole unit was relieved by the 10th Battalion and moved back to Wulverghem once more, "A" and "C" Companies being in huts in the main camp, "B" Company at Bristol Castle, and "D" Company at Bethlehem Farm.

The two outstanding features connected with this tour in the line was the amount of work done in the sector and the abnormal quietness of the enemy.

When we first arrived in the sector, we were somewhat surprised to see the comparatively unbroken state of the country after the battle of Messines, and also to find that although the whole of the summer and autumn had passed since the ground had been captured, very little effort had been made to construct any lines of defence. A comprehensive scheme was therefore at once formulated by the Brigadier, and every unit in the Brigade entered whole-heartedly into the work and made wonderful progress during our occupation of the sector. As far as our front was concerned, the front line garrison worked exclusively on the improvement of their own posts and wiring the front, which was badly needed. The support companies worked on the S.P. line, by constructing a series of strong posts in rear of the front line and providing them with cupola dug-outs, the intention being that they should form part of the front line system when completed and sufficient accommodation provided.

The Brigade Mining Company worked like Trojans on Pollard Support, by extending and improving the actual trench and providing more dug-outs for the congested garrison.

The 10th Battalion (or support battalion) were employed on the Brigade Reserve line, just in advance of Battalion Headquarters, by constructing

CLOTH HALL, YPRES

(Copyright by Australian War Museum)

a series of well-sited strong posts, which should prove a formidable obstacle to any advancing enemy, if held by good troops.

Units in rear were similarly occupied in constructing and wiring a Corps line of defence.

As stated, the enemy was unusually quiet at this time, but in view of the fact that he was quieter still during our next tour in the line, the fact will be more fully commented upon at a later stage. Our casualties were not many, but at the same time, proportionately speaking they were extremely costly, being 3 officers 2 other ranks killed and 3 officers and 2 other ranks wounded.

The period January 2nd-9th was spent at Wulverghem, when the Battalion furnished nightly working parties, whose varied duties consisted in continuing the work on the Brigade Reserve line, supplying large carrying parties for conveying R.E. material to the forward dumps, and also pushing parties for pushing the loaded trucks up the light tram-track as far as the Headquarters of the Battalion in the line. Every opportunity was taken to care for the men's feet, and the R.M.O. and his stretcher-bearers were untiring in their efforts to insist upon and supervise the application of the special talc powder issued for this purpose. The baths were also requisitioned on more than one occasion and the men given the opportunity of having some hot showers and clean clothing.

On the night of 9th-10th January, we again moved back into our old sector and relieved the 10th Battalion by 11.45 p.m. During the afternoon a very heavy fall of snow covered the ground to the extent of nearly four inches and after midnight a rapid thaw set in, which made the forward area very objectionable and covered in mud. During the night a patrol went out and was fired upon by the enemy and one man was wounded. L.-Cpl. A. E. Dilger, of "B" Company, very pluckily volunteered to go out to bring him in, and while doing so was himself wounded, as a result of which he was afterwards awarded the Military Medal.

The company cookers at this time were located at Stinking Farm, situated on the River Douve in rear of the Messines Ridge. Lieut. Bensley had a small command of men here (mostly sore-footed men and others selected by the R.M.O. as unfit for line work) and assisted the Quartermaster in the preparation and despatch of hot meals. He also had a drying room and sent a consignment of dry socks and gum boots up to the line every night and received the wet ones back in the morning by the returning ration parties.

The Q.M. store was located at Daylight Corner, on the Neuve Eglise-Kemmel road, whilst the Transport Section were in a paddock near Neuve Eglise.

January 15th was a disastrous day, for it rained from early morning till late at night with unceasing steadiness, and in consequence all working parties had to be cancelled. Very few of us, however, anticipated the view which greeted our eyes in the morning, for the River Douve was high in flood, and from a stream averaging only a few feet in width it was now swollen to such an extent that in some parts it reached as much as 100 yards from bank to bank. Two of our line posts in its vicinity were flooded and had to be evacuated, while pitiful messages reached us from the company commanders in the line to the effect that in many cases the sides of the trenches had literally slid in, owing to the absence of revetting frames, and that the trenches were now knee-deep in semi-liquid mud and totally unfit for occupation. The Germans were in a similar condition, for many of them could be seen walking about in the vicinity of their trenches and apparently trying to dry their blankets. So the day passed by, most of the fellows adopting the attitude of the Hun and sleeping on the ground in rear of the ruined trenches, or attempting to improve them ready for occupation during the night.

At mid-day an excited messenger arrived from Stinking Farm with the news that a field cooker had been washed away down the river, together with an unknown quantity of hot food containers, gum boots and socks. When the water ultimately subsided the cooker and the hot food containers were salvaged, but the gum boots and socks—never.

We were almost shamefaced when we handed over the command of the line to the 8th Battalion on the evening of the 16th January, but endeavoured to explain the damage done by the flood in the short period of twenty-four hours, and at the same time were sincere and profuse in our expressions of regret at not having had time to repair more of the damage.

On relief, we once again moved back to our old familiar camp at Wulverghem, where Lt.-Col. Elliott rejoined us on 18th January on completion of his thirty days' leave. During his absence the administration of the Battalion had run very smoothly under Major MacPherson's command, and he proved himself a very practical soldier while commanding the unit during its two recent tours in the line.

The same day "B" Company moved *en masse* to Liffey House Dug-outs on the left of the Brigade sector and in rear of the Messines Ridge, where they worked on burying cables, under the supervision of the Divisional Signalling Company, and lived under very adverse conditions.

A very violent form of diarrhoea affected the whole Battalion during our "rest" (if it could be called such), and although every precaution was taken, the cause could only be ascribed by the R.M.O. to the water supply. The effect of this was very weakening, and quite a number of men had to be evacuated, while a still greater number were left at Stinking Farm to recuperate, and a very sick Battalion went into the same sector of the line and relieved the 8th Battalion by 7.45 p.m. on 23rd January.

The outgoing Battalion had made good headway in improving the front line posts during our absence but there was still a considerable amount to do. Extra parties were put on to this work during our sojourn of eight days in the line, and on relief we left every post in a dry state with a raised duckboard bottom, the sides well revetted, and dry shelters for the garrison. The rapid progress of this work was made possible by the abnormal quietness of the enemy. His attitude was very difficult to understand, for day after day passed without a hostile shot being fired by his artillery, while machine-gun fire and sniping was practically "nil." Many suggestions were offered to account for this apparent apathy, such as a projected withdrawal, shortage of ammunition, saving up of ammunition for a big *strafe*, or presence of Bavarian or other similarly less aggressive troops, but the matter was never solved to our satisfaction.

It is with regret that the fact must be recorded that during our tours of duty in this sector, one man walked over to the enemy's line; his action appeared to be so deliberate, and repeated warnings were so totally disregarded, that the front line garrison were firm in their opinion that it was a case of deliberate desertion. If so, it was the only known case in the whole of the Battalion's existence, and even before admitting this, it should be remembered that the man has had no opportunity of tendering an explanation.

The 30th Battalion (5th Division) relieved us on the last day of the month, and we moved back to a Nissen hut camp, known as Shankhill Huts, at Neuve Eglise, without having sustained any casualties in the line.

During the month the following movement of officers took place, other than the casualties already recorded:—

> Capts. S. R. Houghton and C. N. Richardson to hospital. Lieuts. Gandy, Jacob, Anderson, Kelly and Lambert rejoined the Battalion, whilst 2nd-Lieuts. King and Muir joined from Cadet Battalions, 2nd-Lieut. Clemes from the Training Battalion, and 2nd-Lieut. Sayer from reinforcements.

Major James also rejoined the Battalion and afterwards transferred to the 9th Battalion.

The whole of the month of February was spent at Shankhill Huts, which proved to be quite the most comfortable camp occupied by the unit since its arrival in France. The camp occupied two large paddocks, and the Nissen huts, in most cases, were constructed under the tall elm trees and behind the hawthorn hedges in order to reduce their visibility and minimise the result of any hostile shelling or bombing. There was a sufficient number of these to allow comfortable billetting, while most of the Headquarters details had a hut to themselves. An officers' mess was once again started, and for the first time we used special "12th Battalion" cutlery, purchased out of mess funds. The regimental band was put to good use, and, in addition to playing the Battalion on and off parade, used to render items during the changing over of "duties," and also during the officers' mess in the evening.

Great credit is due to Padre Hayden, who obtained a very large tent from the Church Army and converted it into a reading, writing and recreational tent for the men. In conjunction with Lieut. Geo. Gandy, he also organised concerts, lantern lectures, euchre and boxing tournaments for almost every evening, while on Sundays the tent was utilised for early morning service and the Battalion's church parade.

The usual syllabus of progressive training was issued and carried into effect, commencing with "steadying-up" drill (which is always so very essential after a tour in the forward area), and afterwards extending to specialists' training in all branches under company arrangement. In addition to this, we also had to supply a fairly large daily fatigue party (approximately 150 men) for unloading duties at various railway sidings.

Afternoons were invariably spent by each company carrying on organised games, and before long football, soccer and Rugby were in full swing throughout the Battalion. Inter-company matches developed into inter-battalion matches, until eventually a Divisional competition, held under Australian rules, was organised. In the Brigade heat we were defeated by the 10th Battalion, who were afterwards defeated by the 8th Battalion in the final. A happening worthy of record occurred on 28th February, when the unit had the first real opportunity of mingling freely with their comrades in the 40th Battalion, which was located a comparatively short distance away, as only a small number of the men had previously availed themselves of this pleasure when at Steent-Je. We invited them over to a friendly game of football, and we were pleased to see them bring a large number of "barrackers" with them. Great excitement prevailed during the match, which resulted in a narrow-margin win for the "white over blues."

February 19th was declared a holiday, and arrangements were made to celebrate the Christmas Day we had spent in the line. Sports were held both morning and afternoon, and gift boxes from the Australian Comforts Fund (on behalf of our homefolks) were issued to every man. In the evening, the 3rd Brigade concert party, known as "The Boomerangs," gave a free performance to the whole unit, utilising the large hall in the village.

An increased percentage of men were allowed to go on both English and Paris leave, a fact which was appreciated by everyone—at least, everyone with a decent credit in his paybook. During the month, the C.O. again temporarily commanded the Brigade during the Brigadier's absence, and Major MacPherson acted in his stead, until he himself proceeded on Paris leave, when Major J. A. Foster commanded. I also applied and received permission to spend eight days' leave in the south of France, instead of Paris, and during my absence Lieut. A. D. Tynan acted as Adjutant.

A party of 30 officers and 600 other ranks from the Brigade proceeded to Tilques (in the Wisques area, near St. Omer and the 2nd Army School) and carried out a ten days course of musketry on the specially constructed rifle ranges which were situated there. Brigade Headquarters also organised short courses of instruction within the Brigade in elementary engineering and map reading, Capt. B. J. Andrew being the chief instructor at the latter class.

During the month a Divisional rifle competition was held, for which the Army Rifle Association (England) presented medals for each member of the winning platoon. The conditions of the competition were for a Lewis machine-gun team of three and seventeen riflemen, under the command of one officer, to fire at disappearing targets from three different ranges, trenches being used on each occasion, in and out of which the competitors had to jump. The competition within the Battalion was held on 16th February, when 2nd-Lieut. A. W. Clemes with No. 2 Platoon, "A" Company, was successful. The same platoon won the Brigade heat with an easy margin, and similarly won the Divisional championship. Our only regret was that it was not possible at the time to extend the competition to the other divisions of the Australian Corps. Clemes afterwards said that his biggest difficulty had been to beat the other fifteen platoons in his own unit, for the actual scores were as follows:—

12th Battalion heat (leading platoons only)—
  No. 2 Platoon 337
  No. 16 ,, ... 332
  No. 4 ,, ... 311

3rd Brigade heat—
  12th Battalion 405
  10th ,, ... 333
  11th ,, ... 326
  9th ,, ... 303

1st Divisional final—
    12th Battalion 322
    7th   „   287
    2nd   „   283

Capt. Holyman did wonderful work during our stay at Shankhill Huts by keeping the canteen well stocked with goods. To do this, it meant that, as many as two or three times a week, he had to go out in a motor lorry and scour the whole of northern Flanders in his efforts to procure a sufficient quantity of produce to satisfy a whole Battalion during the first few days after a pay day. The B.E.F. canteens at Hazebrouck, St. Omer and Boulogne were very soon sold out, and on many occasions he had to go as far as Calais and Dunkerque to satisfy his needs.

The Quartermaster's staff worked at high pressure in re-equipping the Battalion, while every rifle in the unit was overhauled by the Armourer-Sergeant. The rations generally were rather good at this particular period, especially the meat ration, although the quantity of vegetables issued left much to be desired. These, however, were supplemented as much as possible by purchases from the French peasants out of regimental funds, while individual purchases from the canteen brought the daily ration to a fair pitch of perfection.

Major Johnston rejoined us again as R.M.O. on 27th February, having recovered from the wounds received at Polygon Wood. Although we welcomed him back with open arms, we were equally sorry to lose Doc. Henderson, and everyone was of the opinion that, as we wanted to keep both of them, *our* Battalion ought to have two M.O.'s.

Some extremely interesting lectures were given by Capt. Bles, 2nd Army lecturer, in the concert hall, Neuve Eglise. His subjects covered the Retreat from Mons, the First Battle of Ypres, the Battle of Verdun, and other strategical movements connected with the early stages of the war, all of which were excellently delivered, and illustrated by large maps and diagrams. At first they were given only to officers, after which N.C.O.'s were allowed to attend, who showed such marked appreciation that, ultimately, Capt. Bles was lecturing to crowded halls of "Diggers." Not a sound was heard as the lecture proceeded, and each man intently followed the strategic movements of corps and armies across the north of France in the early days, in a most intelligent manner, which the lecturer afterwards admitted surprised him. On many occasions he stopped and said, "Have you had enough?" when a babel of voices urged him to "Keep going, sir," and "You're doing well, Dig," and also testified to the interest being shown.

After a month of almost perfect winter weather, an extremely pleasant spell within three to four miles of the front line was brought to a close on 2nd March, when we "embussed" at Neuve Eglise at 10.30 a.m., in a piercing cold wind, and proceeded to Voormezeele. From here we marched a short distance to the Ypres-Comines canal, and thence along the southern bank for about half a mile, crossing at Lock No. 6 to dug-outs in the vicinity of The Bluff. On either side of the canal there was a huge spoilbank, from twenty to thirty feet above ground level, which had been tunnelled from end to end, installed with electric light, and consequently gave accommodation to many hundreds of troops. Indeed, the allocation of space and impartial billetting of units necessitated an Area Commandant, who was situated at Norfolk Bridge (Lock No. 6).

The initial *role* of the Battalion in this new area was Support Battalion to the right Brigade, for which purpose we were distributed as follows:—

Battalion H.Q., "A" and "D" Coys.—Crater Dug-outs,

"B" Coy., less one platoon.—Gasper Cliff.

"C" Coy. and one platoon "B" Coy.—Canal Dug-outs.

all being on the northern bank of the canal.

The Q.M. store and Transport Section were at Bedford Farm on the Kemmel-La Clytte road, where the Nucleus Company was also situated.

R.S.M. Joe Cooper organised a very decent rifle range from Gasper Cliff to the southern bank of the canal, firing at bottles, biscuit tins, etc., until some of the men of the 10th Battalion occupying some dug-outs in Spadger Lane nearby, lodged a justified complaint regarding *ricochets*, which caused the range practice to cease abruptly.

The works programme of the Brigade was promulgated immediately on our arrival, and the whole of the Battalion was detailed for duty the first night, either in carrying R.E. material to the forward dumps for the use of the Battalion in the line, or in the construction and improvement of communication trenches (*viz.*, Oak Avenue on right of canal, and Imperial Avenue on the left), and also construction of support lines—Oak Support on the right and Railway Trench on the left.

The enemy on this front was proving himself to be quite different from the one we had recently in front of us at Messines, for on the night of their taking over in the line, the 10th Battalion were heavily raided by a party of 3 officers and 120 other ranks. The line was penetrated and the raiding party reached a "pill-box," which served as a platoon headquarters, where Major Henwood, the Company Commander, was killed. It also became very noticeable that, as our tour of duty in the forward area continued, so the attitude of the enemy on our front became more aggressive. His artillery activity increased considerably, particularly with regard to gas shelling; our patrols constantly came in touch with hostile parties, and on more than one occasion he attempted to raid the Brigade front.

A part of the Brigade defence scheme was to locate and organise a line of "pill-boxes" on the crest of the ridge, which ran about 1,000 yards behind our front line. This duty was allocated to the 12th Battalion and effectively carried out, and in addition we stocked each strong post with cases of bully beef, tins of biscuits, and water, and a plentiful supply of ammunition to enable a garrison to put up a protracted fight in case the enemy barrage in rear made it impossible to replenish supplies. This entailed a considerable amount of work, in addition to the carrying of the stores and ammunition, for many of the "pill-boxes" were water-logged and needed to be pumped out and made weatherproof, after which it was necessary to build a staging inside to keep the stores dry.

The sector occupied by the Brigade was quite near to the famous Hill 60, and while in the support area, many men who had not served with the Battalion in September, 1916, applied for permission to leave the Battalion sector for an hour or so to visit this historic battlefield. Another notable feature was the establishment of the Battalion canteen in a sandbagged "possie" on the spoilbank on the northern bank of the canal, this being the first time it had been brought into the forward area.

The 9th Battalion Headquarters (left battalion in the line) were situated in "pill-boxes," which occupied a position in a gully in Fusilier Wood on the left of the canal. During the early hours of 7th March, the enemy bombarded this gully with gas shells, with disastrous effect. The morning was particularly still, and in consequence the deadly fumes hung about in the low ground and offered no warning note to the impatient "Diggers," who were anxious to take off their gas masks after wearing them for such a long time. As a result of this gas shelling, practically the whole of the 9th Battalion Headquarters staff became casualties, totalling 9 officers and 150 other ranks, including the Commanding Officer, Lt.-Col. L. M. Mullen. Orders were at once received by us from Brigade that Major MacPherson, Major Johnston (R.M.O.), together with signallers, runners and medical personnel, were to re-establish their headquarters in a new locality and to carry on the administration of the Battalion until relieved at night by the 11th Battalion. In the meantime, the Divisional Gas Officer arrived on the scene and placed the whole of the area "out of bounds," posting sentries along the tracks to prevent anyone from wandering into the tainted area, where the fumes still lingered.

We relieved the 10th Battalion in the line on the night of 10th-11th March, and were disposed as follows:—

Battalion Headquarters.—Bow Dug-outs in spoil-bank on the right of the canal and on the forward fringe of Chateau Wood.

"A" Company (left company in the line).—Posts 4.0.6 and 5.0.6 in front line; Support Platoon and Coy. H.Q. in Oak Support.

(On right of the canal)

Posts 6.0.6, 7.0.6, 8.0.6 (Platoon H.Q.), 9.0.6 and 10.0.6 in front line, and Support Platoon in Railway Trench.

(On left of the canal)

"D" Company (right company in the line).—Posts 2.0.12, 3.0.12, 4.0.12 (Platoon H.Q.), 1.0.6, 2.0.6, and 3.0.6 in front line; two platoons and Coy. H.Q. in Oak Support.

(On right of the canal, in front of Hollebeke)

"B" Company (Support Company).—Dug-outs underneath White Chateau.

"C" Company (Reserve Company).—Two platoons and Coy. H.Q. in White Chateau; two platoons in Strong Posts 2, 3 and 4 in the Reserve Line.

Patrol Platoon (Lieuts R. W. Fletcher, E. B. King, A. D. Anderson and 50 men).—White Chateau.

Wiring Platoon (Lieut. B. Vaughan and 36 men).— Bow Dug-outs with Battalion Headquarters.

As soon as the relief was complete, Capt. Harry Webber, of "D" Company, decided to move his Company Headquarters, and finally selected another dug-out about fifty to one hundred yards along the trench. The gear was transferred to the new "possie" and the signaller was in the act of connecting the 'phone when the enemy artillery opened fire, and a direct hit from a 4.2 landed on the dug-out, with deadly effect. Capt. Webber was killed at once, Signaller Furmage was very badly wounded and died at the Regimental Aid Post, C.S.M. F. H. Ripper was badly wounded, and ultimately sustained an amputated arm and a stiff leg, whilst Capt. Webber's batman was the only man who got off with nothing but a thorough fright. The distressing news soon filtered through the Battalion, and everyone expressed the deepest regret that such a popular officer as Harry Webber had proved himself should have gone to answer the "last roll call." From Pontville, onwards, he had always proved himself a good N.C.O., but after receiving his commission in August, 1915, some latent qualities seemed to come to the surface, and, as the Battalion's first Lewis machine-gun officer, he was always regarded as one of the most brilliant of our junior officers, while afterwards he administered his company in an equally capable manner.

As it was now well-known at General Headquarters that the enemy contemplated launching a big offensive in the very near future, it became necessary to obtain identification of hostile units along the whole front in order to trace the movements of German divisions and corps. With this end in view, Lieut. Mead, 10th Battalion, with twenty-five other ranks, left our lines at Post 4.0.12 in "D" Company's sector, on the night of 13th March, as a fighting patrol with the object of gaining touch with the enemy and capturing a prisoner or obtaining identification from casualties. Strong opposition, however, was met in No Man's Land, and bombs were thrown by both parties, but, on account of the enemy's superiority of numbers, our patrol retired precipitately, having suffered five casualties. For the next two hours, a light barrage fire was kept up on Oak Support, which culminated in a hurricane bombardment at 2.15 a.m., extending to front line posts, which also suffered from light and medium *minenwerfer* fire. All telephone lines from Platoon Headquarters to Company Headquarters in the support line, and to Battalion Headquarters in rear, were cut, and it was not until about half-an-hour later that we discovered what had happened. An enemy raiding party, consisting of 3 officers and 60 other ranks, especially trained for the purpose, had attacked our posts in front of Hollebeke with the object of getting behind them and taking the garrison back as prisoners as they returned. (This was the same spot that was raided on 1st March, when held by the 10th Battalion). The party had been assembling in No Man's Land when Lieut. Mead's patrol encountered them, and the *fracas* which followed somewhat disorganised the party and caused the raid to be postponed until midnight. The posts which were being raided were situated in low-lying ground, where the digging of trenches was impossible, and protection was obtained by sheltering behind a barricade of tree-trunks, ammunition boxes, etc., and a plentiful supply of earth. The artillery and *minenwerfer* barrage gave sufficient warning to the garrison of the approach of the enemy, and in consequence rifle and machine-gun fire was brought to bear on the raiding party, while bombs were freely used as an attempt was made to get through the wires.

Wonderful bravery was displayed by Pvte. E. A. Reading, who was the sole survivor of Post 3.0.6, and absolutely refused to surrender, although called upon to do so, but, on the contrary, used his rifle and bombs to such good effect that he repelled all efforts of the enemy to make an entry into the post. He was eventually found by the officer, who came along shortly afterwards to ascertain the casualties suffered, holding the post on his own and covering three wounded Germans with his rifle.

A pathetic incident occurred in one post, where

two brothers formed part of the garrison, one of whom was mortally wounded and fell back into his brother's arms and died.

As a result of the raid, the enemy not only failed to take back any prisoners, but, on the other hand, left twelve of his own men in our hands, six of whom were wounded. Our casualties totalled four killed and eleven wounded.

Capt. Richardson, who commanded the Company, reported the incident by the following message:—

> "To Adjutant.—Fritz had a go, but came a thud. Can I have two platoons to repair the support line? Our casualties are fairly slight. About six more wounded squids are on our wire yet.—O.C. 'D' Company."

Simultaneously with the above raid, a smaller party attacked Post 6.0.6 on the left of the canal, endeavouring to approach it under cover of the railway embankment, but they were easily driven off by machine-gun fire and bombs.

S.O.S. signals had been fired from both platoon and company Headquarters, but owing to a thick ground fog they had not been observed by any of the relay posts, and so the raid was beaten off without the assistance of any artillery.

In recognition of gallantry and devotion to duty in repelling the raid, the following decorations were awarded:—

Distinguished Conduct Medal.—Pvte. E. A. Reading.

Military Medal.—Sgt. A. Kelling; L.-Cpls. F. Cole,

H. G. Brown; Pvts. L. O. Monks, C. W. Witzerman, H. Shreeve, D. Sullivan, J. Cox, W. H. Glover.

In addition, Lieut. A. T. Wertheimer, Pvts. V. Ferguson and H. Hull also did good work, the first-named carrying a wounded man from the front to the support line under a heavy machine-gun fire, when the morning twilight had almost grown to broad daylight.

The prisoners captured proved to belong to the 7th Inf. Regiment, 31st Division, and had only recently arrived from the Russian front.

During the next day we were badly troubled by 7.7, 4.2, and 5.9 artillery fire from the direction of Wervicq, which required a lot of silencing, whilst Railway Trench and the front line posts on the left of the canal suffered considerable anxiety from *minenwerfer* fire, many of them being filled with gas, which appeared to originate from the direction of Locks No. 5 and 6 bis.

An inter-company relief was effected on the night of 15th-16th March, when "B" Company went into the line on the left and "C" Company on the right, the only difference being that "B" Company established their Headquarters in Railway Trench, on the left of the canal.

During our occupation of the forward area, the allotment of leave to the United Kingdom was considerably increased, as many as six and seven men receiving leave passes daily, although on 21st March the military situation caused all leave, both to England and Paris, to be stopped immediately.

A violent gas-shell bombardment was experienced

on the night of 17th-18th March, which lasted from 10 p.m. to 1 a.m. and, it was afterwards reported, extended from Passchendaele in the north to Warneton in the south, enveloping the whole of the forward area (including the front and support lines and the artillery belt). No casualties were sustained in the 12th Battalion, and very few in the whole Brigade. Duckboard tracks were smashed considerably, and many of the trenches were damaged. Working and carrying parties, wherever possible, took shelter in the tunnels along the canal banks, but many of them had to obtain cover in the open during the whole bombardment. This was almost the first time that the small box respirator had been used continuously for such a lengthy period, and, although keeping the wearer entirely immune from the effects of the gas fumes, its presence became irritating after a while and the nose-clip very painful. The garrison in the front line also stated that the eye-pieces were practically useless at night, as it was not possible to see more than a yard or two with the mask on, and in many cases the men took the mask off and merely used the nose-clip and breathing tube.

A similar bombardment occurred on the morning of 21st March, although H.E. shells were freely interspersed with the gas. The S.O.S. signal was fired on our front, but on investigation it turned out to be a repeat signal from the left Battalion sector, on account of the morning mist. A fighting patrol had attempted to approach a post occupied by the 11th Battalion, but was effectively repulsed, three prisoners being taken and the remainder—without exception—being killed. On being interrogated, they were found to belong to the 153rd Regiment, which was an abnormal identification, proving that once again new troops were on our front.

Later on in the day, the following message was received from 2nd Army Headquarters:—

> "Intense bombardment started 4.30 a.m. against whole of 3rd and 5th Army fronts and against French, leaving out Rheims sector. It has since slackened in places, but is still intense between Sensee and Moy and against French. No attack yet."

The expected German offensive had started!

Chapter XVIII.

THE GERMAN OFFENSIVE — SPRING, 1918

THE Germans actually launched their attack against the 5th Army front on 22nd March, this fact being conveyed to us later on in the day, together with the news that the front line in general was being held, although in isolated parts the enemy had penetrated to depths not exceeding 1,000 yards.

To celebrate this fact, we carried out an inter-company relief the same night without incident.

The next day the news was a little more disconcerting, for we learned that the enemy had captured 16,000 prisoners and 200 guns, together with the villages of Bullecourt, Lagnicourt, Louverval and Doignies. It was also rumoured that they had penetrated as far as Fremicourt. It was just heartrending to read of the rapid loss of these villages, with all of which we were so closely associated, and which had been captured and held by us during the spring of 1917, after many acts of astonishing bravery and heavy casualty lists.

Alterations were made in the dispositions of the Corps front, which indicated that Divisions were being drawn into support and reserve areas and thus made more accessible if required at short notice.

The 10th Battalion relieved us on the night of 24th-25th March, the movement being complete at 9.56 p.m., when we found ourselves disposed as follows:—

Battalion H.Q. and "D" Coy.—Crater Dug-outs.

"B" Coy.—Gasper Cliff.

"A" Coy.—Canal Dug-outs.

"C" Coy.—White Chateau.

On account of the Brigade extending its front to the north, "D" Company were instructed to occupy Larch Wood Tunnels on 25th March, in order to give more even support to the Brigade front.

The war news indicated that the number of prisoners had now increased to 40,000; Bapaume had fallen; heavy fighting around Le Transloy. Unconfirmed rumour also reported that the 3rd and 4th Australian Divisions were on their way south and that the Germans were using a 60-mile gun to shell Paris. The first portion of this rumour was very easy to believe, but the latter portion was regarded as the biggest joke we had heard for a long time.

During our first occupation of the dug-outs and tunnels along the canal bank, a considerable number of the men suffered from colds and scabies (a very contagious and irritating skin trouble), due to the close and confined living in the deep dug-outs. These inflictions, however, almost entirely disappeared during our occupation of the line, but were once again making a re-appearance on our return to our subterranean residences. To prevent the spreading of scabies the R.M.O. recommended more frequent baths, and in accordance with this advice, we improvised some baths at Norfolk Bridge and arranged for them to be frequently used by the various companies, with excellent results.

War news received from 26th-28th March informed us that there was heavy fighting around High Wood; Bernafay Wood had been lost and retaken by counter-attack; fighting around Miraumont; the New Zealanders had recaptured Beaumont-Hamel; 4th Australian Division had successfully replused two big counter-attacks; 3rd Australian Division was fighting near Morlancourt; the line at present ran through Beaumont-Hamel—the brickfields at Albert—Morlancourt. Thus, in six days we had lost practically all the territory captured during the twelve months commencing July 1st, 1916.

At 4.30 a.m. both on March 27th and 28th, the S.O.S. signal was fired on the 10th Battalion front and the enemy attempted to raid posts in front of Hollebeke, and on each occasion was successfully repulsed. The 11th Battalion also encountered hostile patrols which showed "fight," all of which tended to prove that the morale and fighting spirit of the units opposed to us were good, and that he was still determined to obtain identification, which up to the present, in spite of his determined efforts during the past month, had been denied him.

The Brigade was eventually relieved on April 3rd by units of the 9th British Division, which had suffered many casualties and hardships in the recent retreat on the 5th Army front. Being in support and in rear of the main ridge, our relief was effected during the early part of the evening, being complete at 8.35 p.m., in the following manner:—

> H.Q., "B" and "C" Coys. relieved by Black Watch Regiment; "A" Coy. relieved by Cameron Highlanders; "D" Coy. relieved by K.O.S.B.

After handing over to the relieving units, we proceeded along the canal bank to the head of the Spoilbank, where we were conveyed by light railway to Barbados and Jamaica Camps at La Clytte; the strength of the unit being 63 officers and 1,077 other ranks.

The casualties sustained by the Battalion during the month of March, while holding the Ypres-Comines Canal sector, amounted to:—

1 officer, 12 other ranks Killed
    4 ,, ,, Died of Wounds
   27 ,, ,, Wounded
    7 ,, ,, Possible gas cases
    6 ,, ,, Possible shell-shock cases.

The movement of officers, other than casualties mentioned, included:—

> Capt. Houghton, Lieuts. Keen, Tynan and Priddey returned to the unit from hospital, and Lieut. Dadson from 1st Training Battalion.

> Capt. Vowles was transferred to the Indian Army, and Lieut. T. A. Lay detached for duty with 3rd A.L.T.M.B.

The Brigadier congratulated all units on the amount of work accomplished, both in the front and support lines, and compiled the following information:—

Work done by the four battalions during March, 1918—

- 9,930 yds. barbed wire entanglements, being mostly double-apron, about 700 yds. being double-apron over French wire.
- 1,107 „ parapet sandbagged and revetted
- 740 „ parapet thickened by banking with earth
- 505 „ trench revetted
- 291 „ trench and drains, lower, revetted
- 231 „ trench, upper, revetted
- 500 „ drains dug
- 347 „ trench dug
- 650 „ cable trench dug 6 feet and electric cable laid
- 583 „ track cleared for duckboarding
- 606 „ duckboards laid
- 57 cupola dug-outs erected to accommodate three men each
- 3 footbridges constructed across the canal.

Material used on above work—

- 2,176 coils barbed wire
- 111 „ French wire.
- 9,822 corkscrew pickets
- 26,940 sandbags
- 279 cupolas (large and medium)
- 698 sheets corrugated iron
- 656 "A" Frames
- 1,153 duckboards
- 539 panels (revetting)
- 886 angle iron pickets
- 124 windles (stay wires)
- 96 yds. expanded metal (duckboards)
- 5 rolls camouflage.

Any credit reflecting on the Battalion in connection with the above work was largely due to Lieut. M. Bensley, who acted as Works Officer, together with the men who actually did the work.

Although there is a natural tendency to inflate the figures when furnishing a Works Report, by erring on the right side, yet after a fair discount is made on the above figures, the net result will still indicate a wonderful volume of work carried out by one brigade, exclusive of the operations of the Brigade Mining Company.

The Battalion spent one night only at La Clytte and "embussed" at 9 a.m. on 4th April and proceeded to billets at Borre, on the Strazeele-Hazebrouck road, which we left again at 4 p.m. the next day, and marched to Caestre, entraining at 6.10 p.m. It was surprising to hear the confidence placed in the Australian troops by the French peasantry, and to witness their visible distress at our leaving the area. On more than one occasion I heard an old *madame* reiterating to a group of "Diggers" at the front door of her house, which opened on to the street, gesticulating freely to support her French-English conversation, *"No bon!* Australian *parti; Allemands* come *tout de suite."* It almost seemed as if she had the power of prophecy, for although there was no indication of an attack of any kind on this part of the front, yet within eight days these people were homeless and we were back again defending the village from the advancing Hun.

We travelled all night in the troop train and proceeded *via* Calais and Abbeville to our destination at St. Roch Siding, on the outskirts of Amiens. We detrained at 6.10 a.m. and had breakfast by the side of the road just outside the station yard, after which we marched through the town to billets at

APRIL, 1918

Coisy. Here we stayed for forty-eight hours and allowed the men to rest, and gave the company commanders an opportunity to reorganise. Another move was made on 9th April, when the Battalion marched to Flesselles, where shortage of billets caused the officers and men to be very crowded.

Astonishing war news reached us the next day, April 10th, to the effect that the Germans had broken through on the Portuguese front and had already captured the villages of Laventie, Estaires, Sailly-sur-la Lys, Bac St. Maur and Steenwerck (although the Messines Ridge was still held) and that they were continuing the advance.

On April 11th we received warning that the 1st Australian Division (being the only Australian division not absorbed into the fighting on the Amiens front) would return north the next day, to assist in the defence of Hazebrouck, which was of considerable strategical importance, being a railway junction.

The same day, 74 reinforcements joined the Battalion, accompanied by 2nd-Lieuts. Cooper and Simmonds (from reinforcements), and Glozier and Dollery (from Cadet Battalions).

At 11 a.m. on 12th April, the Battalion marched out of Flesselles back to the entraining point at St. Roch Station, and on the way the 4th Army Commander, General Rawlinson, took up a position and watched us march past. We bivouaced in a large paddock just near the citadel and remained there the whole of the afternoon, but as soon as darkness fell the Germans sent over several squadrons of bombing 'planes, which carried out their allotted tasks with disastrous effect. For fully three hours the distinctive drone of the 'planes could be heard, and as soon as the bombs had been dropped and a squadron started on its way back, another lot could be heard approaching, and thus the raid appeared to be continuous. In some instances, inflammatory bombs were utilised, which caused many fires to start in the city, lighting up the surrounding countryside. We were congratulating ourselves that we were not actually in the city, and therefore were unlikely to be molested, when suddenly a bright light appeared in the sky, like a brilliant Verey light flare, but instead of dropping and gradually going out, it floated in the air and increased in intensity, and, together with two other similar parachute flares, illuminated the whole surroundings, making it as bright as daylight. The effect was appalling, and everyone, more or less, went cold with fright. It is difficult even to visualise the scene—a whole battalion bivouaced in close formation in an open paddock, entirely devoid of cover, with the knowledge that similar concentrations of troop were in the near vicinity, offering an ideal target to hostile aircraft. To commence moving about in an attempt to seek cover would have been suicidal and would have attracted attention at once, so we had to lie there in the open, watching these monster arc lamps suspended in the air and thinking all the time that they *must* soon burn out, and instinctively offering a silent prayer for the friendly darkness to envelop us once again. At the same time, the humming of the invisible 'planes could still be heard, and the explosions of the bombs began to come nearer and nearer, until eventually fully a dozen fell within a radius of 200 yards from our bivouac. The nerve-strain at once appeared to be relieved, and the thoughts of all immediately turned towards possible casualties. The R.M.O. and his A.M.C. staff were soon on the scene, but fortunately no casualties were sustained by the Battalion. We afterwards heard that the railway siding at St. Roch fared very badly in the raid, and the 2nd Brigade, which was entraining at the time, suffered about 80 casualties. After midnight the intensity of the bombardment decreased considerably, although at hourly intervals the approach of 'planes could be heard, followed soon afterwards by explosions in the city. "A" Company had left us earlier in the evening to proceed by an early train, and spent a very trying time in the goods yard during the whole of the raid, the only cover available being in goods sheds and underneath trucks, both of which were totally inadequate. They finally left by a train at about 11.30 p.m. The remainder of the Battalion left the bivouac area at 2 a.m. and proceeded to the station, finally entraining at 4 a.m., expecting every minute that the raid would recommence. We waited and waited for the train to pull out, until half-an-hour became an hour without a move having been made. Enquiries were then instituted, but it was difficult to find anyone to supply information. However, eventually we were told by the entraining officer that the civilian linesmen and signalmen had thought that discretion was the better part of valour, and had taken shelter in the cellars of different houses in the district and could not be found. This was a serious state of affairs, for the men were now crowded into a troop train, and one single bomb might cause irreparable losses. Just as dawn was breaking more 'planes came over, dropping a considerable number of bombs, most of them falling in the city, although two fell close to the station yard. Our troubles were not yet over, however, for as soon as it was fully daylight, a long-range high velocity gun commenced firing and several shells burst within 200 to 300 yards of the troop train. Just before the train pulled out, at 7.30 a.m., one of these shells struck the base of a very high chimney stack nearby, which was seen to tremble and then to commence to fall, ending up with a tremendous crash and a volume of brick dust. As soon as the train began to move, the troops gave a cheer, but their joy was of short duration, as we only shunted on to another line, where we remained until 8.45 a.m. The next move took us to a cutting just clear of the city, where we stagnated for another two hours, and finally we left at 10.30 a.m., after having been waiting in the train for six-and-a-half hours, every moment of which was valuable, as we knew how urgently we were required.

We travelled by the "short cut" *via* St. Pol, Frevent, Chocques and Lillers, and discovered that the line had been heavily bombed all the way along. At one spot, a direct hit had been obtained on a truck, which now lay in a mass of wreckage at the bottom of a slight bank, while several mutilated bodies belonging to a kilted regiment gave the tragic scene a gruesome appearance. As we neared Hazebrouck, we were enabled to estimate the extent of the German advance, for at one spot the train actually passed through a belt of 18-pounders, with guns firing on either side of the railway line.

We eventually detrained at Hondeghem Siding, on the north of Hazebrouck, at midnight, and after unloading the transport and gear in pitch darkness, we marched along strange roads and through the centre of the town, until finally we halted on the outskirts of the village of Borre, where we had been billetted only a few days previously. The Commanding Officer instructed company commanders to issue a dry ration and to allow the men to have breakfast, while he reconnoitred the position and obtained more definite instructions. He then discovered that the 1st and 2nd Brigades had gained touch with the advancing enemy on the fringe of the forest of Nieppe and had temporarily checked his advance. The 3rd Brigade was being utilised as a Divisional Reserve, and our immediate task was to construct a defence line in front of Borre capable of defending the ridge which ran from Strazeele to Hazebrouck. Company commanders were then sent for and the C.O. explained the situation to them, showed them where the line of posts was to run, the Battalion's sector, and finally allotted frontages for each company. Without any delay, the four companies moved off independently, and while the Battalion reserve of entrenching tools was being issued, officers were placing their platoon posts, and shortly afterwards had the digging of them well under way. We then discovered that the 11th Battalion were on our right and a French regiment on our left.

Battalion Headquarters were established in the first house on the left entering the village from Hazebrouck, and the interior not only presented a pitiful appearance, but also gave evidence of the rapid evacuation of the owners only some thirty-six or forty-eight hours before. On the kitchen table was a bowl of potatoes, and alongside it a saucepan half full of some already peeled, while on the table itself one had been hastily dropped, half pared, with the knife still inserted.

About noon, the Brigadier accompanied the C.O. round the new lines and was profuse in his praises, both regarding the quantity and quality of the work done. The posts were all completed and sited in the most advantageous positions, in many instances—on the right flank in particular—commanding a field of fire of from 400 to 600 yards. All newly exposed earth had been carefully camouflaged with turf and other vegetation to correspond with the environment of each individual post, and consequently the posts were difficult to detect from quite a short distance away, even by one who knew of their existence.

The Q.M. store, transport lines and "N" Company were situated at Morbecque, on the south of Hazebrouck, and during the morning both the Q.M. and transport officer came up to ascertain our requirements, but were told that a normal supply of rations was all that was required at present until further orders were received.

Very few shells had fallen in the village up to this time, although on inspection the interior of the houses presented a wantonly disordered appearance, having been ransacked from top to bottom either by the retreating units or troops moving up to check the advance. Contents of chests of drawers were littered about the floor, wardrobes were stripped bare, while pantries and kitchens had shared a similar fate. Of course, it was the inevitable result of war, but at the same time the thought instinctively passed through one's mind that it was regrettable that the question of loot should have been uppermost with any troops acting on the defensive at such a critical moment. How tragic it would have been if we had only occupied the village for twenty-four hours and had driven the enemy back and so enabled the peasants to return to their ransacked homes!

It must not be thought that our own men were blameless in this regard, for as soon as the line of

PRADELLES CHURCH
(Photo. by Lieut. L. M. Newton, M.C.)

posts was completed and some of the men had spare time on their hands, a tour of inspection was commenced and the littered contents of the various houses were many times overturned in the hopes of finding suitable souvenirs. A humorous touch was given to the whole affair by seeing a couple of unmistakable "Diggers" coming down the main road, one wearing an ill-fitting suit, worn, no doubt, recently on special occasions by the village blacksmith, while the other coyly hung on to his arm and fumbled in an uncertain manner with dress, blouse and furbelows as though ascertaining whether everything was still there.

Discipline, however, had to be maintained, and in view of the fact some of the men had already discovered the contents of various wine cellars, officers and N.C.O.'s quickly rounded them up and allotted additional tasks.

In the rapid evacuation of the area, live stock had been left to look after itself, and consequently cows, pigs, ducks, fowls, etc., roamed about everywhere. Parties were at once organised to scour the country and round up all the cattle into one big paddock, which was accordingly done, and altogether 95 beasts were handed over to the Military Mounted Police for transmission to the French Mission. A few pigs, together with the ducks and fowls, were considered more or less legitimate plunder, and during the next few days the Battalion's menu was varied considerably, and the savoury odours which issued from many of the houses were an indication of the meal which awaited the majority of sections and platoons. Meals were once again set out on tables with white table-cloths, whilst almost every man (other than the garrison in the posts) discovered a comfortable bed in which to sleep.

II.

We remained here two days, during which time a very good beginning was made in wiring the defence line. On April 16th we moved to Pradelles and relieved the 1st Battalion as support battalion to the 1st Brigade, completing the movement at 10 p.m. Battalion Headquarters were situated in the basement of the Brasserie, or brewery, which was in the centre of the village and opposite to the church. The four companies were distributed over the countryside, with headquarters in farmhouses and the platoons sheltered behind hedges and dug into the banks of sunken roads. During the morning of the following day, about 10 a.m., the enemy started a violent bombardment, concentrating at first on the high ground around Strazeele and on the village itself, and afterwards extending it right along the ridge, enveloping the villages of Pradelles and Borre. Several direct hits were registered on Battalion Headquarters, but Cpl. Sheppard, of the Signalling Section, was the only casualty. The companies, however, suffered badly, as the only available cover—ditches and banks at the side of the roads—proved totally inadequate. Many of the men rushed for shelter in the surrounding farm-houses, but in many instances these became crowded and were therefore veritable death traps. During the two hours of continuous shelling we suffered 30 casualties in all, mostly from "B" and "D" Companies. Lieut. E. Bromley King was wounded in "D" Company Headquarters by a shell penetrating the roof and exploding in the kitchen. A lamp, suspended from the ceiling, crashed on to the table as a result of the explosion, and a fragment badly cut one of King's fingers. This was believed to be the only wound he received, until, after running fully fifty yards away from the house, he stopped exhausted and admitted being wounded in the back. Stretcher-bearers were at once called for and he was evacuated after having his wound attended, and it was with sincere regret that we afterwards heard he had died of wounds. He had been an extremely useful member of the Battalion, having arrived with an early batch of reinforcements on the Peninsula. As an N.C.O. he had been quiet and unassuming, but his work was always reliable, both in and out of the line, and he commanded the respect of his men at all times. Cpl. Mills, of "B" Company, was killed on the same day. He, also, had joined the Battalion during the early days at Anzac and had seen much fighting with the unit. He had earned his stripes by consistently displaying the sterling qualities of a good soldier, and had never given his company officers any reason to regret the confidence placed in him.

During the early part of the evening, "C" Company received orders to move up in close support to the 4th Battalion, and occupied some trenches on the rear slopes of the village, almost in the exact spot where we received our first gas demonstration on arriving in France two years before. The next twenty-four hours were damp and overcast, whilst hardly any artillery fire was experienced in the Battalion area.

April 19th was very cold, and it snowed on and off during the day. We left Pradelles at 9.30 p.m. and moved into the line in front of Meteren, relieving the 102nd and 32nd Chasseurs Rapides, 133rd French Division. This was the first and only time the 12th Battalion relieved a French unit. The handing over was really funny, although much of the humour was lost on account of the seriousness of the situation. Brigade Orders informed us that interpreters and guides would be made available during the relief, and, although there was an interpreter at Battalion Headquarters, the company officers had to rely on gesticulations and crude pencil drawings in order to gain any idea of our dispositions and the situation in general. Indeed, Capt. W. R. Jorgensen, of "C" Company, in reporting "Relief complete," sent the following message:—"Adjutant, 12th Battalion.—Absolutely tickled to death; he can't speak English and I can't speak French, so there you are. I know as much now as when I started. Everything O.K." The guides supplied by the French regiments were very little different to many of the guides supplied by British regiments and A.I.F. battalions at various times, their chief qualification being, apparently, total ignorance of the roads and the country over which they were "guiding" you. Lieut. A. D. Cooper and one of "D" Company's platoon were being led down the Fletre-Meteren road by a guide, when suddenly Cooper noticed that there were no longer any troops marching a short distance ahead of him, and drew his guide's attention to the fact. The latter casually retraced his steps—quite oblivious of the fact that he had approached within a hundred yards of the front line—and took the party across cultivated fields and left them behind a hedge. His disappearance might have been disconcerting had not another Frenchman approached from out of the darkness and ultimately agreed to take the platoon forward, a section at a time. During the relief in the front line, the experience of each post was more or less the same, namely, as soon as the Australians set foot in the trench the French garrison said, *"Tres bon,"* and disappeared into the darkness. The actual handing over, if this was their normal method of relief, was done at Company Headquarters, where elaborate pencil sketches showed the disposition of posts, machine-guns, areas subjected to machine-gun and mortar fire, known enemy positions, etc.

The Battalion held, approximately, 1,000 yards of frontage astride the Fletre-Meteren road, with three companies in line ("B" Company line right, "C" Company centre, and "D" Company line left) and "A" Company in support. The line was composed of a series of small posts, mostly commanded by N.C.O.'s, which were formed into platoon groups under an officer. Company Headquarters were invariably situated in dwellings immediately in rear of the line, while Battalion Headquarters and the R.A.P. were situated in two farm-houses about 800 yards behind the line.

The next two days were comparatively quiet and were utilised in improving the front line posts, although the German snipers were particularly active and never missed an opportunity of firing when a target presented itself, Lieut. B. Vaughan being killed in this way on 22nd April. Enemy aeroplanes were active over the whole of the area and did a considerable amount of low flying along the roads, bringing machine-gun fire to bear on individuals moving about in rear of the lines in daylight. On one occasion, Capt. Sid Houghton and I were walking along the road from Battalion H.Q. to the R.A.P. when a German 'plane swooped down and dropped fully a dozen egg bombs around us without result. Pineapple bombs were also dropped around billets and farm-houses by enemy aeroplanes during the hours of daylight, but without inflicting any casualties. Artillery fire was below normal, although Lieut. J. Simmonds was slightly wounded from this cause. The front line companies were subjected to much annoyance during the night from machine-gun and light *minenwerfer* fire, although no casualties were sustained.

On April 22nd, advice was received from Brigade Headquarters to the effect that "the Brigade has been ordered to capture Meteren. The operation will be carried out gradually by advancing our line on the flanks, with the idea of squeezing the enemy out and then mopping up the town itself."

The method of attack did not appeal to us at all, although in theory it was very excellent and, provided the enemy acted "according to plan," should prove entirely successful. It reminded us too forcibly of the attack on Boursies, which was carried to a successful issue during the second phase, only after suffering heavy casualties and nerve strain. (Chapter XIV.—The German Withdrawal). However, orders issued are not to be queried, but obeyed, and in consequence on the night of 22nd-23rd, the 11th and 12th Battalions commenced an enveloping movement by advancing the line on the northern and southern flanks of the village.

The burden of the work fell upon "B" Company, although "D" Company advanced their line in order to get into closer striking distance of the village, and "C" Company merely advanced to conform with the movement on either flank.

Capt. Holyman was in charge of "B" Company on the right, and as soon as he received his instructions, about 10.30 p.m., he immediately pushed his two left platoons forward, Nos. 6 and 7, where they established a new line of posts about 100 yards in advance of the old line, without any opposition. At 1.30 a.m., No. 8 Platoon, under Lieut. G. F. Gould, moved out cautiously along the Meteren Becque (a small stream or ditch) with a view to capturing a known strong post between 250 and 300 yards out in front. At the same time, No. 5 Platoon, under Lieut. R. B. Goode, moved out and took up a position about 200 yards in No Man's Land and awaited Gould's readiness before concerting with him and rushing the new position. All was ready at 2.30 a.m. and both platoons rushed forward and dislodged the enemy with very little effort, the greatest factors of the attack being surprise and dash. Invaluable assistance was rendered by three Lewis and two Vickers guns, which were operated by the 1st Battalion on our right, by giving covering fire to the attacking platoons.

Goode exploited his success by capturing another small post on his left, which might have proved troublesome if allowed to remain. Gould anticipated a counter-attack on his front and asked for assistance, which Holyman gave by sending forward Lieut. A. W. Clemes and a platoon from "A" Company, which had been placed at his disposal. Two local and half-hearted counter-attacks were attempted before dawn against the new position, but were easily repulsed, although Clemes was slightly wounded. The whole operation was complete and the new line dug and consolidated by 5 a.m., 2 other ranks having been killed and 1 officer and 4 other ranks wounded, to compensate for which 17 prisoners and 4 machine-guns had been captured.

The attack on the left of the main road by "D" Company (Capt. B. J. Andrew) was successfully carried out with very little loss, which reflected credit on both the Company Commander and Lieut. H. M. Sandy, who commanded the attacking platoon. Two objectives were allotted, making the total advance about 200 yards. A preliminary bombardment by Lieut. T. A. Lay and three Stokes mortars at 3 a.m. produced excellent results, for direct hits were registered on the first objective, as well as on a house which the enemy was believed to be occupying. As soon as the trench mortar barrage lifted, a bombing section moved along the northern bank of the road and rushed the trench which formed the objective, and met with little opposition, although it was garrisoned by twenty Germans, twelve of whom were taken prisoner. Only one man was wounded in this initial advance. Lieut. P. F. Sellick, who was utilising his platoon as a support, now moved two of his sections forward in order to occupy the trench as soon as Sandy took his men forward to the second objective. Lay again opened up with his mortars, after which Sandy advanced once more, supported by Lewis gun covering fire from Lieut. Cooper on the left. A little more opposition was encountered this time, but Sgt. Vickers was the leading spirit of the attack, and used some lurid language when dealing with the obstreperous Hun, who (if he was wise) invariably threw up his hands, yelling *"Kamerade, Kamerade!"* ("Comrade, Comrade!"). The position was ultimately captured and consolidated by 4.30 a.m., and 14 prisoners were sent back to Battalion Headquarters, whilst the only casualties were Pvts. Bradford, Preston, Senior, Ray and Pryor, all of whom were wounded, the last-named very slightly.

"C" Company (Capt. W. R. Jorgensen) in the centre, had the least to do, and yet, unfortunately met with the greatest opposition. The enemy in front of them was thoroughly aroused, and, therefore, when an attempt was made to conform to the advance on either flank, heavy machine-gun fire was encountered from a hedge in front, which entirely prevented any movement and kept them in their trenches until after dawn. In an attempt to move forward, Lieut. G. H. C. Hart was badly wounded and lay about thirty yards in front of our position for the greater portion of the day, until two stretcher-bearers accepted the risk of exposing themselves under cover of the white flag, which was respected on this occasion, and brought him in. When taken to the R.A.P. he was still cheerful, in spite of two badly fractured legs, and the R.M.O. endeavoured to restore some warmth in his body by the careful use of a Primus stove. The result was only of a temporary nature, and he afterwards died of wounds owing to the terrific shock to his system.

The 23rd April was spent quietly, the only activity being from hostile snipers, who on this occasion claimed Lieut. W. W. S. Sayer as a victim. The Battalion was relieved during the night by the 9th Battalion (complete at 12.45 a.m.), and, with the exception of "A" Company, moved back to a locality in the support area known as Phincboom.

The second phase of the attack on Meteren was carried out on the night 23rd-24th April by the 9th and 10th Battalions, assisted respectively by one company of the 12th and 11th Battalions for "mopping up" purposes. The method of attack was for the flanks to advance and to link up on the far side of the town, leaving the two "mopping up" companies to clear the isolated garrison by capture or otherwise. Owing to the preliminary advance on the previous night, which was of an indicative nature, the enemy seemed to be fully aware of our intentions, and as a result the outskirts of the town were bristling with machine-guns. The attacking battalions encountered considerable opposition, and only in isolated parts were they able to advance at all.

Our own "A" Company, therefore, when moving off at 1.30 a.m., the pre-arranged time, did not carry out their "mopping up" duties, but in reality attempted to make a *frontal attempt,* unaided, on a strongly fortified position held by an enemy who was literally waiting for them to come. It was a forlorn hope from the very onset, and although officers, N.C.O.'s and men alike acted in an irreproachable manner, they could not attain the impossible. As soon as a move was made, concentrated machine-gun fire swept the whole front on either side of the road and made movement extremely difficult. Lieut. P. F. Heurtley-Reed showed more than his usual amount of fearlessness in urging and leading the men forward, until the buildings on the outskirts of the town were reached. Sgt. Whittle and L.-Cpl. "Josh" Patmore had also handled their men well and joined in the house-to-house fighting which now took place; Cpl. T. Cairnduff had been less fortunate and had already sustained a lacerated wound in the right upper arm, which ultimately resulted in amputation. It was a fight between bombs and machine-guns, and although many Huns were accounted for before we admitted defeat, the machine-guns, which were placed in advantageous positions, proved their superiority and demanded our withdrawal. Heurtley-Reed was last seen rushing in between two sheds with his revolver in his hand, when suddenly he was seen to reel backwards. His body was recovered three months later after the town was captured, together with those of Cpls. Whitelaw and Killalea. The total number of casualties sustained by "A" Company was 1 officer and 6 other ranks killed, 21 other ranks wounded.

At the conclusion of the operation, "A" Company were withdrawn to Phincboom and "D" Company moved up in close support to the 9th Battalion, while Battalion Headquarters (which had remained with the 9th Battalion Headquarters during the attack) also withdrew to the support position, moving back just before dawn, when it could be seen that many fires had been started and were burning fiercely in Meteren.

As a result of the two-day operation, the following decorations were awarded:—

Military Cross.—Lieut. R. B. Goode.

Distinguished Conduct Medal.—Sgts. N. A. Vallance, M.M.; W. Vickers, M.M.

Second Bar to Military Medal.—Pvt. J. B. McCulloch, M.M.

First Bar to Military Medal.—L.-Cpl. F. H. Williams, M.M.

Military Medal.—Sgts. C. B. Timothy, R. Lapthorne, A. F. Adams; Cpl. F. O'Neill; L.-Cpls. J. W. Cruthers, S. C. Freitag; Pvts. J. F. Duggan, J. Goodwin.

The following officers and men were also specially mentioned as having done good work:—

Lieuts. G. F. Gould, M.C.; H. M. Sandy; Sgts. J. Whittle, V.C., D.C.M.; J. W. Quinn; L.-Cpls. J. B. Patmore, S. J. Smith, A. Raabe, C. Shirley; Pvts. L. F. Foley, A. J. Baker, E. J. Oates, J. R. Turner, T. L. Kingsley, C. T. Arnol, J. Moody, W. Kaine, F. J. Watt, J. Caulfield, F. J. Dougall, G. Pout.

The Battalion remained at Phincboom for four days, during which time the enemy fired a considerable number of phosphorous shells, with the object of firing the billets. Two direct hits were obtained on Battalion Headquarters' billet, which occupied an exposed position on the crest of a ridge. The first one completely wrecked the room which the R.M.O. was using as a bedroom, the explosion occurring while the C.O. was holding a conference of Company Commanders. The second one landed in the kitchen as the batmen were preparing breakfast, and wounded Pvt. E. J. Joseph in the knee.

We were relieved by the 4th Battalion on 28th April and marched *via* Courte Croix and Rouge Croix to Le Peuplier Camp, which in reality consisted of huts at Borre railway siding.

The only movement of officers to report during the month of April, other than casualties already recorded, is Lieuts. Blacklow, Gibson and Taylor to hospital.

The strength of the Battalion on coming out of the line, inclusive of "N" Company, which was waiting to rejoin us at the Divisional Reinforcement Camp at Sylvestre Cappel, was:—

	Officers	Other Ranks
Actually with unit	30	593
Sick in Divisional Area	3	29
On leave, detached duties, etc.	23	286
	56	908

Casualties for April:—

	Officers	Other Ranks
Killed	4	33
Wounded	2	123
Wounded and Missing	1	—
Missing	—	8
	7	164

In closing this phase of the Battalion's career, it is pleasing to record that on 29th April our Commanding Officer, Lieut.-Col. C. H. Elliott, D.S.O., was awarded the French Legion of Honour.

Chapter XIX.

THE DEFENCE OF STRAZEELE—SUMMER, 1918

THE camp we occupied at Borre Siding was very comfortable, being composed of well-built huts used previously by the Ordnance Corps attached to the Broad Gauge Railway Unit, which was at that time situated many miles behind the line. The huts, however, were quite near to the Hazebrouck-Poperinghe railway line, and as they were now surrounded by batteries of guns and were less than three miles from the front line, their use for the close billeting of troops was very injudicious and was the cause of a dire calamity to the 12th Battalion. The enemy fired many shells in his efforts to locate the guns in the vicinity, but they all passed over the camp with a margin of 150 to 200 yards. On 1st May, however, at 9.30 p.m., just as it was growing dark, a stray shell landed in the middle of the camp and burst on the ridge-pole of one of the huts. It had an instantaneous fuse, and consequently the occupants of the hut received the full effect of the explosion, the casualties amounting to the large number of 10 killed and 14 wounded, four of the latter afterwards dying of wounds. The scene inside the hut was pitifully tragic, for when the shell exploded many of the men were asleep in bed, while others were reading and chatting before turning in. Four others had been playing a game of cards, and one man was found with a writing pad and a half-written letter in front of him. They were all buried in the one grave at Le Peuplier, and, after the grave had been covered with turf, a cross was erected:—

IN MEMORY OF

2374	L.-Cpl. J. McKENZIE	6471	Pvte.	M. AMOS
6358	Pvte. W. VAN DRIELL	7477	,,	L. B. DALE
2031	,, D. McFARLANE	7747	,,	B. IVORY
2842	,, K. DOWNES	7786	,,	A. W. SHOOBRIDGE
6297	,, D. J. KING	7740	,,	W. HENDERSON

12th BATTALION, A.I.F.
KILLED IN ACTION, 1/5/1918

No further risks were taken after this, and the various Company Commanders were instructed to bivouac their men and spread them out as much as possible behind the hedges in the near vicinity. Three days later, Lieut. E. E. Terry was also wounded while at Brigade Headquarters acting as Brigade Bombing Officer.

Another unfortunate incident happened at this camp, when two members of the band were wounded while attending a Lewis gun class of instruction. One of them, Pvte. Fox, who was a fine trombone player, received a lacerated wound in the upper arm, which resulted almost immediately in amputation.

We were not at all sorry, therefore, when we left the camp on 4th May and relieved the 8th Battalion in the line immediately east and south-east of the village of Strazeele. The relief was complete at

11.30 p.m., with "A" Company occupying the right sector of the line, "C" Company in the centre, "D" Company on the left, and "B" Company in support. The line consisted of a series of posts, which were rapidly being improved, and was situated on the top of the high ground occupied by the village, but not sufficiently forward to give an extensive field of vision or fire. Wiring and patrol work were assiduously carried out, while chloride of lime was in great demand for freely sprinkling on the dead cows which were numerous in this area, and were making their presence more noticeable every day.

We were very pleased to have our old friends, the 29th British Division, on our right, the unit being the King's Own Scottish Borderers, afterwards relieved by the Worcestershire Regiment.

The weather was rather wet during our four days' tour of duty in this sector, which apparently accounted for the comparatively quiet time we experienced. During the early hours of May 8th, hostile artillery fire was considerably increased on the front line, and Lieut. E. W. D. Laing, while standing upon the parapet to direct a working party, was killed by a 77-mm. shell. His loss was felt keenly by the Battalion, for, being one of the original members of the unit, he had done sterling work at the Landing, and, since receiving his commission, had proved himself one of the most dependable of officers, being keen, thorough, brave, and a strict disciplinarian. Pvte. Lopez was also killed about the same time.

We were relieved by the 10th Battalion that night, and just as their companies began to approach Battalion Headquarters, the enemy attempted to raid Lieut. A. D. Anderson's post on the right of the line. The S.O.S. signal was fired,

THE RUINS OF STRAZEELE VILLAGE

(Photos by Lieut. L. M. Newton, M.C.)

but through the sentry at Battalion Headquarters not seeing and repeating it, no artillery support was received, but frontal and flanking Lewis gun fire was sufficient to repulse the raid before it reached the post. The artillery barrage which accompanied this effort caught the 10th Battalion in its progress to the front line, causing several casualties and delaying the relief considerably, but our only loss was about three men wounded, including Lieut. E. M. Dollery.

The Battalion now moved back to a support position at Pradelles, when Headquarters were once again situated in the cellar under the brewery (now furnished with furniture from the local *chateau*), and companies occupied farm-houses and trenches in rear of Strazeele and formed the garrison of the second line of defence.

Before coming out of the line, "A" Company had been warned that they would have to carry out a raid during our next tour of duty, in order to obtain identification. On the evening of 10th May, Capt. D. McLeod asked permission to go on patrol in order to reconnoitre the front (although it was afterwards discovered that his intention was to capture a post and thus save his company from having to carry out the raid). He took with him C.S.M. W. Sheedy, Pvt. "Snowy" Carrick and one other man. They penetrated fully 1,200 yards along the railway line before encountering an enemy post, but machine-guns and bombs were turned on to them and made them retire. McLeod was wounded in the leg and Sheedy afterwards died of wounds. The other two men were posted as "missing," although their bodies were afterwards found a considerable distance in front of our line.

The weather now improved considerably and
III.

living in the open was more or less pleasant. Rations were supplemented by growing crops, and many individuals discovered allotments of new potatoes in the gardens of the ruined houses of Strazeele, which proved very acceptable. During the next month or so it was quite a common occurence to send a message to a Company Commander "to supply a party of one N.C.O. and twenty men to pick peas from the crop at the rear of 'C' Company's billet. Bags, when full, to be forwarded to the Q.M. by ration limber to-night for culinary purposes." Each company also had its cow, which was invariably handed over as trench stores. The A.P.M. had instructions not to allow any cattle to be taken forward, so that when once taken to the rear they were irretrievably lost, and in order that possession of them might be retained, they became "trench stores," and remained always in the forward area.

A considerable amount of engineers' material was still located at Strazeele station, which had been an ordnance depot before the German advance, and we supplied a salvage party every night to assist in its recovery. Although the station was within 200 yards of the line, a G.S. waggon was used to take back the recovered material.

We moved to an old Chinese camp at La Kreule (just north of Hazebrouck) on 13th May, when the men occupied bivouacs constructed behind the hedges. Training was again commenced, and continued for five days, when we were relieved by the 2nd Battalion and moved back to a tented camp in the reserve area at Sercus. The country in this vicinity was delightfully fresh and everything was wonderfully green, both facts having a very pleasing and soothing effect on the men after their strenuous experiences of the last month.

Our eight days' sojourn in this camp was employed in specialists' training, interspersed with the supply of large fatigues for burying cables for the XV. Corps Signallers.

The Divisional Commander, General Sir H. B. Walker, reviewed the Brigade on 22nd May, when each battalion marched past in column of half-companies, and, in spite of the fact that the ground was exceedingly rough for ceremonial work, we undoubtedly created a good impression.

In view of the warm weather now experienced, parades were held from 7 a.m.-10.30 a.m., and recreational training from 5 p.m.-7 p.m. Before leaving the area, a very successful Battalion sports meeting was held on 23rd May, as a preliminary to the Brigade sports, which were to take place at a later date.

We moved again on Sunday, 26th May, back to the camp at La Kreule, when the opportunity was seized to bathe the men during our brief stay, and the next day we moved forward into the line, relieving the 3rd Battalion in the sector astride the Hazebrouck-Armentieres railway. "A" Company occupied the frontage on the left of the railway, with "B" Company on their right, "C" Company was in support, with their Headquarters in an old farm-house just behind the station yard, while "D" Company were billetted in the outbuildings of a farm about 600 yards along the railway line. The R.A.P. was situated in one of the many buildings in the precincts of the station itself.

It had become the custom of the 1st Australian Division, at this time, to harass the enemy continually by means of minor raids and fighting patrols. Indeed, the raids became quite a feature of our occupation of this particular frontage, for not only would a N.C.O. and some three or four men go out and capture an enemy post, but frequently individual N.C.O.'s and privates crawled through the long grass and growing crops in broad daylight, capturing and bringing in anything from one to six prisoners. This audacious procedure, together with numerous minor operations on our own and adjacent divisional fronts, had the effect of reducing the enemy's morale to a very low ebb, and his intense nervousness caused him often to fire the S.O.S. signal for no reason whatever. As a result of this activity the front line experienced a fair amount of barrage fire, particularly during the night, while the whole area was intermittently shelled during the day in an effort to locate the numerous batteries scattered about.

The 10th Battalion carried out a minor operation on our left on 29th May, by occupying a line of enemy listening posts about 100 yards in front of our line, and our left flank post conformed by moving out about fifty yards at 11.30 p.m. The whole affair took place without much incident, and a weak counter-attack on the 10th Battalion front was easily repulsed.

Another original member of the Battalion was killed on 30th May, in the person of Lieut. K. G. Jacob, who was standing in the doorway of a small house near the support line, when, without any warning, a stray shell fell in the road immediately in front of him, with the tragic result recorded above.

A larger operation was carried out on the morning of 3rd June by the 11th Battalion on our left, when, covered by a substantial artillery and trench mortar barrage, they stormed and captured the high ground known as Mont de Merris, which overlooked

Strazeele and the rear areas south of the main Hazebrouck road. The attack was a wonderful success and caught the enemy in the middle of a relief, with the result that altogether 5 officers and 253 other ranks were taken prisoners, together with 27 machine-guns, 18 trench mortars, and 1 77-mm. quick-firing field gun, beside a considerable amount of equipment. It was necessary for the left of our line to assist in this operation in order to straighten the new line, and consequently "D" Company advanced their line to a maximum distance of 400 yards on the left, at the same time taking 16 prisoners. Sgt. W. Vickers was the outstanding character as far as the 12th Battalion was concerned, and not only led his men with wonderful skill, but, with never-tiring energy, tackled post after post without bothering at any time to discover whether anyone was near him in case of need. His strength and bravery were miraculous and his language fiery, but he received recognition for his valiant services by being awarded a Bar to his Distinguished Conduct Medal.

At 11 p.m. the same night an attempt was made to improve our line on the right of the railway line, when Lieut. A. T. Wertheimer and a party of men moved out with the object of capturing a wooded copse about 200 yards in front. The enemy, however, was fully roused and strong opposition was encountered, in the course of which Wertheimer was believed to be killed, a fact which was afterwards confirmed. Indeed, the party might have had great difficulty in returning to our lines had not Lieut. A. L. Wardlaw, Sgt. G. W. Turner and a party of men moved out from the railway line and engaged the enemy from that flank.

Some very excellent patrol work was carried out

almost every night without a break by Sgt. G. W. Turner, accompanied by Pvts. L. R. Saltmarsh and F. T. Reynolds. On one occasion they located an enemy post, and after holding a conference in No Man's Land they decided to storm it. This was done with entire success, and in the *melee* which resulted three of the German garrison were killed and a machine-gun captured.

The 7th Battalion relieved us on June 4th, when we moved back to a camp at La Kreule, near to Ana Jana railway siding. As a result of this tour of duty in the line, in addition to the officer casualties mentioned, Lieuts. W. C. B. Daly, A. S. Webb and E. R. Facy were wounded.

The following decorations were also awarded:—

Bar to Distinguished Conduct Medal.—Sgt. W. Vickers, D.C.M., M.M.

Distinguished Conduct Medal.—Sgt. G. W. Turner, M.M.

Military Medal.—L.-Cpl. E. R. Stewart; Pvts. L. R. Saltmarsh, F. T. Reynolds, A. R. Goss.

We remained at La Kreule for four days, during which we furnished large parties for work on the Corps line of defence.

An incident occurred on the evening of June 7th which will remain long in the memory of everyone who witnessed it, when a German aeroplane entered into a duel with four or five of our own fighting 'planes. The fight took place in our immediate vicinity and lasted fully half-an-hour. The Hun put up a wonderful fight and was forced down time after time, but always effected a marvellous recovery, which earned for him the admiration of every spectator. Overwhelming odds eventually forced him to the ground and he made a landing within fifty yards of Battalion Headquarters, when both he and his machine escaped without injury. He was escorted to the Orderly Room, accompanied by fully half the Brigade, and while he was drinking a cup of coffee, we conversed with him in French, and congratulated him on the clean fight he had put up and the bravery he had displayed.

We were relieved by the 1st Battalion on June 8th, when we moved by route march to the Sercus area and occupied the same camp as on the previous occasion, with a strength of 46 officers, 893 other ranks (including detached duties).

A week's rest in this locality proved very acceptable and full advantage was taken of it. The weather, on the whole, was very fine and enabled us to carry out the following programme:—

First Day.—The day being a Sunday, Brigade church parade was conducted by Padre H. A. Hayden, at which the Corps and Divisional Commanders were present.

Second Day.—The Battalion was reminded that the war was still on, and went *en masse* to dig trenches for burying signalling cables.

Third Day.—"Application" and "rapid" practices were carried out on the long musketry range at La Belle Hotesse, about two miles away.

Fourth Day.—Brigade sports were held in perfect weather, when the 10th Battalion beat us by two points for the General's Cup. However, Capt. W. R. Jorgensen won the 100 yards championship and the 12th Battalion team won the tug-o'-war.

Fifth Day.—Training under company arrangements and preparing for the move the next day.

At this period the authorities realised that some members of the A.I.F. had been away from Australia nearly four years, and individual N.C.O.'s and men who could furnish substantial private or business reasons, were granted leave to return home for a period. One of the first to benefit from this concession was Sgt. Roy Chivers, who had seen continuous service with the Battalion and much front line work.

While we were at this camp, a most contagious epidemic of influenza broke out, generally known as "Spanish influenza," but more often referred to as the "dog's disease," Its main symptoms were a high temperature, aching limbs and complete prostration, and it may well be imagined that it was the cause of much anxiety when the evacuations from our own unit amounted to 200 within a few days. Major Johnston was untiring in his efforts to check its progress and ordered all men to sleep apart in the open. He also paraded the whole Battalion twice a day and issued them with a prepared liquid which was used as a gargle and nasal douche. The good results of a rest in the reserve area were therefore discounted to a large extent by this virulent epidemic, and we were a somewhat sick Battalion that marched to a bivouac on the outskirts of Hazebrouck on June 15th.

Sunday, June 16th, saw us again on the move to a support position in rear of Strazeele, with Battalion Headquarters once more at Pradelles. There was considerable uneasiness with the higher command at this period, and an attack on our front was expected daily, but never eventuated. A "precautionary stage" was declared, when all units had to be prepared for rapid movement, especially the 1st Line Transport; in fact, the G.S. waggons and ammunition limbers were always kept packed. "D" Company were utilised as a special garrison and occupied Strazeele Avenue, which formed part of the trench system known as the inner defences of Strazeele. As far as the man in the ranks was concerned, there was nothing apparent to indicate an impending attack, and it was very difficult to make him realise the importance of being prepared. The general opinion was that "the 'heads' had got the wind up." (Which may or may not have been true in this instance). Indeed, on one night the password was "Chess," but a company humourist suggested that it ought to be "Draughts."

Second-Lieutenants A. Montgomery and B. N. Butler joined the Battalion on June 18th, and a week later we relieved the 9th Battalion in the right sector and once again occupied the frontage astride the railway line, with "A" Company line left, "C" Company line right, "B" Company support, and "D" Company reserve. The first portion of this tour in the line was rather quiet, the only really objectionable features being increased gas-shelling of rear areas, and nervous bursts of machine-gun fire, which proved very disconcerting to ration and carrying parties when crossing the flat, exposed country in order to approach the front line.

An inter-company relief took place on the 30th June, when dispositions were somewhat altered on account of taking over a large portion of the support and reserve lines of the Royal Fusiliers on our right. "B" Company was now in the right sector of the line, and "D" Company on their left. "A" Company was in support on the left, and "C" Company on the right. The companies in the lines garrisoned the posts with three platoons each, while the support line was held with nine platoons, the remaining one being accommodated in Moleghein Farm.

The Divisional Commander, Major-General Sir H. B. Walker, also took the opportunity of coming round to wish us "good-bye," having been transferred to a unit on the Italian front, and Major-General Glasgow succeeded to the command.

The enemy at this particular period was very nervy, and any slight artillery activity on either flank would bring down an S.O.S. barrage on his whole divisional front. The Battalion experienced this on the night of 2nd-3rd July, when the 8th Battalion raided the enemy—two battalion frontages to our left—and extremely heavy retaliatory fire was put down on our whole front, but by sheer luck we suffered no casualties at all. At this time we had some American officers and N.C.O.'s attached to the unit for experience, and this was the first time that they had heard or seen shell-fire to any great extent, and, according to the report they submitted to their Company Commander, they were greatly impressed by the intensity of the fire, the flare signals used by the Germans, and, most of all, the coolness of our men through it all.

Just before dark on the evening of July 4th, the enemy put down a violent barrage on the front line, particularly on Mont de Merris, which the 10th Battalion occupied, and the left of our sector, which "D" Company occupied. This soon extended over the whole of the Strazeele defences and along the main road to Pradelles. Communication was soon lost to our left front line and support companies, but the lines held to our right companies, and, fortunately, a direct line laid laterally to the 10th Battalion kept us in touch with them. It afterwards transpired that the enemy attempted a twilight raid on our "D" Company and the 10th Battalion on the left, but was completely repulsed without his obtaining identification of any kind. The whole incident—although intense—lasted only about three-quarters of an hour, after which we passed an abnormally quiet night.

After being relieved by the 1st Battalion on July 5th, we moved back to a camp at Weke Meulin, situated about half-a-mile to the north-west of Hazebrouck. The men were accommodated under trench shelters and in camouflaged bell tents, pitched as near to the hedges as possible in order to minimise the chance of detection from hostile aircraft.

Training grounds in the vicinity were very limited and parades were carried on under company arrangements, the majority of the time being allotted to specialists' training.

Hazebrouck was placed "out of bounds" to the troops, although many accepted the risk and made cautious visits into the town. Considerable surprise was experienced one morning when a "salvaged" piano was discovered in the large tent which served as an officers' mess; nevertheless, very few questions were asked regarding its delivery, etc., and much pleasure was derived from its use during the next few days.

The nearby village of Hondeghem was also forbidden to the units of the 1st Australian Division, being just outside the Divisional boundary. It was in this village that the notice was placed, advising that a certain *estaminet* was "out of bounds to Chinese and Australians." It was never discovered whether the last two words originated from some person in authority or from a would-be humourist.

With a "paper" strength of 47 officers and 850 other ranks, we moved on July 15th and relieved the 8th Battalion in a reserve position in rear of Rouge Croix. Battalion Headquarters were situated in a farm-house near to Borre Siding, and would have been comfortable but for the fact that a 12-inch gun close by, on a railway mounting, fired regularly throughout the night and was the cause of much hostile searching fire during the day.

Forty-eight hours later, owing to a readjustment of the Divisional front, we became the left supporting Battalion of the Brigade, when "B" and "C" Companies occupied Courte Croix Switch and "A" and "D" Companies garrisoned Rouge Croix Switch. Battalion Headquarters were considerably more than a mile in rear, at Mango Farm, and the area occupied by the unit was so considerable that it took the Works Officer, Lieut. R. G. Walduck, and myself four-and-a-half hours to visit all the companies and inspect the works in progress.

We moved into the line on July 22nd and relieved the 9th Battalion shortly after midnight, but, owing to the fact that both the right flank of the 9th Battalion and the left flank of the 11th Battalion had moved forward at dusk, the enemy had become thoroughly roused and the changing over was effected with great difficulty, Capt. I. N. Holyman being wounded about dawn. "A" and "D" Companies were in the line, on the right and left respectively, while "B" Company was in support and "C" Company in reserve. Battalion Headquarters were at Ionic House.

The left company in the line was subjected to a great deal of shell-fire, and on the night of July 23rd, the Company Headquarters (Ewe Farm) were completely blown in and Capt. B. J. Andrew and his runner had a narrow escape.

The 9th British Division on our left (on the opposite side of the dividing stream or ditch known as Meteren Becque) was raided on the night of 25th-26th July, and, without advising us of their plan of action, evacuated their front line posts and retired to the support line. This left our flank "in the air," so the Platoon Commander on the left of the line sent out a fighting patrol with a Lewis gun across the Becque. They surprised a party of Germans in the captured post and promptly engaged them. Very little opposition was encountered, however, and our patrol was able to capture a machine-gun. The remainder of the raiders withdrew hurriedly and we were able to inform our neighbours that their front line was once again ready for occupation.

An inter-company relief was carried out on 26th-27th July, when "B" and "C" Companies moved into the line (the latter on the left), and the R.A.P. at the same time moved forward to Moolenacker.

Instructions were received from Brigade Headquarters that it was essential to discover the identity of the unit on our front, and in consequence a fighting patrol, consisting of Cpl. W. Hammersley, ten men and a Lewis gun, went out on July 27th. They soon located an enemy post, and, leaving the gun on a flank to protect the party, Hammersley and his men rushed the post. In doing so he was badly wounded, but still continued to take an active part in the fight which ensued. The Germans put up a stout resistance, and, when eventually there were only two left in the post, they refused to be taken prisoners and had to be shot. When our men attempted to withdraw, it was discovered that a party of the enemy had moved out from a flanking post and were endeavouring to cut off their retreat, and the patrol had to fight its way back to our front line. The No. 1 Lewis gunner performed excellent work in covering their retirement, and was the last to reach our lines.

The 10th Battalion on our right, delivered an attack on the night of July 29th, on a well-devised plan, and captured the village of Merris with 180 prisoners and 36 machine-guns, suffering only 39 casualties themselves. We co-operated in a small way on their left flank, with the object of diverting attention, and were able to capture three prisoners, who were hiding in a ditch in a very demoralised state of mind.

Our relief in the line was effected by the 7th Battalion, and was complete at 1.40 a.m., on July 31st. We then had a long march back to a bivouac ground near L'Hoffand (north-east of Hazebrouck), where we remained for forty-eight hours, "embussing" at 3 a.m. on August 2nd for the Heuringhem area. Just before we left the bivouac, and while the Lancashire Fusiliers were relieving us, some enemy 'planes flew over the locality and two bombs were dropped within 100 yards of the paddock we were occupying, but no casualties were suffered.

The 'buses conveyed us as far as Heuringhem, which we reached at 6 a.m., and the Battalion then marched to a scattered area around the villages of Coubronne and Le Rons.

As a result of the recent tour in the line, the following decorations were awarded:—

Bar to Military Medal.—Cpl. W. H. Hammersley, M.M.

Military Medal.—Cpl. J. G. Watt, Pvte. A. H. Daniels,

while special mention was made of the excellent

work performed by the following N.C.O. and men:—

L.-Cpl. E. J. Starling; Pvts. J. H. Albert, C. W. McFarlane.

It was now generally known that the 1st Australian Division was leaving the XV. British Corps and was on its way to the Somme area to rejoin the Australian Corps and participate in the forthcoming Allied offensive.

The promulgation of the following letter received by the Divisional Commander was, therefore, gratifying to all ranks, who were pleased to know that their efforts had been appreciated:—

"XV. Corps Headquarters,
"4th August, 1918.

"Major-General T. W. Glasgow,
C.B., C.M.G., D.S.O.,

"Commanding 1st Australian Division.

"Before your magnificent Division leaves my Corps, I wish to thank you and all ranks under your command for the exceptional services rendered during the past four months.

"Joining this Corps on April 26th, during the Battle of Lys, the Division selected and prepared a position to defend the Hazebrouck front, and a few days later repulsed two heavy attacks, with severe losses to the enemy. This action brought the enemy's advance to a standstill.

"Since then, the Division has held the most important sector of this front continuously, and by skilful raiding and minor operations has advanced the line over a mile on a front of 5,000 yards, capturing just short of 1,000 prisoners, and causing such damage to the troops of the enemy that nine divisions have been replaced.

"The complete success of all minor operations, the skill displayed by the patrols by day as well as by night, the gallantry and determination of the troops, and their high state of training and discipline have excited the admiration and emulation of all, and I desire that you will convey to all ranks my high appreciation of their fine work and my regret that the Division is leaving my command.

"(Sgd.) BEAUVOIR DE LISLE,
    "Lieutenant-General, Commanding
        XV. Corps."

Chapter XX.

THE FINAL ADVANCE—AUTUMN, 1918.

THE transfer of the 1st Australian Division from the 2nd Army to the 4th Army took place between 5th-7th August, 1918, when we rejoined the Australian Corps on the Somme and participated in the final advance which resulted in the Armistice.

The 12th Battalion entrained at Arques on 6th August, and left at 5.30 p.m., although "D" Company proceeded by a subsequent train and left four hours later. We journeyed *via* Abbeville, and detrained at Hangest about 3 a.m., and left "C" Company at the station as an unloading party, while the remainder of the Battalion marched along unknown roads in the cold dawn and eventually arrived, very tired, at our billets in the village of L'Etoile.

As soon as the cookers arrived, breakfast was prepared, after which many of the men attempted to get a few hours sleep, for we were all very tired after a night in the the troop-train, and a warning order had already been received regarding another move the same evening.

This took place at 7.30 p.m., when we commenced "embussing," but we did not finally leave L'Etoile until 9 p.m., and, after a protracted journey, we reached some crossroads on the outskirts of the village of Rainneville, where we "debussed" at midnight. Our guides, however, were not there to meet us, and as the night was very foggy, all efforts to discover our bivouac ground at a "map-reading" near Poulainville proved fruitless. The only thing to be done was to pile arms on the roadside and try to snatch a few hours sleep while waiting for dawn to break.

We found our guides (or they found us) soon after daylight and proceeded to our bivouac site, where we at once had breakfast and then urged the men to rest.

It was the morning of August 8th, and even though we were situated a considerable distance behind the front line, there was evidence in plenty of the fact that the British attack had been launched. The bombardment, which had been intense during the early hours, had now ceased, which rightly indicated that a successful advance had been made. The sky was thick with our 'planes, coming and going in all directions—some on reconnaissance work, others on contact work, while bombing squadrons were continually passing overhead to carry out daylight raids. During the morning, long columns of prisoners, numbering many thousands, were seen marching in an almost continuous stream on their way to the P.O.W. Cages.

As the day advanced it became very hot, and at 2.45 p.m. we commenced a long march through Allonville, Pont Noyelles and Corbie, finally arriving at Vaire about 11 p.m., when we bivouaced in a field near the church. Although we had marched twenty miles (without a man falling out), we found the latter part of the journey very interesting, as the country was new to us, and the many ambulances and medical relay posts situated in positions which had only this morning been in the support area indicated the extent of our advance. The observation balloons had moved forward almost as fast as we marched, and the men jokingly said that they were our objective, which we had failed to reach at nightfall.

Lt.-Col. Elliott returned to the Battalion that night, after having relieved the Brigadier during a period of "Blighty" leave, and took over the command again from Major MacPherson.

The men were roused at 5 p.m. on August 9th, and Company Commanders were warned to be ready to move by 7 a.m., although it was actually 10 a.m. before we marched off by platoons with intervals of 100 yards.

The route taken was *via* Hamel and then by a track across country, skirting the ruined villages of Warfusee and Lamotte, until we reached an assembly point south-west of Bayonvillers.

It was very apparent to everyone that the front line trenches and support areas occupied by the remainder of the Australian Corps during the spring and summer months had not been subjected to nearly the same amount of shelling that the 1st Australian Division had experienced in the Hazebrouck area, and the knowledge came somewhat as a surprise, although the village of Hamel and country immediately surrounding it showed signs of heavy fighting.

There was every indication that the preceding

day's attack had been extraordinarily successful, for the large number of dead, and the quantities of war litter usually found in the wake of an advance were conspicuous by their absence, and one or two derelict tanks were practically the only signs of the recent attacking troops.

To show how open the fighting had already become, it will be necessary merely to state that, although we were only about two miles behind the front line troops, the Battalion cookers brought right up to the assembly point, a hot mid-day meal, which the companies issued to their men in the bivouac.

At dusk we moved in an artillery formation to a position south-west of Harbonnieres, when companies were instructed to pile arms, and permission was given for the men to take off their boots, and they were urged to settle down to sleep as an early morning move was expected. The move came, however, much sooner than this, for at 9.30 p.m., orders were received to advance to another assembly point south-east of Harbonnieres, and within striking distance of the enemy. The Battalion then accomplished a truly remarkable feat, which had been carried out many times on the parade ground in daytime, but now for the first time in reality, over strange ground on a pitch dark night. The whole unit moved in its present formation (line of half-platoons on a two-company frontage) across 3,000 yards of unknown country, and successfully crossed two thick belts of barbed wire and a deeply sunken road, without at any time losing touch or direction.

The companies accommodated themselves as best they could in the darkness, while Battalion Headquarters were established on the outskirts of the village itself.

Orders were received about dawn for the Brigade to attack, but as the dispatch runner had found difficulty in locating our headquarters, we were late in receiving them. Companies were immediately roused and we moved off at 7.15 a.m., in a thick morning mist, in the same artillery formation as adopted on the previous day.

The 10th and 11th Battalions had been ordered to attack at 8 a.m., and we were allotted the task of supporting the latter unit. We continued to advance in the above-mentioned formation until within 1,000 yards of the enemy position, when we came under extremely heavy and well directed machine-gun fire. The platoons immediately extended into skirmishing order and commenced advancing in short rushes. It was at this moment that the C.O. was wounded, whilst making a rush to take cover behind a heap of dirt. Willing hands soon carried him to a disused trench, and Major Johnston was quickly on the spot to render first aid. Many of us feared that the wound would prove fatal, but although it was serious, he was able to immediately Lieut. Frank Priddey, who had gone forward to reconnoitre and obtain information rejoin the Battalion just after the Armistice. Major MacPherson once more commanded, and almost immediately Lieut. Frank Priddey, who had gone forward to reconnoitre and obtain information generally, returned with a nasty gash in his left cheek, caused by a machine-gun bullet.

Companies were now instructed to take all available cover and to await orders, and during the morning the 11th Battalion dislodged the enemy from the ridge he had been occupying, and it was once again safe to walk about in our immediate neighbourhood.

During the day Lieut. M. W. Blacklow received a serious scalp wound from a bursting shell, and it was with the deepest regret that we learned later that he died at an old German field hospital which had been captured and converted into an Advanced Dressing Station. He was universally known as "Billy," and popular with both commissioned and non-commissioned ranks. To give him an order to do anything was equivalent to considering it done, and consequently his superiors had every confidence in him, while his own platoon trusted him.

About 1 a.m. on the night of 10th-11th August, Major MacPherson was sent for by Lieut.-Col. Neligan, 10th Battalion, and informed by him that the 12th Battalion had been placed at his disposal for an impending operation, the object of which was to capture the "Blue Line" which included the large village of Lihons, and that zero hour would be at 4 a.m. Details of the attack had then to be arranged, and it was 2.30 a.m. before the C.O. returned, and, in consequence, Company Commanders had to have the attack explained to them, the men had to be roused, given a meal and prepared for battle, and the whole unit had to proceed 1,700 yards to the assaulting position *within an hour-and-a-half*.

We were heavily shelled by a gun of large calibre as we proceeded to our position, and although the column was broken, fortunately no casualties were sustained. We barely reached the jumping off tape (an imaginary one) by 4 a.m., when the barrage opened up, and the companies advanced in perfect order, although heavy hostile machine-gun fire was experienced, and Lieut. T. E. C. Bridger (Signalling Officer) was badly wounded in the leg.

The actual attack was made by "B" Company, commanded by Lieut. L. Dadson, which advanced in lines of half-sections, and supported by "A" and "D" Companies in lines of sections in single file, only about 150 yards in rear, while "C" Company was kept in reserve.

It was a thick, foggy morning, and the tanks, which were to assist in the attack, proved to be quite useless, as they had no means of ascertaining their direction in the fog and floundered around in big circles.

During the attack, the 11th Battalion was on our left and the 10th Battalion and 2nd Brigade on our right. Our line of advance took us through Auger and Crepey Woods, which the enemy saturated with gas, thus making it difficult for our men to proceed, as the undergrowth was very thick, and retarded progress as well as harboured the gas.

By 6 a.m. we had enveloped Lihons and reconnoitring patrols were pushed out in front to gain touch with the enemy. One patrol was commanded by Lieut. G. T. Gandy, who took a Lewis gun with him, and afterwards estimated that his patrol penetrated from 1,000 to 1,500 yards in the misty light, and finally espied a team of horses dragging a gun out of position. They opened fire, and a horse was seen to fall and the gun crew dispersed.

On settling down in the new line, we very soon discovered that a large gap existed between ourselves and the 11th Battalion on the left, and patrols failed to gain touch. "D" Company was at once sent to fill this gap, but before this was effected, the gap had apparently been noticed by the enemy, and a party, estimated at about 50, was seen to filter

through, evidently with the object of turning our
flank. However, they were quickly engaged by
"D" Company in a very determined manner and
disposed of, after which they ("D" Company) proceeded to the line. Even then the gap was not
filled.

Battalion and company runners, when proceeding to and from the line, persistently reported that
they were fired upon as they moved through Crepey
Wood, and "C" Company were now detailed to
"mop up" this area thoroughly, before going into
the line on the left of "D" Company to link up with
the 11th Battalion. No sign of the enemy was discovered in the thick undergrowth of Crepey Wood,
but quite a number of Germans were found secreted
in the north-west corner of Auger Wood, and as
they were ejected and endeavoured to reach their
own lines, were shot by "B" Company gunners.

During the latter part of the morning, the enemy
made several half-hearted counter-attacks which
were easily repelled, but at 1.30 p.m. a strong attack
carried out by more than 100 men, gave the enemy
temporary possession of a military hospital on the
northern outskirts of Lihons. Only after sharp
fighting at close quarters by "C" Company, and
parties from both 10th and 11th Battalions, were
we able to regain possession of it.

Throughout the day the front line, Battalion
Headquarters and neighbouring woods were heavily
shelled with 5.9's, while shells of smaller calibre
were noticeably absent. Many of the H.E. shells
contained gas which brought on violent sneezing
attacks.

The 2nd Battalion relieved us that night at 2 a.m.,
and we moved back to the position we had occupied
before making the attack. We spent a rather quiet

day and enjoyed two good meals, when orders were received for "A" and "C" Companies to relieve two companies of the 11th Battalion in the line. It is interesting to note that in this vicinity the front line was on the fringe of the old French trench system in front of Vermandovillers, which was in use before the offensive of July, 1916.

Heavy "counter-preparation" barrages were fired by our artillery at dawn and shortly afterwards, with the object of breaking up any counter-attacks which might be forming. The men had rather a good time in the line, for they were quite comfortable, and there was little shelling. Some of them discovered a German canteen, although most of the contents had disappeared, either taken by the enemy before retiring, or by some of our fellows who had "got in first." However, there were several dozen bottles of mineral water—something like soda water—which proved very acceptable.

"C" Company was relieved by the 23rd Battalion on the evening of August 13th, and "A" Company by the 11th Battalion on the following day, and these reliefs concentrated the whole unit, once again, in a support position.

The 16th Battalion relieved us during the early evening of August 15th, after which we marched back to a bivouac position in an old brickfield near Guillaucourt, being bombed heavily on the way, but suffering no casualties.

As a result of the two days' strenuous fighting, the following decorations were awarded:—

Second Bar to Military Cross.—Lieut. L. Dadson, M.C.

Military Cross.—Lieuts. G. T. Gandy, H. M. Sandy.

Distinguished Conduct Medal.—C.S.M. A. Keeling, Sgt. T. T. Smith; Pvts. S. Lyden; H. J. Wegener.

Bar to Military Medal.—Cpl. H. V. Weighill, M.M.; Pvt. T. Burgess.

Military Medal.—Cpl. A. G. Petterd; L.-Cpl. H. J. Pedley; Pvts. H. Stevens, J. H. Albert, W. Craig, H. Turmine.

Special mention was also made of the valuable work done by the following officers, N.C.O's., and men:—

Capt. W. R. Jorgensen; Lieut. F. E. Priddey, M.M.; Sgt. E. J. Nicholls; Cpl. J. G. Watt; L-Cpl. W. H. Leonard; Pvts. W. J. Crothers, J. P. Murphy, J. H. McBain.

We left the next morning at 8.30 a.m., and marched back to Vaire, where the whole unit was bivouaced in the woods on the bank of the River Somme. We stayed here for five days and during the time the weather was delightfully hot, and the men took full advantage of the fact by swimming in the river practically all day long. Parades merely consisted of roll-call twice a day, inspection of arms, re-equipping and general smartening up.

Major G. D. Shaw joined us on August 18th from the 10th Battalion, and was appointed to command temporarily.

Orders were received on August 21st for another move forward, and at 1 p.m. we marched out by platoons and relieved the 32nd Battalion in a wood and an adjoining gully south of Morcourt.

A captured gun of large calibre was situated on the outskirts of the wood, and during the thirty-six hours that we remained here, it was firing continuously in order that all the captured ammunition might be fired back at the Hun before he got out of range.

It was now known that the 3rd Australian Division was going to attack north of the River Somme, on August 23rd, with the object of capturing the large village of Bray, and the 1st Australian Division was to attack simultaneously on the south of the river in order to protect their flank and at the same time advance the line.

We moved off in bright moonlight at 2 a.m. for our assembly position in St. Germaine Wood, north of Proyart, as the 3rd Brigade was acting as a reserve in the initial stage of the attack. The Battalion looked like a huge serpent as it wended its way, in single file, along the numerous valleys which we had to traverse. As we neared Proyart, an enemy gun began to fire at regular intervals, and as it was enfilading the whole column, we soon saw that it was only a matter of time before casualties would be incurred. The inevitable happened, and a shell burst almost at the rear of the column, and Lieut. A. L. Wardlaw, one of our best officers, was seriously wounded in the leg. His injuries were so severe that for some days it was doubtful whether he would pull through, but a good constitution and strong will power prevailed, although it was a long time before he fully recovered from the shock of amputation.

The Battalion, meanwhile, proceeded onwards, when it was regretfully discovered that instead of following the route that we had reconnoitred, the C.O. was following in the rear of the 10th Battalion, and consequently we approached our assembly position from an entirely different angle. This resulted in everyone having a very hazy idea of our front, the position of the enemy, and our line of advance.

The head of the column reached a deep gully in the vicinity of St. Germaine Wood at 4.15 a.m., and as the barrage was timed to commence in another half-hour, no time was to be lost in getting the companies under cover. "B" Company was placed in a large quarry, which it was thought would be immune from shell-fire, while fully half of "D" Company took shelter behind some big earthworks. The remainder of the companies were distributed in the near vicinity.

Just as dawn was breaking, at 4.45 a.m., our barrage opened with a roar, and before long we were experiencing heavy retaliatory fire, when, to our consternation, we discovered that the gully offered no cover at all and was almost enfiladed. Shells began to land right in the quarry where "B" Company was sheltering, and casualties were incurred, whereupon Major Foster shifted them out and told them to scatter. Daylight now disclosed the fact that the earthworks behind which "D" Company sought shelter, were in reality a magazine of *minenwerfer* ammunition, and a local explosion resulted in the death of C.Q.M.S. White. We suffered nearly 50 casualties in all in this gully from hostile shelling.

As the attack progressed, the enemy fire slackened somewhat, and Company Commanders were enabled once more to re-organise their companies and dispose them in the numerous German shelters in the Wood, which provided moderate cover. By this time the Quartermaster had brought the cookers up (again *right to the assembly position*), and as the men had their breakfast, we had the pleasure of witnessing a wonderfully impressive sight, when the field artillery galloped into action, unlimbered, and opened fire.

During the latter part of the morning we learned that the 1st Brigade had reached the "Red Line" (a position east of the village of Chuignolles), and the 3rd Brigade was instructed to pass through them at 2 p.m., and to continue the advance. In accordance with this order, companies began to move forward at 1 p.m., and crossed the high ground west of Chuignolles in artillery formation. As they came into the open ground flanking the village, they were subjected to heavy machine-gun and rifle fire, originating from the high ground, almost resembling cliffs, about 900 yards away. "C" Company suffered quite a number of casualties from this cause, in addition to shrapnel fire, when crossing an exposed wheatfield, and were compelled to take temporary shelter in the village, where they rested a few moments, as the men were already becoming exhausted in trying to keep up with the barrage, which was advancing much too fast.

"D," "B," and "A" Companies (in order from the left) now made a determined effort by dashing down the valley beyond the village, and made straight for Marly Wood and the steep slopes in front. Reports had been received that Long Wood, on the left flank, was clear of the enemy, but heavy sniping fire was encountered from this quarter, which necessitated "D" Company detaching a platoon to "mop up" the Wood and thus retarded their progress. "A" and "B" Companies, therefore, were the only two companies able to keep up with the barrage in the assault on Marly Wood and the heights beyond, while "C" Company was in close support on the left, and "D" Company practically had to form a protective flank, as no sign of the 9th Battalion had been discovered on the left.

The work of ejecting the enemy from the Wood proved to be somewhat easier than was expected, and no protracted fighting took place, and under cover of the trees an effort was made to re-organise the companies. Major Foster superintended this task to a great extent, and having completed it, was just emerging from the Wood in advance of the troops in order to indicate the direction of the advance, when he was killed by machine-gun fire coming from Garenne Wood on the right front. Major Foster was one of our original officers, whose numbers were now terribly depleted, and he had proved himself, both in and out of the line, a most capable Company Commander, administering his command with marked impartiality, and yet always making the welfare of his men his first consideration. The esteem with which he was held was proved by stretcher-bearers and members of his company, who carried his body many miles to the rear, in order that he might be buried in the military cemetery at Morcourt.

It has always been difficult to explain why the Germans allowed themselves to be dislodged from an almost impregnable position on top of the cliffs previously referred to, in a daylight attack, for it held complete command over an approach of more than 1,000 yards of open and exposed country.

The dislodgement of the enemy was effected, however, and all the more credit is due to "A" Company, who was largely responsible for it, under the leadership of Lieut. Geo. Vaughan. Although the men were feeling the effects of the rapid and strenuous advance, and, in addition, were more or less out of breath after their climb up the steep hill, a sharp fight ensued at the top, and before long the enemy was seen to retire in the direction of Garenne Wood.

The attack on the Wood itself was carried out in a most able manner by "A" Company (Lieut. G. Vaughan), and "B" Company (Lieut. E. E. Terry), attacking it on the right flank and "C" Company (Lieut. G. T. Gandy) on the left. Their concerted action made the enemy see that his rear was threatened, and the garrison (less 70 who were taken prisoners) soon retreated precipitately in the direction of Chuignes.

"D" Company, meanwhile, under Lieut. P. F. Sellick, had continued the advance on the left front, and in the absence of the 9th Battalion, occupied a very large frontage extending from the banks of the Somme, fully 400 yards to the right. They had not met with a great deal of opposition, and in consequence were able to follow up the retreating enemy, inflicting many casualties, almost to the outskirts of the village of Cappy itself.

During the night, Lieut. R. W. Fletcher and Sgt. A. V. Chadwick did particularly good work in holding their several posts, and the responsibility of holding such a large frontage with a handful of troops must have proved very trying. Although the 9th Battalion was repeatedly advised that our company was not only holding their frontage, but was actually in front of their troops, it was not until the Brigadier visited the line the next night and gave explicit orders on the subject, that "D" Company was relieved by that unit, and on relief withdrew to a quarry at the foot of the cliffs, where they carried out the functions of a support company.

August 24th proved to be a somewhat quiet day in every respect, and "A" Company was able to occupy some disused trenches about 200 yards in front of Garenne Wood, without opposition. "B" Company endeavoured to advance their bomb-stop along a communication trench, but encountered the enemy, and a sharp bomb fight ensued, which ultimately resulted in their post being advanced about 150 yards along the trench.

Advice was received on August 25th to the effect that the 3rd Australian Division had advanced on the left of the River Somme, and as the 1st Brigade had also outflanked us, orders were received for the 3rd Brigade to advance during the afternoon. The instructions were terse and to the point: "You will attack and advance as far as possible."

Prior to this, the C.O., Major G. D. Shaw, had been wounded in the arm at about 1 p.m., when making a reconnaissance of the front line, and remained with the unit until 4 p.m., when his wound became painful, and he was forced to leave just before the arrival of Major MacPherson. For a while, therefore, every Company Commander and the Adjutant (acting for a short period as Battalion Commander) was of the rank of Lieutenant, and under these conditions the attack, referred to above, was launched.

At 4 p.m. the three companies in the line began their advance towards the enemy under cover of a very weak and ragged barrage, while "D" Company moved up to a support position in rear of

THE VILLAGE OF CHUIGNOLLES

From the Official History of Australia in the War of 1914-1918, Volume VI. By permission of the Editor and the Publishers, Angus & Robertson Ltd.

Garenne Wood. The country over which they had to advance was as flat as a billiard table, and "C" Company on the left had few, if any, disused trenches along which they could operate. Heavy machine-gun fire was encountered, originating from Earl and Olympia Woods on the left, and from an occupied trench in front, from which a considerable number of casualties were suffered, and which entirely frustrated any efforts on the part of "C" Company to advance. "A" and "B" Companies on the right (afterwards joined by "D" Company) commenced bombing their way along the old French communication trenches, and very fierce fighting ensued, in the course of which the Hun fought well and hard. It was not long before our supply of Mills bombs was expended, and a plentiful supply of German stick bombs (left behind as he retreated step by step) were used to force the enemy back.

During this period of strenuous fighting, excellent work was performed by Lieuts. Geo. Vaughan, "Toc" Terry, Dick Fletcher, A-C.S.M. Nicholls, Sgt. Dean and Cpls. Lord and Phillips.

While commanding his company, Terry got out of the trench in order to direct a team of bombers, and was unfortunately killed by a machine-gun bullet. Cpl. H. E. Lord was also wounded in the middle of a particularly fierce bomb fight, and as he fell a Mills bomb rolled out of his hand with the pin withdrawn. Lord's wounds were very serious and would probably have proved fatal, but even at this trying moment he apparently realised the danger in which he had placed his comrades, and covered the exploding bomb with his own body, and thus made his death an heroic sacrifice.

v.

Lieut. E. M. Dollery was responsible for a neat little affair on the left flank, when he and his party successfully dislodged an enemy machine-gun post from a small gravel pit near Olympia Wood, and thus saved his company many casualties.

At dusk the enemy put down a heavy smoke barrage, and it was thought that he was going to attack, but it was afterwards learned that he was withdrawing his rearguard troops to a prepared position some distance in rear.

The 11th Battalion was instructed to occupy a line considerably in advance of us at dawn on August 26th, when the command of the front line automatically passed to the C.O. 11th Battalion, and our companies were withdrawn to a support position on the fringe of Garenne Wood, where they spent a quiet day. The 3rd Brigade was relieved by the 6th Brigade during the evening, and as they passed through our lines, we withdrew our companies, and the unit moved back and bivouaced once again in St. Germaine Wood.

The casualties sustained by the Battalion during the four days' fighting, were as follows:—

	Officers	Other Ranks
Killed	2	32
Wounded	5	154
Missing	—	1
Gassed	—	7
Total	7	194

which reduced our effective strength to approximately 400.

As a result of the operation, the following decorations were awarded:—

Bar to Military Cross.—Lieut. G. Vaughan, M.C.

Military Cross.—Lieuts. L. M. Newton and E. M. Dollery.

Bar to Military Medal.—Cpl. W. E. Phillips, M.M.

Military Medal.—Sgts. E. J. Nicholls, R. J. Wynyard; L.-Sgt. R. H. Box; Cpl. L. G. Layton; L.-Cpls. H. E. Brooks, A. J. Baker; Pvts C. T. Buckpitt, J. Fox, L. V. Lewis, S. J. Carnell, E. W. Saltmarsh, G. Nichols, W. Kaine, A. Aitken, L. W. Hill, E. H. Ping, V. Ferguson, C. Whish-Wilson, H. E. Harvey, K. L. Moore, H. Wilkins.

The following officers, N.C.O.'s, and men were also specially mentioned for valuable and gallant services:—

Lieuts. G. T. Gandy, R. W. Fletcher, P. F. Sellick; Sgts. J. I. Powell, J. Doyle, J. O'Loughlin, R. W. Stretton, C. Byng, W. H. Benson; Cpl. C. J. Allen; L.-Cpls. R. W. Williams, J. J. S. Rogers, H. J. Wegener, T. Burgess; Pvts. W. H. Pickering, J. P. Orky, C. F. C. Maingay, W. Russell, R. G. Billet.

The stretcher-bearers did excellent work throughout, and the headquarters' runners, Pvts. Gherkie and Huxley, excelled themselves in carrying messages in daylight to exposed positions in the line, and in displaying a wonderful sense of direction at night time.

The next morning, August 27th, we marched along the Canal bank *via* Mericourt-Chipilly-Cerisy, to a deep gully at the south of the latter village, where we bivouaced. It was on this march that we saw a crude home-made cross erected over a grave, and inscribed:—

"Here Lies an Unknown German,"

underneath which a grim humourist had scrawled:—

"Who Met an Unknown Aussie."

The work during the next fortnight consisted, as was usual after every period of fighting, of bathing and smartening up the Battalion, plenty of recreational training, promotion of N.C.O's. to replace casualties, and re-organisation. The Orderly Room staff was also kept busy preparing a "Report on Operations," and forwarding "Recommendations for Honours and Awards."

The re-organisation was somewhat different and more drastic on this occasion than usual, for the heavy casualties we had sustained during the last fortnight, and the rapidly decreasing number of reinforcements from Australia had caused all Battalions in the Brigade to be considerably below the required establishment, and too weak to administer in their present form. They were, therefore, re-organised into three companies, each of three platoons, and thus "A," "B," "C," and "D" Companies now became "X," "Y," and "Z" Companies.

Other divisions were experiencing the same difficulties, and many Battalions (including the 52nd Battalion) had already been disbanded and amalgamated with other units. It was rumoured, however, that a promise had been made that the first four Brigades to leave Australia (i.e., 1st, 2nd, 3rd, and 4th Brigades) would be the last to be so treated.

On September 7th, the Battalion "embussed" and

proceeded to Peronne, where they bivouaced on the outskirts of the town on the famous Mt. St. Quentin, and during the 48 hours spent there, large parties were detailed to bury the German dead, which were numerous in this vicinity.

Another forward move was made on September 10th by marching to the Tincourt area, where the Battalion was billetted in huts in Millen Copse, more often referred to as the Tank Wood, from the number of tanks which were parked in the wood for purposes of concealment.

While in this area the Brigade carried out the role of Support Brigade to the Division, and a portion of the time was utilised in digging a defensive position, consisting of a line of posts, about 2,000 yards in front of the bivouac position.

An incident of comparative importance occurred on September 14th, when the first draft of 1914 men, consisting of 15 other ranks, left the Battalion in order to return to Australia for six months furlough.

Warning was now received of another impending attack in the vicinity of Jeancourt, and officers proceeded daily to the forward area in order to become familiar with the geography of the new sector.

The Battalion actually moved out at 1.45 a.m. on September 18th, in a drizzly rain, led by Major H. A. MacPherson (C.O.), Lieut. G. Vaughan (Acting Adjutant while I was finishing some "Blighty" leave), Lieut. R. G. Walduck (Intelligence Officer), and Lieut. R. D. Radford (Officer responsible for direction in the attack). The assembling of the troops was not noticed by the enemy, and the last platoon was in position about ten minutes before zero hour, which just gave time for gaps to be cut in the wire, when the barrage opened at 5.20 a.m.

"Z" Company, under Capt. S. R. Houghton, attacked on the right of the Battalion sector, and "Y" Company (Capt. I. N. Holyman) on the left. One platoon of "X" Company followed each line company for "mopping up" purposes, while the third platoon, under "X" Company Commander (Capt. L. E. Burt), was kept as a small local reserve, and carried 50 Stokes Mortar shells and a proportion of picks and shovels.

The morning turned out to be very foggy, and the smoke barrage in addition made it very difficult for the line companies to advance, while the Directing Officer (Lieut. R. D. Radford) had an extremely hard task, and found it almost impossible to convey his information.

The artillery barrage was quite thick and effective, although many of the shells were falling short and we sustained several casualties from this cause. At this early stage Capt. Burt had his foot blown off (by one of our own shells, it was generally believed), and for a moment his company was thrown into confusion, until Radford quickly assumed command, and, assisted by Lieut. E. R. Facy, continued the advance.

Opposition was encountered on the right flank by intense machine gun fire from a small wood. Lieut. B. N. Butler and a small party gallantly attempted to rush the position, but a thick belt of wire prevented their progress, and in their efforts to pass through a gap, Butler and five of his men were killed. Another platoon of "Z" Company now attacked the wood from the other side, and were able to capture 20 prisoners.

"Y" Company, meanwhile, on the left, had experienced very little opposition, and had been able to advance nearly 1,000 yards, when they suddenly met with stout resistance as they attempted to enter Brosse Wood. A sharp fight ensued, and eventually the same tactics as related above were pursued, and "X" Company's platoon entered the wood from the left flank and drove the enemy into the open, where those who were not shot down surrendered.

Fierce fighting took place, for a while, in the system of trenches on the outskirts of Grand Priel Wood, but the Australian soldier proved his superiority in initiative and dash, and dislodged the Hun, at the same time capturing two 77-mm. field guns, several machine guns, and numerous prisoners.

The trees in Grand Priel Wood had all been cut down, but the rapidly growing shoots from the stumps gave ample cover to advancing troops, and "Y" Company was thus enabled to advance down the forward slopes of the hill and approach the "Brown Line," this being our objective.

Capt. Houghton and "Z" Company had, in the meantime, struck some determined opposition in the vicinity of a *chateau* on the eastern fringe of Grand Priel Wood, and some fierce fighting took place. The enemy used his machine guns to such advantage, that it was quite a considerable time before our fellows could get within striking distance. Bomb fighting took place in and around the framework of a large conservatory adjoining the main building (the glass having disappeared long since), but eventually we gained the upper hand, and captured a considerable number of prisoners from deep dugouts, including Captain Von Streseman, a Machine-Gun Battalion Commander. He afterwards stated that the Germans knew that the 1st and 4th Australian Divisions were attacking, and had reinforced the line accordingly, as the Australians were regarded as "storm troops." His first knowledge of our close proximity was when his sergeant-major had come down the dugout and said, "The English are here." He had not expected the attack to come so far or so fast, the line having been advanced a mile and a half in the hour.

Capt. Houghton was badly wounded in the leg during the early part of this fighting, but still remained and directed operations until the line was established on the 1st objective, when Lieut. R. W. Fletcher assumed command and supervised the consolidation and organised the posts. While this was in progress, a considerable number of casualties were caused by a German machine-gun firing from a small quarry, about 400 yards away, where a Red Cross Flag was flying. This was afterwards discovered to be a German Aid Post. Capt. Houghton and his company gained the distinction of capturing more prisoners than the strength of the company with which they attacked.

At 8.45 a.m. the 10th Battalion passed through our line on their way to the "Red Line" (2nd objective) and as they passed into the valley in front of us, we were in a position to give them some very useful overhead covering fire, which undoubtedly assisted their progress materially.

The 12th Battalion advanced the line a little less than two miles, and the 10th Battalion continued the forward move to a line of posts about 600 yards short of the famous Bellicourt Tunnel (Canal du Nord) and the Hindenburg Line, making a total advance of three miles.

September 19th was abnormally quiet, and we suffered very little from shell fire of any kind. It was with sincere regret that we learned that Lieut. J. G. Simmons, who had been badly wounded the previous day while on liaison duty with the 11th Battalion, had died of wounds at the Casualty Clearing Station at Doingt. Although he had only joined us in the spring, his cheery disposition had soon won him a place of affection in our hearts.

During the evening of September 21st, we relieved the 10th Battalion in the line, "Y" Company being on the right, "Z" Company on the left, and "X" Company in support. A line of posts was occupied by us for the next forty-eight hours, without any incident of particular importance happening, and on the evening of September 23rd we were relieved by "K" Company, "A" Battalion, 118th Regiment, 59th Brigade, American Army. The strength of the unit may be estimated, when it is pointed out that one company of the American troops relieved our whole Battalion. We were somewhat surprised to see the relieving troops arrive at Battalion Headquarters (situated in a dugout known as "Harrods Stores") in "column of fours," and in full marching order. They explained, however, that this was their *first* appearance in the forward area, and that they had no idea how far they were from the line, and promptly acted upon any advice we gave them. After relief Lieuts. K. T. Payne, L. D. Rafferty, and E. A. Potts, and four N.C.O's. remained behind to render any assistance and advice that was needed, and unfortunately Payne was wounded by one of the American Lewis gunners, who proved himself to be too keen. As Payne approached his post, he challenged him by saying "Halt! Who goes there?" but fired before Payne could declare himself.

The decorations awarded for the above operations were as follows:—

Distinguished Service Order.—Capt. S. R. Houghton, M.C.

Military Cross.—Capt. I. N. Holyman; Lieuts. R. W. Fletcher and W. Lambert.

Military Medal.—Sgts. W. T. Young, D.C.M., S. Horne; Cpls. H. G. Crooks, W. C. Gardiner; L-Cpl. T. C. Doherty; Pvt. R. B. Harrington.

Casualties:—

	Officers	Other Ranks
Killed	2	17
Wounded	5	74
Missing	—	3
Total	7	94

Material Captured:—

> 38 Machine Guns.
> 2 77-mm. Field Guns.
> 2 Trench Howitzers.

After relief we moved back once more to the huts in the Tank Wood, near Tincourt, and did not know at the time that we had completed our last tour of duty in the front line in the Great War.

Chapter XXI.

CONCLUSION.

THE usual procedure of calling rolls and preparing correct casualty lists was carried out during the next morning, and orders from Brigade for an anticipated move to the rear areas for rest and training were awaited with customary eagerness.

The 1914 men were even more anxious for advice regarding further drafts for Australia. Capt. Richardson had taken a batch of men from out of the line during the recent operations, and it was now known that efforts were being made to get them all home in time to spend Christmas with their homefolks.

A movement order was received from Brigade on 24th September, and the next day the transport section moved—part by road and part by rail—to our new area near Abbeville. The Battalion itself entrained in open trucks at Tincourt on 26th September, about noon, and proceeded *via* Peronne and Amiens to Longpre, where we detrained at 7 p.m. Considerable interest was shown as we proceeded through Lihons, for we passed within a few hundred yards of the spot where we had carried out operations on August 10th-12th.

The night was extremely dark, and the roads were very difficult to follow, and in spite of the murmurs which could be heard coming from the column, the 1: 100,000 maps once again proved their usefulness, and we arrived at the village of Ergnies about 11 p.m.

A tour of inspection next morning disclosed the fact that we had been billetted in many better villages than Ergnies. It was, no doubt, a charming village in the summer-time, for it was enveloped by beautiful elm and chestnut trees, but unfortunately these prevented the weak wintry sun from penetrating, and, in consequence, the roads remained in a shocking state of mud which reminded us to no small degree of the 1916 winter. The billets, also, were damp and cold, and quite a considerable amount of Regimental Funds was expended in the purchase of straw.

Major MacPherson received a preliminary warning of his approaching 1914 leave on September 28th, on which day Captain (afterwards Major) E. W. Tullock, 11th Battalion, arrived to take temporary command of the Battalion. There was a Brigade Church Parade the next day at the adjoining village of Brucamps, and as we marched home through Gorenflos, Major MacPherson halted the men on the roadside and bade them "good-bye."

Our time was occupied at this juncture in reorganising, promoting N.C.O's. to replace casualties, commencing a comprehensive training syllabus, and occasionally marching the Battalion to baths at Bouchon.

The weather was particularly inclement, and our murky environment was not having a good effect on the men, so representations were made to Brigade

Headquarters, which resulted in a move to the nearby village of Surcamps on October 7th. Two of the companies were billetted in Nissen huts, Battalion Headquarters were accommodated at the Chateau de la Haie, but the other company occupied uninviting and inadequate billets in the village itself.

Lieut. Dadson had, by this time, taken a draft of 1914 men away, and he was soon after followed by Lieut. MacDonald, to compensate for which, 2nd. Lieuts. T. McCredie, C. H. Johnson, and E. C. Stephens joined us from the base.

The country in this vicinity was particularly suitable for training purposes; in fact, until the recent advance an adjoining tract of country, comprising 50 acres or more, had been used as an aerodrome, and served as an excellent parade ground. On October 11th, the Brigade was to have been reviewed by the Hon. W. M. Hughes, but the weather was very indifferent, and, as a result, the Divisional Commander, Major-General T. W. Glasgow, arrived alone and inspected us. The parade was impressive and unique, for we took up a position of "Brigade in line," and the "presenting" of arms when the "General Salute" was given was well worth seeing. We afterwards marched past the saluting base in *battalions in line*, and the 12th Battalion was specially congratulated by both the Divisional Commander and the acting Brigadier (Lieut. Colonel Wilder-Neligan), for they told us that there was not a man out of step and the "dressing" along the whole line was perfect.

We returned to Ergnies on October 20th, and occupied our old billets. During our sojourn in this village, the efforts of Padre Hayden to provide additional comforts for the men during their leisure hours were most praiseworthy. He rented an old barn from a local French farmer, and with the assistance of improvised tables and forms, made out of boxes and Q.M. Stores, he provided a reading and writing room, which was greatly appreciated by the men. Stationery and reading matter was obtained from the Brigade Y.M.C.A. representative and other sources, and large maps of North-West Europe were nailed on to the wall, and the rapid advance of our troops was indicated daily as the news was received from Brigade. It was with regret that we lost the Padre's services on October 23rd, when he was transferred to the 2nd Australian General Hospital. Padre Douglas returned to us to fill the vacancy.

Towards the end of the month, Divisional Musketry Competitions were held on the range at Bouchon, and the 12th Battalion distinguished itself by winning *every* event, which included champion company, champion platoon, champion team of ten, and champion individual shot.

The scores for the champion company event were:—

12th Bttn.	493	6th Bttn.	328
4th „	386	11th „	308
10th „	366	M.G. „	294
8th „	360	3rd „	277
9th „	355	1st „	216
5th „	330	7th „	211
2nd „	329	Pioneer Bttn.	106

There were only three 1914 officers now remaining with the Battalion, *viz.*, Capts. I. N. Holyman, H. E. Spotswood and myself. Holyman had elected to take the alternative 90 days leave in England, and so Spotswood and I "tossed" to see which of us should be the next to go—and I won. I left the Battalion on October 31st, after having completed two years unbroken service as Adjutant of the unit, my successor being Lieut. Frank Priddey, M.M., who had already proved himself invaluable as an Intelligence Officer and Assistant-Adjutant.

The Battalion entrained, for the forward area once more, at Pont Remy, on November 9th, and after nearly 36 hours in the train, arrived at Tincourt on the night 10th-11th November. The following day, the memorable "eleventh day of the eleventh month," the Battalion was to proceed by 'bus to the Cambrai area, but through a miscarriage of orders, the 'buses were not at the appointed place, and the unit had to return to billets. It was a miserable day, cold and foggy, and a drizzly rain began to fall. Rations were not available, as they had been sent to the new area, and any attempt to make a fire only resulted in dense clouds of smoke issuing from the wet fuel.

This was how matters stood at 11 a.m. Everyone was miserable, out-of-sorts, and thoroughly "fed up." Suddenly hooters and sirens could be heard in the distance, followed by the beating of tins and gongs nearer at hand, but no one seemed inclined to interest himself in the matter, and one enthusiast who jumped up and exclaimed, "The war's over," was told to sit down and not be a blanky fool. So many rumours had been circulated during the last week concerning a fictitious Armistice and cessation of hostilities, that when it did actually eventuate it was not believed.

The Battalion left Tincourt the following day, 12th November, and proceeded by 'bus to

Mazinghien, where they stayed two days, after which they marched to Bohaine and rested for about a week. The next move was to Sars Potteries, where they stayed a short while, after which, a long march by daily stages, brought them to Chatelet, on the outskirts of Charleroi, about two or three days before Christmas.

This was the commencement of a very enjoyable time for the whole of the Battalion, as both officers and men were comfortably billetted with the civilians of the town, who could not do sufficient to prove their gratitude at being released from German occupation. The men also made themselves wonderfully popular and created a marvellous impression on the civilian population.

Christmas Day was spent under these happy conditions, and Regimental Funds were freely spent to supplement the rations, and an enjoyable dinner, accompanied by a free issue of beer, was appreciated by the men.

On New Year's Day, 1919, the officers, N.C.O.'s., and men of the Battalion gave a dance in a large hall to the local residents, as some slight return for the many acts of kindnesses they were receiving. It was a great success, and enjoyed by all ranks and all classes of guests. It was rather humorous to see the democratic touch given to the assembly by the obvious "Sunday clothes" of the working man and their woman folks intermingling with the evening dress of the more influential guests.

It was now realised that the continuance of military training was out of the question, and yet some occupation had to be found for the men, while waiting for demobilisation. Sports of all kinds were freely indulged in, and Lieut. G. T. Gandy was appointed Battalion Sports' Officer.

An Educational Scheme was also commenced, the object of which was to prepare the men once again, in some small measure, for their return to civilian life. Lieut. E. Crofton Stephens was placed in charge of arrangements in the Battalion, and very soon had several classes organised, including general education, book-keeping, and French, R.S.M. J. R. Hickey being the instructor in the latter class. This effort was greatly appreciated by the men, and large classes were formed, although they, more or less, dwindled down to a few enthusiasts as time proceeded.

Increased leave was granted to England and to Paris, while a percentage of the Battalion were given leave passes to visit Brussels. A limited number of officers were also permitted to visit the German frontier towns on the Rhine. Educational tours were arranged, and organised parties were conveyed by motor lorries to the battlefield of Waterloo and the interesting towns of Namur and Dijon.

By this time drafts had been formed, and were gradually being transferred to camps in England to await returning transports. The effect of this was to reduce the strength of the Battalion to such an extent that administration became difficult, and, in consequence, on February 5th, 1919, the 11th and 12th Battalions were combined to form one unit. Lieut.-Colonel C. H. Elliott returned to the Division about this time, but did not take the command of the combined unit, the appointment being given to Lieut.-Colonel R. A. Rafferty.

As further drafts left, the concentration of troops

was continued, until one complete unit was formed of all 3rd Brigade troops, when Lieut. C. H. Johnson took charge of the remnants of the 12th Battalion.

While the Battalion is educating and enjoying itself at Chatelet, and gradually being pared away by the departure of drafts to England and ultimately to Australia, it may be interesting to observe the Battalion's four-and-a-half years existence from a perspective point of view.

Although an effort was made, it has not been possible to discover the actual number of men who passed through the Battalion from its inception to the period of demobilisation, but a conservative figure would be about 8,500, although some of the reinforcements who joined up after the Armistice possessed regimental numbers of 10,000 and over.

The number of officers who passed through the Battalion amounted to no less than 187 (exclusive of officers attached) and may be summarised as follows:—

	Originating from 12th Battalion	Originating from other Units
Original Officers	31	—
Transferred from other Units	—	6
Reinforcements	40	5
Commissioned from the ranks	89	16

Major-General Sir J. Gellibrand attained the command of a Division, and no less than nine others held the rank of Lieutenant-Colonel.

At one time (certainly for a very brief period) the officers commanding the 9th, 10th, 11th, and 12th Battalions, 3rd M.G. Company and 3rd A.L.T.M. Battery all originated from the 12th Battalion.

Major G. Tostevin, O.C., 3rd. A.M.G. Company, was the only officer promoted from the ranks of the 12th Battalion who received his majority.

The decorations awarded to members of the Battalion may be summarised as follows:—

Victoria Cross (V.C.)	2
Commander of the Bath (C.B.)	1
Companion of St. Michael and St. George (C.M.G.)	2
Bar to Distinguished Service Order	1
Distinguished Service Order (D.S.O.)	3
2nd Bar to Military Cross	1
Bar to Military Cross	2
Military Cross (M.C.)	24
Bar to Distinguished Conduct Medal	1
Distinguished Conduct Medal (D.C.M.)	22
2nd Bar to Military Medal	3
Bar to Military Medal	15
Military Medal (M.M.)	150
Meritorious Service Medal (M.S.M.)	5
French Legion d' Honneur	1
French Croix de Guerre	1
Belgian Croix de Guerre	4
Cross of Karageorge (Serbian)	1
Serbian Silver Medal	1

Personnel attached to the unit:—

Distinguished Service Order	1
Military Cross	4
Military Medal	2

A considerable number of officers, N.C.O's, and men were also mentioned in despatches and in Army Corps Orders, but it has not been found possible, at this late date, to obtain a full and complete list of these. It may here be said that the standard set for immediate awards in the 12th Battalion was very high, and the recipients may well feel proud of any they possess. It was not until late in 1917 that the C.O. reluctantly lowered the standard slightly in order to prevent our own unit being penalised and to bring it more into alignment with other units in the Brigade.

The casualties of the A.I.F. Infantry Battalions throughout the war, have been published by the Defence Department, and those sustained by 1st Australian Division may be summarised as follows:—

CASUALTIES FROM 1914-1918.

Battalion.	Total Battle Casualties (excluding "gassed" and prisoners).	Battalion.	Killed and Wounded only.
3rd	3582	3rd	3409
12th	3531	12th	3387
4th	3525	11th	3382
11th	3517	1st	3306
1st	3504	4th	3302
9th	3485	2nd	3236
2nd	3423	9th	3154
8th	3271	10th	3084
10th	3189	8th	2980
7th	3103	6th	2840
6th	3072	5th	2836
5th	2975	7th	2803

CASUALTIES IN FRANCE.

Battalion.	Total Battle Casualties (excluding "gassed" and prisoners).	Battalion.	Killed and Wounded only.
12th	2927	12th	2783
3rd	2857	3rd	2684
9th	2846	11th	2605
11th	2840	1st	2589
1st	2787	10th	2584
4th	2777	4th	2554
8th	2715	9th	2515
10th	2689	2nd	2495
2nd	2682	8th	2424
5th	2354	5th	2217
7th	2350	6th	2104
6th	2336	7th	2050

It is therefore interesting to note that the 12th Battalion suffered the largest number of casualties in the 1st Australian Division whilst in France, and, incidentally, the 40th Battalion gained a similar distinction in the 3rd Australian Division.

The casualties sustained by the 12th Battalion in the major operations, may be summarised as follows:—

	Killed		Wounded		Missing		Total	
	Off.	O.R.	Off.	O.R.	Off.	O.R.	Off.	O.R.
Anzac ..	17	139	17	501	1	54	25	694
Pozieres ..	3	68	6	242	1	97	10	407
Mouquet Farm	—	42	3	148	1	48	4	238
Boursies .	2	60	5	179	—	10	7	249
Lagnicourt	—	29	4	55	—	37	4	121
Bullecourt	3	31	12	213	—	25	15	269
Polygon Wood	1	16	—	138	1	16	2	170
Meteren ..	3	8	2	31	1	4	6	43
Proyart ..	2	32	5	154	—	1	7	187
Jeancourt .	2	17	5	74	—	3	7	94

As a unit we are proud to record that:—

(1) We have never been known to retire (except one company at Lagnicourt when they were overwhelmed by 10 to 1 odds, and even then the lost ground was recaptured);

(2) We failed on one occasion only (Meteren) to gain our objective, and no blame was attachable to the Battalion in this case, as a previous phase of the engagement had not been successfully carried out;

(3) We fired the S.O.S. Signal twice only. Once in a thick fog, when it was not seen by the relay post, and once when the sentry at Battalion Headquarters was asleep and failed to report it. On each occasion the enemy was repelled without artillery assistance.

It may be interesting to record that during our $2\frac{1}{2}$ years fighting in France, our time was occupied as follows:—

Training Areas in Rear .... 550 days
Forward Area:—
    Reserve .... 100 days
    Support .... 120 „
    Front Line (normal tours of duty) .... 145 „
    Major operations ...... 35 „
                                                  400 „
                                                  950 „

The subject matter of this narrative has necessarily dealt primarily with the company officers, N.C.O's., and men, and recorded their fighting, training and resting. The fact must not be lost sight of, however, that there were many officers and men who held administrative appointments, and whose duties did not permit them to "hop over" with the assaulting troops.

The Transport Section was one of the most important units of the Battalion, and their task at times was anything but enviable. Long working hours, irregular meals, unfavourable climatic conditions, and numerous journeys through belts of country subjected to intense artillery fire, were some of the privations they had to suffer through the campaign. They were particularly fortunate in having competent officers throughout, the principal ones being Lieut. (afterwards Lieut.-Colonel) L. M. Mullen, Lieut. (afterwards Captain) J. E. Newland, Lieuts. E. A. Shepherd and E. A. Potts. Similar remarks can also be applied to such N.C.O's. as Sgt. (afterwards Captain) W. F. Wilmot, Sgt. (afterwards Lieut.) J. R. Taylor, Sgts. E. J. Bradley and W. E. Johnson; the work of both officers and N.C.O's., however, was made considerably easier by having men in their section, such as Dvrs. W. J. Matthews, W. Tooley, C. S. Tegg, F. Norbury, J. J. O'Loughlin, W. J. Hart, and others, who knew the work so thoroughly and upon whom great reliance could be placed.

The appointment of Quartermaster, at different periods of the Battalion's existence, was in rotation filled by Lieut. (afterwards Capt.) N. D. Fethers, Capt. (afterwards Lieut.-Colonel) D. A. Lane, Lieut. (afterwards Capt.) W. Kennedy, Lieuts. C. H. Lyne and G. P. Potter, and Capt. H. E. Spotswood.

The Quartermaster had a varied command to administer, and comprised, in the main, his R.Q.M.S., a Storeman, the Butcher, Sgt. Bootmaker, Sgt. Cook, Armourer-Sergeant, the Regimental Tailor and general supervision over the C.Q.M.S.'s and Company Cooks.

His duties were numerous, and if enlarged upon, would almost fill a book themselves. To show the variety and scope of his duties and the amount of responsibility he carried, it may be stated, that, *inter alia*, his duties were to feed, clothe, and equip the Battalion; joint responsibility with the Transport Officer for the carriage of rations to Battalion Headquarters in the line; to replace all shortages; to supplement the rations by purchases out of Regimental Funds (when so instructed by the C.O.); to keep the boots of the Battalion in repair; to maintain a supply of gas helmets and other equipment for protection against gas; to dispatch the personal effects of deceased and wounded officers; to forward all captured trophies and salvaged material to Ordnance; the issue of clean underclothes and dry socks in winter; and so one might continue. It was also his pleasant duty to advise the C.O. of the receipt of the invaluable parcels of socks forwarded by the 12th Battalion Comforts Fund, the O.A.S. Fund, Lady Brown and Mrs. Tom Barr-Smith (both of Adelaide), the Loyal Ladies of Perth (W.A.), and other patriotic bodies and war-workers.

During our four-and-a-half years of campaigning, the various Q.M's. were ably assisted in their store by R.Q.M.S's. J. E. Newland, C. H. Lyne, J. Cooper, and H. J. Cassidy; also as storemen, S. G. Salt, S. Kershaw, J. Youl, R. Winspear, G. Mulrennan, G. Windridge, A. Waddington, and others.

Sgt. C. Dand and Cpl. J. Patmore both, at different times, acted as tailors to the Battalion and converted "Tommy" slacks into Australian breeches by the score.

Sgts. Z. Poulteney and Maggs followed one another as Bootmaker Sergeants, and during our periods of long marching, their staffs were kept fully employed.

Sgt. H. J. Cassidy acted as Armourer-Sergeant through a strenuous period on the Peninsula, and also for a time in France, until being promoted R.Q.M.S. He discovered that if the barrel of the S.M.L.E. Rifle was cut down to half its length, it was capable of firing a No. 23 Mills grenade an additional 50 to 70 yards, and although the improvement was forwarded on to 1st Anzac Corps, and he received much praise, they would not sanction its adoption. He was afterwards succeeded by Sgt. W. O. Blyth.

The Quartermaster's whole staff gave him their unqualified support at all times, more especially during the later period in France. When the Battalion was in the line their work was indeed strenuous. Rations had first to be drawn from the A.S.C. dump, after which they had to be divided between the four companies, various Headquarter units in the line, and numerous detached sections in the rear areas, according to their "ration states." This, however, did not complete the issue, for to assist the companies in the line, all dry rations, such as bread, biscuits, cheese, jam, bully beef, cigarettes, etc., were again subdivided into quantities representing five men's rations, which were then put into sandbags, tied up, and labelled, ready for the line. It should not be difficult to appreciate the amount of work this involved.

On Gallipoli, the Quartermaster's scope, as regards liberality, was very limited, but in France it was customary, particularly with Spotswood, to have some sort of meal waiting at all hours of the day or night, for any member of the Battalion who was sent out of the line through exhaustion, from nervous breakdown, or other similar reason.

VII.

During the latter part of the war there was a great shortage of certain articles in England, and in consequence, units in the field were instructed to conserve all waste paper and cardboard, and all fatty waste from the cookhouse had to be rendered down into dripping and despatched in biscuit tins. A ½d. per lb. was paid into Regimental Funds for all dripping sent back in this manner, and it may be imagined that the Quartermaster allowed no waste in this direction. It is said that some units resorted to the collection of dead horses for this purpose— not necessarily to supplement their funds, but to keep their "fat figures" up to standard. A Divisional Return was issued every month, and often accompanied by a curt note stating, "that the Divisional Commander notices, with regret, that your unit has only forwarded — lbs. of fat (paper or cardboard) to D.A.D.O.S. during the month. Please explain." Oh! those "please explains."

The Battalion Post Office was an institution which usually sought shelter under the Q.M's. wing, generally owing to the failure of the billeting officer to provide accommodation. The first Battalion "post master" was Pvt. W. McCulloch, who collected and delivered the mails in an exemplary manner on the Peninsula. He was followed later by Cpl. Peter O'Loughlin, who held the appointment from Serapeum days right through to the Armistice, with the exception of one period when he was wounded by a H.V. gun at Montauban railhead. Many an insufficiently addressed letter has he delivered, and many a message from home has he forwarded on to catch some wounded member of the unit at the Base Hospital.

The Regimental Canteen formed an integral part of the Battalion in France, in so much as an officer was put in charge of its administration and supply. This was largely effected by Capt. I. N. Holyman, as referred to in the narrative, but he was ably assisted by Pvts. Harold Bird and Tim Ward, who alternately helped in the buying, transporting, and selling of the produce.

I have intentionally left an appreciation of the work of the Battalion Orderly Room Staff until last, because from the inception of the Battalion I have been so closely associated with it.

The duties of Orderly Room Sergeant were, in rotation, carried out by Sgts. C. H. Lyne, R. Latta, and myself on Anzac and in Egypt, and Sgts. Fred Green, D. G. Bishton and Sherwood while in France. The three latter N.C.O's. assisted me in my duties as Adjutant to a greater extent than perhaps they themselves realised. The compilation of returns, the filing and recording of correspondence and other office routine in a tent, broken down billet, under a trench shelter, or in the open, is not the easiest of duties to perform.

Pvts. Brockett, Dove and Sherwood (before promotion) were also invaluable as typists and manipulated our little "Corona" typewriter under many curious and unenviable conditions.

Sgt. (afterwards Lieut.) Powell was the first Pay Sergeant, and accepted the task of instituting the new pay book and the somewhat elaborate (though exceedingly efficient) system relating thereto. Members of the Battalion obeyed Powell's little notes to attend the Orderly Room with mixed feelings of doubt and wonder, and breathlessly asked "is it a debit?" The Pay Office made the pellets, but Powell had to fire them—and accept the abuse. He was afterwards succeeded by Sgt. Gilbert, who carried on the work in an equally efficient manner.

The Company Orderly Room Clerks were also an efficient lot of fellows, taken collectively, although now and again a "dud" was unearthed.

The manner in which they did their work, compiled returns, and collected information, was indeed creditable when one remembers the conditions under which they existed at times.

It is difficult to say when the 12th Battalion ceased to exist; from a composite unit, it joined with the 11th Battalion and formed half a unit, and later, a still smaller unit in the Brigade and Divisional concentrations, until individuals commenced to return singly. No special ceremony marked the cessation of its existence, as none had marked its commencement.

For purposes of administration and centralisation of command, a routine order of the 3rd Australian Infantry Brigade was issued at Charleroi, ordering the consolidation of the 11th and 12th Battalions to take effect from noon on 5th February, 1919, but from the "diggers'" point of view, the Battalion retained its individuality until the last man was demobilised. There was no bugle call or executive word of command to order its dismissal. Just as the reinforcements came from Australia to maintain its fighting strength, so the drafts left for the homeland and gradually sapped the life-blood from the unit.

During its existence the Battalion saw service in four of the continents of the World, in the course of which it laid its honoured dead to rest in the shadow of the Pyramids of Egypt, beneath the towering heights of Gallipoli, on the sunny shores of the Mediterranean, in rural England, in devastated Flanders, and beneath the scarlet poppies of Picardy—the flower that suggests sleep and remembrance, and which gently reminds us that—

"THEIR NAME LIVETH FOR EVERMORE."

Map of ANZAC

From "The Official History of Australia in the War of 1914-1918," Volume I. By permission of the Editor and the Publishers, Angus & Robertson Ltd.

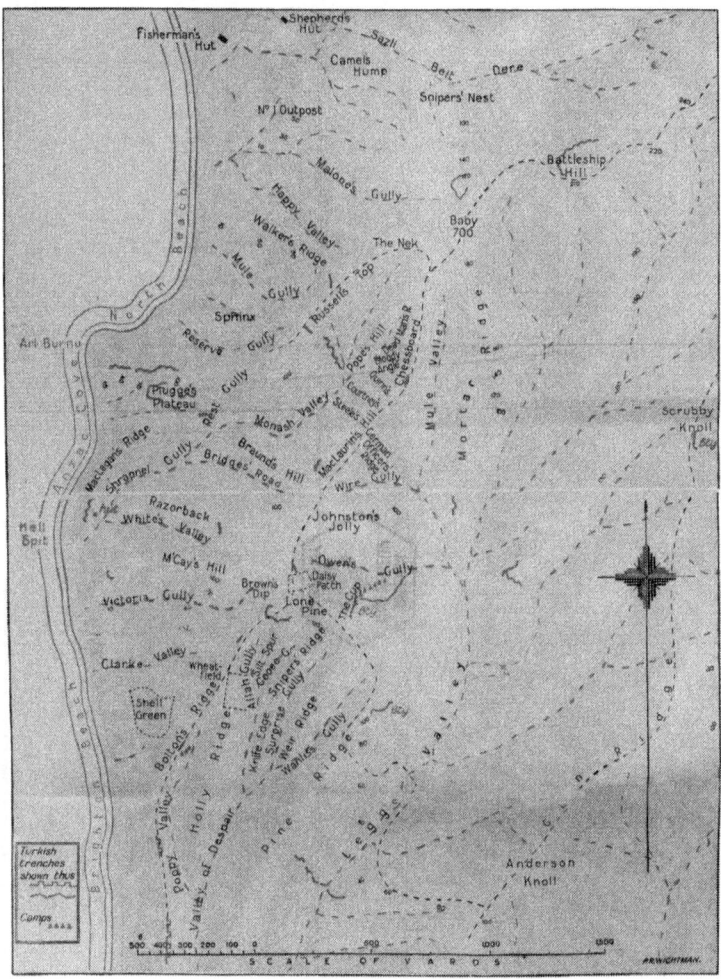

Map of TASMANIA POST

(Chapter VII)

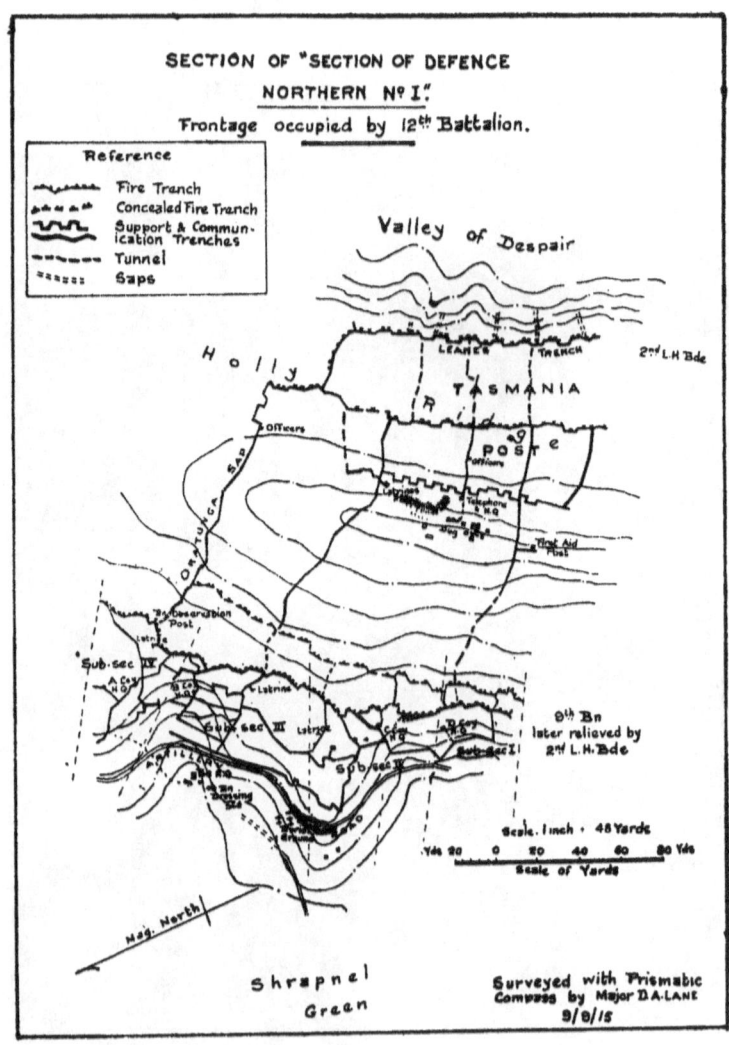

Portion of LENS 11 Map
1:100,000

See Chapter XI.—The Road to the Somme
Chapter XV.—The Summer of 1917

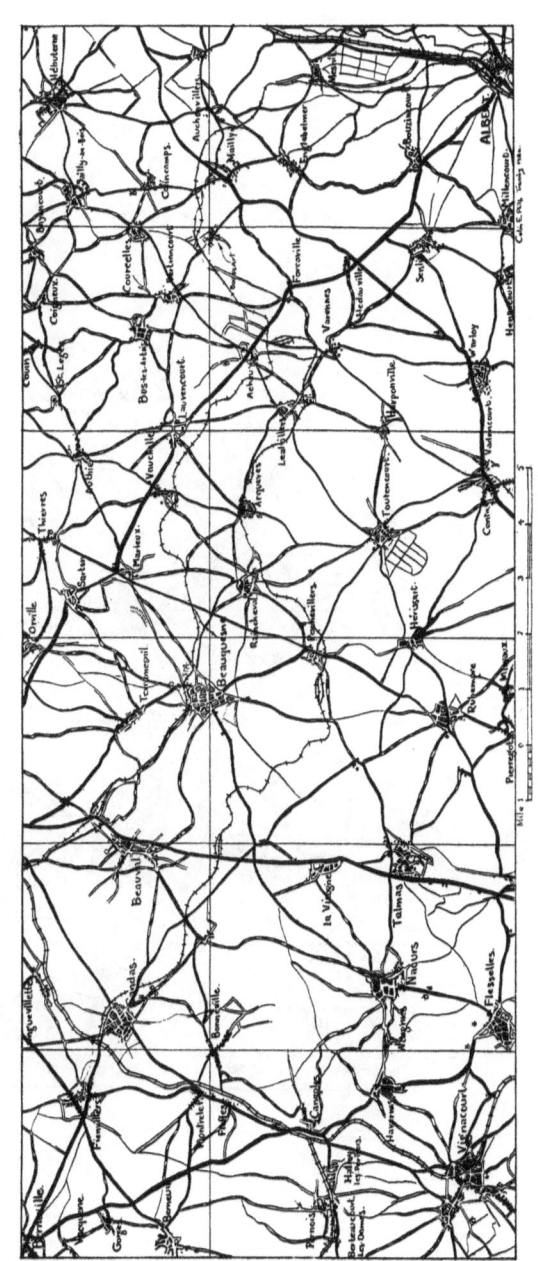

Portion of "MARTINPUICH" Map
1 : 20,000

See Chapter XII.—Pozieres and Mouquet Farm.

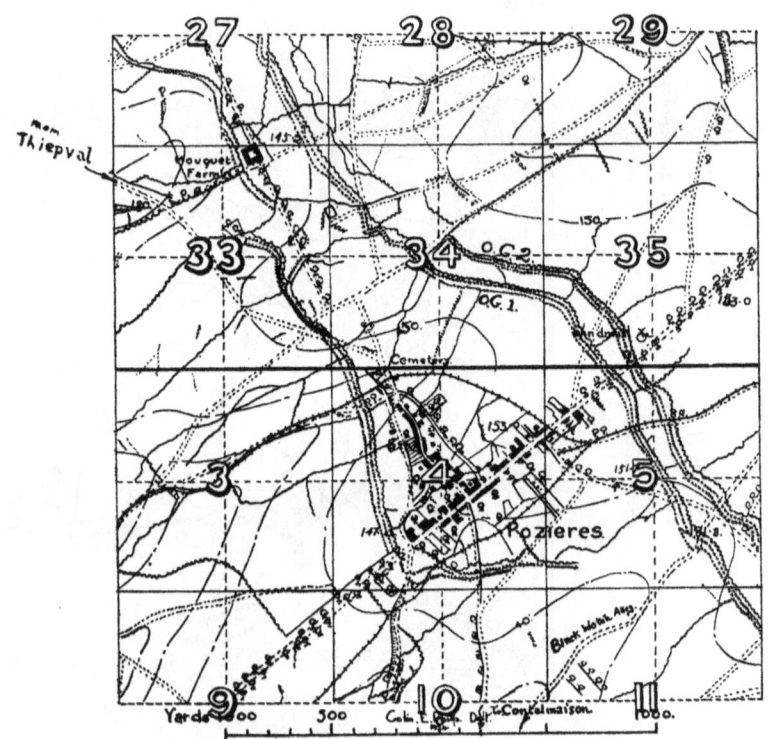

Portion of "ALBERT, Combined Sheet"

1 : 40,000

See Chapter XIII.—Pozieres and Mouquet Farm

Note.—The shaded line indicates the British front line prior to the attack on July 1st, 1916. When the 1st Australian Division attacked Pozieres from the direction of squares X 10 and 11, the Germans were still in possession of High Wood and Delville Wood. This may help to satisfactorily explain the erroneous report that our own guns were continually firing into our rear.

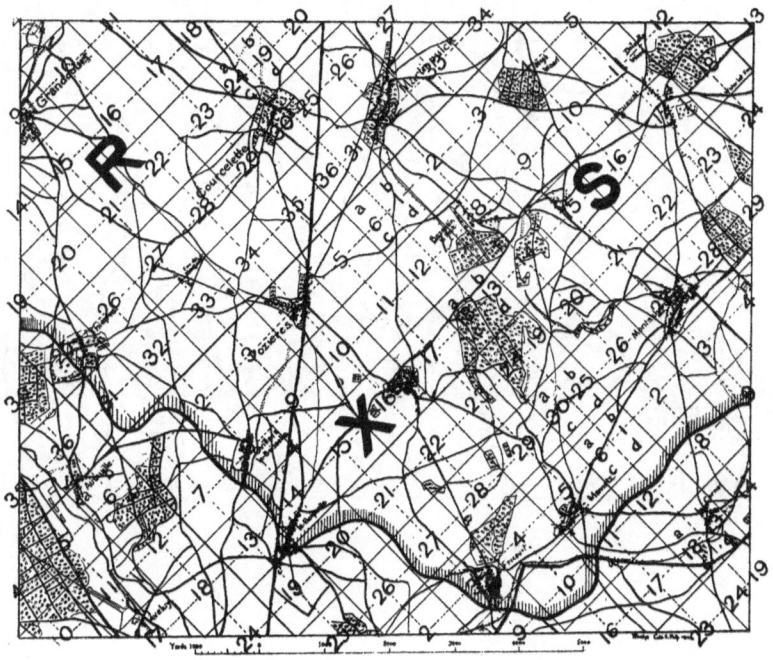

Portion of LENS 11 Map
1 : 100,000

See Chapter XIII.—The Winter of 1916
Chapter XIV.—The German Withdrawal—
Spring, 1917

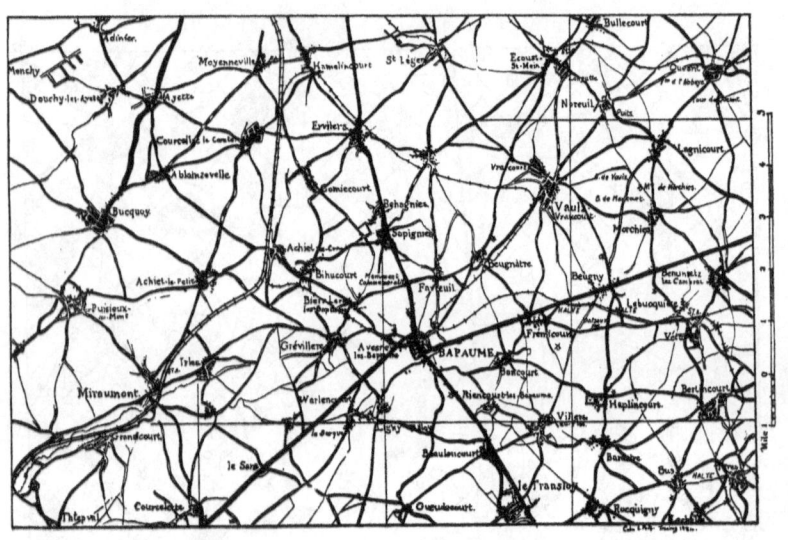

Portion of AMIENS 17 Map
1 : 100,000

Showing the Somme valley and the junction of the Rivers Somme and Ancre.

See Chapter XIII.—The Winter of 1916

Chapter XV.—The Final Advance—Autumn, 1918

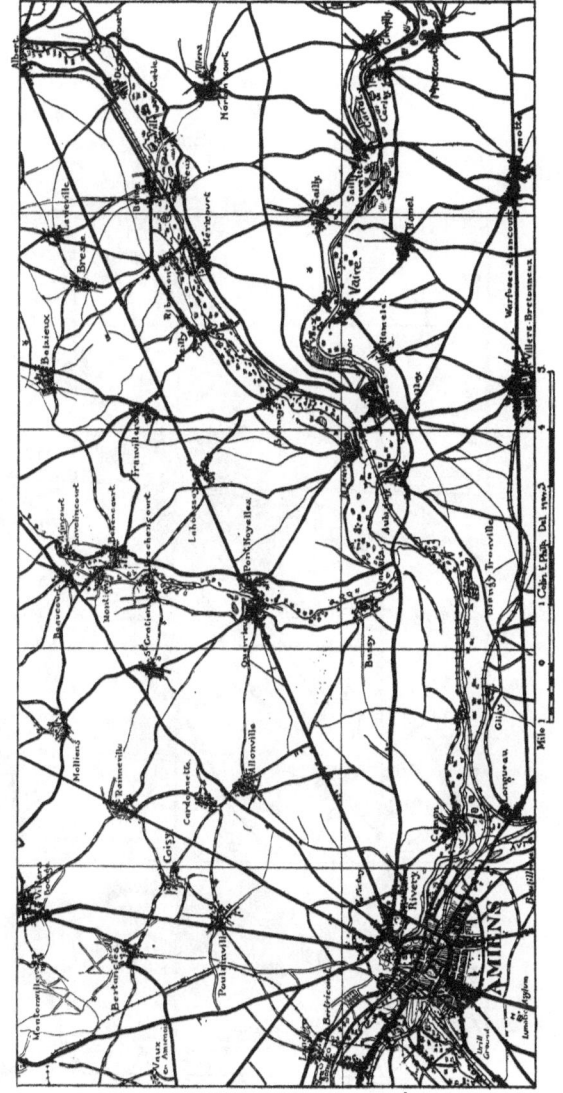

Portion of "GUEUDECOURT to BAPAUME"
1 : 10,000

See Chapter XIII.—The Winter of 1916
Chapter XIV.—The German Withdrawal—
Spring, 1917

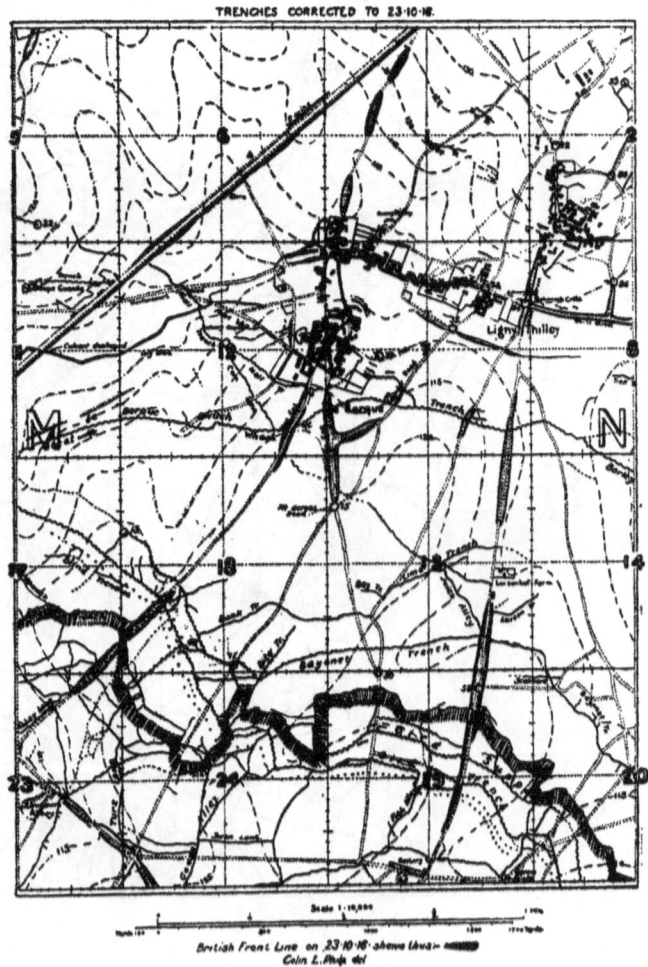

Portion of "WESTHOEK" Map
1 : 10,000

See Chapter XVI.—The Battle of the Ridges—
Autumn, 1917

(Illustrating the Artillery Barrage in the Battle of
Polygon Wood)

The thick lines represent the objectives referred
to in the narrative.

The thin lines represent the successive lifts of
the artillery barrage.

The figures represent the number of minutes
after "zero hour."

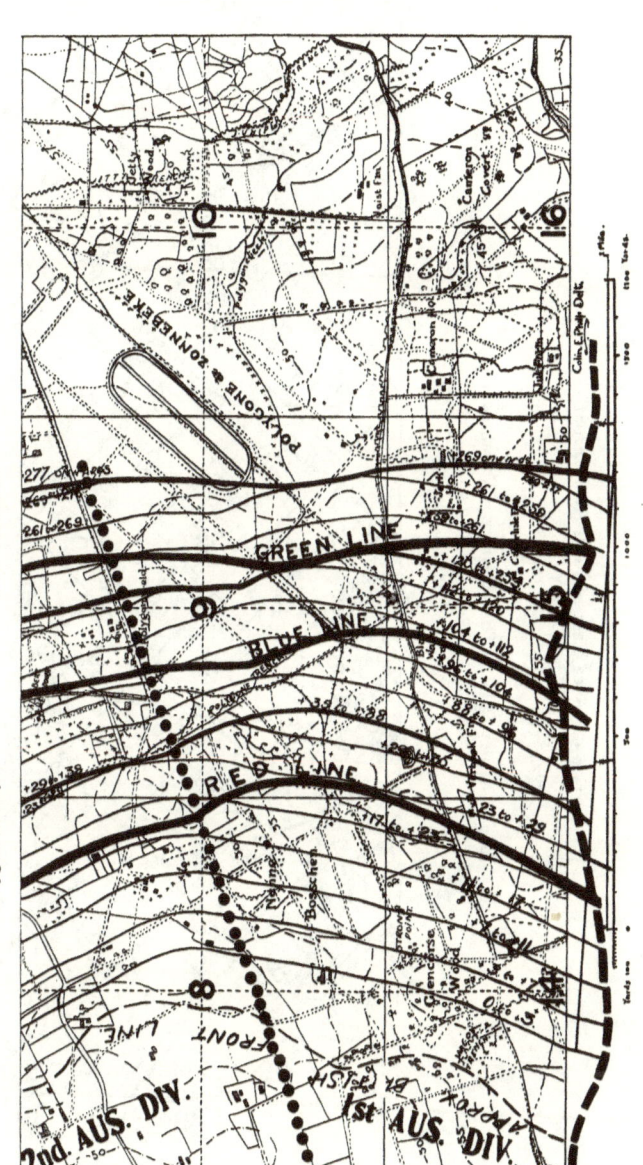

Portion of "Area East of Fifth Army Front"
1 : 40,000

See Chapter XIV.—The German Withdrawal—
Spring, 1917

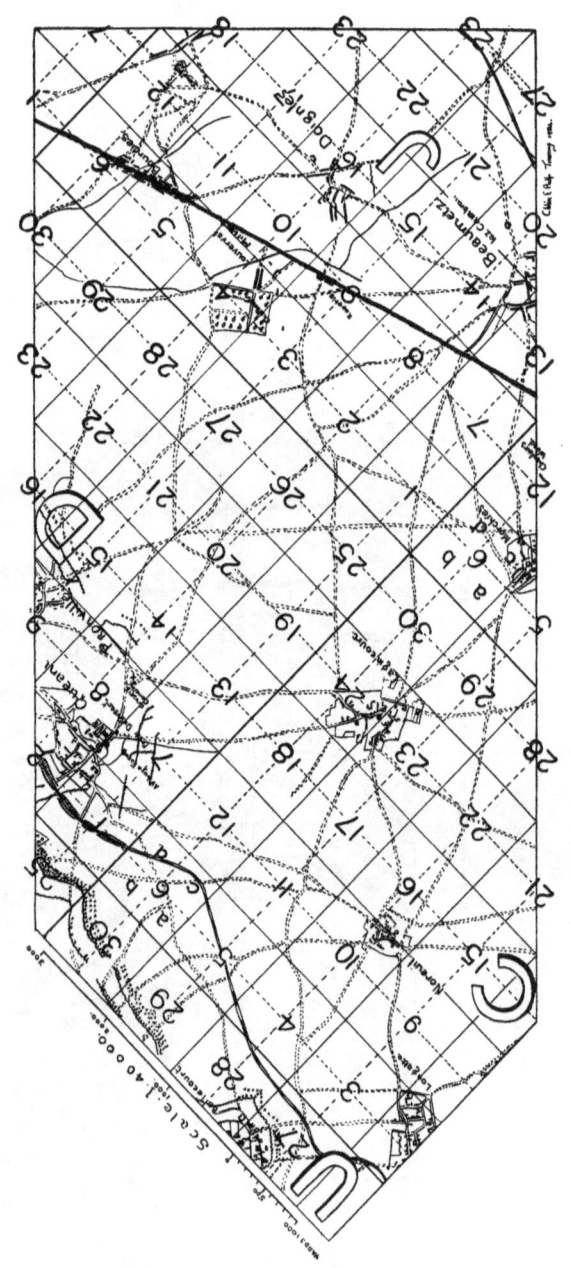

Portions of "Belgium and part of France, Sheet 28."
1 : 40,000

See Chapter XVII.—The Winter of 1917

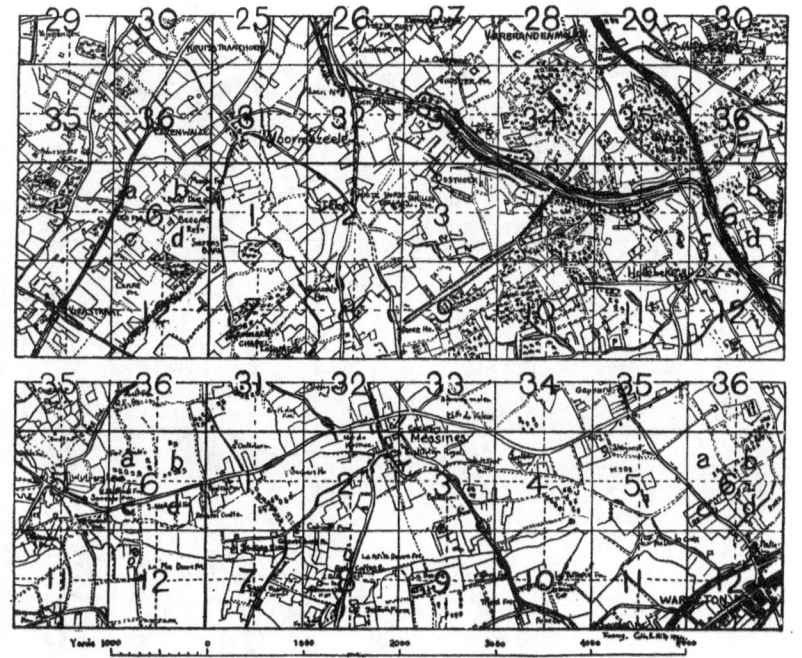

Portion of AMIENS 17 Map
1 : 100,000

See Chapter XX.—The Final Advance—Autumn, 1918

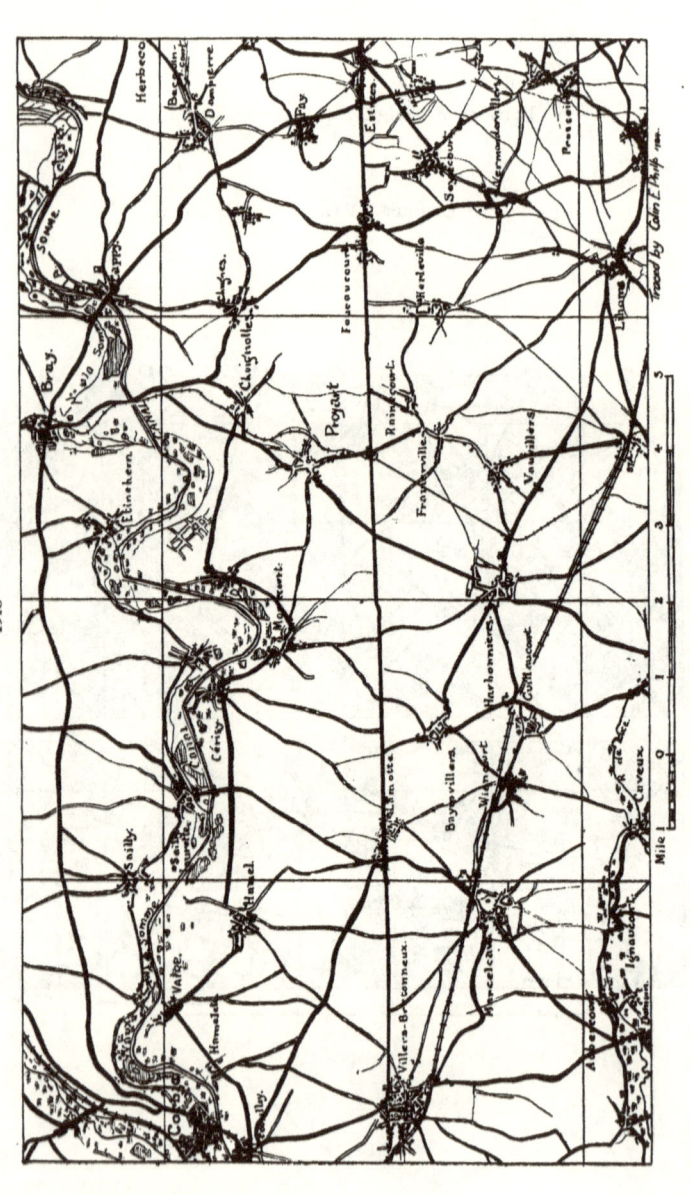

www.ingramcontent.com/pod-product-compliance
Lightning Source LLC
Chambersburg PA
CBHW021823220426
43663CB00005B/108